NEW YORK ROCK

FROM THE RISE OF

THE VELVET UNDERGROUND

TO THE FALL OF CBGB

STEVEN BLUSH

ST. MARTIN'S GRIFFIN 🞶 NEW YORK

www.stmartins.com

Library of Congress Cataloging-in-Publication Data

Names: Blush, Steven, author.
Title: New York rock : from the rise of the Velvet Underground to the fall of CBGB / Steven Blush.
Description: First edition. | New York : St. Martin's Griffin, 2016.
Identifiers: LCCN 2016007627| ISBN 9781250083616 (trade pbk.) | ISBN 9781250083623 (e-book)
Subjects: LCSH: Rock music—New York (State) —New York—History and criticism. | Rock musicians—New York (State) —New York.
Classification: LCC ML3534.3 .B58 2016 | DDC 781.6609747/1—dc23
LC record available at http://lccn.loc.gov/2016007627

Research Editor: George Petros
Editorial Assistance: Deanna M. Lehman, Tony Mann, Jerry Williams

Our books may be purchased in bulk for promotional, educational, or business use. Please contact your local bookseller or the Macmillan Corporate and Premium Sales Department at 1-800-221-7945, extension 5442, or by e-mail at MacmillanSpecialMarkets@macmillan .com.

First Edition: October 2016

10 9 8 7 6 5 4 3 2 1

To Alyssa Fisher and Jacqueline Fisher Blush

Toilet love: CBGB Men's Room, 2005. Photo by Tony Mann.

CONTENTS

ACKNOWLEDGMENTS

Writing a book on the definitive history of New York Rock was no easy feat.

Maximum respect to executive editor Elizabeth Beier for all her professional insight, and for always keeping me inspired, focused, and moving forward.

Much thanks to editorial assistant Nicole Williams, for dealing with my correspondences and pulling all the disparate pieces together. Freelance copy editor Ian Gibb and lawyer Henry Kaufman really helped strengthen the manuscript. Heartfelt appreciation for production manager Janna Dokos, production editor Eric C. Meyer, and designer Steven Seighman for making everything look so clean and simple, and to jacket designer Lisa Pompilio for taking me back to 1977. Extra thanks to publicist Rebecca Lang, marketing director Laura Clark, marketing manager Lauren Friedlander, and sales director Brian Heller for all your efforts. The biggest thank-you of all goes to Griffin publisher Jennifer Enderlin, for bringing this 20th-century subculture to the 21st-century mainstream.

I could never have written this book were it not for my personal editor and dear friend George Petros, and the editorial assistance of Deanna M. Lehman, Tony Mann, and the late great Jerry Williams. The scores of interview subjects, photographers, archivists, and musicians hassled for this project all deserve serious accolades—you know who you are.

Mad props to my agent, Jim Fitzgerald at the James Fitzgerald Agency, for taking my career to another level. Much love to the Blush, Fisher, Goldstein, and Radick families for putting up with my nonsense. Alyssa Fisher and Jackie Fisher Blush, I am always touched by your presence.

INTRODUCTION

TO THE FIVE BOROS

New York City and New York Rock mean different things to different people. Everyone has ideas of "what it's all about." There are no absolutes. New York's a city in constant flux, so it's tough to call anything quintessentially NYC.

The city represents endless possibilities. It's a cross-collision of art and commerce, style and substance, subversion and illusion, and tension and danger. Walking down the street, one can feel the ghosts of players past. Every inch of terrain has been trod. There's relatively little new artistic ground to cover. So it's all about reinvention, reflection, and retrospection.

New York Rock breaks down the rock scene's half-century connection to art, film, theater, poetry, and politics, in relation to the city's kaleidoscopic socioeconomic, racial, and sexual variants. It analyzes New York Rock's distinct subculture through the prism of influences, crosscurrents, and psychoactive distractions.

New York's rockers range from a handful of impressive stars to a glut of historically relevant washouts. The point of the 1,500-plus musicians, clubs, and labels discussed in this book isn't to retell every fact—books have been written on many of these characters—but rather spell out how they played into the making of New York Rock. So, the prerock "Precedents" sections don't even try to recite well-known facts about New York City jazz, blues, disco, minimalism, et cetera; rather they identify how each of those fed into the creation of the city's rock subculture.

My years as a New York journalist, editor, publisher, promoter, DJ, and filmmaker (the latter with director Paul Rachman) have made me privy to some unreal behind-the-scenes situations. I was not onstage, but I was more than a cultural voyeur taking mental notes.

My father was born on Rivington Street in the Lower East Side. He and my grandfather ran a small printing shop at 195 Christie Street. That's where I spent much of my youth in the '70s. There I picked up an understanding of publishing, and discovered at a young age the sins of the city. At around thirteen, I heard a weird band rehearsing upstairs that I peeked in on. Years later, I realized that was Talking Heads. During my forays, I frequented the local bars serving minors, one of them CBGB. I also stumbled upon the punk subculture on St. Marks Place. My father knew plenty of riffraff. One of them was Arthur Weinstein, to whom he was like a father figure (he attended my father's funeral). Arthur owned the "new wave disco" Hurrah, and then the after-hours clubs the Jefferson and the Continental, and then the legendary World. Arthur brought me to his clubs and other nightspots, so I saw a lot of crazy action firsthand, at an early age. This book was born of years of lifestyle, not Web research or Facebook interviews.

In my four years in Washington, D.C., I was lucky to live through and be involved with that city's burgeoning hardcore punk explosion. Then, back in New York, I booked a few Downtown club shows that some people still talk about. I spun records at more than a few cool clubs and parties, and wrote for, edited, or published great magazines. Regarding Don Hill's, Cat Club, Mars, Love Club, Carmelita's, 428 Lafayette, Metal Bar, the Pyramid, *Paper, Details, RIP, Seconds,* et cetera—I likely had a hand in it. Of the post-'80s bands, I worked in some capacity and/or socialized with most of them.

One thing I've learned from this process is that the more things change, the more they stay the same. Each generation goes through the same bullshit, each subject to the same egotism and petulance and foibles, sparring over who's "legit" or "old-school" and who's "fake" or a "sellout." The research also shows that most every genre or movement in the annals of modern culture traces straight back to New York, and if anything, New York rock musicians and scenesters deserve way more credit than they've received. Most of these folks were too busy livin' it to ever monetize it.

American rock has two epicenters: New York and Los Angeles. Los Angeles is a story unto itself that I will tell at a later date.

New York Rock was a twentieth-century art form, and means something very different in the twenty-first. Some "hipster" bands refer to what they do as "post-rock." They are correct: we are living in a post-rock era.

The New York Rock of the Velvet Underground, New York Dolls, and Ramones symbolically ended when CBGB closed. New York Rock is a relic, like a museum piece, removed from its original intent as the soundtrack of the radical fringe.

Perhaps some kids are about to come along with a new sound to blow us all away, worthy of a new chapter for the next edition of *New York Rock*.

—Steven Blush
New York City, 2016

Hey, ho, let's go: Joey Ramone and Dee Dee Ramone, Bowery, 1977. Photo by GODLIS.

FUNKY BUT CHIC

THE NEW YORK ROCKER

Love comes in spurts: Richard Hell and the
Voidoids, CBGB, 1977. Photo by GODLIS.

INTRO

It's hard times in the city
Livin' down in New York town
—Bob Dylan, "Hard Times in New York Town"

Everyone knows about the Yankees, the Statue of Liberty, Wall Street, and King
Kong climbing the Empire State Building. They also know about New York rockers like Lou Reed, Deborah Harry, David Johansen, and Joey Ramone.

LOU REED (The Velvet Underground): I need New York City to feed
off. Like I run dry and I've got to go out and do things, and build up
new people to write about. There's nothing about me especially interesting. All I do is change clothes and hairdos. (1972)

New York inspires great art and music. Talented, energetic, ambitious characters
come from near and far in search of a tolerant artistic milieu—to be among
the best, to fully express themselves, and hopefully to "make it." Many move
to the city chasing a dream that might not even exist.

CHRIS STEIN (Blondie): I lived in New York to be part of something. Our band couldn't have come from anywhere else. The Downtown scene was great, and the city gave us the inspiration. The city didn't start going downhill till somewhat recently. But New York will always be New York. (1999)

New York Rock reflects a New York state of mind. It's an amalgam of styles, yet it's its own unique thing. It manifests as larger than life, yet it's stripped down. It's more than a sound; it's a cacophony of noises, like the streets themselves. Despite endless attempts to categorize or describe New York Rock, it's indescribable—yet you know it when you hear it. New York Rock means rock from Manhattan, mostly Downtown, with a bit of Brooklyn. It's a confluence of harsh urban realities, moody artistic dispositions, self-promotion, and intoxication rituals.

JAMES MURPHY (LCD Soundsystem): New York is the world's greatest city and has been for a long time. Other cities have their moment but none of them come back—like Seattle had its moment. Hurray! But New York's consistently there whether it's the art or writing or music or ideas. It's the most idealized part of America, and to me it's the most ideal part. (2005)

New York Rock is a story of great successes and great failures. It's not a good business model, trying to swim upstream against pop music's flow, as most of these musicians had trouble getting it together personally, professionally, or pharmaceutically. Maybe that's why New York Rock resonates so deeply, and stands the test of time.

LOU REED: Relatively few people make it out of New York. So many people come to New York, competing with each other like crazy. There's only so many clubs, there's only so many venues. It costs more to be here. There's a lot more opportunities to get yourself in trouble here. There are things available—distractions. (2000)

Haircut & attitude: Miss Guy, Toilet Boys, 1999. Photo by Frank White.

ATTITUDE

I live in the city, I breathe dirty air
I ride trains with b-boys, junkies, queens and squares
—Manitoba's Wild Kingdom, "New York, New York"

NYC is at once the best and worst place in the world, where amazing and awful things happen. It's a harsh terrain, with no sanctuaries. There are untold diversions: people to meet, vices to try. You can't "get away from it all." It is no place for the weakhearted.

WILLY DeVILLE (Mink DeVille): All kinds of things happen in New York, and if you can live under that kind of pressure you can live anywhere. (1977)

DON HILL (club owner): New York's a tough place to survive. It's no amusement park. You gotta earn it; it's not a given. You need a killer instinct, a self-destructive attitude, always living on the edge. No rules here. It has its own state of mind. (2004)

New York musicians face crushing survival issues. The bar for success is high. That "You talkin' to me?"/"Get outta my way!"/"Mind your own business" chutzpah sets the tone. To survive in the city is to pass an acid test of legitimacy. The payback for getting roughed up mentally and physically is a chance to get famous.

> **ALAN VEGA (Suicide):** New York can space you out. But I can spot trouble a mile away, even spaced out, and I know how to deal with it because I know the speed. (1989)

> **CHRIS HARLOT (Harlots of 42nd Street):** The speed of the city has a lot to do with it. People move faster here, where things are bigger and better. You're not in a laid-back mood—New York style is not laid back—there's no time, everyone's too busy, always something to do. To slow down, you move to Florida. (2011)

The city breeds powerful personalities: hard-charging, tough and cynical, with plenty of "attitude." New Yorkers have a reputation for being on top of their game. They think quick and talk fast. The city serves as a stage for the angry, alienated, and discontented.

> **BOB GRUEN (photographer):** The New York Rock attitude is just New York attitude. There's this confidence, an aggressive determination to succeed, and this cynical seen-everything, done-everything, "show me what you can do" attitude. A New York Rock band has a cocky attitude. There's a certain coolness that goes back to the '50s rockers in Brooklyn. You're not in awe of the world, the world's in awe of you. But when you live here it's not a pose—you gotta be tough to walk down the street. (2004)

> **THEO KOGAN (Lunachicks):** One of the many great things about New York is people here are sarcastic, we have attitude, we're realistic, and we deal with people every day on top of each other on the subway or on the streets. People here are very honest—and angry. The New York attitude comes through in the music. (2004)

LENNY KAYE (Patti Smith Group): Here's my word for it: "spunk." It's like, "We may not listen to what you tell us, but if it's a good idea, we might borrow it." I believe the flow of blood's a little faster here. It's just a fast city and your metabolism has to keep up with it. That's why you should live here and work here. (2004)

JOHN CALE (The Velvet Underground): Here's how I'd define it: "Stubborn as hell, designed to lose, yet somehow wins." (2004)

Walk on the wild side: Lower East Side, 1983. Photo by Ted Barron.

GENTRIFICATION

We are from the Lower East Side
We don't give a damn if we live or die
—David Peel & The Lower East Side, "Lower East Side"

New York Rock history isn't the minutiae of musicians' lives, or at what club who saw whom. It's a real estate tale of funky 'hoods where creative types drawn by cheap rent and a sense of identity create and immerse themselves in a subculture, and later get edged out by gentrification. In the '60s, the combination of creative types within the urban squalor of the Lower East Side made a rock scene with a distinct sound, style, and spirit.

KEMBRA PFAHLER (The Voluptuous Horror of Karen Black): In 1979 and 1980 people like me who had dyed-black hair, who were young punk rockers, we were a minority in the Lower East Side. A lot of people got killed and overdosed. You were getting picked on a lot for your appearance. (2006)

CYNTHIA SLEY (Bush Tetras): People didn't like us moving in. We were the minority. We looked very different. The attitude fed the fire. We were fearless, which kept you safe. It was extremely tough down there. (2004)

Downtown musicians lived, loved, learned, drank, drugged, and jammed within walking distance of other unconventional artists, poets, authors, and actors. "Alphabet City," the no-man's-land between Avenues A and D, nurtured '70s–'80s rock subculture.

IVAN JULIAN (Voidoids): People who moved there felt like it was their last refuge to be creative and to be who they were. This was the one place you could write and play—the environment was immediate and urgent, which reflected in the music. (2004)

JIM THIRLWELL (Foetus): When I first came here in 1983, it was steeped in a kind of urban decay, which I found very beautiful. There was a high amount of energy, a lot of character as well. And it was so centralized. Lydia Lunch and I had an apartment on Twelfth between A and B and that was when Alphabet City was still Alphabet City. You didn't go east of Avenue A at that point, unless you wanted to score drugs. (2004)

WALTER STEDING (artist/musician): I never wanted to play outside of New York or outside of Manhattan or outside of the Lower East Side. Going to Hurrah on like 60th Street was as far as I'd go. (2011)

Downtown subculture was protected by moats. But instead of alligators, it was crime keeping away jocks, yuppies, normal people, and other interlopers. Eventually, the crime subsided and the real estate developers did their magic, and the 'hood became livable. New York could've gone either way at the end of the twentieth century. But the fin de siècle real estate boom forever transformed the city's styles and attitudes. The freaks lost the turf war. Many rolled with the changes; others pined for "the good old days."

DAVID JOHANSEN (New York Dolls): The East Village was the template of that worldwide urban renewal gentrification craze. It's probably the first place where artists moved in and made the place attractive, and then the gentry moved in. We've been all around the world and we see it happening everywhere. (2006)

NICK MARDEN (The Stimulators): It's like sending in the missionaries first to see how few get killed and can be righteous with the neighbors. Then you bring in the rest of the abusive immigrants. The art world has always been like that. A weird artist will move in and tolerate the abuse in order to have the space to create, and their friends move in and it becomes an artistic community. Then like what happened in SoHo, the landlords started interjecting white people and others who disrespect the community. (2011)

DIANE DI PRIMA (artist): Bit by bit, all the life of Downtown is being turned off. The coffeehouses have had to fight to keep going. The License Bureau has lessened the numbers of Off Broadway theaters. Screenings of experimental films—which were flourishing and just developed a large audience—have stopped altogether. The Living Theater has been seized, and the New York Poets Theatre has been effectively stopped. Painters and sculptors are again facing the possibility of losing their loft situation. . . . New York is in many ways over. (1964)

Too much junkie business: *East Village
Eye* covers story on Operation Pressure
Point, 1984. Collection of the author.

DRUGS

*I try to reason why
But end up getting high*
—The Dictators, "Stay"

Creative types have a buzz in their brains causing varying degrees of mental illness and chemical reliance. Most "cool" New York scenesters took drugs, and for many, it got the better of them. Others indulged in drugs, and it helped.

LOU REED (The Velvet Underground): I take drugs just because in the twentieth century in a technological age living in the city there are certain drugs you have to take just to keep yourself normal like a caveman. Just to bring yourself up or down, but to attain equilibrium, you need to take certain drugs. They don't getcha high even, they just getcha normal. (1973)

BILL BRONSON (The Spitters/Swans): It comes down to shortcuts. If you want to get somewhere in terms of spiritual or musical enlightenment, I don't think it's bad to use drugs to get there. (1994)

New York beckons as a land of excess, an inebriation vortex where the drugs find you. There is no escape from the 24/7 lifestyle, with many ODs, freak-outs, and funerals. Psychoactive trends reached their zenith in the City That Never Sleeps. All these psychic intensities played into New York Rock. Musical styles, rehearsal spaces, practice times, sleeping hours, living arrangements, friends, and lovers all tied into intoxication rituals.

> **HANDSOME DICK MANITOBA (The Dictators):** The drug environment in the '70s was plentiful, an open supermarket. My first favorite drugs were pills, they were easy to pop, you didn't need to get drunk, and you didn't get sick. Seconals, Tuinals, real 714 Quaaludes were available. I dabbled in coke, but then I found heroin, and loved it. It was a love affair, even though I threw my guts up for eight hours the first time I did it. (2003)

In drugs, there's everything else, then there's heroin. Downtown sounds, from jazz and blues to punk and no wave, capture the spirit of smack. The jagged, drawn-out whirr, pained groans, and droning stupor embody the drug experience. Heroin is as much a part of New York Rock as CBGB or black leather jackets. The VU's "Heroin," in the great bluesman tradition, detailed scoring and getting high. The drug had long been musicians' dirty secret, so the frankness was audacious.

> **KEMBRA PFAHLER (The Voluptuous Horror of Karen Black):** I do feel drugs have a parallel existence to the music and art created. In the late '70s and early '80s there was an infiltration of heroin. Bands were making loud, viscous, and sloppy but intelligent music. That was the spirit of the times. Whether or not you were on heroin, it played into the sound and subject matter. (2006)

> **SONNY VINCENT (Testors):** Heroin had both a positive and negative effect on the New York scene. I've seen Johnny Thunders play sets more energetic and passionate while fully whacked on heroin than other people who were straight as a judge. But of course it did wreck some of the momentum of some of the artists and their output. The drug does have an alluring "pull" to say the least. Just the fact that you bring it up makes me feel these feelings. . . . Actually I'd like to shoot some right now! (2011)

The big daddy of all intoxicants entranced generations of enthusiasts with its own lore and allure. New York looms as a heroin hub, where dope makes sense. For some, it offered escape from urban strain and pain. To those who could handle it, heroin offered transcendence and artistic liberation.

JOHNNY THUNDERS (The Heartbreakers): I take smack because I enjoy it. I enjoy all it makes me feel. I don't do it to be in with the in crowd or shit like that. I do it because I enjoy it. If I didn't enjoy it I'd never do it, and if it interfered with my music I'd never do it. I can rock out with it. I can rock out without it. It doesn't affect my performance at all. (1980)

MIKE DOUGHTY (Soul Coughing): When I later became addicted to booze I woke up with the shakes, and I'd drink a beer before I brushed my teeth, and then try and stay a little bit drunk, but not super drunk, all day. That was when I said to myself that the game was done. (2012)

The name of this band is Talking Heads: CBGB, 1977. Photo by GODLIS.

CHARACTER TYPE

I don't have to prove
That I am creative!
—Talking Heads, "Artists Only"

You can't discuss New York Rock without discussing the characters creating it. Offbeat artists with art-school training built New York Rock—very different from clichéd images of four L.A. dudes rockin' out in a garage. Music made by aspiring painters, poets, actors, filmmakers, and designers makes for a distinct product.

MOBY (DJ): New York Rock is the cross-pollination of rock and art. Talking Heads are a perfect example: they all went to RISDI and were all artists. That element introduced an air of erudition to the New York scene. (2004)

DON HILL (club owner): There's an artistic pretense here that you don't get anywhere else. You're never gonna play Lincoln Center if you're from Nebraska, but New York bands get to do that. New York band members have abilities to conduct symphonies and do soundtracks. You really only get that in New York. Dimensions here are much deeper. We are cultural snobs in New York. Bands here read books. (2005)

JEFFREY LOHN (Theoretical Girls): There were a lot of artists involved. That was what was unique about it. Some of the bands that were around at the time were "arty." That's the best word to describe it. They were not just commercial pop kinds of people; they were connected to the art world in some way. They were more philosophical, idea-oriented people. We were just making a more creative, noncommercial kind of music, more experimental, connected to ideas. Not slick. (2002)

JIM JARMUSCH (filmmaker): I feel more comfortable around musicians and I've met a lot of people through music. I used to hang out at Max's and CBs. A lot of the reason I even make films started from New York music culture in the late '70s. That scene gave me the courage to express myself in film without having to be a virtuoso. (1996)

THURSTON MOORE (Sonic Youth): Filmmakers like Richard Kern and Jim Jarmusch, people who are the same age as us, could've easily been switched around. It just happened that they're filmmakers and we're musicians. (1987)

RICHARD HELL (The Voidoids): Also, I think it was a moment in cultural history when it occurred to kids who liked to read and liked to write that they could also form bands. I don't think it's because there's much in common with rock and roll and poetry, except that the kids who also ended up writing had seen the power of physical music and how it could be combined with all the possibilities of writing, too. Anyway, it's boring. (2006)

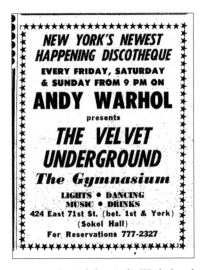

Artists only: Ad for Andy Warhol and The Velvet Underground, The Gymnasium, 1967. Collection of the author.

Warhol forever changed rock music when he conferred his artistic blessing on a band: "Andy Warhol's Velvet Underground." They brought a new attitude and new rules, tied to Warhol's emphasis on social scenes and "being fabulous." His Factory scene of freaks and wannabes exuded egotism and camp, culminating in "fifteen minutes of fame." Gatekeepers shielded Andy from those not "au courant."

WALTER STEDING (artist/musician): From working as his assistant, what I can say is Andy really understood the big picture. He had such an open mind. He'd have lunch with museum directors then meet up with his transgender junkie decadent friends making movies. He knew what would be collectible. He encouraged people and he did not interfere. Like with the Velvet Underground, he let the artist speak. (2011)

LEEE BLACK CHILDERS (photographer): I started taking photos of all these incredible drag queens in Greenwich Village, and I was taking photos of the Velvet Underground. The next thing I know Andy said to me, "You're a photographer!" I was pronounced a photographer and at that moment I think I turned into a really good one. Before that, it never even dawned on me I was a photographer. (2011)

New York Rock's Warhol "look"—austere in black—was born of the city's *noir* nightlife. We know the French had Parisian intellectuals dressed in black, in berets and turtlenecks. And black looked terrific in early B&W films; avant-garde filmmakers knew how to dress actors to enrich chiaroscuro. The VU set the tone for the '60s: cynical and in all-black. Then came the '70s punks in black leather, dressed straight outta *Lords of Flatbush*, in as much of a defensive posture as an antifashion one, bolstered by an "I'm no stereotype of anything" attitude. People still try to attain such New York cool.

RICHARD KERN (filmmaker): The no-wave look was all black. I remember peeking at Beth B's wardrobe, and everything was black. Lydia's, the same: all black. I had two pairs of straight-leg black jeans; that's all I wore. You just needed black clothes. (2004)

BEBE BUELL (musician): Black is the best color: it's slenderizing, it's mysterious, it's hot, and it makes you look dangerous. To be a great rock-and-roller, you gotta have a great pair of peg-leg black jeans. If you don't have your pair, you're pretty much out of it. Those and your studded black belt and leather jacket. These are the mainstays. (2004)

JOHN CALE (The Velvet Underground): I loved black. I thought priests had a really good idea because you could never tell if they're clean or dirty. It gave a certain businesslike patina, which is scary as hell mixed with what we were singing about. (2004)

Gays, women, blacks, and other outsiders were always involved in the process with no questions asked, and invoking no progressive multicultural imperative.

JAKE SHEARS (Scissor Sisters): One thing I love about living here is how gay it is. But to me, to be a rock singer, you have to have gay in you. It's like being a hairdresser or ballet dancer or a fuckin' flight attendant—it's gotta be in there somewhere. (2004)

ADELE BERTEI (The Bloods/The Contortions): It wasn't about being gay or bisexual or straight. It was just about being free sexually, it wasn't about hiding or the kind of ambiguity that comes from shame. It was the most exciting time I ever lived in. Every lesbian in the Lower East Side had a copy of *Junkie* and a needle by her bed. That's a big part of the gay experience, getting fucked up. (2000)

KEMBRA PFAHLER (The Voluptuous Horror of Karen Black):
Sexually it was anything goes; girls were not just holes with heart-beats. In other cities people had to identify themselves like, "Oh, we're gay," but here nobody cared. You come here to get away from all that. New York was a place you came to be free and to have your dreams come true, where you weren't going to be ostracized for being too dark. Back in the early days you couldn't wear five-inch stiletto heels and pastel-colored chiffon dresses. You'd be on your bike in tennis shoes or combat boots because it was so rough. Most girls in this 'hood today didn't grow up with Wendy O. Williams or Gyda Gash or Lydia Lunch as their role model. They grew up with a corporate view of female sexuality. TV shows like *Sex in the City*, which I hate. (2006)

LINDSEY ANDERSON (New York scene): The women-in-rock thing, I didn't even hear of that until way after I started playing. It wasn't even an issue. You'd get together with friends and make a band. I hate the whole women-in-rock thing because it's like the Special Olympics of music. Like, "Oh, you're cute. Go over there." That's exactly what I don't want. It was the reverse here. Women in New York were hanging out. (2005)

New York's melting pot meant many creeds and colors propelled the city's sounds and styles. Nonbelievers of all faiths, from secular to agnostic to anti-religious, discarded religion for the right to rock. They all went through various alienations, but arrived at similar conclusions. Blend a few ethnic stereotypes with the status quo of Jews, Italians, and WASPs, and the city's rock sounds colorful.

HANDSOME DICK MANITOBA (The Dictators): Being a Jew-boy, people had Afros, so they called mine a "Jew-fro" because it was an Afro but it wasn't super-kinky and in some spots it was straight. It was so un-kempt and ridiculous looking that I'd wake up in the morning, spread my fingers apart, and just pull it out and down—that was my comb. It was covering my eyes and about a foot off my head. (2003)

New York Rock reflects the city's kosher nature, heavy on hubris, kitsch, Borscht Belt, and Tin Pan Alley. It's the difference between Kiss and Kansas, the Ramones and the Rolling Stones, the Beastie Boys and the Beatles. It's lots of wayward Jews slumming it in a goy realm. None became doctors or lawyers or wore yarmulkes or read Talmud. One can't imagine rock today without Lewis Rabinowitz (Lou Reed), Jeffrey Hyman (Joey Ramone), or Chaim Witz (Gene Simmons).

JEFF WENGROFSKY (New York scene): Jews were behind most radical political and social movements. Then there's the Jewish history in avant-garde art: they change names and noses, definitely not hanging out Downtown to meet other Jews. It was people trying to escape their Jewishness but yet not assimilate with the dominant culture. And part of being Jewish is a reaction against Jewishness. In rock, it was lots of Jews not parading Jewishness. They weren't going for knishes afterwards, or going home to see Grandma. Likewise, make no mistake that the Ramones would've had a very different trajectory with Jeffrey Hyman as the singer's name. In my formative years, I had no idea all these people were Jewish. If I knew it was a Jewish thing, I would've been put off. (2012)

The scene is now: CBGB crowd, 1977. Photo by GODLIS.

THE SCENE

I was at the bar, where I'm a superstar
Livin' on free drinks, "Hey man, your band stinks"
That's the way we live Downtown
—Warrior Soul, "Downtown"

People from everywhere are drawn to the New York scene. "The Scene" is a kaleidoscopic blur of geniuses, wannabes, schmoozers, winners, losers, and hangers-on who socialize and publicize within the city's late-night mix of art and depravity. Starving artists mingle with millionaires and megastars, all indulging in varying degrees of sex and drugs and rock & roll.

MOBY (DJ): It's not a puritanical scene; drugs and sex fuel it. And you can't disregard the sexual component. People buy into a lifestyle. It's a crucible of self-expression; everyone in art and music gets the benefit of the doubt here. (2004)

SHAYNE HARRIS (Luger): The scene's all about networking with the right people, and getting accepted with the beautiful people, hipsters and businesspeople connected. It's about partying with people you'd only dreamed of, even crashing at their homes if you're too stoned or drunk. In New York you cared very much about making the scene. (2011)

New York bands understand the city's intellectual currency and countercultural legacy (and, of course, their perceived role in it). Big Apple musicians long profited from the city's critical machine, where if someone made interesting music or had something to say, there'd be a phalanx of critics, pundits, and people watchers to grease the skids.

GABE ANDRUZZI (The Rapture): Being in a New York Rock band you're conscious of the myth you're making. You're conscious of the element of art and appearance—an aesthetic look and style is very important here—so there's a lot of mystery. (2004)

RUSSELL WOLINSKY (Sic F*cks): Any true New Yorker has a colloquial view, like "This is the epicenter, the rest of the world doesn't matter." It's a big deal to play in the city, so many people here have this "I live in New York, I accomplished my goal" mindset. But that doesn't pay the rent. (2011)

JESSE MALIN (D Generation): It's easy to get caught up in all the attention you receive in the local bars and clubs. But you don't wanna end up as a legend in your own mind. That happens too often here. I know too many people like that. It's tragic, kinda pathetic. (2005)

New York Rock is largely about what did *not* happen. So many people come to the city and play the same venues and run in the same circles but don't attain the legend. Most fail, despite talent and tenacity. For every Lou Reed or Debbie Harry, there are thousands of broken dreams. It's a crapshoot, where many are called but few are chosen.

DON HILL (club owner): I've seen 'em come from as far as Japan and play here to three people. There are thousands of bands from all over the world playing to huge crowds and making a living, but no one cares about 'em. This is the entertainment capital of the world, and it lives by its own rules. You gotta earn it here—it's not a given. (2004)

HANDSOME DICK MANITOBA (The Dictators): It rarely takes off. Bands get signed, act like big shots, and six months later they're back bartending. I've been through it—it's a humbling experience. (2003)

LENNY KAYE (Patti Smith Group): The scene is—by the time it gets recognized—it's probably already over. (2004)

Picture this: Deborah Harry and Chris Stein of Blondie, CBGB, 1977. Photo by GODLIS.

THE SOUND

Heart breathing, eyes splashing
Walls humming, soul crushing
—White Zombie, "Drowning the Colossus"

New York Rock ain't rocket science. The sound's not ornate and flowery. At its best it's direct and to the point, with a simple rhythm, maybe a counter-rhythm, and sing-along lyrics a step or two above nursery rhymes. The objective is more to simplify the chops than to dumb down the idea.

TOM WYNBRANDT (The Miamis): There's a rougher edge to New York bands. It's a suspicion of slickness; anything too slick is seen as inauthentic. The kids making music are more into getting a point across than wanting to be clean on their instruments. In L.A., the Eagles were studio cats; Toto were four trained musicians who decided to be a supergroup, and did. In New York you had four kids who got beat up in high school and never got love at home. They're gonna get their point across, as they believe in what they're doing. (2011)

Most New York Rock bands sounded like their physical environs: tense, noisy, jittery, and irritated, reflective of the hustle and bustle on the subways and the streets.

MARTIN REV (Suicide): The sound of New York comes from the city: the drama, the theater, the certain energy, the subways, the excitement, the culture, and the culture that came before us. It is no accident that the New York movements—and punk was a New York movement—didn't come out of thin air. (2005)

PAGE HAMILTON (Helmet): There's a kind of industrial hum in New York you're aware of when you first come here. Things like the subway and its rhythm always stuck with me, and created noise loops in my head that became riffs for Helmet. You'd have to look at all the New York bands and compare them to bands from anywhere else, and there's no question that there's a distinctive musical vocabulary. (2006)

MITCH SCHNEIDER (publicist): The music sounds like night. It doesn't sound like daytime. I think of the rumble of the subway, the blinding fluorescent white light in the train when you're underground and how everybody just looks so mean and hard-core—though they might be nice. That's the face of New York and that totally seeps into the music. (2005)

Loudness and atonality prevail, with very little "party music." It's antithetical to pop in that it's not trying to appeal to everyone; it's trying to find like-minded listeners, and fuck everyone else.

DAVID HERSHKOVITS (*Paper*): You dressed a certain way and you acted a certain way and it came through in the music. (2005)

DEB O'NAIR (The Fuzztones): The groups here sound meaner. Living in New York tends to make a person more ruthless by the day-to-day scraping along. (1984)

ROB ZOMBIE (White Zombie): If you live in a disgusting city, you tend to think about disgusting things. (1989)

IKUE MORI (DNA): It's much more fun to play in a New York band than it is to be in an audience in a club. (1997)

JON SPENCER (Pussy Galore): As far as the music being hard to get through, that's kinda the point. (1988)

ALCHEMY

THE PRECEDENTS

You can't put your arms around a memory: Manny Roth's Cock & Bull, Greenwich Village, 1966. Photo by Ron Da Silva/Frank White Photo Agency

INTRO

New York Rock did not happen in a vacuum. The VU, New York Dolls, Ramones, Blondie, et al. came from a long tradition, with jazz, R&B, folk, and pop melodies etched into their brains. They created something unique based on bits of shared sounds and experiences.

New York once reigned as the music industry's epicenter. Sheet music, piano rolls, instruments, phonographs, radios, and records were all made here. Most major labels, and many smaller ones, were headquartered here. Every decade had a sound, style, and inspiration connected to the city, and to the music that followed.

New York became the center of songwriting because there was a chance to earn a living. Many of the greats also honed their ideas elsewhere, and then moved to the city to make it.

New York Rock grew from the collision of art and commerce. Rock's intensity is diluted for market by an army of label execs, producers, writers, arrangers, lawyers, managers, and would-be managers. Welcome to the thorny milieu in which New York Rock blossomed.

They're singin' our song: Tin Pan Alley, circa 1925. Photographer uncredited.

TIN PAN ALLEY/BROADWAY

I'd rather be on old Broadway with you, dear
Where life is gay and no one seems to care
—Sheppard Camp, "I'd Rather Be on Old Broadway with You"

George Gershwin and Cole Porter may seem like a far cry from New York Rock. But rock stars like David Johansen, Gene Simmons, and Joey Ramone owed much to Tin Pan Alley's theatricality, the great NYC songwriters and their abilities to turn a phrase.

GEORGE GERSHWIN (composer): True music must repeat the thought and inspirations of the people and the time. My people are Americans and my time is today. (1935)

The most important connection was not the music but the alternative lifestyle. The aura of Tin Pan Alley stars living in "gay bohemia" brought to New York a signature style that would earn the city its reputation for decadence. That era's trendies pushed boundaries, setting the stage for much to come, and for much of what people today take for granted.

OSCAR HAMMERSTEIN II (lyricist): I would like to talk about sentiment in distinction to sophistication. The sophisticate is the man who thinks he swims better than he can and sometimes drowns, he thinks he can drive better than he really can and sometimes causes great smashups. So in my book there's nothing wrong with being sentimental because the things we're sentimental about—the birth of a child, falling in love—I can't help but to be sentimental about such basic things. I think to be anything but sentimental about these basic things is to be a poseur. (1958)

Tin Pan Alley's demise came with the rise of the Brill Building, and bold new sounds like jazz and R&B. The new emphasis on electric gear and musicians writing their own songs diminished the Alley's role. The old Broadway pros could never reproduce rock & roll on sheet music, or compete with street-smart record labels and amateur artists.

DEE DEE RAMONE (The Ramones): We hated all those old fucking show tunes but a lot of them and other stuff are stuck in my brain. That's why we make the music we do. (1986)

Here's to Swing Street: 52nd Street jazz clubs, 1948. Photo by William P. Campbell/ Library of Congress.

NEW YORK JAZZ

In the Bronx of New York City
lived a girl, she's not so pretty
—THE ORIGINAL DIXIELAND JASS BAND, "LENA FROM PALESTINA"

One cannot overstate the black influence on New York Rock. During early-twentieth-century racial segregation, with racial mistrust high on both sides, jazz and blues helped bring the races closer together. Jazz clubs offered taboo drug use, where one could easily score loose joints or some heroin. White youth coming home from late-night miscegenation at Harlem clubs caused moral outrage.

JAMES BLOOD ULMER (guitarist): Jazz was always about New York. It seemed like you had to go to New York to play jazz. If you weren't in New York, it was R&B. (1994)

The hardscrabble New York jazz archetype set a standard to which all New York rockers aspired—purist, no-sellout, and cool, with an emphasis on licentious clubs and high-energy shows.

SAM SHEPARD (playwright): The way those musicians presented themselves onstage in New York, like Coltrane and Eric Dolphy and Charles Mingus and Roland Kirk, they were the heroes of that era. I still find it hard to believe the whole jazz era is over. It seemed like such an active force in the '60s, a real expression of the times—and, of course, it was essentially black and angry. (2011)

Downtown soul: The Glories, live at The Gold Bug, 1967. Photo by Ron Da Silva/
Frank White Photo Agency.

R&B/DOO-WOP

I know of a fool you see
For that fool is me
—FRANKIE LYMON & THE TEENAGERS, "WHY DO FOOLS FALL IN LOVE?"

The first black-vocal-group big acts came from, or resettled in, New York—the
Ravens (hit in 1950), Billy Ward & the Dominoes (1952), the Crows (1953), the
Chords (1954), and the Cleftones (1955). They created the first R&B records,
because motivated New York labels found them first. The music appealed to
baby boomers; the first teenagers who were not called "young adults."

GENYA RAVAN (Goldie & The Gingerbreads): I don't think there
was a rock and roll band back then. It was all R&B groups. It was at the
Brooklyn Paramount where all the black groups first appeared. All
these teenagers were all of a sudden swooning over the black artists at
the time. (2005)

Vocal groups sprang up across the city, harmonizing in schoolyards, subway stations, and on random stoops. The Willows (1956's "Church Bells May Ring"), the Bop Chords (1956's "Castle in the Sky"), the Channels (1956's "The Closer You Are"), the Ladders (1957's "Counting the Stars"), and the Charts (1957's "Desiree") all lived in the same building at 115th and Lenox. Battles for street-corner supremacy arose, like at Queens' St. Albans Park between Herbie Cox's Cleftones, James "Shep" Sheppard's Heartbeats, and Gene Pearson's Rivileers (the latter in matching white leather). Before Phil Spector's girl groups came sassy Uptown ladies like the Chantels and the Bobbettes.

JOHN COLLINS (John Collins Band): Bands back then had the whole package: the dance steps, the pronounced doo-wop vocals, and the nice outfits. It was fun to see a show band come out in matching jackets, all these attempts to create an image. It was very different from what was to come with the Beatles. Not just the hair, which was an extremely important issue—but that time in rock and roll was a different sound. (2011)

Many of the city's stars succumbed to the lifestyle. Heroin derailed Frankie Lymon ("Why Do Fools Fall in Love?") and Dion ("Runaround Sue"), which was shocking at the time. Then came the sudden shift from doo-woppers to hip-shaking soul singers. But a decade-plus of Alan Freed and Murray the K on the dial inspired most early New York rockers.

SEYMOUR STEIN (Sire Records): I miss it a lot, the excitement of the charts. I'd come back on Saturday mornings from synagogue, and have my radio under the pillow so my father wouldn't hear it when he came home, listening to Martin Block play the Top 25 off the *Billboard* charts. That's what got me started. (2009)

The hungry years: Brill Building song-writer Neil Sedaka, 1976. Photo by Lynn McAfee/Frank White Photo Agency.

BRILL BUILDING

You had your way
Now you must pay
—Connie Francis, "Who's Sorry Now"

By the '50s, music business activity shifted from Tin Pan Alley to Broadway's "Great White Way." The Brill Building (1619 Broadway), a ten-story, Art Deco 1931 edifice on 49th Street's northwest corner—named for Brill Brothers cloth-iers, which once operated on street level—bridged Tin Pan Alley panache with baby boomer energy.

JOE RENZETTI (arranger): The industry's big spurt was technology. As the 45 came in, it became easier for the average person to make a record, especially with the rise of Top 40 syndication. At first there was no such thing as a national hit, it was all local; records big in Philly could be unknown in New York. But as the electronics got cheaper and the distribution made it all more available, there was a groundswell. You could make a record, get it pressed, and played on the radio. That's why we all got work. (2011)

The Brill Building was a hit factory. At its 1962 apex, 1619 Broadway stirred with 150-plus music firms: writers, publishers, singers, players, and "pluggers" plying their wares. For a hit, one could one-stop shop: going floor to floor, select a song, and record its demo on acetate. Small-time hustlers lined the lobby pay phones as their "offices." Meetings upstairs resulted in big breaks and broken dreams. Brill "hacks" worked nine to five in cramped cubicles with upright pianos. Fueled by pastrami on rye, they cranked out pop hits, selling an idealized teen lifestyle to a new young crowd with disposable income.

MARK BARKAN (songwriter): It was so easy to get cheated in this business. The publishers ripped you off—they'd take off money for publicity before royalties then take a third for themselves. On this one record, I wrote both sides, played the piano and did the arrangement and got paid ten bucks total! At parties these guys were great and fun, but they'd stab you in the back when it came to business. I could never understand that. I mean, these were my friends! One guy with our wives we'd double-date, and he said, "How could you sue me?" and I said, "Hey, it'd be nice to get paid!" That was the mentality. They thought they were hooking you up. (2011)

JOEY RAMONE (The Ramones): All the artists were artists, and left their business to the crooks that stole their money and got them hooked on drugs. Buddah and Roulette were known as drug labels. That's what happened to Tommy James, to Hendrix, and to Bobby Fuller of Bobby Fuller Four. He did "I Fought the Law (And the Law Won)." He ended up dead with tar poured down his throat by mobsters. (1986)

The Brill Building's demise came fast, starting in 1963 with the sale of Aldon Music—songwriting employers of Neil Sedaka, Carole King, Cynthia Weill, and Ellie Greenwich—to Columbia Records for $3 million. Phil Spector's Wall of Sound (the Brill at its edgiest) crumbled with the rise of folk (Bob Dylan), rock (Beatles), and soul (Motown). Artists creating their own music sapped the control of the professional songwriters. Without that hierarchy in place, music changed forever.

CRAIG LEON (producer): A lot of those CBGB and Max's Kansas City bands came wanting to not copy but to go back and capture the same feel of bands from years earlier. Ramones and Blondie were big fans of, and trying to emulate, that Brill Building '50s/early '60s thing. It was very immediate, and it really hit you. (2006)

Bring the noise: Minimalist composers David Tudor and John Cage, 1971. Photo courtesy of Merce Cunningham Archive.

MINIMALISM

The city's art and music had traditionally come from Uptown. Art—ornate, rigid, and literal—hung at museums and got debated at salons. A new scene of avant-gardists at dodgy Downtown spaces set standards that still apply today. Downtown experienced a nexus of new art and ideas in the '50s and '60s: splattered canvases or flushed toilets and calling it art, composers playing one note (or none at all) and calling it music.

> **YOKO ONO (artist/musician):** Those early days in New York were quite exciting. There was an influential beatnik movement, and then gradually the big hippie movement. Between all that, art movements like Fluxus were on such a fringe that it was not really recognized in the big picture—though we felt like we were the center of the world. (1996)

The story began with John Cage teaching "Experimental Composition" from 1957 to 1959 at the New School for Social Research. New School classmates in 1959 included La Monte Young, George Maciunas, and Allan Kaprow, pioneers of the music and art movements Minimalism, Fluxus, and the "Happenings."

JOHN CAGE (composer): I'm not interested in telling people what to do. I mean that as a social statement. I think we need more of a society without government. We can give examples of its practicality in art, and those can be imitated in society. We can make our concerts instances of the practicality of anarchy. (1969)

Cage redefined classical composition with his concepts of Minimalism. His ideas of the economy of sound—in contrast to ornate Old World classicism, included "micro-macrocosmic rhythm structures" and "embracing of any sound and no sound as music" based on mathematical randomness free of manipulation. Cage caused outrage with his "4'33"'—not playing piano for four-plus minutes as he opened and shut the cover. The interface of Cage-taught composers along with abstract expressionist painters at the "10th Street Galleries" inspired Yoko Ono to Steve Reich to Philip Glass.

PETER GORDON (composer): Cage taught us that anything could be music: any type of sound, any gesture. That also means music can be treated as music, which was very freeing. (2010)

New York Rock's first spasms were felt in 1961 when drummer Angus MacLise and filmmaker Piero Heliczer of Dead Language Press rented the top-floor apartment at 56 Ludlow Street. That's where Angus's new troupe, La Monte Young Trio, rehearsed. Young fell in love with the artist downstairs, Marian Zazeela. In September 1962, she moved in with La Monte and gave her place to Tony Conrad. Tony took cellist John Cale as his roommate. The two joined LMY's ensemble Theatre of Eternal Music that portended the VU.

THURSTON MOORE (Sonic Youth): This music wasn't about being easy or hard, it transcends that. Anybody can play this. Yet there is a certain restraint to it that guarantees it to have this elegant quality. It's all about listening, and group interplay, and your own sense of dynamics. It was the musicians making the music, as opposed to being primarily about the composer. (2000)

'Bout changes 'n' things: Eric Andersen, Gaslight Cafe, 1966. Photo by Ron
Da Silva/Frank White Photo Agency.

FOLK

Move on over or we'll move on over you
The movement's moving on
—Len Chandler, "Move on Over"

Folk music began as a merging of American campfire ballads, cowboy jingles, hillbilly howls, and union songs. "Protest music" voiced opposition to the status quo, supporting emotional issues of the day like labor rights, desegregation, and nuclear disarmament. While not rock music, many of rock's constructs of artistic attitude and stage presentation came from trails blazed by folk musicians.

JOHN HERALD (The Greenbriar Boys): I was in on a bohemian revolution in the folk part of art: folk craft, folk culture and so on. There I was in lower Manhattan, and it was happening all around me. People like Bob Dylan and Jerry Jeff Walker, Tom Paxton and Dave Van Ronk were arriving every month. (2000)

Youth descended on Washington Square Park to hear bluegrass and ragtime revivalists and other "young turks" busking for spare change and a chance to be heard. Sounds soared, as did egos—over the fastest picker, truest "traditionalist" or biggest "sellout." Dingy cafés opened around the park's periphery; the Gaslight, Gerde's Folk City, and the Bitter End threw weekly open-mic "Hootenannies," propelling a postwar subculture.

ERIC ANDERSEN (musician): The start of the folk explosion was a handful of writers on Fourth Street. Somebody called it the Big Bang of the singer-songwriter. People who had feelings and ideas wrote songs to perform. It was a far cry from the other thing happening at the Brill Building with Carole King and Gerry Goffin, Neil Sedaka, and Neil Diamond; their job was to sit in cubicles and write songs for others. The Village was an intersection of other forces from Beat poets to Woody Guthrie. (2005)

Folk faded with Beatlemania and psychedelia. Police enforcing Washington Square Park's Sunday 5 p.m. curfew hassled and billy-clubbed young fiddle-pickers, Frisbee tossers, and freedom-seekers. Bob Dylan opened a Pandora's box with his electric band, dividing an uncompromising scene of roots traditionalists. Such purists—like those behind the blacklisting of Pete Seeger for his TV gig on *Hootenanny!* that purportedly commercialized their scene—concur on folk's demise by this 1964–1965 era. Young players like David Crosby, John Phillips, and Judy Collins fled for West Coast fame and fortune. Bitter bards left behind kvetched. Open-minded types rolled with the changes.

DAVE VAN RONK (musician): I formed a rock-and-roll band in 1965. Frankly, I was making a grab for the brass ring. I couldn't see why not to. Subsequently, I saw reasons why not. I found it musically boring and I quit, even though it was my band. Maybe we didn't give it a chance. Maybe we needed better representation. But that isn't why I left. I left 'cause I got tired of doing the same damn songs every night. (1998)

We ain't got nothin' yet: Blues Magoos, The Night Owl, 1966. Photo by Ron Da Silva/Frank White Photo Agency.

GARAGE ROCK

Hot town, summer in the city
Back of my neck getting dirty and gritty
—The Lovin' Spoonful, "Summer in the City"

New York Rock began in earnest with the impact of the Beatles, the first democratic rock band, like a gang, writing their own songs and not playing standards. Prior to this, rock & roll still sprung from the Brill Building pipeline of songwriters, publishers, and producers directing a magnetic vocalist (or singers) backed by musicians, with a chain of command (Joey Dee and the Starliters, Jay and the Americans). The British Invasion razed the Brill Building. Carnaby Street redefined fashion. A new energy was in the air.

BINKY PHILIPS (The Planets): In 1964, I got my brains fried by the Beatles on *Ed Sullivan*. I was only eleven but like everyone I'd been affected by JFK's assassination like ninety days earlier and was looking for solace and freshness. Murray the K played "I Wanna Hold Your Hand" in Christmas 1963; I remember the raw guitar and the voices. Up until that point every act was a singer or a group choreographed.

There was something about these four guys playing and writing their own songs, it seemed such a complete package, so novel and unusual, and there was such a cultural buildup to it all. Then I saw the Beatles at Forest Hills Tennis Stadium hosted by my favorite radio jocks, the WMCA Good Guys. I spent the entire summer learning to play guitar. (2011)

The Beatles "made it" in New York. On December 29, 1963, WMCA DJ Jack Spector first played "I Want to Hold Your Hand." February 9, 1964's *Ed Sullivan Show* appearance, at CBS Studio 50 (1697 Broadway), aired to 73 million viewers, inspiring "garage bands" everywhere. Their 1964 tour began August 28–29 with shows at the 16,000-seat Forest Hills Stadium, launched by their famed first American press conference in the Delmonico Hotel. August 15, 1965's Shea Stadium show, with 55,000 screaming teens, revolutionized rock and pop culture.

PEPPY CASTRO (The Blues Magoos): The British Invasion was as if they swallowed up American R&B and put it in a blender; it was an amazing onslaught of creativity, so radical and inventive. By the time the Beatles came, no one ever saw or heard anything like that, it was so fresh and new. The buzz was pure frenzy; it was such a shot of adrenaline that anyone into music had to take a look at it. I was in that first wave of American kids that wanted to be part of it. Once Americans came up with our own answer to the British Invasion, with its own mindset, we really hit on our own thing again. (2011)

New York Rock evolved from two 1960s "schools." Uptown scenesters connected to the music business and the city's society elite. Discothèques like Arthur, Ondine, and the Cheetah—swank spots tweaked for mod culture—supplied a sensory overload of cover bands, go-go dancers, psychedelic lights, and swanky types doin' the Twist. Downtown, folk clubs adapted to the new teen energy. Many of these spots were "ice cream bars" and didn't sell booze. The Night Owl catered to finding "the next Beatles." Village kids like the stylish Blues Magoos and the rootsier Lovin' Spoonful cut some of the first garage rock.

GENE CORNISH (The Rascals): Two revolutionary albums were *Pet Sounds* by the Beach Boys—it wasn't that surfer crap they were playing—and *Sgt. Pepper's* by the Beatles, which Paul McCartney has said many times was inspired by *Pet Sounds*. It was the iconic album of albums. Before the Beatles, you just did singles. If you got a hit, you just threw a bunch of crappy songs together, and put the hit on there to sell the album. The Beatles made it so the album was a whole picture of the group. Even when we did a B-side, we wanted to be sure it was quality. We didn't put out crap just for filler. (2012)

Kill for peace: Ed Sanders, The Fugs, 1965. Photo by Ron Da Silva/Frank White Photo Agency

FREAKS

Slum goddess from the Lower East Side
Slum goddess gonna make her my bride
—The Fugs, "Slum Goddess"

The first cracks in the postwar American façade started in the '50s in New York with the beatniks, espousing alternative thought and bodily expression, to a soundtrack of ribald poetry, cool bebop, and pensive folk. That mindset segued into the Beatles revolution, to create a distinct New York City hippie subculture.

DAVID PEEL (David Peel & The Lower East Side): There was your West Coast "peace and love," but the Lower East Side was different. We were hippie-anarchist-whatever. We believed in revolution. The Vietnam War had a lot to do with that. People now talk about punk rock: what we did was punk rock ten years before punk rock. (2009)

Modern rock began with the Fugs, their name a sanitized version of the F-word. They were the first group not teeny bop, the first meeting of underground art and rock, in New York if not ever, transforming pop's cuteness into something mind-blowing. The Fugs were so far out that only now can their music be fully appreciated.

KEN WEAVER (The Fugs): It was 1965! I don't even remember what the hell was popular back then, but it wasn't freaks. There weren't any hippie bands back then—there was shit like this band the Dave Clark Five—all these Beatle imitators, all these cute people. We weren't cute. (2005)

ED SANDERS (The Fugs): "Mustang Sally" was in all the jukeboxes that summer. We'd go to all the Happenings. I knew Steve Weber and Peter Stampfel who had this band the Holy Modal Rounders. I got them to play at my bookstore opening in February 1965. Andy Warhol made the banners. James Michener was there, so was William Burroughs. It was a groovy time. (1994)

New York's "hippie dream" crashed and burned with the violent criminality of a city in decline, and a rising netherworld of hucksters, hustlers, panhandlers, pickpockets, narcs, and other bad seeds scamming, robbing, assaulting, and raping. Lower East Side light poles were plastered with flyers from distraught parents in search of their runaway teens. The perpetrators of the Groovy Murders and other heinous events fueled white flight.

PETER STAMPFEL (The Holy Modal Rounders): The Lower East Side collapsed by 1968. The murder of Groovy was the first shot over the bow, so to speak, signifying a decaying social situation. The neighborhood got more dangerous; friends were dead of overdoses or murders. Cities were burning with race war, and got worse after Martin Luther King got shot. Forty-second Street sleaze started hanging out Downtown, not just artists but ex-cons and spare-changers and runaways. The darker aspects continued to spiral down. The 1965–1966 hippie scene by 1967 was a confluence of runaways, ex-cons and bad drug dealers. It was a catastrophic collision course of sleazoid criminals, doe-eyed innocent kids and a burgeoning bohemia. Plus all the cuckoo lefty politics, extremists deeply batshit like the Black Panthers and Weather Underground manipulating kids. It was a real nightmare bunch of shit, which doomed and completely discredited the hippie scene. There were all these sociopath types on the scene, and one of these guys killed Groovy. This was during the Summer of Love, a utopian ideal doomed to failure due to human nature. (2011)

Some time in New York: Yoko Ono and John Lennon, outside the Dakota, 1977. Photo by Greg Oese/Frank White Photo Agency.

'70S ROCK

Nobody came to bug us, hustle us or shove us
So we decided to make it our home
—JOHN LENNON, "NEW YORK CITY"

Today, New York Rock of the '70s gets discussed in terms of glitter rock or punk rock, but those were slow-moving subcultures that popped up years later. The city hosted plenty of intense and unorthodox '70s mainstream rock scene action.

MICK JAGGER (The Rolling Stones): A lot of interesting music and art made it through the New York squalor. There was a vibrant art scene back then, lots of new things, new people. And a great music scene, too, with dancing, and clubs. It was a big interesting time to be living in the city: the place falling to bits, going broke and Son of Sam and all that. It loomed large as an object in your imagination. (2011)

The press splashed images of British rock stars playing and partying in NYC. Dandies like David Bowie and Gary Glitter at Max's Kansas City made waves. The aura of Led Zeppelin or Yes at Madison Square Garden defined the era. New York's big rock stars were still the Beatles (John and Yoko at the Dakota) and the Stones (Mick and Bianca at Studio 54). The city's lure for these stars was twofold: the 24/7 action, and lower taxes.

MITCH SCHNEIDER (publicist): Mick Jagger and Bianca spent a lot of time in New York in the '70s, so did Lennon, so you could feel these people's presence in New York and it really helped New York Rock. They were going to shows so it was given more attention. (2005)

John Lennon loved New York, exemplified by his 1972 album *Some Time in New York City*. He also loved Yoko's SoHo friends' lofts, so he redesigned their Dakota apartment into a Downtown-like loft. John and Yoko's funky NYC days had immense influence, and their bohemian lifestyle fanned '60s radicalism's last burning embers. Then on December 8, 1980, Mark David Chapman laid in wait outside the Dakota allegedly for an autograph. He pulled out a five-shot Charter Arms .38, got into a combat stance, and pumped five slugs into Lennon's chest, as Ono watched in horror. NYPD spokesman Lt. John Schick called the tragedy "as important as the assassination of John F. Kennedy."

BOB GRUEN (photographer): John came here to be part of the New York scene and New York art world. Yoko had been part of the SoHo art world years earlier, so she came up with Nam June Paik and Andy Warhol and John Cage and Ornette Coleman; people she knew as young friends who'd become successful. John came here to meet Yoko's art friends. (2004)

Under the blade: Twisted Sister, L'Amour, Brooklyn, 1983. Photo by Frank White.

HEAVY METAL

My heart is black and my lips are cold
Cities on flame with rock and roll
—BLUE ÖYSTER CULT, "CITIES ON FLAME WITH ROCK AND ROLL"

Heavy metal remains a big part of, yet totally removed from, New York Rock. Many NYC hipsters cut their teeth on metal before moving on to more cultured sounds. First came the original "heavy metal." Then came "glam metal" or "hair metal," a macho suburban rebirth of New York Dolls–style glam. After that came "thrash metal" or "death metal," a crossover with CBGB punk rock and hardcore. Metal bands came into the city to play, to do business, and most importantly, to party.

EDDIE TRUNK (DJ): It's true other geographical spots get looked at as centers for metal—like L.A.'s Sunset Strip or blue-collar England or the Bay Area thrash scene—and for good reason. But New York was always different and grittier and more metal. You had bands not even from New York, like Metallica coming here because of Megaforce, and how Anthrax showed them the ropes. All that thrash music that started at

L'Amour had that New York attitude. There was something special happening at that time. (2013)

As much as British groups like Led Zeppelin and Black Sabbath created it, heavy metal goes back to Long Island, and the amplified blue-eyed soul of the Rascals and Vanilla Fudge. These acts played Phil Basille's Action House in Island Park, and recorded for Atco, Atlantic's rock division.

When that scene faded, the Fudge's Carmine Appice formed Cactus, "The American Zeppelin." Cactus rocked stages with proto-stoner-rock legends Sir Lord Baltimore, and Dust, with sixteen-year-old drummer Marc Bell, later Marky Ramone. LI also launched Stony Brook dropouts Blue Öyster Cult, the first underground metal band, like brainy bikers with Luftwaffe imagery and sci-fi lyrics. Another big one was Blackjack, which made two major label albums with airbrushed covers before their guitarist Bruce Kulick joined KISS and singer Michael Bolotin became lite legend Michael Bolton.

GLENN-MAX (Naked Sun): That culture occurred before people had such an acute awareness of being an artist. Now people are savvy about what it means to write your own songs and produce your own music and have a Web site and being creative. If you were some kid in the suburbs, and your main interests were partying with your friends and fixing up your car and cranking Zeppelin on a really good car stereo, writing original material wasn't a huge priority. The priority was to have a fuckin' good time and play loud music and drive a muscle car. Those people, even though they loved original bands like Stones or Zeppelin or Aerosmith, they didn't talk about the artistry. They just liked the riffs and thought it kicked ass; they didn't really analyze it. I never wanted to see Swift Kick play in Farmingdale, Long Island, though I could have. It was all about cars and bong hits and cranking stereos in the parking lot. It was about having nowhere to go; that movie *Dazed and Confused* captured it perfectly. Now people have somewhere to go with the Internet. People more readily have ideas now. (2013)

Brooklyn's '90s tough-guy, blue-collar, punk-metal scene of Type O Negative, Biohazard, and Life of Agony went off in unforeseen directions. The menacing Pete Steele of Type O died a broken man at forty-eight. His onetime roadie, Biohazard's Evan Seinfeld, pursued a porn career and other notoriety. Life of Agony's Keith Caputo went all the way, undergoing sexual reassignment surgery to live as Mina Caputo.

Good times: Chic, 1979. Photo by Laurens Van Houten/Frank White Photo Agency.

DISCO/FUNK

At Twelve West, the sound is the best, I guess you can come in your jeans
But I still prefer getting dressed up, getting dressed up for Regine's
—ANDREA TRUE, "N.Y. YOU GOT ME DANCING"

Disco, like almost every modern dance form, was born of the city's late-night underbelly. It began in the early '70s in reaction to drab hippie-dom, with an anything-goes mix of glam and gutter, driven by ribald desires and stoned delirium. Disco ranged from Halston, Bianca Jagger, and Sir Monti Rock III at posh Regine's, to West Side rough trade hustler bars. Ever since, New York Rock raged in action or reaction to NYC disco glory.

DREW STONE (Antidote): Disco was seen as something that poisoned the rock scene. It was a bourgeoisie, elitist movement. You couldn't get into Studio 54 unless you had lots of money and cocaine and pretty women. That was a whole other galaxy, man. We rock people despised disco, but it had a strong presence in New York at the time. (2008)

The end came cold and hard. Nearly every in-demand disco artist packed it in by 1982 due to lack of interest. The labels turned their backs on multimillion-dollar sellers because they were no longer popular. Comparisons to such overnight cultural ruin included the Beatles' obliteration of the Pat Boones or Nirvana's deflation of hair metal. On the other hand, disco never really died. Future NYC-created sounds based upon disco include house, electro, and techno. Disco forever changed rock, and the city's rock scene always had a love/hate affair with the dance floor. Punk clubs mutated into "rock discos" like Mudd Club and Danceteria, upsetting many diehards. New York rockers to successfully "go disco" included Blondie and Talking Heads.

CHUCK RUSINAK (2001 Odyssey, manager): By the '80s, the nightclub business was turning sour. Drugs were rampant. Studio 54 was closing. There was no direction in music. You had everything from new wave to rap. I didn't know where to go with the club. There was no more dancing. No one was doing the Hustle. (2005)

King of rock: Run DMC, Madison Square Garden, opening act the Beastie Boys, 1987. Photo by Frank White.

HIP-HOP

Tear a nigga's head off for lookin' at ya wrong
But won't touch a little white man for stealin' your songs
—Kid Capri, "Creepin'"

Hip-hop began within a ten-square-mile radius of Harlem, the South Bronx, and Queens. The cutting and scratching and braggadocio reflected NYC: rhythmic and raucous. Rap may have started Uptown but it exploded in the Downtown clubs, and that hype is what put rap on the map. Its influence on New York Rock cut both ways—hip-hop fueled sounds/styles, while punk and new wave shaped rap's presentation and evolution.

AFRIKA BAMBAATAA (DJ): Punk rockers were the first whites to accept hip-hop and they started mixing with us. We both looked at each other crazy at first, but after a while everybody was cool and hanging. People thought there was gonna be race wars but we shut them the fuck up. You had all dancing under one roof whether it was Downtown or in the South Bronx. (1995)

ADAM HOROVITZ (Beastie Boys): Rap is no huge thing—it's like punk rock or something. (1985)

The tale of Def Jam, with Rick Rubin, Russell Simmons, and the Beastie Boys, dates back to the 99 Records shop on MacDougal Street, where owner Ed Bahlman educated those kids on rare grooves and new trends. The store's label released Liquid Liquid's "Cavern" with its unmistakable riff sampled on Grandmaster Flash's "White Lines." Native Tongues Posse (Queen Latifah, De La Soul, Jungle Brothers, A Tribe Called Quest) took off Downtown at parties like Nickel Bag, Payday, and Hotel Amazon. Rockers John King and Steve Ett ran Chung King House of Metal, the studio behind the Beasties' *Licensed to Ill* and Public Enemy's *Fear of a Black Planet*. The city's rap legacy has filled books. It all brought a dope mindset to New York Rock.

BILL ADLER (Def Jam): Punk was the revolution that failed; rap is the revolution that succeeded. Of course there were great punk bands like the Ramones at CBGB but they never meant anything on the charts. The entire movement was a critic's wet dream. Whereas "Rapper's Delight" charted in a dozen countries, and the song was fifteen minutes long. Rap came along at exactly the right time to reinvigorate rock and roll. Objectively, it was exciting in the way you wanted rock and roll to be, it was sexy and aggressive, and it occurred at a moment rock was flat on its back. Punk understood that. They wanted to reinvent it because too much Pink Floyd made them sick. They tried to bring it back to basics, and people by and large did not bite. Half a decade later, rap music became the new rock and roll, and it did so on its own merits. On its own merits, rap won. (2014)

Get into the groove: Madonna,
Radio City Music Hall, 1985.
Photo by Frank White.

GARAGE/TECHNO

Let's get this party started right
Let's get this party started quickly
—STRAFE, "SET IT OFF"

House music, garage, freestyle, and techno played into New York Rock via "clubland," a decadent underworld where rockers mingled with dance-floor scenesters. Disco's early-1980s demise resulted in its reinvention by DJs like Larry Levan at Paradise Garage, Jellybean Benitez at the Funhouse, Junior Vasquez at Sound Factory, and David Morales at Red Zone. Such late-night scenes delivered new highs in pansexual adventure.

STRAFE (musician): I feel like a painter working with montages. It's like a coloring book. The freedom of jazz is synonymous with the freedom of dance. I also like the abrasiveness of Led Zeppelin. I just try to tune in to what's happening around me. I'm turning off the TV and just listening to the New York environment. (1986)

There will always be such an audience for a late-night soundtrack to nefarious nocturnal activity. The urge to "go clubbing" remains stronger than ever. Modern club culture is a replica of a twentieth-century Manhattan model. New York Rock intersected, often uneasily, with dance clubs. The scenes collided, as places to party, to maybe play, or to find a job. Many jaded rockers got into the groove.

MOBY (DJ): I've always felt a strong connection to New York, and in some ways my music is paying homage to what I've learned living here. In terms of rhythms and soundscapes, I think it reflects the realities of living Downtown, with all its attitude and energy. (2004)

WAITING FOR THE MAN

THE VELVET UNDERGROUND

1965–1973: Lou Reed, John Cale, Nico, Andy Warhol, Exploding Plastic Inevitable, Tom Wilson, Steve Sesnick, Doug Yule, *White Light/White Heat, Loaded, Squeeze*

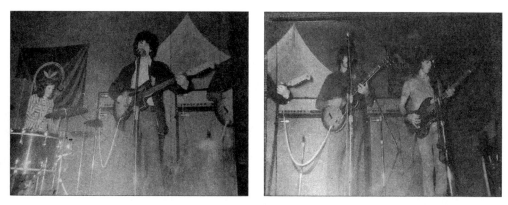

All tomorrow's parties: The Velvet Underground, The Matrix, 1969. Photos by John Aes-Nihil.

THE VELVET UNDERGROUND

I'll be your mirror, reflect what you are
In case you don't know
—THE VELVET UNDERGROUND, "I'LL BE YOUR MIRROR"

The Velvet Underground struck an un-groovy, dark urban pose, ill at ease with the Summer of Love. Their poetic Downtown noise, once critically panned as sub–Simon & Garfunkel, now reads as legendary. Met with mixed reception in their day, the VU's four studio albums barely cracked the Top 100, yet they still sound fresh fifty years later.

JOHN CALE (The Velvet Underground): We started in 1965. We were there because of the Beatles revolution. We thought because Lou was a poet and I was a composer that we could really give Bob Dylan a run for his money, and never have to do records because we'd perform different music every night and set different standards and improvise and go about it aggressively. Lou was especially attuned to that paranoid flavor people may have been thinking. (1999)

LOU REED (The Velvet Underground): I never cared if what we did was counterculture or not, I didn't care about anything like that. I tried to write something good, to elicit an emotion, or to take one to a certain place. I didn't care what was going on outside, I didn't care about other people, I was doing it for me. But I will say one thing for that time: we never ever bluffed. (2000)

The VU cannot be compared to other rock bands because of the blessing conferred upon them by Andy Warhol. That, combined with the band's look and feel—dressed in black, cool and aloof—made them read as "arty." Bands have tried ever since to attain such attitude and such loftiness.

LENNY KAYE (Patti Smith Group): The Velvets made an adult music. It wasn't kids' music, it wasn't teen rock and roll, and it wasn't garage rock. It was the equivalent of film and art. They were the Jean-Luc Godard of New York Rock. It had theory, it had great songs, and they had an intelligent cultural platform. (2004)

PAUL MORRISSEY (filmmaker): It was the first time the art world had any connection to the rock-and-roll world, and the art world's been craving it ever since. And the rock-and-roll world's been craving a connection to the art world ever since. (1999)

DOUG YULE (The Velvet Underground): The theatricality of their presentation was such an intense step up from any other band I'd been exposed to, it immediately gave me new ideas I'd never even considered before. It was like a *Sgt. Pepper's*, it was an awakening of bold new ideas. So when they called me out of the blue and offered the job, I was stunned and said yes right away and left for New York within an hour. For me, it was an instant connection. (2011)

JOHN CALE: We had advanced ideas. We were fascinated by subliminals: subliminal advertising and images and techniques—the subconscious being the best way to control people's behavior. But we also believed setting people off was the best way to advance the human intellect; which came from having a fucked-up attitude about people. (2004)

LOU REED: William Burroughs was running around way before us, as was Hubert Selby. Those ideas were so interesting that we moved those things into the arena—for the lack of a better word—of music. People think we invented it but of course we literally didn't do anything. It's not even a blip on the radar. Andy made it possible by encouraging that kind of stuff, but I just had a job as a songwriter. The precedent of this stuff goes back centuries. So you read these books, and you run with it. (2000)

Here comes two of you
Which one will you choose?
—THE VELVET UNDERGROUND, "BEGINNING TO SEE THE LIGHT"

In the '60s, New York's two big "underground rock" bands were the Fugs and the Velvet Underground. Both came from Downtown and both came from a similar visceral subculture. But they're far from twin pillars. They represent two distinct currents of the city's psychedelia, two twisted types of college-educated rockers.

STERLING MORRISON (The Velvet Underground): The only people playing in New York City at the time were the Fugs and ourselves. We were all lurking around the old Cinematheque and occasional gala underground events at the Village Gate downstairs. It was them and us living in the Lower East Side with, like, twenty-five dollars a month combined. (1981)

The Fugs and the VU reflected their particular muses. The VU worked with Warhol and ran in SoHo art circles. The Fugs worked with Allen Ginsberg and embodied East Village radicalism. The VU offered something chic, akin to Carnaby Street but in black. The Fugs crowd was stoner beatnik freaks. The VU played along to silent art films and as a soundtrack to Warhol's Exploding Plastic Inevitable. The Fugs raged with a proto-punk fury around gritty Tompkins Square Park. The Fugs' Ed Sanders and the VU's Lou Reed shared a Dylanesque propensity for poetry with dark literary references, but Sanders's came of the idiosyncratic William Blake, while Reed's sprung from the libertine Marquis de Sade. The Fugs were the more popular of the two bands in those days. Sanders dismissed the VU as phonies, but then again, he thought everyone was. There was minimal Fugs-VU interplay, like both opening for the Grateful Dead in Pittsburgh on February 7, 1969.

Reed had more in common with fellow angst-ridden New York Jewish singer-songwriter Paul Simon. Reed and Simon both began in high school doo-wop acts: Simon and Art Garfunkel went Top 10 in 1958 as Tom & Jerry; Reed's 1958 single with the Jades, and his 1961 songs with aging hit-maker Bob Shad, went nowhere. Both writers had Brill Building credentials. But one lived Uptown and shot to fame, while the other slowly arose from the Downtown underground. The acts also shared Dylan producer Tom Wilson, but whereas S&G's folk sounded ornate and flowery, the VU depicted the dark and debauched.

Went to the candy store but you weren't there
Somehow I knew deep down that you weren't fair
—THE JADES, "SO BLUE"

The Jades, originally the Shades, was a doo-wop vocal act-cum-loose-knit band with a sixteen-year-old Lou Reed on guitar. Producer Bob Shad (Charlie Parker, The Platters) caught wind of their set at a Freeport High senior variety show, and signed them to his Time label. The 1958 single "Leave Her for Me" b/w "So Blue," cowritten by Lewis Reed and vocalist Phil Harris, is notable as Lou's first recording. After Syracuse University, Lou reteamed with Shad on two 1962 Lewis Reed tunes ("Merry Go 'Round," "Your Love").

> **PHIL HARRIS (The Jades):** When we got to the session Shad had gathered some top musicians for the recordings. King Curtis was part of that band. There was a pianist and a drummer. Curtis is heard on the intro to "So Blue" and "Leave Her for Me." (2003)

> **LOU REED:** Our big moment came when Murray the K played it, but he was sick and someone else stood in. He played it once. I got royalties of seventy-eight cents. We were still in school. We'd open supermarkets, shopping centers, and things like that. We had glitter jackets. It was what was called style—later on people would call it punk but at that time what we meant by punk was a pusher, you know, "He's just a fucking punk!" (1992)

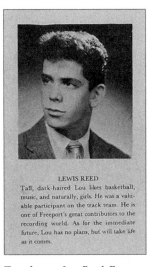

LEWIS REED
Tall, dark-haired Lou likes basketball, music, and naturally, girls. He was a valuable participant on the track team. He is one of Freeport's great contributors to the recording world. As for the immediate future, Lou has no plans, but will take life as it comes.

Transformer: Lou Reed, Freeport High School *Voyageur* yearbook, 1959.

In 1964, Reed landed a Brill Building songwriting gig working for Jerry Vance and Terry Phillips (Jerry Pellegrino and Philip Teitelbaum) at Pickwick Records. There, from nine to five, he wrote novelty songs and knockoffs, cut with C-list session players and pushed as having come from real groups like the Primitives, All Night Workers, the Roughnecks, and the Beachnuts. His finest Pickwick work may be 1965's "Soul City" 7" released as the all-girl act the Foxes.

The Primitives came out on Pickwick City (a sub-label with a logo depicting the 59th Street Bridge). Lou cowrote and sang 1964's "The Ostrich," which failed to start a dance craze like the Twist. The B-side, "Sneaky Pete," foretold Lou's VU style. To promote the 45, Pickwick asked Lou to put together a live group. Tony Conrad heard the recordings and told John Cale about them. The two were bandmates in Theatre of Eternal Music. Conrad and Cale joined Reed's band, as did La Monte Young's drummer Angus Maclise. Lou reteamed with his college pal Sterling Morrison, and put him in the band. The brainy Cale identified the similar tunings of Lou and La Monte, and relished a chance to rock for young ladies.

The All Night Workers, the next step to the VU, featured the first collaborative work between Reed and Cale. Reed socialized back at Syracuse with a frat band called Otis & the Headliners, then Otis & the Elevators, that included Reed's roommate, guitarist Steve McCord (who turned down the Young Rascals to finish college), future Blues Magoos guitarist Mike Esposito, organist

Lloyd Baskin (pre-Seatrain), and drummer Herb Flower. Their bassist, Billy Elmiger, wrote the A-side of the All Night Workers' 1965 "Don't Put All Your Eggs in One Basket." That 45, "A Lee Harridan Production" on Pickwick's Round Sound imprint, offered the Philips/Vance/Reed/Cale–credited flip side "Why Don't You Smile." Lou quit Pickwick when they wouldn't let him do "Heroin."

STERLING MORRISON: When the whole thing with Pickwick fell apart, we sat around and said, "There's no way we can put a band together that can work in this city." Because all that was going on in Manhattan in the early '60s were these slick Midtown club acts like Joey Dee and the Starliters who wore matching suits. So we decided to forget about competing and just play songs we liked. (1981)

> *What goes on in your mind?*
> *I think that I am upside down*
> —The Velvet Underground, "What Goes On"

Reed and Cale honed a sound born of both bohemia and suburbia, with haunted lyrics and a hypnotic whirr. Cale, a Welsh classical violist, trained under Aaron Copland before La Monte Young. Reed grew up living the Jewish-American dream with his bookkeeper father and beauty queen mother at 35 Oakwood Avenue in Freeport, Long Island, right by Nathan's Famous in Oceanside. Lou never overcame his family allowing electroshock to "cure" his homosexuality. After therapy "failed," Lou moved in with Mike Quashie in the Village.

STERLING MORRISON: I was afraid of Lou's parents. There was this constant threat of them seizing Lou and throwing him into a nuthouse. That was always over our heads. Every time he got hepatitis his parents were waiting to seize him and lock him up. (1981)

Sterling Morrison (Holmes Sterling Morrison, Jr.) was studying at City College when he ran into Reed on the C train in late 1964. The trumpeter-turned-guitarist/bassist studied creative writing with Reed under Delmore Schwartz (muse to the first VU LP's "European Son [To Delmore Schwartz]"). Reed and Morrison were of a similar mindset, their literary aims cloaked in urban drug culture. Angus Maclise, an obstinate artist, ran by his own schedule. Reed,

Cale, Morrison, and Maclise toyed with various band monikers like the War-locks or Falling Spikes before settling on the title of Michael Leigh's 1963 soft-core novel. Tony Conrad and Gerard Malanga gave their copy to them.

STERLING MORRISON: We owe that legacy to Gerard Malanga who in his infinite wisdom did outrageous things. Suppose that title we took for our name had been on a detective novel. It just happened the book was about that. It was a dumb book. (1970)

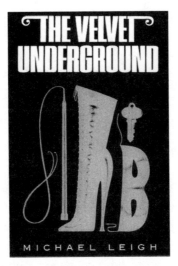

That's the story of my life: *The Velvet Underground*, by Michael Leigh, 1963. Design by Paul Bacon Studios. Collection of the author.

> *Just like I figured*
> *They're always disfigured*
> —THE VELVET UNDERGROUND, "HEAD HELD HIGH"

The Velvet Underground applied Minimalism to Phil Spector's Wall of Sound, their melodic patterns buoyed by Cale's low-end bass/viola drone and Reed's and Morrison's down-tuned guitars. July 1965's first rehearsal tape—with Cale, Reed, Morrison, and Conrad, and Maclise MIA—eighty minutes on Cale's Wollensack reel-to-reel, included "Heroin," "Venus in Furs," "All Tomorrow's Parties," "I'm Waiting for the Man," and "Wrap Your Troubles in Dreams" (the latter on Nico's 1967 solo album *Chelsea Girl*).

STERLING MORRISON: The antecedent was done in the old Cinematheque, all done by film people; things Angus called "ritual happenings." Underground film didn't mean a thing in 1964 in New York. You were just sneaking around with no money. (1970)

Angus quit the band over the commerciality of accepting a $75 show offer. So Maureen Ann "Mo" Tucker, younger sister of Lou and Sterling's Syracuse friend Jim Tucker, replaced him. The Westbury, LI, native became the first female drummer in a prominent male-dominated rock band, playing mostly bass drum and toms, and very little cymbals.

That first $75 gig came through rock journalist and fleeting VU manager Al Aronowitz. It was on December 11, 1965, at Summit (NJ) High School, opening for the Myddle Class, a popular garage band Aronowitz also managed. Al then booked the VU a late-December residency, doing six sets a night at Café Bizarre in Greenwich Village.

ROB NORRIS (The Bongos): I was at that first Velvet Underground show at my high school in 1965. My friend John was the usher for that Myddle Class show and he called me from the sound check and said, "You will not believe this band." It changed my life. It was a total wake-up call, unlike nothing I'd ever imagined. As you could imagine, it pretty much caused a riot of disapproval, but I was magnetized and mesmerized by the stage. The first record didn't come out for another year and a half. (2011)

CHARLES LARKEY (The Myddle Class): I don't think we knew who they were. It was the very beginning of their career. The kids who came to the show, I don't think they were ready for it. It was eventful in that there was no anticipation. I don't recall anything before the show, not that there would even be another band that night. I was surprised to hear such different music. But it more surprised the audience. We were straight-ahead rock, and that band was something else, so there was confusion in the crowd. (2015)

The VU with Maclise had been performing at the Cinematheque, behind projected art films. Filmmaker Barbara Rubin—the link between the VU and Al Aronowitz—loved what she saw and became the band's first advocate. She spread the word to Andy Warhol, who went to see them play at Café Bizarre.

Café Bizarre fired the VU as the house band for playing "Black Angel's

Death Song" too many times. But Warhol loved their rockin' dance music with blaring shards of noise, and brought them into his realm. He made them part of his Exploding Plastic Inevitable (EPI)—a prerock video multimedia spectacle blending music with strobes, projections, and light shows done by oil refragmentation. The EPI began in April 1966 at the Dom, later called the Balloon Farm, on St. Marks Place; an old Ukrainian Hall packed with receptive art students.

ANDY WARHOL (artist): Barbara said something about this group, and mixed media was getting to be the big thing at the Cinematheque, so we had films, and Gerard did some dancing and the Velvets played. Then Nico came around, and Paul [Morrissey] started the Exploding Plastic Inevitable. We just rented a club, the Dom, by the week, and then when it was doing well, other people just took it away from us. (1977)

What Goes On: *Village Voice* ad for Andy Warhol's Exploding Plastic Inevitable, The Balloon Farm, 1966. Collection of the author.

Andy bankrolled and managed the VU, with his filmmaker Paul Morrissey (*Heat, Trash, Chelsea Girls*). The VU debuted for Andy on January 13, 1966, at the Delmonico Hotel, playing at a New York Society for Clinical Psychology banquet at which Andy spoke. The VU became Warhol's de facto orchestra, and "All Tomorrow's Parties" his favorite song.

ANDY WARHOL: They were just playing loud. They always wore black. They were great. They were somehow a New York kind of band. California kind of won out with all the hippie kind of music. (1980)

PAUL MORRISSEY: I discovered the Velvet Underground, managed them, made their first album and paid for it with Andy's money—which made Andy look like a producer. Andy paid their bills; rented them a place to live, got them amplifiers, and gave them allowance. Andy invested in it; he was the producer as he invested the money. In reality, I produced and managed them with Andy's money. As manager, I saw it as a good way to promote Andy's name, and the way to make money then was to go into rock and roll. It paid off huge as it made his name more famous and situated in that rock-and-roll era—which he was not a part of and didn't want to be a part of. (1999)

> *She's knocked out on her feet again*
> *She's down on her knees, my friend*
> —The Velvet Underground, "There She Goes Again"

Andy's biggest gift to the VU was hiring the striking Teutonic chanteuse Nico (Christa Päffgen) to enhance their sound. The Stones' Brian Jones first brought the Budapest-born model to the Factory, where she stood out among the swingers, wannabes, and debutantes. Nico's hiring caused problems with Lou, who saw the act as his vehicle and her inclusion as diminishing his stardom. But no one can deny that the move worked. It made for some of Reed's best music, such as "Femme Fatale" and "I'll Be Your Mirror," which he wrote for Nico's voice. Morrissey wanted Nico to sing every song. Live, their biggest hurdle was what to do with Nico when not singing (she'd gawkily stand stage-center on tambourine).

PAUL MORRISSEY: Nico came around and wanted to sing. She had a little record she'd made in England and I thought she was wonderful. I said, "We'd like to have a girl sing with you." John and the others saw no problem, but Lou was jealous and hated the idea. When the record was made, he wouldn't let her sing more than two songs. Tom Wilson, who bought the album from me, didn't like Lou and wasn't crazy about the group; he thought they were too peculiar to sell, but he said, "This group has potential because of Nico." When Lou realized they got signed because this guy was crazy about Nico, he was incensed. To Lou, he was the whole thing. Then Tom said, "We need another song with Nico. A song we can put out as a single." Lou said, "I have a single." It was "Sunday Morning," an awful Simon & Garfunkel wannabe. It was to be for Nico but Lou only let her sing background. It was unpleasant to see somebody so ambitious and mean and jealous of Nico, who was very innocent. She was a fascinating performer with a wonderful voice. Before she'd gone into heroin and was on her death trip, she was so beautiful it was unbelievable. She was tall, refined and stood perfectly still with a very deep voice. She didn't jump up and down and scream. She was a class act. (1999)

In May 1966, Warhol and former Columbia studio engineer Norman Dolph ponied up $1,500 to make a VU album. The bill came to $2,000, so the band paid the final $500. They booked eight hours at run-down Scepter Studios on Broadway near Warhol's Factory. "Produced by Andy Warhol" meant that Andy merely sat at the board with Dolph, but his presence impacted the sessions. Verve/MGM producer Tom Wilson (Dylan, Zappa) signed the VU and cleaned up the mess in Los Angeles (like reworking "Heroin") over two days with engineer Omi Haden at either T.T.G. Studios or Cameo-Parkway Studios.

STERLING MORRISON: Andy was "producer" in the sense of producing a film. We used some of his money and our money. Whoever had any money, that just went all into it. Andy was producer but we were "executive producers" too. We made the record and brought it around and MGM liked it. We never cared to do it how most people do. (1970)

LOU REED: We thought it would seem better with his name on it. We were all having fun and didn't care about credits and things like that. "Produced by Andy Warhol," we liked that. It was like being on a soup can. (1972)

Between Verve's unease with the dark material and production snafus with the cover's peel-off banana graphic, it took over a year for the first VU album to see the light of day. In the interim, Verve put out two 1966 singles: "All Tomorrow's Parties" b/w "I'll Be Your Mirror" and "Sunday Morning" b/w

"Femme Fatale." The VU also unleashed 100 seconds of "Noise" to ESP-Disk's *East Village Other Electric Newspaper* compilation.

The Velvet Underground & Nico—with Warhol's name on the cover, not the VU's (!)—hit stores on March 12, 1967. Richard Goldstein proclaimed in the *Village Voice* (4/13/67): "The Velvets are an important group, and this album has some major work behind that erect banana on the cover."

STERLING MORRISON: The album was ready April 1966, but I don't think it even made a '66 release. We were going crazy wondering what was going on while things got lost and misplaced and delayed. I know what the problem was: it was Frank Zappa and his manager Herb Cohen. They sabotaged us in a number of ways, because they wanted to be the first with a freak release. And we were naive. We didn't have a manager who'd go to the record label every day and drag the whole thing through production. (1981)

Sales stalled during the Summer of Love (peaking at #171). It didn't help that Warhol scenester Eric Emerson sued MGM to get his photo airbrushed off the back cover. But despite weak sales, the album impacted future generations of music. Even in communist Czechoslovakia, future Czech Republic prez Vaclav Havel and his resistance members listened to the smuggled LP for inspiration.

JOHN CALE: We'd really stuck to our guns on our first album, and we really believed in ourselves, and did the arrangements. There was something about the band that stood apart. There was a lot of abandon about the attitude. But it was a complete mishandling of the situation. I guess Lou worked for his father's accounting firm, so he had a strong background in the business side of things, and took care of that, and his feet never left the ground. Mine definitely did. (1977)

Warhol cut ties with the VU before their next album; he felt that funding a rock band and all the music business nonsense did not suit him. The VU played at the final EPI on April 7–8, 1967, at a gym, the Gymnasium (424 East 71st Street). In a fired/quit scenario, Lou declared no longer would they be "Andy Warhol's Velvet Underground." Despite their fallout, Lou, John, and Sterling all backed dates of Nico's residency at the Dom's first-floor bar. Cale and Reed played on her *Chelsea Girl*, and Cale produced her 1969 *The Marble Index* and 1971's *The Desert Shore*.

MAUREEN TUCKER (The Velvet Underground): I guess Andy got bored with it, and we wanted to make records and be a group. I don't feel either he or us ever entered into it as a five-year proposition. It just sounded like a good thing to do. As we got into it, it got more fun and interesting, but then he had other interests and so did we. So we parted as friends. (1990)

White Light/White Heat, issued by Verve on January 30, 1968, barely charted (a week at #199). The Tom Wilson–produced album included the 17-minute "Sister Ray" and the anti–Vietnam War tirade "Kill Your Sons" (the latter referred to in David Fricke's 1995 box-set liner notes as Lou's ode to his shock therapy). With that album, the VU became the first American group with a Vox distortion pedal endorsement deal.

STERLING MORRISON: No producer could override our taste. We'd do a whole lot of takes, and then there'd be a big brawl over which one to use. Of course everyone opted for the take where they sounded best. It was a real hassle, so on "Sister Ray," which we knew was going to be a major effort, we stared at each other and said, "This is going to be one take. So whatever you want to do, you better do it now." And that explains what's going on in the mix. There is a musical struggle— everyone's trying to do what he wants to do every second, and nobody's backing off. (1981)

Cale quit after a September 28, 1968, show at the Boston Tea Party, where they gigged so often, they were seen as a Boston band. Cale, married that April to fashion designer Betsy Johnson, had tired of both Reed's power plays and new manager Steve Sesnick's machinations. Plus, Lou told Mo and Sterling that he could no longer work with John.

STERLING MORRISON: Lou said, "He's out." I said that we were the band, that was it, engraved on the tablets. So a long and bitter argument ensued, with much banging on tables. Finally Lou said, "You don't go for it? All right, the band is dissolved." It was more important to keep the band together than to worry about Cale, but that wasn't what decided me. I just wanted to keep doing it. So I weighed my self-interest against Cale's interests and sold him out. I told Lou I'd swallow it, but I didn't really like it. (1981)

Over you: John Cale and Lisa Robinson, Black Sabbath
press conference, Butler's Restaurant, 1972. Photo by
Leee Black Childers. Collection of Tony Mann.

That's the story of my life
That's the difference between wrong and right
—THE VELVET UNDERGROUND, "THAT'S THE STORY OF MY LIFE"

The VU's usual opening band at the Boston Tea Party was the Grass
Menagerie, so it seemed natural when Sesnick and Reed asked that band's
young bassist Doug Yule to step in for Cale. Days later, on October 2, a new
VU premiered at Cleveland's La Cave.

DOUG YULE: I met Sterling and Maureen and Lou, and out of that
came the notorious VU. I was just practicing guitar trying to get better, looking around for the next thing, and John and Lou had a big
argument and John was leveraged out of the group and they needed
someone who could come in. That was a Wednesday night and on Friday
we were in Cleveland playing La Cave. I didn't know all the songs but I
was a fast study. (2010)

STERLING MORRISON: The band was never the same after John left.
He was not easy to replace. Doug Yule was a great bass player, but we
moved more towards unanimity of opinion, and I don't think that's a
good thing. I always thought that what made us real good were tensions
and oppositions. (1981)

ROB NORRIS: Doug Yule was as integral as anyone in the Velvet Underground. It really was a five-person band. Those who discount him miss the whole picture. Just look what he did with *Loaded*, it's amazing, his playing and how he holds things together. He was young and naive and dazzled by Lou, and had to fend for himself with Sesnick. But Yule was central to the band, always. (2011)

From 1967 to 1970, the VU played numerous markets but not New York, due to Lou's avoidance of shady characters from his past, and the band's issues with its local standing.

STERLING MORRISON: The radio wouldn't even accept advertising for the album, because it was about drugs and sex and perversion. A rational response would've been to rent a hall in New York and play there every night. Instead we said, "Fuck 'em, if they're not going to play us on the radio, we're not going to play here. It was a good way to generate mystique, but that wasn't our intention. We wanted to punish New York. (1981)

During a string of November 1968 West Coast dates—in San Francisco, Bill Graham banned the VU for exiting the Fillmore stage with their amps feeding back full volume—this new lineup entered L.A.'s T.T.G. Studios with engineer Val Valentin to do a third VU LP. March 1969's *The Velvet Underground* (MGM), remixed by Reed, had cover photos by Warhol boytoy Billy Name and graphics by staff artist Dick Smith. It offered twelve-string flourishes, as on Lou's "Pale Blue Eyes," the Yule-sung "Candy Says" (about Warholite Candy Darling), and Maureen's vocals on "After Hours." The atypical sound had to do with their Vox boxes getting stolen at JFK. Lester Bangs in *Rolling Stone* (5/17/69): "The real question is what this music is about: smack, meth, deviant sex, or something deeper?"

The VU began demoing a fourth album for MGM at the Record Plant in October 1969, until the label's new president Mike Curb, an avowed Christian fundamentalist, fired all the freak bands, which meant the Cowsills stayed and the VU and Mothers of Invention had to go. (Most of that demo's fourteen songs later appeared on two outtake compilations: 1985's *VU* and 1986's *Another View*.) Atlantic's Ahmet Ertegun and Jerry Wexler, through publicist Danny Fields, signed the group after a March 1970 set with Chambers Brothers at Salvation.

Loaded, released on September 19, 1970, on Atlantic's Cotillion label, featured early takes on future Reed solo hits ("Sweet Jane," "Rock & Roll"). Mike Jahn oozed in *The New York Times* (7/4/70): "The Velvet Underground plays a hard rock that is powerful and tight as a raised fist: so unified and together it just rolls itself into a knot and throbs. They make 80 percent of today's popular rock groups seem pointless and amateurish."

The record also signaled the band spiraling out of control. In the credits, Sesnick billed Yule over Reed and Morrison. Tucker got listed as the drummer but was in fact on maternity leave, replaced by a blend of Yule's teen brother Billy, session player Tommy Castanaro, and album engineer Adrian Barber. Reed quit to go work for his dad in Long Island. Then he briefly returned to play the band's nine-week summer 1970 stint at Max's to launch *Loaded* (their first NYC shows in three years), in what would be Lou's final VU shows. Lou asked Sterling to form a new band, but Sterling chose to keep playing with Doug. That lasted until August 1971, when Sterling quit after some lousy gigs at Houston's Liberty Hall. *Loaded* may have been the VU's biggest album in that it never went out of print.

STERLING MORRISON: I'd hardly spoken to Lou in months. Maybe I never really forgave him for wanting Cale out of the band. I was so mad at him, for real or imaginary offenses, and I just didn't want to talk. So in his last days with the group I was zero psychological assistance to Lou. (1981)

MAUREEN TUCKER: We kept playing shows. When I think back on it, I think Sterl and I just would rather play music than get a job, that's why we stuck to it. The band was good but it wasn't anything special, just something to do instead of "growing up." (1998)

> *Somebody's got the time, somebody's got the right*
> *All of the other people, tryin' to use up the night*
> —THE VELVET UNDERGROUND, "COOL IT DOWN"

Live at Max's Kansas City (Cotillion) was mastered from a cassette recording of Reed's final VU show at Max's on August 23, 1970, taped by Lou's Warhol friend Brigid Berlin. Mercury A&R man Paul Nelson—a former *Rolling Stone* writer and founder of the *Little Sandy Review* that introduced Bob Dylan—

helped facilitate the May 1972 release. Between songs one can hear crowd banter, including Jim Carroll trying to cop heroin.

DOUG YULE: We were playing at Max's when Lou left. Nobody in the band knew. Steve Sesnick knew ahead of time but none of us knew till the first night of the week when he didn't show up. When Lou initially left, it was kind of exciting because I got to do the two things I hadn't done a lot: one was to sing lead, the other was to play guitar. But with Lou not there, a strong center was gone and it was less focused. I had enough of a reputation that I couldn't just go out and form a garage band, but I didn't have the cache to go to a big label and say, "I've got a new band and I'm ready to do an album." (2010)

Sesnick kept the franchise alive for another year or so with lineups built around Doug on guitar/vocals and Billy Yule on drums, with Doug's old Grass Menagerie mates Walter Powers on bass and future Boston punk star Willie "Loco" Alexander replacing guitarist Sterling Morrison. (In those pre-MTV days, few people even knew who was in bands. David Bowie spoke to Doug Yule after one UK show and thought that he'd spoken to Lou.)

BILLY YULE (The Velvet Underground): The Velvets were four people part of a dark scene or various scenes, real or created in the interest of celebrity, and they were adults. Doug was twenty-three at the time of *Live at Max's*, and even younger when he first joined the Velvets. Later, when I went to play at Max's, I was still living at home and searching for who I was, still in high school in Great Neck, Long Island, still immersed in the safety and comfort of middle-class suburbia. The core Velvets were older and well entrenched in urban angst. (2005)

WILLIE "LOCO" ALEXANDER (musician): I never had a rehearsal with them, or ever played the songs with them until the first gig at some festival in the Midwest. I had a sheet of paper with a few things written, like keys of songs and some chords. I had to learn all the Velvet Underground songs. I got most of them some of the time. It was weird. (2004)

Squeeze (Polydor UK), February 1973's swan song, did not come out in the States. Made in London during a 1972 tour, the eleven tunes were intended for a Yule solo recording but the VU name got affixed. Doug arranged, produced, and played the instruments, with Deep Purple's Ian Paice on drums; no original members were involved. In their interviews, upon mention of Sesnick's name, both Doug Yule and Rob Norris hurled invectives, claiming to have never gotten paid.

> **DOUG YULE:** Looking back, I think I was mostly oblivious to everything. I don't think I understood anything in the world, I was just living it. It was very immediate, just looking for the next thing to do. . . . But it took me years to learn my craft. That's why I look at *Squeeze* as being the equivalent of a tenth-grade term paper—it's a piece of work that I did not do my best work, but it shows where I was heading. (2011)

> **ROB NORRIS:** I played on the *Squeeze* tour. For years that embarrassed me but it was great fun. It was so good to play VU music in any situation! It was supposed to be a European tour but Sesnick grabbed the money and ran before the plane landed in London so it was just nine shows in England and Wales. No equipment, and low or no money. One show, we escaped with our lives. Lou was not pleased. We were both there at the same time; he was on his *Transformer* tour. But I will say, wherever we played, people came and were not at all concerned it was just Doug. It was not that big a deal. (2011)

The VU lost their buzz with Warhol's departure, their soul with Cale's, their heart with Reed's, and their credibility on *Squeeze*. Maybe the best thing about *Squeeze* was the British new-wave act named for it. Fans and critics revile the album, but songs like "Mean Old Man" and "Dopey Joe" possess a VU spirit. While not as good as their classics, it was no worse than other filler tracks. By mid-1973, Doug distanced himself from Sesnick.

> **DOUG YULE:** From the day I joined the band until the day I left, I never received a paycheck. If the rent was due and I didn't have money, I'd go ask for it, but mostly I lived at my parents' house and commuted in. There was never any reckoning. There was no, "Here's your share of what we made." Nothing like that ever happened. It was all based around Sesnick's vision of the future for himself. That was one more thing that soured me on the music business and caused me to just go away from it for years and not be involved in the music business. Not to leave the music but the music business. (2011)

For all their legend, the VU performed to little applause, and went out with a whimper. By the time it was over, few people cared.

JOHN CALE: From the very beginning, it was us against them. Absolutely, we got no help from anyone. We'd play Boston—at a movie theater playing for *The Trip*—and nobody was there. Our whole attitude was, "Fuck 'em if they can't take a joke." (2004)

Waiting for my man: Lou Reed, glam rocker, 1972. Photo by Laurens Van Houten/Frank White Photo Agency.

I've been set free and I've been bound
To the memories of yesterday's clouds
—THE VELVET UNDERGROUND, "I'M SET FREE"

June 15, 1990's Cartier-sponsored Warhol fête in Paris—where the four original VU members did ten minutes of "Heroin"—gave rise to a summer 1993 European reunion (sans Yule, who has been written out of VU history).

MAUREEN TUCKER: We didn't do that tour thinking we'd restart the Velvets. That wasn't the idea at all. For me, it was just going to be fun. Especially in Europe, those are the people who've supported us for all these years and we hadn't played there ever. It was great to play for these people who'd been paying my rent! I thought it was going to be great because I knew they'd be thrilled to death. So, that was my thing. That's what I wanted to do, but I can't speak for the others. It was like a "thank you." (1998)

Morrison earned his PhD in Medieval Literature at University of Texas, and then quit in 1986 to pilot tugboats in Houston harbor; he died on August 30, 1995, of non-Hodgkin's lymphoma. Maureen raised a family, worked at a Walmart, and jammed with Workdogs and Half Japanese. Yule, through Lou's then-lawyer Dennis Katz, played on Reed's 1974 *Sally Can't Dance* and then in American Flyer with Dennis's brother Steve Katz (Blues Project), Eric Kaz (Blues Magoos), and Craig Fuller (Pure Prairie League). Nico went home to Europe, and recorded sporadically until her July 18, 1988, death in Ibiza from a bicycle crash. Cale and Reed reconciled after Warhol's death, on 1990's *Songs for Drella*, named for Warhol's nickname, a blend of Dracula and Cinderella. Reed died on October 27, 2013, at age seventy-one, after a liver transplant.

PAUL MORRISSEY: That first album's stayed in print thirty years and it must've made a lot of money. John Cale told me it all went to Lou. Someone manipulated the publishing rights. It wasn't a pleasant experience in retrospect but it was an interesting idea. (1999)

LOU REED: I don't like to talk about gossip—what color sneakers I like or who I fucked the night before. But a lot of people think there's something to be forthcoming about, when there really isn't. It's hard to understand from the outside. (2000)

LOOKING FOR A KISS

GLITTER ROCK

1970–1975: New York Dolls, Magic Tramps, Harlots of 42nd Street, Max's Kansas City, Mercer Arts Center, Nobody's, *Interview, After Dark, Rock Scene,* Kiss

Too much too soon: Sesu Coleman and Eric Emerson, Magic Tramps, School of Visual Arts, 1972. Photo by Chris Stein. Courtesy of Moonlight Dust Archives.

GLITTER ROCK

Something must have happened over Manhattan
Who can expound all the children this time?
—New York Dolls, "Frankenstein"

THE RISE

By 1970, New York had hit the skids. Economic insolvency drove America's business and cultural capital into a criminal hellhole of muggers, hookers, bums, pickpockets, and con men. *The French Connection* or *Kojak* captured the intensity and the blight, but not the olfactory overload of garbage, car exhaust, and excrement of unknown origin.

DAVID JOHANSEN (New York Dolls): By 1970 everything was boarded up, it was over. When we started with the New York Dolls, there was nothing happening, as far as places to play. Besides forming a band, we had to make things happen. (1997)

NITEBOB (soundman/producer): The city was on the edge of collapse and everything was cheap: records were $2.79 and you could eat at Wo Hop for six bucks. Because it was so cheap to live, things were very different. For good rock you really had to search it out. There was no Internet "what's happening tonight." It was all word of mouth, or you had to find that Dolls ad in the back of the *Voice*. (2011)

BEBE BUELL (musician): When I first moved to New York in 1972, I lived with Todd Rundgren on 13th Street between Second and Third, and back then it was a dangerous neighborhood. They filmed a scene from *Taxi Driver* on my doorstep. You couldn't walk around there quite as freely but of course we did—in feathers and sequins and platform shoes. We walked around like a bunch of crazy people. (2004)

The East Village and Lower East Side, historically one of the city's poorest areas, had bottomed out. The hippies were gone, and the tenements and housing projects were in ruins; all that remained were a few tough blue-collar Eastern European types: printers, die-cutters, and glaziers working behind triple-bolted doors with baseball bats for security.

DAVID JOHANSEN: We had a real colloquial view of the world. The East Village was this lab of new social concepts, and when you're involved on a daily basis, you forget there's a world out there. Some people harassed us but they'd inevitably regret it. (1997)

As America underwent post-Vietnam fatigue, rock suffered post-Woodstock fatigue after the deaths of Jimi, Jim, and Janis. Rock turned rootsy and introspective, bands wore fringy leather and buckskin, evoking cowboys and Indians. Rock's nadir may have been George Harrison's August 1971 Concert for Bangladesh at the Garden (the first rock star benefit show), a poorly managed, egotistical affair that browbeat the public, but whose proceeds almost never reached those starving children. Flower Power felt ages ago. Pot and acid gave way to coke, speed, and heroin.

RICHIE FONTANA (Piper): The hippie thing was disintegrating, and people started to dress up, and that made things better. The British

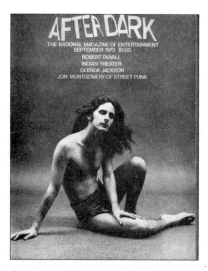

Creatures of the street: Jon Montgomery,
Street Punk, cover of *After Dark* Magazine,
1973. Collection of the author.

influence was big—coming out of the '60s was the dirty hippie scene, funky and dirty with no style—so when innovative British artists like T. Rex and Bowie dressed up, we did too. All of a sudden you wanted a nice tapered jacket and nice shoes, not the dirty sandals worn at the Fillmore. (2011)

JOE VALENTINE SAUSA (The Rags): Music just got stale, the Fillmore closed; there was no scene in New York City. We didn't relate to Southern rock with jeans and beards, and instead of standing around like statues, it was time to play some fun rock and roll again. The Dolls may have generated that. Lou Reed and Bowie were the first to come on strong with some drag, but in New York it was all about the glitter rock. (2011)

ELDA STILETTO (The Stilettos): In 1971, there was this thing coming from the West Coast, they called it "The Avocado Mafia"—the Eagles and "Blue Bayou" and all that. And here we were, a bunch of New York people, living in the art scene going, "Wow, that sounds really boring." So what happened? People started doing music and it didn't matter if you were schooled or not. Didn't even matter if you could play or not. Just get on the stage and figure it out. And that daringness, that's a very New York thing. (2008)

Psychedelia turned on people to an inner quest to break down barriers and inhibitions. So the next logical step in rock's sexual revolution was to transcend the hetero. It's like, "We've made all the free love possible in every position, so let's take that next step." Flower Power gave way to a new thing: London called it glam rock, NYC, glitter rock.

BEBE BUELL: Glam was T. Rex and Slade—more British than American. The people who took trash and glam and married it was the Dolls. They added smut to glam, which gave it a unique delivery. They gave birth to Kiss and stuff like that. They were the first straight guys wearing lipstick and makeup. It was exciting; it was fabulous. (2004)

DAVID JOHANSEN: When the Dolls got together, that was a time when everybody, at least in the East Village, had taken a lot of acid, and was real into this utopian idea of androgyny. This was when real radical feminism started, and the "Up Against the Wall Motherfuckers" types—I used to run with those people, too. We'd be dressed like that all the time. It wasn't like we all got together and said, "Let's dress outrageously"—that's what brought us all together in the first place. (1997)

JOY RYDER (Joy Ryder & Avis Davis): Rock in the '60s was very male driven, a very butch world: Stones, Beatles, Doors, all of 'em. There were no female musicians to speak of. Women were relegated to be singers, like Janis Joplin or Grace Slick. I do remember one or two girl bands and they were mainly gay girls banding together, not many women playing instruments. When I moved home to New York in the early '70s, all the guys wore high heels in quasi-drag but they still didn't want any girls in their band. (2011)

The first London glam-rockers—David Bowie, Marc Bolan, Gary Glitter—beautiful stars with bisexual glamour, evoked British elite effeminacy. NYC's answer—New York Dolls, the Magic Tramps, and the Harlots of 42nd Street—merged Times Square trash and transvestite camp, taking rock's bad-boy cross-dressing impulse to its logical extreme. The merging of UK glam and NYC glitter was Lou Reed's 1972 Bowie-coproduced *Transformer*—the gender-bending title and provocative images said it all. More hands-on than Lou's VU muse Warhol, Bowie cowrote and produced it in the studio.

KEITH WEST (The Brats): We wore all those clothes: the velvets, satins, lames, and all those thigh-high platform shoes. We all shopped for clothes at Jumpin' Jack Flash and Granny Takes a Trip. We loved Bowie, the Faces, Mott the Hoople, and Queen, and got very into it. It was a real androgynous look; everyone was being creative and different. It was a very exciting time, a great time for rock. (2011)

MIKE MILLIUS (Five Dollar Shoes): The only rule was there were no rules. It was all starting to mesh: music, art, and theater. It was an all-night scene; everyone knew each other and hung out. It was full of this wild New York attitude that was like nowhere else, with lots of old and new drugs all over the place. We were punk before they were using those terms. And back then people took great pleasure in getting a rock musician high—an ounce of coke or a big bag of whatever; no one was saying no. (2011)

T. ROTH (Another Pretty Face): When glam started—I'm gay, hello, and have always been into performance as much as music—it took me by storm. Before that, it was long hair, jeans and no style. Everything looked and sounded the same; we needed something to happen. This was before Bowie, with T. Rex, though "T. Rextacy" didn't happen here, or melodic British stuff like Sparks and Cockney Rebel. People saw us in makeup and thought we were insane! In those days, I can't believe the clothes I'd wear fearlessly. And it was so not scary, maybe because of the drugs we were doing. (2011)

SAL MAIDA (Sparks/Roxy Music): I thought it was a weak scene here. In my view, it hadn't kicked in yet. The Dolls tried at Mercer Arts, and then you had all these others like Ruby and the Rednecks, what turned out to be very minor. Only the Dolls happened and it was the beginning of Suicide—all underground and indigenous to New York. In England they had Slade and T. Rex; people forget how big those bands were. What we knew here as Beatlemania, that's the way it was there. It was a phenomenon; these bands would play 20,000-seaters for a week. I needed to go there and see. (2011)

Critics dismissed glitter rock as insincere. But at its core was a deep emotive honesty. It was a scene of motivated aspirants out to conquer the world.

TIMOTHY A. JACKSON (Dorian Zero): Glitter, the metallic dust you can buy in art supply stores, was used in vast quantities in campy stage productions like the Angels of Light and Theatre of the Ridiculous. Eric Emerson of the Magic Tramps used it as makeup and decoration, as did the rest of that band. We played many gigs with the Dolls and the Tramps, and we all started wearing glitter. *Variety* dubbed us all "glitter rock." The Rags and Teenage Lust also played these gigs. Dorian went to the UK during this time, and had contact with some UK glam bands. But we saw our glitter rock as a New York original. UK people like Bowie and Jagger were hanging around our scene. (2005)

Glitter recognized sexuality as a grey area, introducing bisexuality and other fantasias into rock's lexicon. As such, glitter did its part to enlighten homophobic rockers, easing society's queer-basher impulse. It prettied up the hippie, bringing haughty pretension to rock. It awoke Oscar Wilde audacity and Kabuki theater-like feminine impulse. But never mistake dandyish for gay: turned-on women flocked to those dolled-up boys.

JON MONTGOMERY (Street Punk): The vibe in those days, you're talking about really talented bands, in and around the rock scene that put on incredible shows with great clothes and attitude—you know, what rock and roll was. In those days, you had to earn your chops and the vibe in the clubs was phenomenal because there were lots of beautiful people. It was very erotic times, very wild; lots of parties, lots of orgies. (2008)

JERRY NOLAN (New York Dolls): We were all girl crazy. And let me tell you, women knew immediately. It was the men who were confused. The women knew and they loved us for it. We had the balls to look and act the way we did. (1990)

BEBE BUELL: The Dolls were the first straight guys to come out wearing lipstick and makeup, and then there was a whole scene of that. It was exciting, it was fabulous and everyone was like seventy-five feet tall because everybody was wearing giant platform shoes. You didn't know how little someone was till you hit the sack with them! (2004)

Private world: Messiah, aka Magic Tramps,
1975. Photo by Betsy Jones, design by R.
Weinstock. Courtesy of Moonlight Dust.

THE SCENE

The downstairs is packed, and the groupies are all dressed up
Upstairs the New York Dolls are kickin' it out, lookin' tough
—WAYNE COUNTY & THE BACK STREET BOYS,
"MAX'S KANSAS CITY 1976"

A club circuit arose—Max's Kansas City, Mercer Arts Center, Hotel Diplomat by Times Square, East Village drag bar Club 82, the Coventry where Kiss
began; Mother's by the Chelsea Hotel, and the original Kenny's Castaways on
East 84th Street, managed by Don Hill. The coolest scenesters drank at
Nobody's, Club 13, and at Kiss flack Ashley Pandel's fleeting Ashley's, or
after-hours at Harold Black of Teenage Lust's 210 Fifth Avenue. December 30,
1972's "First International Costume Glitter Ball" at Hotel Diplomat with the
Tramps, Harlots, and Shaker, put glitter into rock's lexicon.

CHRIS HARLOT (Harlots of 42nd Street): Music was very important back then, and people were looking for a change. I went for a glittery look in silver lamé suits! It wasn't easy to have a band, and we all worked hard to make it happen. It was a great time to be in New York. (2011)

SHAYNE HARRIS (Luger): Everything was all on you. It was legwork, no cell phones or Internet. On the road you waited to get back to the hotel to get your messages, and you had five bucks in change for pay phones. If you got a good gig you'd pass it on to the next band. Like I booked a gig at Max's, and then walked over and took an ad in the *Voice*. It freed us up to have other bands on the bill who'd push their tape too. You knew when club owners were in the office, so you'd check your watch and then go over and see like Paul Sub at the Coventry to book a gig. It was pretty rough. (2011)

Max's Kansas City (213 Park Avenue South) got started by Mickey Ruskin, an NJ-bred ex-lawyer who owned beat cafés and gay bars. He bought a failing Southern eatery by Union Square and renamed it for some story of original owner Max Finstein. The artist-friendly spot opened on December 6, 1965, serving $2.95 steaks. Ruskin amassed now-priceless art, bartering food to starving artists. Warhol began his A-list scene in the back room, holding court at a round table. Artists like Robert Mapplethorpe, Robert Rauschenberg, and Brice Marden shut the bar for, like, five years straight. Every rock star of the era went to Max's.

MICKEY RUSKIN (Max's Kansas City): I don't remember when Andy started coming, but he added an element. He was still on 47th Street when he started coming down, and that shaped the character of the back room, because Andy would always sit at the big round table and everything kind of followed into the back room. (1973)

DAN CHRISTENSEN (artist): Mickey was generous with artists. If you were broke, you could come in. For many people I know, that was their only meal of the day. (2003)

To see bands, one scaled a dark narrow staircase lit by a red bulb. In that room on July 18, 1973, a young Bruce Springsteen opened Bob Marley's NYC debut. Ellen Barkin and Deborah Harry waitressed (the latter served steaks to

Jefferson Airplane before they played Woodstock). Claude Pervis, Chris Cross, and Wayne County were early-era DJs.

> **BEBE BUELL (musician):** Max's was as far uptown as we'd go. Every proper rock star ended up at Max's Kansas City, in this tiny room in the back where everyone looked gorgeous because the light was red. (2004)

A 1969 fire signaled the end of the club's first era (rival owners scoffed that every few years there'd be a fire at Max's, followed by an insurance payout). June 3, 1968 soiled the club's rep after Valerie Solanis shot Andy Warhol. Then Ruskin bit off more than he could chew with Max's Terre Haute (1359 First Avenue) and Broome Street Bar (363 West Broadway). In 1974, after drug and tax charges, Ruskin sold his club to Tommy Dean. (He died of a May 16, 1983, drug-induced heart attack at age fifty.)

> **BOBBY McADAMS (New York scene):** Max's to me was the club to end all clubs; it was the heyday of rock and roll. It was like the day the music died when it finally closed. That place changed the face of music. (2011)

> **MIKE SCHNAPP (New York scene):** My buddy was way into the punk rock so he knew about Max's Kansas City. So we went and get to the front and there's a sign on the door saying CONDEMNED. There was a chain around the door. It was fucking closed, like the party's over. We just looked at each other and said, "We are such losers!" (2003)

Mercer Arts Center (240 Mercer Street) became an early-'70s epicenter. It opened at the decrepit Theater Cabaret, with six theaters (all named for a playwright or writer), a concert hall, drama workshops, boutique, and bar. Off Broadway and classical took place alongside glitter rock gigs. Scenesters mingled by the bar (or in the bathroom stalls). The Mercer's major by-products were New York Dolls, who started in its Oscar Wilde Room, and the Kitchen, granddaddy of performance art spaces that began in its kitchen. David Bowie got ideas going to the Mercer with his wife Angie and Cherry Vanilla. Fire marshals closed "Downtown's Lincoln Center" after August 3, 1973's collapse of the adjacent University Hotel that caused four deaths and $1 million in damage.

SYLVAIN SYLVAIN (New York Dolls): The hotel collapsed. They were renovating something, and they had a few beams that were down and the subway came unusually fast under Broadway and collapsed the whole fucking building. The whole place came down. There were residents found holding each other and stuff. Horrible. (2006)

Who are the mystery girls?: Club 82, East Village, 1969. Photo by Jason Laure/ Frank White Photo Agency.

Club 82 (82 East 4th Street) presented "lavish costumed revues with scads of female impersonators" (*New York*, 1/17/68). The Genovese crime family clip joint opened in 1951, became a rock scene spot, from the fall of the Mercer to the rise of CBGB. Everyone went there—down a staircase, with a stage behind the bar and a dance floor to the side—especially after spicy photos ran in papers of Bowie and Lou Reed drinking cheek-to-cheek. The Dolls played on April 17, 1974, in drag (but Johnny Thunders refused to wear a dress). Television, Suicide, Jobriath, Another Pretty Face, Wayne County's Queen Elizabeth, and the Stilettos all played there. By '76, the 82 went back to what it did best.

T. ROTH (Another Pretty Face): Our first gig at Club 82 was in 1973. Bowie was there as were Zeppelin and Roxy Music; I was hooked. We started playing every other Thursday for a good year. It was in a dingy cellar, an old Art Deco room with fake palm trees, something out of an old movie. It had a tradition of big drag shows there, so when glam came, it was the place to be. It was mind-blowing, black and red like a den of inequity. I was in heaven. (2011)

Nobody's Bar and Grill (159 Bleecker Street) was where rock stars cavorted late night with local scenesters. David Johansen called the Village drinking spot next to Kenny's Castaways "a flash rocker bar where you could pick up chicks." Nobody's had minimal signage, an unadorned corner façade with a single door, and two small windows. The Chin family owned the bar and their son, Charlie Chin, bassist in the Hendrix-produced Cat Mother & the All Night News Boys, bartended and spun albums on the turntable.

JON MONTGOMERY (Street Punk): I walked into this incredible rock-and-roll hangout, probably the best ever. It was a little Chinese bar called Nobody's. You walked in on the right and there was a long bar, stacked with lovelies. On the left wall was a row of banquettes, with tables in front. Robert Plant held court. Rod Stewart was there a lot. For every English band you could imagine, it was their watering hole. They'd pull up in their limo. Straight suits didn't go there because that had nothing to do with rock and roll. You wouldn't step in there because you'd just be scorned. (2008)

RICHIE FONTANA (Piper): Nobody's was the best. We all liked to go there because all the British rock stars went there when they were in town. One time Dave Davies came in with this girl and we were talking, and they excused themselves to leave. Then they went out and traded clothes and came back in. When Zeppelin were in town, Bonham was drinking and my friend goes, "I love the solo on 'Good Times, Bad Times.' How did you do that?" and Bonham played the whole thing on the tables! (2011)

The Coventry (47-03 Queens Blvd.) was like a low-rent Max's, over the 59th Street Bridge in Sunnyside. The 300-capacity mob clip joint first called the Popcorn Pub (with bowls of popcorn at the bar) notably booked Kiss's first show on January 30, 1973, to twelve or so people. Kiss's final club gig that December 22 used full staging (Sapphic R&B act Isis wrongly insisted on headlining). Sniper, featuring a young Joey Ramone, performed regularly. Dolls, Harlots, Dictators, and Heartbreakers all played. Aerosmith never played because they demanded $300. The Coventry ended in 1975 after an owner went to prison.

PAUL STANLEY (Kiss): The Coventry was important for us, because it was so difficult for a band like us to get gigs because we didn't play Top 40, and we weren't part of the Mercer Arts crowd, which was the crowd that took in the New York Dolls and some of the Andy Warhol, Max's Kansas City bands. So, we needed a place that could be ours, and the Coventry was just on the other side of the East River in Queens. It gave people in New York access to see us, and it set us apart from the glitter bands. The Coventry was where we cut our teeth, and it was the first place we ever played. (2008)

GENE SIMMONS (Kiss): The Coventry was in Queens, in a down-trodden industrial area. Two stories above the building was a subway, so when we played, the trains would be going by, and it was loud. It was owned by the boys "who kinda talked like dis." We played a Tuesday, Wednesday and Thursday and got paid $30. (2008)

LYDIA CRISS (Peter Criss's ex-wife): The Coventry was a dump but it was a happening dump. We didn't go see many bands but I went when Kiss played. It was a long room with a bar to the right, and a stage to the left. The first time Kiss played it was me, Gene's girlfriend Jan, and one of Jan's girlfriends and whatever employees. It was comical, like "Where is everybody?" It was a weekday, January 30, the night before our third anniversary. (2011)

PAUL SUB (The Coventry): New York Dolls kept the Coventry going. They played once a month, and whenever they played, seven hundred people showed up. They had the biggest following of all the bands that played there. The Dolls really helped pay my rent! All the other groups who played from Kiss to Ramones didn't bring many people. (2008)

The Music Box (Union Turnpike, Queens), by the Coventry, was more than a record store. Brats singer Keith West (muse for the Ramones' "Beat on the Brat") opened the glitter-scene hotbed in 1970. Keith and James Spina worked the counter, as customers Gene Simmons and Paul Stanley hatched their rock star plans. (They lasted until 1985.)

KEITH WEST (The Brats): I opened the record shop when I was twenty; I owned, like, twenty thousand records. It was a real meeting place; anyone who was anyone in New York Rock came there. Rick

Rivets just left the Dolls and came in and we formed the Brats. The place became Brats Central, where all the bands hung. Everyone came from Queens, even Manhattan. That's how I knew Johnny Ramone and Bruce Kulick. That's how I met Kiss; Paul came to trade records and bullshit. We needed bands to play with so I hooked them up. (2011)

Hotel Diplomat (108 West 43rd Street) a Times Square hotel frequented by junkies, hookers, and johns, had a run-down ballroom with a balcony that hosted rock shows and record conventions. The Dolls' second gig was there on May 29, 1972. Kiss played on July 13 and August 10. Television and Ramones performed embryonic shows in the ballroom.

Come on up: Tally Taliaferrow amd Binky Philips, The Planets, 1977. Photo courtesy of Binky Philips.

Mother's (267 West 23rd Street), a hustler bar across from the Chelsea Hotel, became a glitter-rock spot. Peter Crowley, a Warhol Factory regular dubbed "Peter Gun" (for big reasons), got his start booking folkies at the Night Owl, Café Raffio, and Café Tangiers. His 1974–75 bookings for Mother's owner Tommy Dean (Mills) stole a buzz from Max's, Coventry, and the new CBGB. Mother's was two narrow storefronts sharing a kitchen-turned–dressing room. At the end of the bar was a doorway to a back room to see bands, often for $3. Richard Lloyd (Television) hated "the little teeny crappy club" where Jimmy Destri debuted with Blondie. Linda Stein saw the Ramones there and told her husband Seymour Stein of Sire. Tommy Dean bought Max's, and Crowley quit to run it.

210 Fifth Avenue, a.k.a. "The 210 Club" or "Harold's Loft," was an infamously decadent weekly after-hours joint (December 1973–March 1975) run by Harold C. Black of Teenage Lust. That's where Warhol types mingled with young bands (like Ramones and Television) and rock stars (Mike Quashie brought Led Zeppelin there twice). Wayne County spun vinyl, and Candy Darling worked the door. Customers entered the Flatiron clock tower building, went up the elevator, and signed in to the "private club."

HAROLD C. BLACK (Teenage Lust): I came across a spot at 210 Fifth Avenue, which I originally called Lust Sound Studios, for the band to rehearse. I pulled out a wall and found this beautiful building by Madison Square Garden architect Sanford White, who designed these rooms that needed no furniture. It was the entire block between 24th and 25th behind Madison Square Park from Fifth Avenue to Broadway. So we restored it to its original 1906 period. It was the perfect place for a party.

Our first party was our legal defense fund after getting arrested; seven hundred fifty people came. So a club was born that night of a one-night party, a secret illegal after-hours club. Saturday nights there'd be hundreds of folks banging on the door from the streets late at night.

The illegality was part of the ambience. One night the Stones came, and when the elevator opens, in walked my friend Billy Preston—what a crazy night! And when Zeppelin came up that elevator, you knew it'd be a wild time. It was a great place to be, and the greatest crowd you could think of, doing whatever they wanted, within reason.

Then there was a change in clientele, disco polyester types wanting to get in. You'd have to hide the stars in the VIP room to avoid getting hassled. It got to a point that I didn't even want to open anymore. The last time the cops showed, they went up one elevator, I went down the other, and split to California. (2011)

Mascara queen, I don't know who you think you are,
But I can tell by your face that you just want to fuck a rock-and-roll star
—THE STILETTOS, "MERCER STREET"

After Dark, "The National Magazine of Entertainment," became a voice for closeted '70s America, covering rock music as a pretext to run shots of bare-chested boys. William Como, editor-in-chief of *Dance Magazine* (noted for his weekly NPR ballet show), also managed the waning Danad Publishing title *Ballroom Dance*. In May 1968, Como and Rudolf Orthwine rebranded the latter *After Dark*, as straight enough for the kiosks but rife with faggotry, like ads for hairstylists, Off Broadway plays, and Fort Lauderdale hotels.

JON MONTGOMERY: The photographer asked if I'd take some photos, and "Do you mind doing them nude?" So they took it in little shorts and I didn't really know what it was all about. I was brought over to the table to meet Norma McLain Stoop and William Como, and they said, "Yep, nice to meet you, you're the one." I had no idea what they meant. So I'm walking down the street, going to pick up a young lady, and I see a bunch of effeminate gentlemen, holding something and giggling. I peered in, and there I was on the cover of *After Dark*. It was funny because in Max's back room, I definitely took some kidding. David Johansen said, "Hey Jon, how many dicks did you suck?" (2008)

Rock Scene (1973–1982) championed the underground rock of the day. The magazine got started by "Doyenne of the Downtown Rock Press" Lisa Robinson and her producer-husband Richard. The two, inspired by Lisa's friend Lillian "Mother of Rock" Roxon (of 1969's *Roxon's Rock Encyclopedia*), held court at their Upper West Side flat. *Rock Scene* scribes included Lenny Kaye and Patti Smith, who penned the first piece on Television. Lisa was the first to write about New York Dolls, Aerosmith, Ramones, and Sex Pistols.

BOB GRUEN (photographer): Lisa Robinson put out *Rock Scene* with her husband Richard, Lenny Kaye, Danny Fields and a few others. It was like a magazine and fanzine at the same time. I worked for them. It was very hip. Lisa always had the inside line on who to see and where to go, she was way ahead of everybody else. It was kind of underground, but we made a joke out of it. It was like a twelve-year-old's scrapbook. All the captions said these cutesy things, but it was all double entendre and cynical asides, inside jokes that if you knew who we were talking about, you'd fall out of your chair laughing. (2006)

CHEETAH CHROME (Dead Boys): We read *Rock Scene* and *Creem*, there was no other. We started seeing photos of people that looked like us, and played original music, proof that it actually existed elsewhere. They did a great job of glamorizing the whole thing. It was so cool 'cause it gave attention and made all these nobodies look like huge stars—very groundbreaking in that aspect. It made us wanna move to New York. (2011)

Smoke and mirrors: Magic Tramps promotional shot, 1975. Photo © Joanne Russo-Bryde. Courtesy of Moonlight Dust Archives.

THE MUSIC

Some hip chick, with her hair wet and slick tried to jab me with her comb
I said, "Get out of here 'cause I'm wasted!"
—THE MAGIC TRAMPS, "MAX'S"

Glitter rock began when the L.A. freak band Messiah (friendly with Frank Zappa, Alice Cooper, and Eric Burdon) teamed with Warhol superstar Eric

Emerson while he was in L.A. in 1968 to film *Lonesome Cowboys*. Emerson—a ballet-trained Broadway child star (*Oklahoma!*) turned-Warhol-superstar (*Chelsea Girls, Heat*) who at 1964's premiere of Andy's film *Blow Job* gave a blowjob—officially joined as singer in early 1970 and by March 1971 moved the band to New York, into the East 11th Street four-room railroad apartment of Emerson's lover Elda Gentile or Elda Stiletto, later singer of the Stilettos.

Eric's band visited Warhol's Factory, by Max's Kansas City. Emerson used his "ins" with the eatery's owner Mickey Ruskin to allow Messiah, now called Star Theater, to do a midnight show. Eric's Warhol pals were awed by the band's acid rock jams with Native American mysticism, blitzed by black light and fire-breathing, and bejeweled in glitter, feathers, and whiteface. Turnout inspired Max's to book them and others the act knew or knew of. The band changed their name again, for Lowell Fulson's soul hit, to "Tramp."

> **ELDA STILETTO (The Stilettos):** They wore glitter on their eyes and in their hair and long scarves. This was all pre-Dolls. I didn't see anybody else doing that. Tight, tight pants. Spandex was the thing. That was Natasha, the guitarist Youngblood's girlfriend; she became the East Village spandex queen, when spandex first became popular. (2008)

> **SESU COLEMAN (The Magic Tramps):** Andy, Mickey and Eric opened the door for everyone. I know some people will get upset for me saying this but a lot of people who became famous later with punk rock couldn't get in or were jealous of the Warhol people. The second wave at CBGB was people who got turned away at the door at Max's. (2000)

Magic Tramps' singer Emerson and drummer Sesu Coleman met pianist Michael Tschu, who was starting "The Kitchen" in the basement of a decrepit Mercer Street theater being restored by Sy Kabak. Tschu and Kabak offered, for helping to fix the place, to give the Tramps a night as part of the Kitchen's series. May 5, 1972's "Electronic Exorcise" gig was opened by two acts, Satan the Fire Eater (their rehearsal pad manager "Satan" breathing fire), and Eric's friend David Johansen's new band, the New York Dolls.

> **SESU COLEMAN:** The Warhol scene, as well as what we did at Max's and the Mercer, opened the door. If you're not living it, you can't fake it. Back then there was no punk store, so you had to search to get your look. I'd go to a clown store and the art store to buy crayons to color my

hair. We wore white-faced makeup and glitter and blew fire onstage, and Kiss was in the crowd. Everyone else did stripped-down pretty-boy rock and roll, moldable to the industry. That wasn't our thing. We were different. (2011)

Emerson, the self-proclaimed "Mr. America of Glitter and Gold," was a polysexual free-love-machine in brown leather pants. On May 28, 1975, he died tragically. His murder never got solved. Sesu Coleman and Tramps bassist Larry Chaplan tried with singer Joe Mala and guitarist Steve "Flying Fingers" Caveretta and a Zep feel, but broke up due to punk.

ANDY WARHOL (artist): They found Eric Emerson early one morning in the middle of Hudson Street. He was labeled a hit-and-run, but we heard rumors that he'd overdosed and had been dumped there. In any case, the bicycle he'd been riding was intact. (1980)

ELDA STILETTO: Eric thought he was an icon of the sexual revolution because he made *Chelsea Girls*. And he thought it was his responsibility to have sex with people who wanted to have sex with him, and it got him into trouble. In the end, of course, he's dead. Eric loved me and I loved him. Even [my ex] Sylvain one time said, "You know, I'm not number one, I'm number two; I'm not your guy." He knew, everybody knew. It was difficult for me because I had this absentee person I knew loved me and I wanted to be with him and couldn't be because he'd go off on these tangents, but whatever. (2008)

SESU COLEMAN: We rejected six record deals. We always thought we were artists and wouldn't change or conform. I kick myself in the butt for that. Plus we had weird instrumentation, we did one or two covers but we largely did originals with baroque tunes—it wasn't rock or cabaret: managers and labels didn't know what to do with us. Plus at that point, as more bands got signed, like Chris Stein and Joey Ramone and this thing called punk emerged, we were the furthest thing from stripped-down punk. We were always one step ahead. (2010)

Personality crisis, you got it while it was hot
Frustration and heartache is what you got
—New York Dolls, "Personality Crisis"

New York Dolls, similar to the Fugs and the VU before them, were a new breed of New York rocker. One of the first rock groups not playing the folk cafés, the five-piece infused Off-Off Broadway, old-school R&B, druggy nihilism, and that rock & roll bad boy cross-dressing taken to its limit. They excelled in Downtown, turning on Warholites and Max's habitués, but outside of New York, they remained an anathema.

> **DAVID JOHANSEN (New York Dolls):** We were into tearing down that rock star "gilded cage" vibe. When we'd play at the Mercer, people jumped up onstage and danced. We wanted to be different because we hated all those fucking guys who thought they were better than everyone else. They were all a bunch of prannies as far as we were concerned. (1997)

Bassist Arthur "Killer" Kane and guitarist Rick Rivets (George Fedorick) knew John Genzale (Johnny Thunders) as the guitarist of Actress, who practiced below Rusty's Cycle Shop at 81st and Columbus. Kane met Jagger-ish Staten Islander David Johansen at the June 1970 premiere of *Beyond the Valley of the Dolls*. Rivets bolted after an October 10, 1971, rehearsal, replaced by Sylvain Sylvain (Ronald Mizrahi). Syl got the band name from the New York Doll Hospital (787 Lexington Avenue). Syl and Colombian-born NJ drummer Billy Murcia ran a fashion line, Truth & Soul, so Murcia was asked to join.

> **DAVID JOHANSEN:** At night we'd be at Max's. Nobody had any money, and you could go in there and eat free rolls and salad. That's around the time I met Thunders and those guys. This guy in my building knew Billy Murcia. He'd told me about this band looking for a singer. One day there was a knock on my door, and Arthur and Billy were there. I went to Johnny's house and we played, and we had a band like that day. (1997)

> **SYLVAIN SYLVAIN (New York Dolls):** We got started in the Mercer's back room, called the Oscar Wilde Room, and were there every Tuesday night. We started with our show and then found everyone else there—drag queens and theater groups that came to New York, and your typical artist or writer or poet in the East Village. We became their band. (2006)

Lipstick killers: New York Dolls, 1973. Photo by Laurens Van Houten/Frank White Photo Agency.

The Dolls' crude rock was kitschy yet accessible. Their Downtown shows united the crowds with a ganglike "we're all in this together" vibe. David Johansen, Johnny Thunders, Sylvain Sylvain, and Arthur Kane, with drummer Billy Murcia, set the stage for everything from punk to glam metal.

MARTY THAU (manager): I stumbled upon the Dolls at the Mercer after taking my wife for dinner in the Village, and managed them for the next three years. Working at Buddha, we were geared into what a hit record sounded like, and I heard hits in "Personality Crisis," "Looking for a Kiss" and "Subway Train." I also saw a good-looking band. Back then kids wore army jackets and earth shoes, and I saw them as the next wave. Bowie and Marc Bolan in England, I saw that in the form of the Dolls. (2011)

LEEE BLACK CHILDERS (photographer): The Dolls rebelled visually and musically. They were pretty boys in drag—they wore clothes out of garbage cans, or safety-pinned tablecloths or curtains as a dress, and garish unconvincing makeup—but they also had great rock and roll that we hadn't been hearing. They did a great show, and it turned into a major event; weekly at the Mercer, more and more people came. It brought true rock and roll back, and changed rock and roll permanently. (2011)

BINKY PHILIPS (The Planets): In 1972 I started the Planets, the same summer the Dolls exploded at the Mercer Arts Center. The biggest bands at that time were ELP, Yes and King Crimson, or Zeppelin doing "Stairway to Heaven." I found it all really boring. In August 1972 I went to the Mercer and saw the Dolls, and had my head blown off. I was a better guitarist than Sylvain and Johnny but it didn't matter. Their singer wasn't as good as ours but it didn't matter. It was raw and exciting and my parents would've hated it. It was so nonconformist and against-the-grain, it was breathtaking. The Dolls showed you could still write a straightforward rock song. It made me realize I could do whatever I wanted in my band. I cannot stress how influential they were on the whole scene. (2011)

MITCH SCHNEIDER (publicist): I recall walking into the Mercer as a teenager. I saw all these insanely dressed people and it was so glamorous and shocking and defiant and cool. I remember the Dolls—it was so explosive. The next day we had off and I went back to school on Tuesday. All my friends had just seen the Grateful Dead that weekend at the Manhattan Center. I just felt so highbrow, so above them all. Like "I just saw something that was so incredible, and you'll never be let in." (2005)

David Johansen became the scene's star and focal point. He learned the ropes on St. Marks Place working with the outrageous underground theater troupe Theatre of the Ridiculous, and brought similar Off-Off Broadway stimuli to his rock group.

DAVID JOHANSEN: St. Marks Place, I owned that street when I was a kid. I knew tons of people, and they were all fringe artists. There was a real underground; everything wasn't co-opted. When I was like seventeen, I worked in this tchotchke store on St. Marks Place called Matchless; they'd make like earrings out of beer cans. The store's owner was an amazing costume and set designer who was working with the Ridiculous Theatre as well. So I started working for him, and the pay was shitty. But through him I met all these Ridiculous Theatre people like Bill Vare and Blackeyed Susan; they'd come to the store and hang out. I got in with them, and would help out by doing whatever needed to be done. In early 1972, I was like a spear-carrier at the Ridiculous. Lights, sound; if there had to be an explosion, I turned on the cassette. I also wrote songs for them. Sometimes I'd play guitar badly. So that's what I did, that and hang out on St. Marks Place. (1997)

The Dolls' second show—a May 29, 1972, party for Warhol superstar Jackie Curtis's play *An Invitation Beyond the Valley* in the Hotel Diplomat's Palm Room (later the discotheque Le Jardin)—made them Warhol scene stars. Two weeks later, on June 13, the band began that seventeen-week 9:30 p.m. residency in the Mercer's Oscar Wilde Room (at first advertised as "The Dolls of N.Y."), leading to their signing with Mercury's Paul Nelson.

SYLVAIN SYLVAIN: People think the Warholish crowd embraced the Dolls. But the Velvet Underground was an older generation and we were the younger sort of club kids, and we were taking over their turf. They weren't all that open-armed about it. There were times we played Max's upstairs because we were "86ed" from the downstairs bar. We weren't allowed downstairs. So that's how crazy that got. (1998)

BOB GRUEN (photographer): Clive Davis once told Lisa Robinson not to talk about New York Dolls uptown if she wanted to work in the music biz. They were petrified of the Dolls. They thought they were homosexual. It wasn't just homophobia; it was still illegal to be homosexual. People don't remember that it was the law. To say the Dolls, guys who wore makeup, were your friends was like saying you knew a criminal. (2006)

The sky was the limit until November 6, 1972, during their first UK tour opening for the Faces, when Murcia OD'd on the sedative Mandrax. The band carried on but never rose above Billy's death, much of their junkie death trip masking the pain of his demise.

BUDDY BOWZER (saxophonist): Billy was playing in the band, and these guys were profiling at the Mercer Arts Center. I liked to go out late night, and party and hang out with pretty girls. Billy had lots of girlfriends and boyfriends. He was my drinking buddy and Johnny started hanging with us. They looked at each other and said, "Hey B, why don't you come up and do a few sax solos at the Mercer Arts Center?" I started playing with them before it closed—'cause we rocked the house down—the building collapsed!

I hate to admit this—Billy's body hadn't even been shipped back—but walking home after this I thought to myself that maybe Jerry Nolan could take over because these guys liked him. It was all up to Johnny

Thunders actually liking Jerry. So I pitched it to Johnny the next day on the phone. So to make a long story short that's how Jerry hooked up with the Dolls. At this point he was hanging out with Bette Midler (he told me he had this girlfriend and it was Bette; she might admit to that). (2011)

Man enough to be a woman: Wayne County and the Backstreet Boys flyer, Max's Kansas City, 1976. Collection of Tony Mann.

New York Dolls made headlines for a Halloween 1973 bash at the Waldorf-Astoria that caused $25,000 in damage. More impressive than their jaw-dropping looks or memorable music, was the die-hard, debauched scene that embraced them, largely through word of mouth.

DON HILL (club owner): The Dolls at the Waldorf was the best rock party I've ever seen—lots of chaos without anyone getting hurt. Rex Reed judged the costumes, and the mingling of the rich, beautiful people in the lobby with crazy Dolls fans with dildos hanging around their necks and whatever, was just outstanding. They were a blues-oriented glam band with the hippest crowd in the world. Their whole thing was the crowd. In a way, the scene was bigger than the band. (2005)

THE MUSIC

If you don't wanna fuck me baby
Baby fuck off
—WAYNE COUNTY & THE ELECTRIC CHAIRS, "(IF YOU DON'T
WANNA FUCK ME) FUCK OFF"

Wayne County (Wayne Rogers), a Dusty Springfield imitator from Georgia, moved to the city in 1968. Jackie Curtis cast County in the 1969 play *Femme Fatale* at La Mama (with a young Patti Smith). Fame came in May 1971 in Andy Warhol's play *Pork*; its UK staging wowed David Bowie. County's life changed in 1972 after witnessing the Dolls at Max's, where he'd deejay. County's first band, Queen Elizabeth, with Jerry Nolan, Jeff Salen (pre–Tuff Darts), and Tommy and Jimmy Wynbrandt (The Miamis), notably covered the Barbarians' "Are You a Boy or Are You a Girl?" Wayne then played as Wayne County & the Electric Boys. County's career derailed in London over problems with Bowie's MainMan Management (like if Bowie's "Rebel Rebel" pilfered his "Queen Age Baby"). Wayne then transformed into Jayne, taking the hormones but never making the final cut.

Cherry Vanilla (Kathy Dorritie), a glam groupie star with flaming red hair, was raised in Archie Bunker–style Woodside, Queens. A starring role in that Warhol play *Pork* won her a job as Bowie's flack. After her rock debut ("Shake Your Ashes" on *Max's Kansas City 1976*) Cherry left to London, where she played solo, backed by the Police—who were then fired for her boyfriend Louie Lepore's lineups, on 1978's *Bad Girl* and 1979's *Venus D'Vinyl* (RCA UK). Blondie's "Rip Her to Shreds" may have been about Cherry.

The Stilettos starred Elda Gentile, Eric Emerson's brassy Queens girlfriend who attended SVA, and became a Downtown fixture. She and Holly Woodlawn sang in Puddin', 14th Street's answer to Santana. Puddin' mutated into Holly Woodlawn's Pure Garbage, before becoming the Stilettos. The Shangri-Las-style street-toughs debuted with the Dolls at Club 82, and were one of the first to perform at CBGB. Lineups bore Tommy and Jimmy Wynbrandts (The Miamis), Tish and Snooky Bellomo (Sic F*cks), Fred Smith (Television), and Chris Stein and Debbie Harry (Blondie).

Jobriath (Bruce Wayne Campbell) was to be rock's next gay step after Ziggy Stardust. Manager Jerry Brandt heard in his 1973 demo "a combination of Wagner, Tchaikovsky, Nureyev, Dietrich, Marceau and astronaut," and secured a then-astounding $500,000 deal. Elektra splurged on limos, ads, and a Times Square billboard of a seminude Jobriath. His 1973 *Jobriath* got launched at Paris Opera House, where he reenacted the *King Kong* death scene in a gorilla suit scaling a phallic Empire State Building. *Creatures of the Street* with Jobriath wearing Stephen Sprouse plastic clothing read like post-celestial Liberace in 1974. Natalie Cole introduced his 1973 *Midnight Special* performance as "the act of tomorrow." However, the era's hetero rock press savaged him.

> *Mom, I'm leaving soon*
> *To be the first rock star on the moon*
> —THE BRATS, "FIRST ROCK STAR ON THE MOON"

The Brats starred Rick Rivets, New York Rock's hard-luck story. In 1971, Rick and fellow Van Buren High truant Arthur Kane joined Actress guitarist Johnny Thunders and singer David Johansen to become the Dolls. In 1972, Rick and drummer Kevin "Sparky" Donovan got fired. The two, with vocalist Keith West, shot back as the Brats, named by Alice Cooper who said they looked like a bunch of brats. In Kiss, who opened for them, one can hear the Brats' pop/metal. Label rejections resulted in independent 45s: 1974's "Be a Man" b/w "Quaalude Queen" and 1975's "Keep on Doin' (What You're Doing)" b/w "If You Can Rock (You Can Roll)." In 1976 at Electric Lady, they made "First Rock Star on the Moon" for the flop *Max's Kansas City 1977 (Vol. II)*. In 1978, Rivets's own band fired him.

Street Punk exuded a rock star sexiness and cocksure demeanor that kept them in trouble and unrecorded (rejecting Sire and MGM deals). Jon Montgomery, a Robert Plant type from Hell's Kitchen, began Street Punk at Nobody's with guitarist Nicky Martin and pianist Bobby Blaine. Kiss loved them: they gigged together on August 10, 1973, at Hotel Diplomat, and Kiss bought but never recorded Street Punk's "Master of Flash." Gene introduced them to his manager Bill Aucoin, but they blew that deal too.

The Planets belted out originals and covers with guitarist Binky Philips windmilling Pete Townsend–like and singer Tal Taliaferrow howlin' like a wolf. On December 19, 1972, they opened for the Dolls at the Mercer (Jerry Nolan's Dolls debut) and for early shows by Kiss, Ramones, Blondie, and

Television. Manager/damager Barbara Bothwell got them a Warners demo deal, but the label dumped them. Then the band fell out of favor for firing the black man Tal.

Ruby and the Rednecks began in 1970 after Ruby Lynn Rayner met Johnny "Mondo Cane" Madera at the Theatre of the Ridiculous. Ruby won Drama Desk awards for roles in *La Bohemia* (a put-on of *La Bohème*) and Jackie Curtis's *Heaven Grand in Amber Orbit*. The band gigged regularly with the Dolls. She'd sing Phil Spector's "He Hit Me (And It Felt Like a Kiss)" in boxing gloves, punching herself in the face.

Cool dudes or foxy ladies? Harlots of 42nd Street. 1973. Courtesy of Chris Becker.

Harlots of 42nd Street played a campy rock in glitter, fishnets, and S&M gear. The blue-collar band led by Queens-bred guitarist Chris Harlot (Becker) and Brooklyn singer Gene Harlot and bassist Mugsy Harlot (Franklin) began on December 30, 1972, at the First International Glitter Ball at Hotel Diplomat. David Johansen saw them as the Dolls' big competition. The Harlots only released 1974's "Cool Dude & Foxy Lady" single before ditching androgyny for a proto-punk "New York City Street Rock & Roll."

Five Dollar Shoes played offbeat boogie-woogie during the glam era. Mike Millius, writer of Pete Seeger's "The Ballad of Martin Luther King," made 1969's *Mike Millius Desperado* (with "Lookout for Lucy," sampled on Beck's *Odelay*'s "Lord Only Knows") that sold so few, he formed "The No-Name Band." Hippie queen Melanie's husband Peter Schekeryk saw their debut show at the Electric

Circus and signed them to the couple's Neighborhood label. Melanie had a lyric about "five-dollar shoes," the tale behind 1972's *Five Dollar Shoes*. Shoes kicked ass on December 2, 1972, at the Mercer with Magic Tramps, when Millius smacked a roadie in the head with a two-by-four, grabbed a .38 starter pistol, and "shot" him. But no blood was spilled.

Another Pretty Face appeared when Terry "T." Roth joined a hetero wedding band liberated by the glitter era. The tristate club stars' theatrical rock won them stints at Club 82 and Max's, and raves in *Rock Scene* and *Melody Maker*. Disco producer Tony Camillo didn't get it, so his engineer Ed Stasium (pre-Ramones) oversaw 1974's *21st Century Rock* that RCA shelved. David Fricke raved: "Glitter was a phase, but Another Pretty Face were a phenomenon to those who knew them when . . ." (Drummer Tico Torres found stardom in Bon Jovi.)

Teenage Lust blared an over-the-top proto-punk. Harold C. Black and Billy Joe White of David Peel & the Lower East Side, began their white-trash soul revue that played as "chorus" for John Lennon's "One to One" show at the Garden. The "originators of the New York nasty" shone with "The Lustettes" Laurie Maloney, Loretta Vanacore and Laurie and Leslie Weiss: sexy gal pals who'd frolic onstage and club-hop to push the band. Laurie got lover Keith Richards to cite the band in the Stones' "It's Only Rock 'n Roll" ("Would it be enough for your teenage lust / Would it help to ease the pain?").

Sniper did glam-ish covers and originals. Singer Jeffrey "Jeff Starship" Hyman replied to a *Voice* ad. Jeff (later Joey Ramone) was a sight, 6′8″ in his mother's heels, makeup, rhinestones, and satin jumpsuit. He once got beaten and rushed to Elmhurst Hospital after hitchhiking like that on Queens Blvd. In 1974, Sniper fired Hyman for one Alan Turner. The lion-maned Coventry regulars included guitarist Bob "B.B." Butani (pre–Tuff Darts), who was replaced by Frankie Infante (pre-Blondie). With next singer Michael Harrington, they rocked as Grand Slam (on *Max's Kansas City 1977*).

Luger, equal parts Stones and VU, featured Max's scene star drummer Shayne Harris, and guitarist Ivan Kral, after his stint with the Magic Tramps (and before Patti Smith Group). RCA funded a 1972 album that never came out. Danny Fields hired Iggy to produce a 1973 demo. A highlight was an eight-song set on August 10, 1973, at Hotel Diplomat with Kiss and Street Punk. Dave Marsh wrote in *Creem* (12/73): "an interesting act, with bullwhips, but the songs aren't good."

The Rags rocked glitter-era clubs with the Dolls, Harlots, and Fast. The Queens band with Brats guitarist Ron Blanchard and Joe St. John on vocals were set to debut at the Mercer but it closed down so they began on December 21, 1973, with Kiss at the Coventry. Kiss's Paul Stanley got a Flying V guitar after seeing the Rags' Joe Valentine Sausa's. Their slick 1976 studio single, "We Can Make It" / "Scrambled Eggs," belied their live raunch. The Rags dried up after several almost-deals, the final time with Led Zeppelin's Swan Song Records (for being too polished!).

Dorian (Kenneth Dorian Passante), a glam scene somebody in white-face and top hat, got high with Jobriath and Dee Dee, sang in Sweet Dirt, and fronted: Dorian, Dorian and Sweet Dirt, Dorian & Zero, Dorian Zero Revue (who Television opened for at Hotel Diplomat, April 5, 1975). His self-financed *Dorian* LP of 1977 hired Jeff Beck on "Inside Looking Out" and "Destination Nowhere." The credits read: "I have no one to thank for this album but myself."

> *You little fuck, get out of my way*
> *I need room to rage*
> —HELEN WHEELS, "ROOM TO RAGE"

Helen Wheels (Helen Robbins) worked with Blue Öyster Cult, whom she knew from SUNY-Stony Brook (as the girlfriend of drummer Albert Bouchard). She wrote lyrics on four BÖC albums ("Sinful Love," "Nosferatu"), won two gold and one platinum album, and designed their leather stage-wear. The fashion work funded solo vinyl like 1978's "Room to Rage" 45 and 1981's *Postmodern Living* (produced by Al's BÖC bassist bro Joe Bouchard).

Genya Ravan (Genyusha Zelkowitz) came to the LES after WWII with her Holocaust survivor family. In 1962 she sang for Goldie & the Gingerbreads, the first girl group playing their instruments. In 1969 she sang R&B in Ten Wheel Drive (1970's *Brief Replies* and 1971's *Peculiar Friends*) and Baby (1972's *Genya Ravan with Baby*). Solo work included 1978's *Urban Desire* with songs on the *Warriors* soundtrack. She produced Dead Boys' *Young, Loud and Snotty* and most bands on CBGB Records.

Chris Robison fell through the cracks of history. As a kid in Bridgeport, Connecticut, Paul Leka ("Green Tambourine") hired Chris in an ersatz lineup of Steam ("Na Na Hey Hey Kiss Him Goodbye"). Chris was in Elephant's Memory twice but missed out on their fame as John Lennon's backup band. The "pansexual" proved too much too soon on 1973's debut

Chris Robison and His Many Hands Band with the Fire Island opus, "Lookin' for a Boy Tonight."

Velvert Turner met Jimi Hendrix in 1966 and became "Jimi's little brother." His friend Richard Lloyd of Television claims lefty Jimi taught righty Velvert guitar by playing into a mirror (Velvert in turn taught Richard in Jimi's 59 West 12th pad). Black producer Tom Wilson, who originally rejected Jimi, signed "the next Hendrix." Velvert Turner Group, like Jimi Hendrix Experience, was a power trio with two white guys: Tim McGovern (pre–The Motels) and Prescott Niles (pre–The Knack). Seventy-two's *Velvert Turner Group* with Chris Robison on keyboards had Hendrix-style guitar and vocal timbre.

Isis was like a lesbian Blood, Sweat & Tears. Carol MacDonald and Ginger Bianco of Goldie & the Gingerbreads began the octet named for an Egyptian goddess, and signed to Buddah after a show at Trude Heller's. Their Shadow Morton–produced *Isis* with a cover shot of the ladies in silver metallic body paint cracked the *Billboard* charts in 1974 (#87). The next year's jazzier *Ain't No Backin' Up* made with Allen Toussaint, depicted the girls in spice jars. They got blasted as novelty despite hot gigs with Aerosmith, Skynyrd, ZZ Top, et cetera.

Barnaby Bye presented Peppy Castro (Blues Magoos) and the striking Alessi brothers. Peppy starred in 1970's Broadway cast of *Hair* with eighteen-year-old twins Billy and Bobby. Atlantic's Ahmet Ertegun signed the group after their first show (and five rehearsals) opened for the Rolling Stones–related Mary Clayton. The fourteen months and $200K in the studio couldn't buy a hit for 1973's *Room to Grow*, while 1974's *Touch* felt even 'more out of touch.

Bloontz moved from Houston in 1972 to play sessions for producer Ron Johnsen at Electric Lady. Tony Braunagel, Michael Montgomery, and Terry Wilson performed on the disco-pop album of Lyn Christopher, and met backup singers Gene Simmons and Paul Stanley. Johnsen produced 1973's *Bloontz* and booked Bloontz with a young Kiss at a May 26, 1973, benefit show in Palisades, NY. Evolution Records blew $60K on ad "Bloontzkriegs" and media "Bloontz-O-Grams." (The three played in Free guitarist Paul Kossoff's band Back Street Crawler until Paul's March 1976 coke-induced heart attack on a red-eye from LAX to JFK.)

The Flow, a proto-metal psycho-delic trio that reeked of Mountain and Santana, shared a rehearsal space with a pre-Kiss Wicked Lester. Pete Fine, Monte Farber, and Steve Starer began on an LP with producer Paul Arakian but ran out of money, so they self-released 1972's *The Flow's Greatest Hits* with one side blank.

N.Y. Central rocked a sugary boogie-woogie pop on 1973's 7″ "Underneath the Moonlight" (RCA). Manager Jack Abbott planned to debut harmonica-playing Bob Hamilton's quintet (that gave flight to Joan Jett guitarist Ricky Byrd) at the Mercer, days before the building's collapse. Little happened after Halloween 1973's "The Rock & Occult Show" set at the Manhattan Center with jugglers, sorceresses, and the Harlots of 42nd Street.

Day Old Bread, a Brooklyn-based, Cheap Trick–style trio, cut demos, played the festivals at Max's and CBGB, and got cited in Wayne County's song "Max's Kansas City 1976." Day Old Bread's '70s vibe felt stale in the punk era, so Ed Ryan and Razz rolled on as the Rudies.

The Dynamiters, a teen trio from Oradell, NJ, caught a buzz in the latter glitter days. Epic Records issued fall 1976's "(We Got a) Rock & Roll President," a Raspberries-flavored pop paean to Jimmy Carter's election that dented the charts.

City Lights, Donny Wilkins's Village pop group with guitarist John Berenzy, producer Mark Abel, and photographer Leonard Bobbé, made 1975's Craig Leon–produced *Silent Dancing* (Sire).

Shaker, Jagged Edge guitarist Art Steinman's band briefly with a pre-Dolls Jerry Nolan and Buddy Bowzer, opened for the Dolls at the Mercer and Harlots at the Diplomat. **Flaming Youth** opened for the Coventry's Kiss-Isis fiasco, inspired a Kiss title, and launched writer Deborah Frost. **Wild Honey** gigged with Kiss at the Coventry and Diplomat. **Canon** blew up the Mercer and Max's. **Witch Hazel** gigged with Harlots and N.Y. Central. **Black Rabbit,** **Aura**, and **Whiz Kids** and **Haystacks** rehearsed at Mike Royal's Bacchus Studios on West 19th Street. **Jet Black, Bang Zoom, Ramble On, Rave, Battleaxe, Trilogy**, and the all-girl **Sister Moon** made the Downtown scene.

Hard as a rock: David Johansen, New York Dolls, 1973. Photo by Laurens Van Houten/Frank White Photo Agency.

THE FALL

When everyone goes to your house they shoot up in your room
Most of them are beautiful, but so obsessed with gloom
   —NEW YORK DOLLS, "LOOKING FOR A KISS"

Most of America outside New York was not ready for the New York Dolls. The band's Todd Rundgren–produced *New York Dolls* album of 1973, equal parts Rolling Stones, Shangri-Las, and Young Rascals, failed to gain traction for Mercury Records. The label cut their losses after 1974's aptly titled, Shadow Morton–overseen follow-up—*Too Much Too Soon.*

TODD RUNDGREN (musician): I was at the time a New York guy and part of the New York scene, that pantheon of celebrities and semi-celebs that hung out at Max's every night. I don't know what it'd be compared to today, but in those days it was very intense, especially in light of the number of acts that came out of the area and the associations that went with them. In some sense, I produced the *New York Dolls* album because it was a New York thing. It was people I saw and hung out with. I knew I was about to leave the city, so I did it as a last-gasp tribute to the New York scene of the '70s. (1993)

DAVID JOHANSEN (New York Dolls): I have no idea how many records we sold at the time, not a lot. We'd be like one hundred-twenty on the charts if we were lucky. It definitely wasn't for everybody; it wasn't a mass appeal type thing. We did well where there were a lot of disaffected kids. Or places like Cambridge or Boston, where a bunch of intellectuals would come and observe it and get it. Our record reviews would get like four stars in *Downbeat.* (1997)

PAUL NELSON (Mercury Records): I signed the Dolls. I was fired because of them. I knew they were going to have to be a big success or I'd lose my job, and I did. (2005)

Ego feuds, drug abuse, and money woes disbanded the Dolls. They'd arrive at shows hours late, so the bookings dried up. Manager Marty Thau, followed by Steve Leber and David Krebs, bailed. Final manager Malcolm McLaren dressed them in Marxist-style red leather, to terrible reviews at March 1975's three-night stint at Little Hippodrome Theater (227 East 56th Street). McLaren also tried putting Thunders, Nolan, and Kane into drug rehab. The band broke up that August, dope-sick and broke in Jerry's mother's trailer park near Crystal Springs, Florida.

David and Syl did one final Dolls tour of Japan in 1975. Soundman Peter Jordan often played "second bassist" behind the curtain for a doped-up Arthur Kane (propped against his amp with a hand truck). Drummer/road manager Tony Machine and pianist Chris Robison (of Elephant's Memory) joined; the latter drank himself out of a job. Other Dolls quasi-reunions included Max's final gig with Thunders and Peter Perett (The Only Ones).

JOHNNY THUNDERS (New York Dolls): Jerry and I left because we felt we weren't getting anywhere playing our old songs in tiny clubs. The group was getting stale and staying behind the times, and not advancing in any way. (1977)

JERRY NOLAN (New York Dolls): David had a bad habit of calling the shots about things that he knew nothing about. He'd pick the producer, and settle for a weak mix. He had everything to do with making the wrong moves, and fucked up everything. The first two albums were butchered. They were great songs and we could've done great performances, but David was the type of guy who didn't want to do a song twice in the studio. He didn't give a shit about anybody giving a good performance as long as he sounded okay. (1977)

SYLVAIN SYLVAIN (New York Dolls): We were staying at Jerry Nolan's mother's house, and Johansen was getting lushy drunk. He was an abusive drunk. He'd tell you that you didn't matter, and that he was the singer, and could go on his own without your hang-ups and bullshit. Basically, he said that to us one day after dinner, and Johnny and Jerry, after they heard they could be replaced again and again, walked out. I drove them to the airport. (1998)

DAVID JOHANSEN: I don't remember the exact chain of events, but we were down in Florida, at a Bates Motel place that Jerry's mother owned. There were these old trailers they would use as hotel rooms, and we were gonna base ourselves there, and go off and gig all the time. The band broke up because a lot of these guys, they couldn't function without junk, so it just got impossible to do. You know, big rock stars have nurses and gofers but we never had that shit. These guys wanted to be like Bela Lugosi. (1997)

PAUL ZONE (The Fast): Everyone wanted the Dolls to make it but they never did. And that's what ended up screwing it up for all the other bands that were around those days because the Dolls tried hard but they just weren't accepted by the mainstream. (1978)

The Dolls' over-the-top sound and style inspired punk. McLaren and Vivienne Westwood (his wife), moved back to London, and styled a New York Rock look for their next client, the Sex Pistols.

JOHNNY THUNDERS: The Dolls proved you didn't have to be a technical genius to play rock and roll. It was all down to style, energy and attitude. In that respect we paved the way for today's new wave bands, who nearly all rate the Dolls as innovators. (1977)

JERRY NOLAN: The Dolls were like a gang who turned over to instruments instead of guns. When they started they were great—very raw, a real rock-and-roll band. Nobody could top them. (1977)

SYLVAIN SYLVAIN: When my mother died in 1991, I went through my old drawers and found Malcolm's seven-page letter written in 1975, going, "I can't stand that David Johansen. Come here now. This is your band." He sent me little quarter-booth photos, "We're thinking about calling this guy 'Johnny Rotten.' He can't sing but he's better than Johansen." (1998)

Glitter rock and the the Dolls rose and fell as one. Eric Emerson died of a hit-and-run or was thrown from a moving van. The Harlots dressed straight "street rock" and lost their fans, while real-fag-not-pretender Jobriath got done in by homophobia. The Stilettos snapped as Chris Stein and Debbie Harry began Blondie, and Fred Smith turned on with Television. The Planets lost gravity after a failed deal. The Brats never got what they wanted. Wayne County and Cherry Vanilla left to London to lead the '77 punk explosion.

I'm the king of the night time world
Come live your secret dream
—KISS, "KING OF THE NIGHT TIME WORLD"

Rock 'n' roll all nite: Kiss, 1976. Photo by Laurens Van Houten/Frank White Photo Agency.

Kiss became the big New York Rock stars; ironic as they were considered outerborough outsiders. They arose on the Max's scene's periphery and infused a Dolls style into their circuslike act geared for the masses. Few scenesters heard of Kiss until their first album.

PAUL STANLEY (Kiss): The New York scene was interesting. We were only loosely affiliated with it because we were never embraced by it. The New York glitter scene, the grandfather of what became glam—was people hanging out in clubs, more concerned with the way they dressed than what they played. We were on a different trip. (1993)

Bullfrog Bheer was the first real band of Gene Simmons (Chaim Witz, Hymie Klein, Gene Klein) at Sullivan County College, rocking the Catskills with a mix of covers and originals (1968/69 acetates had "High and Low" in which one can hear roots of "Calling Dr. Love," in "Stanley the Parrot," "Strutter," and in "Little Lady" "Goin' Blind"). **Uncle Joe** was the first legitimate band of Paul Stanley (Stanley Eisen), a bass-less trio with Matt Rael and Neil Teeman. After a 1968 show with Matt's brother John as the Post War Baby Boom (in which Paul wrote "Never Loving, Never Living"), Paul joined Steve Coronel in Tree. Those jams, one with Simmons, led to Gene and Paul's first time together onstage in 1971 as Rainbow at Staten Island's Richmond Community College.

Wicked Lester, from the roots of Rainbow, was a Doobie Brothers–style act in flannel and beards, with Gene and Paul, Steve Coronel (or Ron Leejack), Brooke Ostrander, and Tony Zarrella. That band gigged in 1971 at the Tivoli Theater by Sullivan College, and did three sets in Atlantic City for a B'nai B'rith gala. In 1972, CBS funded a Wicked Lester album but shelved the tapes. An irate Gene and Paul quit to join Ace Frehley and Peter Criss. The rest is KISStory. (In 1976, to exploit Kiss's fame, CBS tried to issue it. The act feared it would ruin their brand, so Casablanca paid $137,500 to squash the masters.)

LYDIA CRISS (Peter Criss's ex-wife): We met them in the Village at Electric Lady Studios. When they first called Peter, they were asking questions like "Do you dress cool? Do you act cool? Are you fat or skinny?" When we first met on the street, Peter dressed so cool, we literally walked right by them! They didn't have their look yet. I heard Wicked Lester and wasn't impressed—but they didn't like the album either. They wanted to start from scratch; that's why they got with Peter. They brought Don Ellis from Epic and he wasn't impressed. That's when they began rehearsing, got Ace, and played the Coventry. (2011)

BOBBY McADAMS (New York scene): Ace was hanging out at his mother's house and I brought over a *Village Voice* and inadvertently left it there. There happened to be an ad for this band Wicked Lester that did original material looking for a guitarist with stage presence. I know he was drunk at the audition, and tripped over himself, in his two different-colored sneakers, which was so crazy to wear back then. I recall thinking Wicked Lester was the stupidest name. But if I didn't leave that *Voice*, he never would've been in Kiss. It was total coincidence that I left it and he circled the ad. (2011)

Peter Criss (George Criscoula), a childhood friend of the Dolls' Jerry Nolan, drummed in Brooklyn bar bands before joining **Chelsea**, the Peter Shepley–fronted quintet on 1970's *Chelsea* (Decca), cut at Electric Lady with John Cale on viola. Peter placed an ad in *Rolling Stone* that excited Gene and Paul. The two went to see Peter's next group **Infinity** at King's Lounge on Flatbush Avenue, and set up a jam at their 10 East 23rd Street loft. Paul "Ace" Frehley played in a few psych-rock acts before joining **Molimo**, a Jefferson Airplane–style six-piece that played the Village Gate and Fillmore East, and recorded part of a 1971 LP that RCA canned. (Ace told *Goldmine* [12/98]: "It was a guy, I think named Tom Lewis. The guy was a fag, man. He was like a fag gigolo.")

Kiss debuted at the Popcorn Club, and wore no makeup: Paul in a dark blazer, knickers, and Beatle boots, Gene in a sailor top and bell-bottoms. They first played the city on May 4, 1973, for $1 at Rick Rivets's Bleecker Street loft opening for the Brats and Queen Elizabeth (with Wayne County eating dog food from a trash can). The legendary tale goes at their next gig, July 13, Sean Delaney brought manager Bill Aucoin to see them at the Diplomat, and Gene and Paul gave Aucoin a month to get them signed. Aucoin's ex-aide Joyce Biawitz had just married Neil Bogart of the new Casablanca label. Aucoin and Bogart stuck by three flop albums until 1975's *Kiss Alive* went gold (five million sold over time).

Sean Delaney (Prentice John Delaney Jr.) was the brain of the operation, creating Kiss's image and their stage productions. He came to New York from Orem, Utah, with $2.98 in his pocket, and lived at the YMCA. He established himself as a singer in the acts Trust and Natural Juice. He cowrote Kiss's "Mr. Speed" and "Makin' Love," coproduced the 1978 solo albums of Gene and Peter, and produced *Double Platinum*. (Delaney's 1979 Casablanca solo album *Highway* involved his pal Luther Vandross on a rendition of Smoky Robinson's "You Beat Me to the Punch.")

BOBBY McADAMS: Sean was a major player in the whole picture. If anything, Aucoin was a TV ad guy, not a music guy. But he was lovers with Sean, who was the music guy. So whatever Sean said, Bill went with it. Anyone there'll tell you Sean was respected on his own as a player. He was a real-life Village People person, they were really into the scene at the Anvil, he'd fuck ten guys a week, it was no big thing, fistings and stuff like that. He was a funny friendly guy; nobody had anything bad to say about him. (2011)

Gene Simmons and Paul Stanley took in and tweaked Downtown glitter rock to fame and fortune much the way Dylan absorbed the ideas of Greenwich Village. Gene and Paul developed their look after seeing the Magic Tramps play in whiteface, breathing fire. They first saw a Gibson Flying V played by the Rags. Paul's High School of Music & Art mate Binky Philips (The Planets), uncredited cowriter of "Love Gun," so struck Gene Simmons that when Kiss cut "Doctor Love," he urged Ace to "do a Binky solo."

BINKY PHILIPS (The Planets): It really felt like something was happening. We thought we'd all be rich and famous but the only ones who got that way were Kiss. Sure they hit that hole in the market perfectly but the makeup and spitting blood and flash pots were just icing on the cake because they couldn't be so big and great without the great songwriting. (2011)

KEITH WEST (The Brats): Kiss wanted to play one of our parties, and right away they blew me away. They sounded so good live; they had the whole shtick down. Most New York bands were into being raunchy and sloppy like the Dolls. We all wanted to be like the Dolls. These guys were more metal and tight—great songs with a metal edge. (2011)

GENE SIMMONS (Kiss): It takes great balls to be an unknown band, without a record out, to put the time, effort, and money into a levitating drum set in the days when John Denver was god. These four knuckleheads from New York in makeup, looking like they crawled out from under a rock, deciding it was vital that the drum kit levitate in the air. (1992)

ACE FREHLEY (Kiss): With Kiss, I had that alter ego. Wherever I went, I wore makeup and the costume. I had enough of it. I felt I'd totally lost control, Gene and Paul really ran the band, and it wasn't a good situation. That's when I started losing it and overindulging in chemicals and alcohol because I was so unhappy. I wanted to blow my brains out. (1988)

FASTER & LOUDER

PUNK/NEW WAVE

1975–1979: Ramones, Blondie, Voidoids, Heart-breakers, Talking Heads, Patti Smith, Lester Bangs, *New York Rocker*, Sire Records, Bleecker Bob's, Manic Panic, CBGB

Gabba, gabba, hey: Ramones, CBGB, 1977. Photo by GODLIS.

PUNK/NEW WAVE

Outside of society
That's where I want to be
—PATTI SMITH, "ROCK N ROLL NIGGER"

THE RISE

TOMMY WYNBRANDT (The Miamis): New York was in bad shape. No one had money. Streets were dirty, subway cars were covered in graffiti, and one going-out-of-business sign after another plastered storefronts. Muggings were everyday occurrences. People sold ratty belongings on the street. It was like an endless loop of *Kojak*. (2011)

SONNY VINCENT (The Testors): The city was rough: gangs roaming, junkies everywhere. Forty-second Street was worse than movies portray. The city was in default, the middle class had moved out. Graffiti everywhere, garbage, violence, drug deals on the street. You name it. But it was ours. There was a flourishing music, an art scene and cheap rents. (2011)

"Punk" was a negative term picked up from prison slang (for homosexuals), and before that from Shakespeare (describing a trollop as a "taffety punk" in *All's Well That Ends Well*). In the '50s, "punk" defined a belligerent twerp. Rock critic Lester Bangs used "punk" to describe Iggy Pop's Stooges, and Alan Vega adopted the tag to promote his band Suicide. *Punk Magazine* plastered posters Downtown in 1975 proclaiming, *"Punk* is Coming!" And people began calling the new acts punk rock.

HILLY KRISTAL (CBGB): "Punk" was a reincarnated term that goes back to Iggy and the Stooges. We called our scene "street rock" back then. It was the aftermath of the '60s, a deep recession, where everyone had $60 apartments and lived on food stamps. That's why everyone wore cheap jeans and T-shirts. (2005)

SCOTT KEMPNER (The Dictators): A punk was misunderstood, a victim, embodied a smoldering rage at one's own ineffectiveness, the little engine that can't. You know the word has its origins in prisons. The one who becomes a sex slave to others was a punk, a humble beginning, for sure. It retained some of the victim vibe of its prison origin until it gets transferred to an actual outlaw and/or criminal—but definitely an outsider. (2010)

Sonically, punk was different from what came before. Before punk, rock guitarists had a blues-based sound—strumming Gibsons and Les Pauls. Punks beat up on Fender guitars played loud through Marshalls and other amps, creating a unique blare. Punk's revved-up, stripped-down amateur spunk defied all previous notions of musical virtuosity. To any "real" musician, being called "punk" was no compliment.

JOEY RAMONE (The Ramones): We were a reaction to all the pretentiousness and clichés and all the bullshit. It was at the beginning of disco, the beginning of corporate rock, like Journey, Foreigner, all that shit. You know, five or six tracks on an album, 45-minute guitar solos or drum solos. All the mega-bands were content writing the worst shit possible and selling billions of records, and they didn't have to get off their asses and do anything. We cut that shit out. We made it fresh again, like it originally was. (1986)

HANDSOME DICK MANITOBA (The Dictators): It was the start of the megastar musician in rock: huge stages with guitar heroes. Alvin Lee and Ten Years After or prog-rock—we hated that stuff. We hated those bands that were overly musical. (2003)

MITCH SCHNEIDER (publicist): New York punk was great because it sounded like the city. It was tightly wound, really urgent, and New York sucked at that time. You think of Son of Sam and the city looked like a wreck. It was not an attractive place. (2005)

Punk quickly evolved into an "umbrella" movement for nonconformists with an edgy new attitude. A major aspect of punk was its intense reaction to the '70s' hippie-esque escapism. Punks espoused "reality," capturing glitter-rock's brashness in a bid to refresh rock. That's why the short hair, fast music, and FU attitude proved so enticing to some, and so threatening to the status quo.

RICHARD HELL (The Voidoids): By the time I was in New York and in a position to do things, the '60s era had passed, and music had become dull, pompous and irrelevant. So I wanted to—and the people I was hanging with wanted to—make music that was about real life again. So, we went that way. (2006)

LESTER BANGS (writer): Each band had a different thing to say that was something of their own. I mean, Richard Hell was a very defeatist sort of nihilism. Talking Heads were a collegian kind of art school—I'm trying not to make them sound so bad because I really love 'em. Ramones were playing with the concept of being dumb but not dumb and being all-American but yet alien mutant—you know, feeling different, an outsider yet yearning for that all-American cars, girls, surfing and all that when you can't even drive. Television was into all that French symbolism poetry stuff. So each of them had real strong personalities and distinct identities. (1980)

RUSSELL WOLINSKY (Sic F*cks): The original scene was eclectic with few punk or even rock bands. It's ironic how punk started with Patti Smith and Television, which was very poetic and Dylanesque. These were people who didn't fit in the neighborhoods they grew up in, so they got into this kind of music. I loved all that, but when the Ramones and Dictators came in, I was like, "That's more like it." Especially when Dead Boys came, it was like, "Wow, a genuine rock band." (2011)

JOHN HOLMSTROM (*Punk Magazine*): There was a thing back then about not playing it safe. You weren't supposed to be commercial yet you were supposed to be able to sell records. There was an idea that if you could be bad enough to make everyone hate you, you could eventually get good enough to make 'em love you. It's like pro wrestling, where the worst heel becomes a good guy 'cause they make people react strongly. (2004)

JOY RYDER (Joy Ryder & Avis Davis): New York was alive again; there was a real groundswell. Kids were dressing up to go see bands again. It wasn't about hippie fests or folk cafés; it was a throwback to a club mentality. It was a working-class-hero thing not based on whom you knew or what school you went to. It felt like a giant high school, with an in-crowd and out-crowd—infantile in some ways but beautiful in others. I could never achieve or want to achieve a lush orchestral sound, so it was great to see people into the raw sound. The vibe in the air was to make it as easy and immediate as possible. It was like haiku: so clean and simple. You felt part of a movement; there was punk dancing, and punk painting with Basquiat and Haring. It was direct and naive, and we loved it and didn't care. (2011)

CHRIS STEIN (Blondie): At the time, the New York punk scene was our lives. Now, I wish there was something like that happening. I wish I could fuckin' go out and see the same two hundred people every weekend, that'd be great. Punk was about people who couldn't really play just going up there—but they knew how to stand onstage, they knew how to hold a guitar. Sure, it was a posed era, but it was also a great time. (1999)

PHILIPPE MARCADE (The Senders): It was great because it was very local and underground. Everybody knew everybody, no one was signed, no money, no Internet! One must also remember these were the freest times in the history of mankind, simply because the pill already existed but AIDS didn't. I miss that sense of freedom. (2010)

CLEM BURKE (Blondie): What went down in the '70s had more impact on modern culture than what happened in the '60s. People today, the way they act and look, I don't see a bunch of hippies running around. They're in black leather or glam clothes, and the music's punk. It had a profound effect on the start of the twenty-first century. (1999)

DAVID JOHANSEN (New York Dolls): I didn't even notice when punk first happened. I remember one incident where the Ramones were rehearsing down the hall from us, and I went in there, hung out for a while, and said, "You guys suck, you're not gonna go anywhere." What did I know? I told Chris Frantz one day, "You're an amazing guy, what are you doing with this band? That's no life." I thought it was great that there was finally a scene happening. But I had no idea there was a movement going on. (1997)

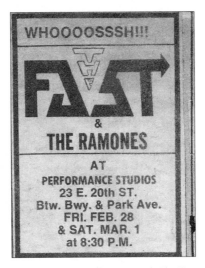

Loud, fast rules: *Village Voice* ad, The Fast and The Ramones, Performance Space, 1974. Courtesy of Paul Zone.

Punk redefined the look and feel of rock. Things would never be the same again.

KRISTIAN HOFFMAN (The Mumps): Being a punk is like being a kid with eyes bigger than his stomach. Their brains are bigger than their abilities—they got the idea but they just can't do it. It's ambition without discipline. (1977)

JOHNNY ZEEK (The Shirts): You gotta look like you're always ready for a fight, even if you wouldn't get into one. And look like you're carrying a switchblade. (1977)

HILLY KRISTAL (CBGB): They'll drink anything—dirty water, if I gave it to them. Punks don't really care about anything but the music. (1977)

GYDA GASH (New York scene): Punk was not a fashionable movement. It wasn't this social scene—it was people who were social cripples. It was a lot of sad, angry, damaged, misfit kids that were not pretty or cool—women like myself who were not beautiful or Playboy Bunnies or models; the shy, angry kids, the ones that never fit in. That's why there was so much drug use. It fit perfectly with that kind of mindset. (2004)

To its fans, punk reenergized moribund rock. To its detractors, it was amateur hour.

ARTHUR ALEXANDER (Sorrows/The Poppees): The late-'70s New York scene was what I imagined it must've been like during the early '60s Liverpool/London scene: all these bands coming out of the woodwork, and all these clubs supporting their growth; musicians and bands hanging out every night, checking each other out, stealing each other's ideas, and record companies actually hitting the clubs and checking out bands instead of conducting focus groups—an explosion of ideas and creativity. (2010)

CRAIG LEON (producer): When I signed the Ramones, a lot of people were interested because they were making a buzz in the newspapers and drawing crowds in New York. But at the time, they were seen as "Oh, they can't play." People were afraid to sign them because they thought they could never make a record. (2006)

JON TIVEN (Prix): People in the business I knew back then had no time for punk. They acknowledged something was going on but couldn't figure a way to pigeonhole it in the way they needed. This was so rough-edged and such a far cry from the slick stuff they were selling, they didn't get that there was an audience. They didn't think that people who bought Queen and Bowie would buy Television records. I figured it wouldn't be a revolution but it more or less became one. (2011)

TOM VERLAINE (Television): I didn't think there was any punk, and I still don't. I think punk is slightly more aggressive bubblegum. Structurally speaking, it's pumping eighth notes, right? It's ramped-up bubblegum, with a bit more of an angry lyric, but not always. Some so-called punk records were just as funny as bubblegum records. (2006)

The UK punk explosion of '77 was inspired by and legitimized the existing New York subculture. Notable scenes occurred in Los Angeles and San Francisco by the next year.

JAYNE COUNTY (Electric Chairs): I was the DJ at Max's for a long time. I was the first to ever spin the Dolls, Sex Pistols, and the Damned. In fact, when I played the Damned, Dee Dee Ramone ran over outraged. He said, "Who's this copying us?" I said the Damned from England. He said, "Don't play them. Play us New York people. Don't play those stupid English bands." He didn't like those bands copping their sound. (1993)

JERRY NOLAN (New York Dolls): The scene in London reminds me of New York four years ago, but they've taken it a step further. It's the same atmosphere with a different type of music. You soon get bored with yourselves if you don't have other bands to look at and learn from, and here we can learn a lot. I notice that they've picked up a few things from us too, which is great. It's very inspiring. (1977)

GLENN DANZIG (The Misfits): Stuff was called punk here way before it was called punk in England. Malcolm McLaren got the great idea for his punk band when he came over here. We'd seen Television in New York in 1973–74. Even in the '60s, you could go in a record shop and find a punk section. It meant garage bands but it said "punk." (1997)

GREG GINN (Black Flag): The common perception was that punk started in London, but we knew better than that. It didn't come out of London, and it didn't come out of L.A.—it came out of New York. We followed the New York bands first. (2004)

Circa 1975, Richard Hell was spotted in the East Village in ripped shirts held together by safety pins. Malcolm McLaren, then working with the Dolls, took that image in his head back to London, and with designer-wife Vivienne Westwood, stylized punk-fringe-Downtown-junkie-artist-squalor to high fashion and pop culture.

BOB GRUEN (photographer): One night Richard Hell apparently had a fight with a girlfriend. I don't know if it was over drugs or whatever but somebody cut up all his clothes. He had to go out, so he took a bunch of safety pins and pinned them together where they were ripped and went out, because he didn't give a shit. Well, Malcolm saw that and he was fascinated by the "unique design." This wasn't fashion; it was more like how do you get out of the house when you've got no clothes left? (2006)

RICHARD LLOYD (Television): Malcolm was managing New York Dolls, who were in a slump. He dressed them in red patent leather with a communist flag backdrop. We did a co-bill in Manhattan. Malcolm fell in love with Television and wanted to manage us. He was turned down, so he went back to England and used the image he got from us, from Richard Hell, and started marketing the image in his wife's clothing shop. Ripped clothing, safety pins, stitches were Richard's idea! So that's where the Sex Pistols came from. (1999)

Joey Ramone became punk's key character, not just for his physical presence and status in the scene, but for his support of bands he loved. You'd always see him out, at CBGB or the Clash at the Palladium, or Robert Gordon and Chris Spedding at the Lone Star.

HANDSOME DICK MANITOBA: The Ramones didn't create something from scratch: they redefined it. Joey was a fan, a historian of sorts. He studied all the pop bands and rock bands, and then spit it back in his own style. (2003)

ANDY SHERNOFF (The Dictators): There was a club called the Coventry. We were the only punk band there so we were outcasts. Joey used to come see us. Then I saw a poster saying the Ramones were playing CBGB. So I went and there were the Ramones and Blondie playing with like a dozen people in the place. Blondie hadn't yet got their shit together, but the Ramones did like fifteen songs in fifteen minutes. It was brilliant. (1996)

JERRY ONLY (The Misfits): My first recollection of being in the Misfits was going to CBGB and seeing the Ramones walk in the door looking like a football team. After that, I knew what to do. (1997)

LESLIE WEST (The Vagrants/Mountain): Johnny Ramone I knew back then because he wanted to be our road manager. He lived across the street. We used to call him Johnny Beatle because he had a Beatles haircut. (2011)

DANNY CORNYETZ (VJ): They just struck me as having a bad attitude. I saw one of their first shows at CBs, and they arrived in a limo. Nobody knew who they were, they had no money, yet somehow had a limo. People crowded around the doors. They looked like made-up rock stars to me. Everyone else at CBs had a fucked-up look, but with the Ramones, it seemed like a marketing technique. I guess I was wrong. (2004)

Go girl crazy: The Dictators, Bowery, 1976. Photo by GODLIS.

THE SCENE

You better come to Max's Kansas City, the Mudd Club or CBGB
And get to the party!
—NEON LEON, "ROCK & ROLL IS ALIVE (IN NEW YORK CITY)"

CBGB (315 Bowery) opened as CBGB & OMFUG (Country, Bluegrass and Blues and Other Music for Uplifting Gormandizers). Hilly Kristal studied violin and opera in Philly and then ran the Village Vanguard. For years he did Ford Caravan of Music, a national college folk-jazz concert series. Then he co-founded, with promoter Ron Delsener, the Schaefer Music Festival in Central Park, which hosted more than three hundred major shows from 1967 to 1976, from Miles Davis and Ray Charles to Bob Marley and Patti Smith.

Hilly's (62 West 9th Street), his first venue (at the site of the Lion where Streisand came to fame), thrived for five years, booking jazz, cabaret, and comedy. They had two pianists, one at the front bar, one at the back. Bette

Midler did breakout shows there. But that was before problems with the "junior mafia." So they reopened in 1972 as Hilly's in the Village (104 West 13th Street), until noise violations necessitated another move.

Kristal discovered the ground floor of a run-down Bowery flophouse. He first called it Hilly's East and Hilly's on the Bowery. Rusty McKenna and Bill Paige convinced him to book rock bands. On October 19, 1973, the Magic Tramps were the first rockers to play what was to become CBGB. The original CBGB, opened December 1973, did not have its own PA, but sold "food" from a filthy kitchen with Kristal slingin' burgers and "Hilly's Chili."

JOEY RAMONE (The Ramones): The first club was CBGB, a slum bluegrass bar that never happened. In the summer of '74 we asked Hilly Kristal, "Can we audition for you?" We played for him and he said, "Nobody's gonna like you guys but I'll have you back." So we tried to play as much as we could. We wanted the kids, but we had to get the Warhol crowd, the art crowd, the gays, because they pick up on everything first anyway. Eventually people started coming. (1986)

Few people back then dared venture to the no-man's-land of the Bowery. CBGB was off the map in terms of the music business, a dumpy bar in one of the city's worst areas with weird bands that nobody knew. One could take a $5 cab down to CBGB, smoke a joint along the ride, and tip the driver a joint.

HILLY KRISTAL (CBGB): It was the edge of civilization. People in the area had no money, and the Bowery was still "The Bowery." It was pretty bad. Upstairs housed four to five hundred men, alcoholics either out of jail or institutions. You had drippings you weren't sure it was wine or urine or water. It was very raw. (2004)

BOB GRUEN (photographer): The Lower East Side was no hip NYU campus, it was a seedy, Spanish, scary fuckin' neighborhood. Just getting to CBGB, you had a sense of accomplishment. You deserved to have an attitude because you didn't get mugged. It was a dangerous place and people felt like survivors. (2004)

Early rock shows at the rebranded CBGB included Neon Boys (pre-Television) in December 1973, and early 1974's debuts by Ramones and Television. Artist Arturo Vega lived upstairs and created the well-famous Ramones logo.

HILLY KRISTAL: Television was the first band that came by; they saw me putting up the awning. They told their manager Terry Ork, who badgered me into putting them in on a Sunday, when I wasn't open. So I started putting in these bands trying to find their way. Television, the first time I saw them, was not very good. Ramones was worse. Their gear'd konk out and they'd yell at each other. It was a mess, especially Johnny. (2005)

Hilly sought out musicians doing originals—in part for artistic reasons but also to avoid costly ASCAP and BMI payments. Bands who auditioned Sundays and Mondays quickly ascended to popular weekend headliners.

ANNIE GOLDEN (The Shirts): I kept reading in the *Voice* of this new band Talking Heads, and in *SoHo Weekly News* about Patti Smith and her boyfriend Tom Verlaine. They lived in a loft on Avenue A and played in this place called CBGB. So we drove over the bridge and got a gig. (2006)

IVY RORSCHACH (The Cramps): We saw pictures in *Rock Scene* of CBGB that showed the New York Dolls standing in front of it. "Wow, let's go there." We went and saw the Ramones at CBGB, and there was no turning back. (1994)

CBGB's July 1975 Unsigned Band Festival was a three-week event with more than forty bands, like Ramones, Heartbreakers (their first show), Tuff Darts, Mink DeVille, the Shirts, and Stagger Lee. Hilly took out large ads for all these unknown acts, and the writers and photographers came, including from London's *New Musical Express* and *Melody Maker*.

CLEM BURKE (Blondie): We felt a connection to one another; there was a sense of something happening, especially among the bands. As for commercial success, that was another story. I don't think that's what people were striving for, at least initially. I felt the momentum—I look back on it fondly. I dropped out of college to go to CBGBs. (1999)

TOM VERLAINE (Television): I wouldn't say there was a bond between the CBGB bands, in terms of hanging out with each other. In some cases there may have been some animosity. I'm not aware of hating anybody in other groups, but certainly the styles were so utterly different that people didn't hang out at each other's shows. I mean, I was friends with Patti Smith before that club became a hallmark of newer bands. (2006)

Live at Max's: Sirius Trixon wedding party with Stiv Bators, Dennis Thompson, and Neon Leon, Max's Kansas City, 1977. Photo by GODLIS.

CBGB Theater (66 Second Avenue) was where Hilly Kristal tried to stage bigger events, in the 1,743-seat former Anderson Theater. On December 27, 1977, Talking Heads, Tuff Darts, and the Shirts unveiled the room, with no heating and production problems (like power coming from a loud generator that angered neighbors). Dictators, Dead Boys, and Orchestra Luna played the next night. The fire marshals shuttered December 30's Patti Smith birthday concert with Richard Hell, the Erasers, and Mars (right after Patti and Springsteen sang his "Because the Night"), both for overcrowding and building code violations. Soundmen worked in parkas, as plumbers dealt with backed-up toilets. The Jam played the final show on March 31, 1978. Hilly lost $150K on the venture.

NORMAN DUNN (soundman): It was an exercise in how many things could go wrong. When it's twenty-seven degrees you don't spray soundproofing under the balcony. It doesn't dry. At the first note, it started falling down. The boiler room was under eleven feet of water because the water main broke. It would've cost $15,000 and Con Edison would've had to rip up the street to make things right. And this thing opened on a shoestring. Plus the chandelier hadn't been cleaned in eighteen years and the mixing board was under it. So every bass note, I was being rained on by eighteen years of soot and grime. (1988)

Max's Kansas City closed for nearly a year, until Mickey Ruskin sold his interest in the club to Chelsea bar Mother's owner Tommy Dean, who brought in his booking agent Peter Crowley. Max's offered the last embers of glitter rock, with scantily clad women, rock stars, and Warhol wannabes—that spearheaded the new punk. Max's hipness differed slightly from the T-shirt and leather jacket set at CBGB seeing the Ramones or Dead Boys.

CHEETAH CHROME (Dead Boys): When we first came to New York there were great bands at CBGB seven nights a week, and a different set at Max's. For the first six months I went out every night. The scene was kids in the bands, and those on the outside. When we got there, there wasn't anything punk about it other than leather jackets. The stores on St. Marks Place were the meeting places but at night it was those clubs. (2011)

HILLY KRISTAL: Things got good—crowds started coming from all over. Max's reopening helped a lot for the scene. Both crowds overlapped, everyone went both places. They did more Johnny Thunders and Suicide; I did more Ramones and Talking Heads. Both clubs were cordial; it was good competition. (2005)

BOB GRUEN: The difference between CBGB and Max's was that CBs was a Downtown Manhattan scene and Max's had become more bridge-and-tunnel. But there wasn't so much of a division between the bands as some people say. But there were definitely CBs bands, and a few, like the Dolls, who only played Max's. (2004)

GEORGE TABB (journalist/musician): As a teenager, CBGB to me was a scary venue—I didn't really understand it. Max's I understood. It was a rock club with bands upstairs, restaurant downstairs, pinball machines in the back, a tiny stage, very dive-y, you could buy 'ludes at the bar, it was fuckin' great—fun, not so damn serious. (2004)

BOBBY STEELE (Misfits/Undead): Max's, the shit that went down there. I don't think I ever bought a drink. You'd hang at the bar and when somebody'd put down their drink, you'd take theirs, and move on to the next person. You could get away with that back then. People at a punk club expected people to act like punks. When I got arrested for slashing a guy at Max's, the first thing the judge asked the prosecutor was "Where did this happen?" The prosecutor said, "Max's Kansas City" and the judge said, "What do you expect?" He wanted to dismiss it right there. (1996)

In the line of duty, in the line of fire
A heartless heart is my proper attire
—TELEVISION, "FOXHOLE"

Insiders like Danny Fields, Marty Thau, Jane Friedman, Seymour Stein, Alan Betrock, Lisa Robinson, and Lester Bangs propagated Downtown's new anti-stars. Mags like *New York Rocker, Trouser Press,* and *Punk* elevated Patti Smith, Joey Ramone, and Debbie Harry. Bob Gruen, Stephanie Chernikowski, David Godlis, and Roberta Bayley shot the fury and frivolity (and became stars in their own right). WPIX-FM (102.7) aired a pioneering new-wave format serving as a pipeline to the burbs. Trash and Vaudeville and Manic Panic sold clothes and tchotchkes. St. Marks Place was a brave new world.

Sire Records—named for the first letters of Seymour Stein (Steinbeagle) and Richard Gottehrer—began in 1965 when Stein promoted the Gottehrer-coproduced "Hang on Sloopy." They didn't become a full-fledged label until the '70s, behind folk/prog LPs by Chicken Shack, Barclay James Harvest, Renaissance, Nektar, and Aum. Their first hits were Fleetwood Mac's "Albatross" and "Hocus Pocus" by Focus. In 1973 Gottehrer brought Climax Blues Band to Craig Leon's studio in Miami, the start of that alliance. In 1976, Sire became a major label with Warners Bros. distribution. Linda Stein, Seymour's wife, turned him on to the Ramones, and then Joey Ramone told him all about Talking Heads. That's how both bands ended up on Sire.

CRAIG LEON (producer): Seymour was a promo man and Richie was the songwriter, and I learned great things working with him. I got a taste of that Brill Building mentality: writing a song at nine in the morning, running a demo at noon, selling it to a label at lunchtime, recording the master that night and having it out on the street a week later. And a lot of that attitude, which was always in New York, is also developed in the sense of urgency about getting it down now and getting it happening. (2006)

Red Star Records began in 1977 under music biz veteran Marty Thau. Named for, and marketed with, the Maoist symbol, Red Star released seminal records by Suicide, Richard Hell, and Walter Steding. *Marty Thau Presents 2x5*, a 1980 compilation with two songs each by five NYC groups—the Fleshtones, the Comateens, the Revelons, Student Teachers, and Bloodless Pharaohs (with a young Brian Setzer)—sold meekly. Other releases yielded three-to-five-figure sales, until 1982. Thau, with employees Miriam Linna and Roy Trakin, even "took to the street" to battle culture's punk snubbing. (The late great Thau died in February 2014.)

> **MARTY THAU (Red Star Records):** Shlackner and Hoffman of Prelude gave me a label deal, and the first group I signed was Suicide. We put out Real Kids, Fleshtones, Suicide, Martin Rev, Voidoids, Comateens and Walter Steding. Suicide didn't sell 5,000 in America. The *Voice* hated 'em: Robert Christgau called them "The Two Stooges," Tom Carson called 'em "meaningless garbage." Steding's album sold 650 copies, but I only spent $1,000 to record it. I was into the artistic end. I ran on pennies compared to most labels. I couldn't compete with the majors. My marketplace was the indie world. (2011)

Spy Records was the indie label of John Cale and manager/publicist Jane Friedman. She handled Cale and Patti Smith: that's how John produced Patti's 1975 album *Horses*. The label, run from 250 West 57th Street, got money from Oxford-educated oil scion Michael Zilkha, introduced to the record business by his Parisian rock critic friend Michel Esteban (the two later did ZE Records). Their first offbeat 7" was released in 1977 by French wavers Marie et les Garcons. Over the next two years came Lester Bangs, Necessaries, Model Citizens, and Harry Toledo.

> **JANE FRIEDMAN (manager/publicist):** We thought we had a great idea with Spy Records. John was the musical genius and I had the connections. There were some great records, but they were not for mass consumption, even in a grassroots way. We tried to compete, the plan to work up to a Sire kinda level. But we just couldn't sell the stuff. (2011)

Venus of Avenue D: Mink DeVille, 1980. Photo by John T Comerford/Frank White Photo Agency.

Live at CBGB's, a 1976 compilation for Atlantic, sprung from Hilly's decision to record the club's Unsigned Band Festival. Producers Craig Leon and Kim King laid it down from a trailer parked outside the club. Patti Smith, Ramones, Blondie, Television, Talking Heads, and Heartbreakers wouldn't/couldn't commit, so the Atlantic release had Mink DeVille, Tuff Darts, the Shirts, and the Miamis. Hilly held tryouts to flesh out the album, leading to the inclusion of Manster, Sun, and Stuart's Hammer. Over time 40,000 units sold (on LP and 8-track). Hilly was the executive producer and his daughter Lisa Kristal took the cover photos of the front and back of the house. Hilly ran out of money on a *Live at CBGB Volume II* with music in the can by Dead Boys, the Planets, the Colors, the Marbles, the Rudies, De Waves, Orchestra Luna, Just Water, Charles St. Choir, Pet Clams, Chemicals Made of Dirt, and Quincy.

CRAIG LEON: I think what you're seeing on that is a very incomplete version of what was done. I was in the truck recording that album, and I can tell you that record really got diluted. By the time it got sold, a lot of the bigger bands were signed to other labels. So what you get is the younger generation of bands on that record. They recorded everybody at the CBGB Festival, except the ones who absolutely refused. Talking Heads recorded but they're not on it because they're contractual [quick to sue or lawyer up]. (2006)

HILLY KRISTAL: I planned to do a double album but nobody wanted it. Blondie then were very sloppy, we couldn't put them on the record. It wasn't getting down on tape and we couldn't manipulate it. We tried and tried. Talking Heads, their lawyers advised them not to do it, even though we'd recorded them. The album eventually made a profit. (2005)

Your face is a magazine
I change my subscription
—THE SHIRTS, "REDUCED TO A WHISPER"

New York Rocker (1975–1982) gave a press platform to the NYC punk explosion. This was before MTV videos, so music fans relied on reliable voices in a printed form. Alan Betrock, a Queens kid rock & roll fanatic, after doing mimeographed zines like *Jamz* and *The Rock Marketplace,* and turned on by CBGB, started the *Rocker* solo for the first ten issues. Alan sold it to his friend Andy Schwartz in 1977, to pursue his Shake! label (The dB's had cut their first demos in the *Rocker* office, where Betrock also launched Marshall Crenshaw and the Smithereens) and to write *Girl Groups.* Schwartz's *Rocker,* run from 166 Fifth Avenue, printed forty-five essential issues, aided by Ira Kaplan (Yo La Tengo), Glenn Morrow (The Individuals), and Chris Nelson (Mofungo). Betrock died of cancer at forty-nine in April 2000.

GLENN MORROW (The Individuals): I joined just as Alan was selling to Andy. The magazine was in a tiny room on Fifth Avenue with a funky elevator in the same room with a religious group, sharing a bathroom. The dB's rehearsed there, so did Information with Chris Nelson. It's hard to imagine how it all functioned. I'd just graduated NYU with a journalism degree, and had written reviews for *The SandPaper* on the Jersey Shore. Alan liked my style and gave me a chance. I started to hang out in my suit looking professional, so they asked me to be ad director. I did that and wrote reviews undercover as Greg McLean. Ira Kaplan and Roy Trakin worked there. Andy Schwartz and Michael Hill ran it. Janet of the Individuals did layouts. The *Rocker* was great. (2011)

Trouser Press (1974–1984), started by Ira Robbins, Dave Schulps, and Karen Rose as *Trans-Oceanic Trouser Press* (for a Bonzo Dog Band tune), offered an

Anglophilia that tied into the birth of punk/new wave. Fans got into the features, especially their "America Underground" column, and the collector "flexi-discs" stapled into each copy. The first issue, 350 copies of 24 pages, sold at gigs for 25¢; by its peak as a 96-page glossy, it printed 5,000. In 1981, Ira, a Bronx High School of Science grad and engineering dropout, tried it full-time, and lasted three years.

> **IRA ROBBINS (*Trouser Press*):** It was seat-of-the-pants, idiosyn-cratic, irreverent and self-indulgence but it was wonderful fun. It sucked getting dicked around by record labels, advertisers, distributors and all the rest. And I took it personally. It wasn't just the money, it was the feeling of powerlessness, that the enterprise we put so much of our lives into could so easily be derailed by others' incompetence or bankruptcy, or record industry suspicions. It was a tough and lonely battle, and we didn't learn until it was over how many people we were important to. (2006)

Punk, New York Rock's comic book, complemented the explosion with a vi-sual narrative. John Holmstrom studied art at SVA under *Mad* cartoonist Harvey Kurtzman. *Punk* was started by Holmstrom, his high school classmate Roderick "Legs" McNeil, and their mutual friend Ged Dunn Jr., and got its na-tional distribution through *High Times* publisher Tom Forçade. From 1975 to 1979, *Punk* printed fifteen issues, notably July 1978's "Mutant Monster Beach Party" with Joey Ramone, Debbie Harry, and Lester Bangs. Legs, at the time a resident of Total Impact, David Sector's commune on 14th and Third, passed out while interviewing Richard Hell. Holmstrom designed the Ramones' *Rocket to Russia* and *Road to Ruin* covers.

> **JOHN HOLMSTROM (*Punk Magazine*):** I always thought the rise of rock and the rise of comics had a cross-cultural influence, and always had the idea of a rock-and-roll comic book. Seeing the Ramones and picking up the first Dictators record inspired us to start a magazine. We walked over to CBs the Sunday after Thanksgiving. The Ramones were playing and the place was empty. We interviewed them, and found out Lou Reed was there and interviewed Lou. That was it; our first issue came out January 1, 1976. (2004)

Bleecker Bob's Golden Oldies (118 West 3rd Street) opened in late 1967 as the hippie record store Village Oldies at 239 Bleecker Street. In 1976, Bob Plotnick moved to 179 MacDougal and redubbed it Bleecker Bob's, focused on the new UK punk vinyl market. Bob's moved again in 1984 to the site of the Night Owl, the shop's ratty rug still from the club's stage. Bob behind the counter dispensed New York attitude. His well-stocked store (sorted by genre, not alphabetically) stayed open until 3 a.m. on weekends, becoming a late-night destination (until April 2013). Other great late-night Village record stores of that era included Freebeing (129 Second Avenue) and Second Coming (235 Sullivan Street).

SONNY VINCENT (Testors): Bleecker Bob was the wisest "wiseass" in punkdom. He offered to be our manager. This meant we'd have to withstand Bob's verbal abuse and jibes more often than if we only met him in his store. Deep down he was a prototypical warm, giving New York Jew with a heart of gold. But on the outside he was very crude and abrasive. This was our manager: "Oh look, those Testors cocksuckers just walked in!" (2011)

> The road not taken to oblivion veers
> And it makes me cry, but they're crocodile tears
> —THE MUMPS, "CROCODILE TEARS"

Manic Panic (33 St. Marks Place) was the first place in New York to sell Sex Pistols T-shirts and electric hair dyes. Bronx sisters Tish and Snooky Bellomo played in early Blondie (Blondie and the Banzai Babies) and the shocking Sic F*cks. Tish & Snooky opened their store/scene clubhouse (whose name was coined by their mother) on July 1977 (7/7/77) for $250 per month. Howie Pyro worked the register, selling $1 band badges and iron-ons. In the '80s, Cyndi Lauper shopped there, Springsteen bought shoes, even Cher got a Sic F*cks shirt. Manic Panic shut their store in 1989 after a 1,200 percent rent increase.

HOWIE PYRO (D Generation): First I discovered the East Village and Trash and Vaudeville. Then I went back, and it was the day Manic Panic opened. That changed me because it was a real punk store. So I ditched my job and school and started hanging out at Manic Panic. I'd work there and sleep in the back, and stopped going home. I think I made six dollars a day. That's where everyone from every band ended up. (2004)

SNOOKY BELLOMO (Manic Panic): We began with a few go-go boots and two racks of clothes brought from home in the Bronx. But people were afraid to come into the neighborhood at first. Some days we'd make fifty cents when somebody bought a button from us. But then we started getting good press and things began to change. (2006)

Chelsea Hotel (222 West 23rd Street) was the historical home to the city's arts underbelly; a crash pad for the creative demimonde. Residents since 1883 included Eugene O'Neill, Jean-Paul Sartre, Frida Kahlo, Dylan Thomas, Arthur Miller, Bob Dylan, Leonard Cohen, Patti Smith, and Robert Mapplethorpe. Stanley Bard's hotel now reads as iconic but it was a sketchy joint. Nico sang in 1967's "Chelsea Girl": "Here's Room 115, filled with S&M queens."

In 1978, Sex Pistols bassist Sid Vicious and twenty-year-old girlfriend "Nauseating" Nancy Spungen lived in Room 100, and cavorted with degenerates like Dee Dee Ramone, Neon Leon, Vinnie Stigma, and Rockets Redglare. On October 12, 1978, Sid got arrested for supposedly plunging a knife into Spungen. On February 2, 1979—one day after spending fifty-five days in Rikers for smashing a beer mug into Patti Smith's brother Todd's face at Hurrah—Sid died at his new lady friend Michelle Robinson's apartment at 63 Bank Street from $200 of dope he got from Keith Richards's dealer/photographer Peter "Kodik" Gravelle. The Chelsea's Room 100 is now a laundry room—it had become somewhat of a tourist shrine. (The hotel was sold in 2013 to a luxury hotelier, but development plans remain up in the air.)

NANCY SPUNGEN (New York scene): On the first night we screwed, Sid had smelly feet and he wet the bed. I taught him everything he needs to know. I put that sexual aura into Sid. (1978)

LEEE BLACK CHILDERS (photographer): I was around at the time of the murder, and Sid did not kill Nancy. It was this drug dealer there. Sid was passed out on the bed, and his knife was there. The drug dealer probably had a fight with Nancy, who was fucking horrible, and said, "Fuck this bitch" and stabbed her, and then just walked out. It was Sid's knife but he didn't do it. The cops were morons and they didn't care. (2011)

Let's dance: Joey Ramone, CBGB, 1977. Photo by GODLIS.

THE MUSIC

D-U-M-B
Everyone's accusing me
—RAMONES, "PINHEAD"

Ramones with their gang-style leather jackets and tattered jeans, and pop-tinged punk, became the template for most hard-edged rock music to come. Joey (Jeffrey Hyman), at first a drummer, cut his teeth with Queens glitter rockers Sniper. Johnny (John Cummings) and Dee Dee (Douglas Colvin) jammed locally as Tangerine Puppets. Manager Tommy Erdelyi urged Joey to sing, and then joined on drums as Tommy Ramone. March 30, 1974's first show at Erdelyi's Performance Studio yielded 2,262 more (last August 6, 1996 in L.A.). *Ramones* (Sire) of 1975 was ignored beyond CBs till a '76 UK tour fueled the '77 punk explosion.

JOEY RAMONE: We started the whole thing, revolutionized rock in 1976, turned the world around musically, culturally, and politically. Everyone followed us. (1986)

TOMMY RAMONE: We play short songs and short sets for people who don't have a lot of spare time. (1975)

JOHNNY RAMONE: We like playing fast songs but we like listening to slow songs. Don't like playing them, I hate to play slow songs, but I like to listen to them. Like, our first album when everything's fast, you've got to be in a certain mood to really listen to it, you have to be a very energetic person. (1978)

DEE DEE RAMONE: I liked the Ramones music before Phil Spector did the albums, but I didn't like the music after. I got tired of the Ramones about the time I quit. (2000)

MARKY RAMONE: Johnny and Dee Dee didn't like each other. Dee Dee always complained that Johnny didn't contribute to the songwriting, but he'd get credit on the songs. That irked him, and the fact that Johnny took Joey's girlfriend from him in 1981, which caused a lot of friction in the band. That festered until the band retired in 1996. Johnny and Joey didn't talk to each other for eighteen years. (2003)

C. J. RAMONE: The early Ramones albums are fuckin' unbelievable if you look at it in the context of what was going on in music at that time and how many people they've influenced, 'cause you measure the true greatness of a band by how many people they've influenced and the Ramones were probably the most influential band of all time. (2001)

> *Say something once*
> *Why say it again?*
> —TALKING HEADS, "PSYCHO KILLER"

Talking Heads eclipsed Downtown to achieve stardom; their preppy good looks and palatably quirky new wave portended pop's future. Rhode Island School of Design grads David Byrne, Tina Weymouth, and Chris Frantz played as the Artistics, who upon moving to NYC, rehearsed at 195 Chrystie Street. TH's first gig was on June 5, 1975, nearby at CBs, opening for the Ramones. In 1976, the trio added Modern Lovers guitarist Jerry Harrison. *Talking Heads '77* (Sire) depicted a city on edge with "Psycho Killer" referencing Son of Sam psycho David Berkowitz. "Fifth member" Brian Eno advanced the act from skeletal art rock to futuristic funk (first on 1981's Eno/Byrne LP *My Life in the Bush of Ghosts*). The band broke up in 1991. Byrne sued over '96's Byrne-less foray as the Heads; *No Talking, Just Head* featured vocals by Debbie Harry, Richard Hell, Michael Hutchence, Gavin Friday, Andy Partridge, and Gordon Gano.

MOBY (DJ): Talking Heads were the definitive New York band. They went through so many permutations, and their music was so obviously inspired by living in New York. *Fear of Music* was such a New York record; they name-check the clubs. It was white academic punk rockers playing funk. (2004)

DAVID BYRNE (Talking Heads): People said we were intellectuals and only smarties would like us. But then kids came and liked us, and that proved they were wrong. (1980)

TINA WEYMOUTH (Talking Heads): People come expecting to see another Velvet Underground. They miss the whole point. (1975)

CHRIS FRANTZ (Talking Heads): It was David Byrne's decision to stop working with the band and it's his decision to continue to stop. What can I say? He's got his head up his ass. (2001)

> *I said don't stop*
> *Do punk rock*
> —Blondie, "Rapture"

Blondie defined NY style with a wide-ranging sense of pop. Their name came from the comic strip, Hitler's dog, or bleached-blond singer Deborah Harry (Angela Tremble). The ex–*Playboy* bunny and Max's waitress sang with '60s folkies Wind and the Willows, cabaret-rockers the Late Show, and glitter-rockers the Stilettos, where she met guitarist Chris Stein. Harry and Stein set off on their own: two gigs as Angel and the Snakes and then five as Blondie and the Banzai Babies before teaming with drummer Clem Burke and by 1974 playing as Blondie. Hilly Kristal told Richard Gottehrer, which led to 1976's *Blondie* for Private Stock, produced by Gottehrer and Craig Leon at Plaza Sound. Frankie Infante, of Joey Ramone's band Sniper, replaced Gary Valentine (Lachman) for 1977's Gottehrer-produced *Plastic Letters*. Chrysalis bought out Private Stock's deal for $500K.

Infante shifted to second guitar with the arrival of Nigel Harrison (of Silverhead with Michael Des Barres and Nite City with Ray Manzarek) on Mike Chapman–produced mega-sellers: 1978's *Parallel Lines* sold twenty million, 1979's *Eat to the Beat* charted for a year, as did 1981's *Autoamerican*. The genre-bending stars disbanded after 1982's *The Hunter* arrived DOA. The next year Stein caught a skin autoimmune disease (pemphigus vulgaris). Bad juju returned at Blondie's March 13, 2006, Rock and Roll Hall of Fame induction, where Infante and Valentine couldn't participate or perform.

DEBORAH HARRY (Blondie): The pin-up thing I used as part of my shtick. Taking the blond silver screen goddess and bringing her into the pop world and making that happen in a musical format, that's exactly what I aimed to do. That was calculated, but within it, what I did was to make it more twisted, and more timely. (1999)

CHRIS STEIN (Blondie): It was hard. Nobody realizes how much criticism Debbie got for being overtly sexual and doing things that were commonplace among male performers. (1999)

HILLY KRISTAL (CBGB): I heard their music and it was a raggedy band, but she was very beautiful and had a sweet-sounding voice. . . . I hooked 'em up with Richard Gottehrer who brought 'em to Private Stock. They had the songs, they had the singer, they were a great band, and they took pride in playing well. (2005)

JIMMY DESTRI (Blondie): We got to a point where we were running into Paul Anka at Teterboro Airport. He'd be boarding his private jet, we'd be boarding ours. A funny thing about that jet was we got it so we didn't have to be around each other as much on the road. But a private jet is actually not that luxurious and since it's so small, we all sat on top of each other, making things worse. That was our final nail in the coffin. (1999)

Till victory: Patti Smith with Lenny Kaye, CBGB, 1977.
Photo by GODLIS.

Outside of society,
That's where I want to be
—Patti Smith, "Rock N Roll Nigger"

Patti Smith pioneered a fiery prose that bridged beatnik and punk sensibilities. She moved to NYC in 1967, and by 1971 earned a rep on the St. Mark's Church poetry scene with crude rants plus playwright lover Sam Shepard on drums. Robert Mapplethorpe released 1974's "Piss Factory" with a B-side of "Hey Joe" (guest guitar by Tom Verlaine). A seven-week stint at CBGB begot an Arista deal that began with 1975's discordant John Cale–produced *Horses*. Her music came to form on 1978's Jimmy Iovine–overseen *Easter* with "Because the Night" and "Rock N Roll Nigger."

Richard Hell, the face of punk, a legend of poetry, music, and fashion, made seminal music in Neon Boys (pre-Television), Heartbreakers, Richard Hell and the Voidoids, Dim Stars, and as a solo act. His Voidoids starred guitarists Robert Quine (who in 1969 issued a noted series of live VU cassettes) and Ivan Julian (of the Foundations ["Build Me up Buttercup"]) with Dust drummer Marc Bell (later Marky Ramone). *Blank Generation* defined 1977-era NYC punk anger and ennui.

Suicide of the same Mercer/Max's scene as New York Dolls, discarded the trappings of rock, emitting cold electronics with sparse vocals that few people grasped. The duo of Alan Vega and Martin Rev earn praise today as pioneers of punk, electro, techno, and industrial. But most self-respecting rockers, upon seeing Suicide, hated them.

Television possessed a mature sound far beyond the other CBs pioneers.

The talented quartet with longish hair and artsy guitar solos, like a punk Grateful Dead, spurred debate in punk circles. "Little Johnny Jewel," the band's 1975 debut single, came out on Terry Ork's label, Ork Records.

The Heartbreakers blared a criminal junkie-rock that paved the way for punk, and '80s glam-metal like Guns N' Roses and Mötley Crüe. Their hostile style won them a die-hard fan base but their bad reputation scared off the biz, so they never "made it." The 1977 studio LP *L.A.M.F.* ("Born to Lose," "Chinese Rocks") portended the junkie revelry of 1979's *Live at Max's*.

The Dictators clicked when roadie Richard Blum jumped onstage at Popeye's Spinach Factory in Sheepshead Bay to sing an encore of "Louie Louie." The Bronx band with Andy "Adny" Shernoff, Scott "Top Ten" Kempner, and Ross the Boss (Friedman) found a singer, dubbed "Handsome Dick Manitoba." BÖC's managers Sandy Pearlman and Murray Krugman knew Shernoff from his *Teenage Wasteland Gazette* (with writers like Lester Bangs and Richard Meltzer). The very first punk album, 1975's *Go Girl Crazy!* (Epic), was for years Epic's lowest-seller. Neither 1977's *Manifest Destiny* nor 1978's *Blood Brothers* for Elektra exploded. Some have suggested they were a bit too Borscht Belt for mainstream rock consumption.

Young, loud, and snotty: Dead Boys, CBGB, 1977. Photo by GODLIS.

Another place, another time
You'll get yours like I got mine
—The Miamis, "Another Place, Another Time"

The Miamis was the wry pop/punk quintet of Tommy and Jimmy Wynbrandt. The bros began in Wayne County's glitter band Queen Elizabeth but got fired when Wayne signed to Bowie's management. The Miamis gigged a lot with the Dolls, and Blondie used to open for them. They cut two demos, one funded by Hilly, another by future Mike Tyson manager Shelly Finkel. So their only release was "We Deliver" on 1976's *Live at CBGB*.

Just Water was a very '70s quartet with smooth vocals and stage presence. Mitch Dancik and Danny Rubin began at Harper College in Binghamton, and moved to Brooklyn in '75. Dancik's pal Binky Philips found them gigs and a manager. *NME* writer Max Bell hailed 1977's *The Riff* LP "better than Television." They excelled on "What We Need Is Some Rock" on *Max's Kansas City 1977 (Vol. II)* and '78's punk rip on "Singin' in the Rain."

Tuff Darts, Jeff Salen's rowdy rock & roll act, made a New York Rock classic in "All for the Love of Rock N Roll," opening 1976's *Live at* CBGB and theme to WPIX-FM's "Live at CBGB." Robert Gordon sang on that comp's songs before his rockabilly solo career. Cig-smoking Tommy Frenzy held his own on 1978's *Tuff Darts!* (Sire) with a new rip on that tune and "(Your Love Is Like) Nuclear Waste." But Sire never got what they desired.

Sic F*cks, the Bronx-based kitschy punk act, with singer Russell Wolinsky and "The Fuckettes" Tish and Snooky (Patrice and Eileen Bellomo) acted out their garish lyrics, the sisters in torn nun habits, bloody axes, and garters. The band auditioned at CBs on August 1, 1977. Members disliked 1982's Andy Shernoff–produced *Sic F*cks* EP with "Spanish Bar Mitzvah" and "Chop up Your Mother" (in horror film *Alone in the Dark*).

The Cramps founded B-movie horror/punk. Lux Interior (Erick Purkhiser) met Poison Ivy Rorschach (Kristy Wallace) at an "Art and Shamanism" class at Sacramento State. They moved to NYC after reading about the Dolls in *Rock Scene*. They auditioned at CBGB on November 1, 1976. After a spell with drummer Miriam Linna came 1978's Alex Chilton–produced "Surfin' Bird" b/w "The Way I Walk" and "Human Fly" b/w "Domino," heard on 1979's *Gravest Hits*. Bryan Gregory (Greg Beckerleg) quit after 1980's *Songs the Lord Taught Us*, to get into Satanism, so they moved to L.A.

Dead Boys from Cleveland came to NY in 1976 and attained instant notoriety, thanks to fan Joey Ramone. As punk's most extreme act, Stiv Bators (Stivin Bator) took Iggy-ish immolation to new levels, fueled by the junked-up axe tones of Cheetah Chrome (Eugene O'Connor). Jimmy Zero (William Wilden), Jeff Magnum, and Johnny Blitz (Madansky) held it down. Kristal became manager, signed them to Sire, and put them in Electric Lady Studios with Genya Ravan to record 1977's *Young, Loud and Snotty*. Everything imploded after 1978's *We Have Come for Your Children* cut with Felix Pappalardi (Cream/Mountain).

The Shirts auditioned at CBGB on Sunday, May 18, 1975, with Talking Heads. Hilly saw them like the Left Banke ("Walk Away Renee") and became manager. Annie Golden backed by her five Brooklyn Italian-American rockers starred on *Live at CBGB* and three Capitol albums. CBGB connected the Shirts to punk, not their Bay Ridge couture. David Byrne wrote in *Thirty Years from the Home of Underground Rock, CBGB & OMFUG*, "One could even say The Shirts were the precursors to the musical *Rent*."

The Marbles played punk-style pop. In the early CBs era the quartet headlined over Blondie, Ramones, and Talking Heads. Columbia freshmen Howard and David Bowler met *New York Rocker* publisher Alan Betrock, resulting in their "Closing Me Down" in Amos Poe's film *Blank Generation*, 1976's "Red Lights" b/w "Fire and Smoke" (Ork), and 1977's "Forgive and Forget" b/w "Computer Cards" (the debut on Jim Reynolds's Jimboco Records).

The Laughing Dogs blared old-school rock & roll in the punk era. Guitarist-vocalist Jimmy Accardi toured with Chubby Checker, bassist Ronny Altaville played blue-eyed soul in Aesop's Fables. The two, along with pianist Carter Cathcart, backed Rupert Holmes (of "Piña Colada" fame). Drummer Marc "Moe Potts" Potocsky exuded punk attitude. CBGB auditions in 1976 won them songs on *Live at CBGB*. Their 1979 debut *The Laughing Dogs* (Columbia) employed artwork planned for a 1973 LP by Wicked Lester, who became Kiss. The follow-up, 1980's *The Laughing Dogs Meet Their Maker*, proved prophetic in a career sense.

Milk 'N' Cookies was a sugary pop quartet that began in Woodmere, LI, with guitarist Ian North and singer Justin Strauss. Sal Maida (Sparks/Roxy Music) replaced bassist Jay Weis (later married to actress Kathleen Turner). A 1975 single, "Little, Lost and Innocent" (Island UK), yielded 1976's delectable Muff Winwood–produced *Milk 'N' Cookies*. North told *Sounds* (3/75), "I hate the word punk."

The Poppees, "The Fab Four of the Bowery," rocked Beatles-style on the Downtown scene. Bobby Dee Waxman (guitar/vocals) and Paddy Lorenzo (bass/vocals), Polish-born guitarist Arthur Alexander, and Bronx-bred drummer Arthur "Jett" Harris did two 45s for Greg Shaw's Bomp! label. "If She Cries" b/w "The Love of the Loved" produced by Craig Leon in 1975 sounded like a dirty "I Wanna Hold Your Hand." Flamin' Groovies' Cyril Jordan oversaw 1978's "Jealousy" b/w "She's Got It," equal parts *L.A.M.F.* and *Rubber Soul*.

Sorrows, not the British Invasion act the Sorrows, captured a '60s feel. Poppees' Jett Harris and Arthur Alexander, with Joey Cola and Rick Street (replaced by Tuff Darts' John DeSalvo) made 1980's Elliot Apter–produced *Teenage Heartbreak* with Ellie Greenwich and 1981's Shel Talmy–overseen *Love Too Late* misplaced on Pavilion/CBS.

The Boyfriends began when Bobby Dee Waxman and Paddy Lorenzo of the Poppees joined bassist Jay Nap and drummer Lee Crystal (pre–Joan Jett). The Heartbreakers-style act briefly managed by Malcolm McLaren did 1978's "You're the One" / "I Don't Want Nobody (I Want You)" (Bomp!) and 1981's "Wrapped in a Dream" / "It's the Same Old Song" (Signal). (Ramones' *Subterranean Jungle* reworked their "I Need Your Love.")

The Cryers, Lowry Hamner's Meridian, Mississippi, pop quintet, moved Downtown in 1976 and played the Max's/CBs loop. Steve Katz (Blues Project) signed them to Mercury and produced 1978's *The Cryers* with "Shake It Up (Ain't It Time)" and "(It's Gonna Be A) Heartbreaker," and 1979's *Midnight Run* (as Lowry Hamner & The Cryers) in blazer-rock attire. Fans hailed 'em a next Big Star, critics panned 'em as REO Speedwagon redux.

Prix made punk-era art-pop 7"s: 1977's EP for Ork and 1978's self-issued "Everytime I Close My Eyes." New Haven–bred Jon Tiven wrote for *Rolling Stone*, was a top session player who worked with the Stones' Andrew Loog Oldham, and produced the Feelies' unreleased debut 45 ("Forces at Work"). Tiven was also in the Yankees, a power-pop act with Voidoids bassist Ivan Julian (1978's *High 'N' Inside* with "Take It Like a Man") and Jim Carroll Band (1982's *Dry Dreams*).

Fotomaker was the power-pop act of the Rascals' Gene Cornish and Dino Danelli with the Raspberries' Wally Bryson. *Fotomaker* of 1978 spewed syrupy like "Where Have You Been All My Life?" (peaking at #81) with lyrics like "I'd rather lose at love than never have loved at all." Robert Christgau railed: "Beat the rush, boycott now, before anyone's even heard of them."

Sylvain Sylvain made bad choices: nixing Malcolm McLaren's offer to form the Sex Pistols to stay with David Jo, and then go solo. Syl spent three months hospitalized after a 1977 van crash on East 13th Street, and the insurance funded 1978's "The Kids Are Back" 45 as the Criminals. He signed to RCA: 1979's *Sylvain Sylvain* contained the NYC opus "14th Street Beat"; 1981's *Syl Sylvain and the Teardrops* peaked on *Billboard* at #123. Cairo-born Syl spent the next twenty-five years wandering a desert of one-off records and indie tours.

Cool metro: David Johansen, 1979. Photo by John T. Comerford/Frank White Photo Agency.

I gotta fly just to get Downtown
I swear where everybody's crazy
—David Johansen, "Funky but Chic"

David Johansen Band, the Staten Island singer's post-Dolls group, bridged old-school barroom rock and new wave. *David Johansen* came out in 1978 and remains a New York Rock classic. Mick Ronson produced 1979's *In Style* that coincided with Shea Stadium shows with the Who and the Clash. Neither 1981's *Here Comes the Night* nor 1984's *Sweet Revenge* even charted. That's why Jo forsook rock to make party music as Buster Poindexter & His Banshees of Blue. His 1987 cover of "Hot Hot Hot" made Arrow a wealthy man.

    Mink DeVille perfected barroom R&B with punk attitude. Willy DeVille (William Boray), born of Basque-Pequot-Irish heritage in Stamford, CT, formed a band that fit Hilly's vision of CBGB (as country, bluegrass, and blues), so Mink DeVille became the house band. John Lee Hooker guitarist Louie X. Erlanger excelled on 1976's *Live at CBGB* cuts. Capitol's Ben Edmunds went to CBs to sign Tuff Darts, and instead signed Mink. The *Mink DeVille* album of 1977 opened with his strident "Venus of Avenue D."

Philip Rambow moved to New York in 1970 to lead the band Saturday Night. In 1973, he left for London to front pub rockers the Winkies (who made a 1975 album for Chrysalis and became Brian Eno's backing band), where he influenced a young Joe Strummer and Mick Jones of the Clash. In 1976 he returned to NYC as Philip Rambow Band, Max's regulars behind the Lou Reed–tinged "Night Time" on *Max's Kansas City 1977 (Vol. II)*.

John Collins, a flashy frontman like David Johansen, sang in Bang Zoom that opened for the Dolls at the Mercer. Collins played Max's 150 times, as John Collins Band (on *Max's Kansas City 1976*) and The Terrorists featuring John Collins, doing reggae with Roland Alphonso and Lee "Scratch" Perry. In his Cajun-style next act, the Hawaiians, John met Wayne Kramer (MC5) and Mick Farren (Deviants). He acted in Mick's musical *The Last Words of Dutch Schultz;* the two rocked Wayne's *Death Tongue* LP and as Tijuana Bible.

Kieran Liscoe performed under several monikers. Kieran Liscoe Band played with the Cramps at Max's and CBGB in 1977 and '78. In 1979, Kieran Liscoe Rhythm Band headlined a Max's benefit for soul singer Jackie Wilson (with Sylvain Sylvain, The Senders, The Rousers, and U.S. Ape). The new wave–friendly soul-pop of 1981's *Kieran Liscoe & The Attitude* (on the Max's Kansas City label) failed to transcend.

Lenny Kaye rocked with Patti Smith, produced Jim Carroll, Suzanne Vega, Allen Ginsberg, compiled *Nuggets,* and wrote rock books and liner notes. The NJ native began in Link Cromwell & the Zoo (1966's "Crazy Like a Fox"). Patti got maternal in '79 so Kaye gigged as Lenny Kaye Connection (often with PS mates Richard Sohl and Jay Dee Daugherty). His 1980 single "Child Bride" featured a live-at-CBs (3/20/80) B-side of "Tracks of My Tears," while 1984's *I've Got a Right* included an "anvil chorus" of Smith, Carroll, and John Giorno.

Jim Carroll embodied New York Rock's edgy poetics. "The Dylan of the '80s," found fame with 1978's *The Basketball Diaries,* an autobiography of his unlikely descent from NYC prep school hoops star to a junkie gay hustler. In 1980, spurred to music by his ex Patti Smith, Carroll recorded his Lenny Kaye–produced debut, *Catholic Boy.* The Atco debut contained "Wicked Gravity" and "People Who Died," a shout-out to drug scene tragedies.

Kids just wanna dance: Paul and Miki Zone, The Fast, 1979. Photo by Donald Marino. Courtesy of Paul Zone.

Kids in the streets, in skirts and pants
Kids just wanna dance
—THE FAST, "KIDS JUST WANNA DANCE"

The Fast kept glam alive in the punk era. It began as a family affair, with Brooklyn's Zone (Cilione) brothers, oldest Miki (guitar), middle Armand (keys), and youngest Paul (vocals). With Max's Kansas City management, the Fast headlined over the B-52's and the Misfits, and near home in Prospect Park at Zappa's. Miki and Paul rocked on as Miki Zone Zoo ('79's "Coney Island Chaos") before Miki and Paul tried a Soft Cell style on "Man to Man" produced by Man Parrish. (Miki died in 1986 of AIDS, Armand in 1996.)

The Mumps starred Lance Loud and Kristian Hoffman, who met in L.A. at Santa Barbara High. Infamous in *An American Family* (PBS, 1973) Lance came out of the closet, to be a gay icon. They moved to NYC in 1976 and made 1977's "Crocodile Tears" (Bomp!) and 1978's *Rock and Roll This, Rock and Roll That* EP (cut at Brian Wilson's studio). Loud left to L.A., to write for *Rock Scene* and *The Advocate* before his 2001 death at age fifty.

New York Niggers began when upstate brothas Aid MacSpade (Elliot Harris) and Leo "Pope" Faison got with Harlem singer Wolf Bonaparte and German guitarist Dieter Osten (Runge). Hilly wouldn't book them, but when the Police played at CBGB they brought a Detroit band, the Niggers. So the 1,000 copies of 1979's "Just Like Dresden '45" came out as "New York Niggers." They claimed the name blended New York Dolls and Patti Smith's "Rock N Roll Nigger."

Stumblebunny began after Chris Robison and Peter Jordan quit one of the final Dolls lineups. On December 1, 1976, they, David White, and Sammy Brown debuted at Max's. As per Henry Schissler (*SoHo Weekly News*, 12/9/76): "Stumblebunny could be a top draw but not before much work is done." Robert Christgau (*Voice*, 3/27/78) called 1977's *Stumblebunny* EP "the only noteworthy New York indie 45 I've come across." Richard Gottehrer re-worked "Tonite" as a 1978 hit on Phonogram Germany. (Jordan and Brown went on to the Nitecaps; 1982's *Go to the Line* for Sire).

Neon Leon came from Philly, where his Neon Leon & the Rainbow Express opened for the Dolls in 1973. *Rock Scene* loved Leon, who lived at the Chelsea in Sid's last days. The Stones funded Leon's "Rock & Roll Is Alive (In New York City)" single. Leon, formerly an alleged coke-dealing pimp whose ladies put his stickers on lampposts and in taxis, also did music for films of porn-star lovers. In 1982 he and a Swedish gal pal went into rehab in Stockholm. Then he totally remade himself as King Leon, a popular Scandinavian ska star.

Pure Hell, the quartet of singer Kenny "Stinker" Gordon, guitarist Chip Wreck (Preston Morris III), bassist Lenny Steel (Kerry Boles), and drummer Michael "Spider" Sanders moved to NYC in 1975 as Philly glam rockers Pretty Poison. "The World's First All-Black Punk Band" tore it up live with the Dolls, Dead Boys, and Richard Hell. They raged on a 1978 UK tour for a "These Boots Were Made for Walking" 45 that charted for Curtis Knight's Golden Sphinx label, but fell out with Curtis after screwing his girlfriend. (The 1979 tapes of *Noise Addiction* amazingly turned up at auction twenty-five years later and got put out in 2005.)

Corpse Grinders, a hard-hitting band in ghoul makeup named for a 1971 gore film, starred Dolls bassist Arthur Kane, Brats guitarist Rick Rivets, Teen-age Lust drummer Jimmy Criss, and London Fogg singer Stu Wylder. They first "played" on October 14, 1977, lip-synching on Manhattan Cable TV; their first gig was that Halloween at midnight at Great Gildersleeves. Cheetah Chrome booked them both nights of May 1978's Johnny Blitz benefit at CBs. That year's "Rites 4 Whites" 45 on Andy Doback's CT-based Whiplash Records raised red flags.

The Slugs, Rick Rivets's post-Grinders punk/rock act, at times gigged as Corpse Grinders. He teamed with rude Long Island rockers, singer Ray Jalbert (Gilbert), guitarist Kenny Lewit, bassist Lenny Lazers, and drummer Mark Gotkin (replaced by Paul Blaccard). Two singles, 1979's "Problem Child" b/w "Suspicion" and 1980's "I'm in Love With You (Again)" b/w "Never Should've Told You," got stuffed into one sleeve as '81's *Slugs 2x7*.

Mistress of taboo: Wendy O. Williams, Plasmatics. 1979.
Photo by Ron Da Silva/Frank White Photo Agency.

Plasmatics upped the ante for punk/metal assault, outré attitude, porno fetishism, and nasty antics (sledgehammered TVs, chain-sawed guitars, exploded Cadillacs). Wendy Orlean Williams sang topless in a vinyl nurse suit and electrical tape over her nipples (she'd get a rare allergy to the adhesive that made her lactate). The 1978 single "Butcher Baby" heard O. Chosei Funahara crazily count off Ramones-style in Japanese. Both 1980's *New Hope for the Wretched* and 1981's *Beyond the Valley of 1984* stiffed for Stiff America. After 1982's *Coup d'État* (Capitol) came WOW's solo career. She did a final Plasmatics LP with a new lineup: 1987's 48-minute "rock opera" *Maggots: The Record.*

The Misfits began in Lodi, NJ. Glenn Danzig (Anzalone) and Jerry Only (Caiafa) auditioned at CBs on September 18, 1977, before the Shirts. The 500 copies of 1977's "Cough"/"Cool" 45 sported a keyboard sound. The band gelled with 1978's arrival of guitarist Bobby Steele. Drummer Arthur Googy (Joe McGuckin) replaced Joey Image (Poole) on 1982's classic *Walk Among Us*. Robo (Black Flag) proved crucial, tuning up their van and drumming on '83's *Earth A.D.* But a year of this Colombian alien in their houses killed the band.

Testors, named for a huffing glue, was Sonny Vincent between reform schools, mental wards, and jail stints. First bassist Rex Pharaoh (Ron Pieniak) quit after he got stabbed on a subway in a "Kill Me" shirt! In 1979 they toured with Dead Boys. Later that year, after a gig at CBGB Theater, Sonny and Lenny Kaye got into an on-air fistfight on WPIX-FM. Nineteen eighty's "Together" / "Time Is Mine," produced and issued by Bleecker Bob, got radio play.

Steel Tips, a shocking five-piece from Edison, NJ, infamous at CBGB and Max's, made a spectacle: Tom O'Leary screaming and playing cowbell, batty bassist Stanly Du Thomas, drummer Patrick McDonnell's organ-playing wife Karen Ann in Catholic school clothes, and Joe Coleman blowing himself up with TNT.

Just because I'm white
Why do you treat me like a nigger?
—GANG WAR, "JUST BECAUSE I'M WHITE"

Gang War was Johnny Thunders and Wayne Kramer in a fleeting drug super-group. Thunders, hating his 1978 solo LP *So Alone,* joined Kramer, off two years in prison for selling cocaine. With Wayne's Detroit pal W. R. "Ron" Cooke (Sonic Rendezvous Band) and Philippe Marcadé (The Senders) flowed songs like "There's a Little Bit of Whore in Every Girl" and "Just Because I'm White (Why Do You Treat Me Like a Nigger?)."

The Idols began when Sid Vicious split to NYC to go solo. His London mates Steve Dior and Barry Jones, along with Dolls' rhythm section Arthur Kane and Jerry Nolan, backed Sid at Max's on September 28–29, 1978. But then Sid died on February 2, 1979. September 1979's single "You" (Ork) ended after Nolan's drug record banned him from England. (Dior and Jones later "coached" a young L.A. Guns.)

The Rattlers featured Joey Ramone's brother Mickey Leigh (Mitchell Lee Hyman) and David Merrill, son of New York Opera/Yankee Stadium icon Robert Merrill. Their quartet with Billy Baillie and Matty Quick opened Ramones gigs and shared stages with the Clash and B-52's, but were too pop for punks. The material on 1985's Tommy Erdelyi–produced *Rattled* reworked 1979's "On the Beach" and 1983's "What Keeps Your Heart Beating."

The Invaders played a cheeky reggae/pop popular at CBGB, zinging one-liners between songs. The quartet's gigs, promoted by large posters splattered across Manhattan by guitarist Gregor Laraque, did not propel 1979's self-released "With the TV On" single of island riddims and Zappa-esque scorn. Their late frontman Bruce Jay Paskow joined the Grammy-nominated Washington Squares, and served in Hot Tuna with Jorma Kaukonen.

The Heat, a multiracial quartet, forged a heavy pop-rock. Guitarist Tally Taliaferrow, dumped by the Planets, exacted revenge with vocalist Dwight "Dwytt" Dayan, bassist Geoff Li (Lee), and drummer Jeff Formosa on 1979's "Instant Love" 45 heard on WNEW and WPLJ. Dwytt quit after being in the Stones' "Waiting on a Friend" video; the others flamed out in a Polydor deal.

The Bees, not the '60s L.A. psych act but an NJ punk quartet, made two self-produced 45s. The first, 1979's *The Bees,* featured "It's a Business Doing Pleasure With You." The buzz died after Brett Cartwright (bass) and David Nelson (guitar) joined David Johansen Band; that's why 1980's "Already in Love" liner notes shot David Jo a "no thanks."

The Dots was the group of first Ramone guitarist Rick Garcia (Grehl). Frontman Jimmi Quidd (James Hatzidimitriou) from Astoria had sung in Socrates, Greek prog-rockers who launched Vangelis. The "I Don't Wanna Dance (With You)" 7″, 100 seconds of pop-punk mania, set in motion a 1979 tour and a DC show with a young Bad Brains. The late Quidd produced the BBs' 1980 "Pay to Cum" single and the Undead's 1984 *Never Say Die* EP before making the Dots' 1985 *Return of the Dots* and 1986 *I Can See You.*

The Rudies played CBGB opening for Dead Boys and the Shirts, and headlining over X and the B-52s. Ed Ryan and Razz of Day Old Bread wooed Mark Charles Lamendola, part of the Gainesville scene with Tom Petty's Mudcrutch, and John Maguire in Plastic Glass with a pre-Aerosmith Joe Perry. Nineteen eighty's Everlys-ish "Sherri Goodbye" and three *Live at CBGB (Vol. II)* cuts fell on deaf ears. Pianist Charles Giordano went on to join Bruce Springsteen.

The Blessed learned the ropes hanging out with older junkie-rockers like Sid Vicious and Johnny Thunders. Fifteen-year-olds Howie Pyro (Kusten), Nick Berlin (Petti), and Billy Stark (Stone) played their first show Christmas night 1977 at Max's with DNA (who also could barely play). Photographer Eileen Polk briefly drummed, replaced by Pyro's Queens friend Brad "BJ" Barnett. Walter Lure was all over 1979's "Deep Frenzy" 45.

Deep frenzy: The Blessed, Max's Kansas City, 1979.
Photo by Eileen Polk.

The Victims from NJ rocked the NYC scene. Frontman Richard Reilly sang in OutKids, who became the Feelies; he also did two gigs in late 1978 with the Misfits after Franché Coma left. Reilly, guitarist Barry Ryan, bassist Steve Berman, and drummer Mark "M.T." Heart did 1978's harmonica-laden "I Want Head" 7″ on the Misfits' Plan 9 label. Max's agent Peter Crowley produced 1979's *Real Wild Child* LP funded by Golden Disc.

Growing up American
Growing up the best we can
—THE COLORS, "GROWING UP AMERICAN"

The Colors, a power-pop band managed by Hilly Kristal and produced by Clem Burke, involved guitarist Paul Sass, star of Robert Stigwood's film *Times Square*. *SoHo Weekly News* chose them as 1979's "Most Destined for Commercial Success." "Growing up American" showed on all their releases: 1980's *Rave It Up* EP, 1981's *Live at the Dirt Club* comp, and 1982's *The Colors* LP (on Dirt Records). *Live at CBGB (Vol. II)* would've included them.

The Speedies, a Fiorucci-clad Brooklyn Friends School pop group, threw Fruit Loops at crowds, did homework backstage, and inspired classmate Adam Yauch to form the Beasties. December 26, 1978's first show at Max's set a turnout record. Seventy-nine's "Let Me Take Your Foto" generated a Danny Cornyetz–directed MTV video. Clem Burke produced 1981's "Something on My Mind." Ira Robbins wrote, "As The Speedies reach drinking age, they'll develop into ace songwriters or lose their charm and disband."

Shrapnel worked with Legs McNeil, who dressed the Jersey Shore teens in Clash-like combat fatigues and marched 'em on Ramones tours. Two 45s, 1979's "Combat Love" and 1981's "Go Cruisin'," yielded 1984's *Shrapnel* (Elektra) with a Billy Idol–ish take on Gary Glitter's "Didn't Know I Loved You ('Til I Saw You Rock & Roll)." Shrapnel members rate for their future work: stoner singer Dave Wyndorf (Monster Magnet); guitarist-producer Daniel Rey (Ramones, Iggy); and bassist Phil Caivano (Blitzspeer) who earned his Masters in Deviant Psych.

The Brattles was a preteen punk act with semifamous parents: eight-year-old frontman Jason Collins's father John Collins, drummer Dagin's was David Johansen, keyboardist Branch Emerson, son of Eric Emerson and Elda Stiletto, and half-brother bassist Emerson Forth, son of Jane Forth (of Lou Reed's "Sweet Jane"). They appeared in *Interview* and *Us*, and on *The Cheryl Ladd Special*.

Fuse was a band of Italian-Irish street toughs with drummer Niki Fuse, singer Tommy Bell, and guitarist Joey Pinter. They played CBs a lot because they owned a PA before the club owned one. They grew a solid base at Max's, until a feud with Peter Crowley got them banned. Fuse burnt out and turned into the Knots (1978's gnarly "Action" 45). Queens-bred Pinter later did stints in the Waldos and Walter Steding before a stint at an NJ prison.

Whorelords, begun by volatile singer Bobby Snotz with guitarist Tarik

Shapli, wreaked havoc in a short time. Members included Bobby Steele and Joey Image (The Misfits) and Howie Pyro (The Blessed) plus "Whorettes" Charlotte Harlotte, Carry Hamilton, Rachel Rage, and Diedre. After 1980's pre-MTV video ("Sociopath"), Snotz served two years in jail. Snotz, "landlord" of the LES's C-Squat, was punk till the end, beaten to death in '92.

Levi and the Rockats began in London with vocalist Levi Dexter, Smutty Smith on stand-up bass, and guitarist Dibbs Preston. Warhol photog Leee Black Childers saw the stylish rockabilly revivalists at the Speakeasy and brought them to NYC, where they exploded on the scene. Jerry Nolan drummed in 1979 because Leee previously managed the Heartbreakers. Rockats roared on 1981's *Live at the Ritz!* (Island), recorded and released in one week. New manager Tommy Mottola got the Rockats on *American Bandstand* in 1982, but 1983's *Make That Move* (RCA) went nowhere.

Buzz and the Flyers, a similar rockabilly quartet, hatched when Buzz Wayne, a black kid from small-town Cambridge, Ohio, sold his Studebaker and moved to NYC with guitarist Michael Gene. The Flyers soared with Jersey bassist Pete Morgan and Brooklyn drummer Rock Roll. Sylvain Sylvain put out 1980's *Buzz and the Flyers* 7″ EP (Sing Sing). Richard Gottehrer coproduced 1981's UK-only *Buzz and the Flyers* LP ("Go Cat Wild"). Buzz flew to London, finding fame as Dig Wayne of JoBoxers ("Just Got Lucky").

> *Some things you never learn*
> *Some things you never earn*
> —Alda Reserve, "Overnite Jets"

Alda Reserve created 1979's dollar-bin classic *Love Goes On* (Sire). Dave Marsh in *Rolling Stone* trashed the Ed Stasium–engineered, Marshall Chess–produced LP of Brad Ellis's Doors-style rock with Roxy Music sheen. They broke up after a terrible Hurrah gig on March 4, 1980, following Sire's rejection of their self-produced follow-up, *Moonjoon*.

Quincy began with Steve and Brian Butler with brothers Alexander and Gerald Takisch as an Eagles-style act in Haddon Heights, NJ (until a 1976 gig in Philly at which Alex got brutally stabbed). The restyled DEVO-ish quintet inspired Hilly to release 1979's "Can't Live in a Dream" on CBGB Records. The 45 read "From LP *Live At CBGB Vol. II*" that never came out. After 1980's *Turn the Other Way Around* (Columbia), label mate Quincy Jones sued Quincy in 1981, so 1983's sax-y *Don't Say No* came out as Lulu Temple.

John Berenzy Group starred guitarist John Berenzy, who played in 1974 with Danny Kalb (Blues Project) and in City Lights (1975's *Silent Dancer* for Sire). By 1977, his "John Berenzy's 20/20" got sued by L.A. new wavers 20/20, so 1978's "Radio Lies" b/w "Vice Verses" (the latter in tribute to Miles Davis) featured a large JBG sticker. **Alan Milman Sect**, crazed Long Islanders behind 1977's *Punk Rock Christmas* EP ("Stitches in My Head," "I Wanna Kill Somebody"), gigged with Dead Boys, Cramps, and Squeeze. Alan Milman and Doug Khazzam carried on new wave-style as ManKaZam, behind 1978's "Spankathon" and an unissued LP (*ManKazaM Goes Surfin* produced by Buck Dharma).

Ryder-Davis Band, or **Joy Ryder & Avis Davis**, starred Joy Ryder (Denise Whelan), who as a teen performed radical guerilla street theater with Living Theater and the Motherfuckers. Her husband-wife new wave duo with Avis Davis became local stars: he the artist-guitarist, she a hot blonde in tight dresses. Seventy-nine's "No More Nukes" single triggered fifteen minutes of fame on September 23, 1979, playing before three hundred thousand at Battery Park City with CSN and Doobie Brothers for MUSE (Musicians United for Safe Energy).

Dirty Looks, Staten Island skinny-tie new wavers, were on the UK label Stiff. Guitarist Patrick Barnes, bassist Marco Sin (Marcus Weismann), and drummer Peter Parker (Minucci) debuted at CBGB in August 1979. Stiff saw them nine gigs later at Hurrah and flew them to London. The 100,000 units sold of 1980's *Dirty Looks* led to the Sons of Stiff Tour with Tenpole Tudor and Joe "King" Carrasco. Everything fell apart after Island tried to remix 1981's *Turn It Up*. It all ended after April '83's death of manager Andy Cavaliere.

Harry Toledo and the Rockets offered an offbeat new wave with quirky vocals that bridged '70s prog and punk. The foursome opened for Television at Max's on November 13, 1975, and had a most taxing cut on *Max's Kansas City 1976* in "Knots." That and '77's John Cale–produced four-song EP (Spy), was all they wrote. **Big Fat Pet Clams from Outer Space**, the unusual art/pop outfit of Lakewood, NJ, outcasts Gary Applegate and Rich Gelbstein, aced their September 1978 CBGB audition. Hilly managed them with a promised slot on *Live at CBGB (Vol. II)*, and coproduced 1981's *The Pet Clams* for CBS's Handshake label, just as that label folded. "OLPB: Oldest Living Punk Band" opened big shows at CBs, and recorded more than fifty demos off its soundboard.

Chemicals Made From Dirt, "avant absurd" PhD students, like Nassau County's answer to Wire, mastered in new-wave uneasy listening. Mark Fred Riegner, Douglas Scott Milman, and David James Martin 3rd made a 1980 four-song 7" and a two-song flexi-disc in spring 1983's *Option* magazine.

Active Ingredients starred Frank "Franché Coma" LiCata after he left the Misfits in 1978 (replaced by Bobby Steele). Coma's new-wave act with Mike Maytag (Morance) on faux-Brit vox, Paul Zot on keyboards, and drummer Ed E. Enzyme made two singles: 1979's "Laundromat Lover" and 1980's "Hyper Exaggeration." Frank gave up the dream for a wife and four kids in Jersey.

The Features featured members of the first Pittsburgh punk band the Fingers (1978's *Isolation* EP), rejected by Sire for being too Ramones-like. Brothers Francis and David Kidd and manager David McGough moved to NYC, changed their name and style, and in 1979 self-produced their coarse "Floozie of the Neighborhood" at Dreamland Studios. **The Visitors** offered a mix of '50s greaser rock, '60s soul, and '70s punk. Seventy-nine's sci-fi-ish "Rocket Me Home" b/w "Comin' from Behind" by the Bay Ridge group said, "Written, Produced & Arranged by M. Ridone" and "Faculty X Records N.Y." **The Sinatras** issued 1979's "Teddy Crashes Blond Dies" with tasteless cover art of the Ted Kennedy–Mary Jo Kopechne–Chappaquiddick incident, to coincide with Ted's primary run against Jimmy Carter. It's been suggested that the Kennedys used their influence to stifle airplay.

Cheese, a Cheap Trick–like quartet fronted by Vic "Ian" Harrison, began when guitarist Jimmy Maresca ran an ad in *The Aquarian*. The height of Cheese came on March 1979's "She Said" b/w "Kids Don't Mind," its 750 copies backed by WNEW-FM airplay by Vin Scelsa, and praise in April 1980's *Trouser Press*. **Arthur's Dilemma**, Montreal's first punk band, starred colorful British expat Arthur May, who moved to NYC in 1978 to create a new Dilemma. He regularly gigged at CBGB and Max's (often with the Victims) and made two 45s—1978's "It's Dirty" b/w "Kristmas Karol" and 1979's "Up to You" b/w "Kicks"—self-issued on Cuntagious. It ended when INS agents chased away May.

I'm not as strong as I look
I'm not as stoned as I seem
—Nasty Facts, "Drive My Car"

Nastyfacts, a Brooklyn teen new-wave band with Jeff "Range" Tischler, Cheri Boyze, Brad Craig, and Genji "Searizak" Siraisi, rocked the Downtown clubs. Ramona Jan (Dizzy & The Romilars) produced 1981's *Drive My Car* EP (Jimboco) and then replaced Craig in the band. (Genji later led the Grammy-nominated Groove Collective.) The **2 Timers** began with guitarist

Audie Willert and Tuff Darts drummer James Morrison. After time in London they moved back to Queens, to gig with Dead Boys, Ramones, Patti Smith, and Teenage Jesus at CBs. Singer John Warnick drove '78's "Now That I Lost Baby" (Virgin UK) and '79's indie "Living for the Week End." Morrison left to join a Voidoids lineup.

Manster played a manic art-rock, straddling Pink Floyd and Pere Ubu. The LI quintet piece in polyester suits led by Warren Stahurski (a 1970 grad of Massapequa's Plainedge High) and Al Hertzberg (Billy Joel's guitarist 1971–74) were on *Live at CBGB*—"(I'm Really Not) This Way" (a ballad about a hobo) and a tense rip on the Yardbirds' "Over, Under, Sideways, Down." **Jah Malla**— reggae band of Jah C (Cleon Douglass) and Ron "Boogsie" Morris with Michael Ranglin and Noel Alphonso (sons of Ernest Ranglin and Roland Alphonso)— shared a space with Mink Deville, the Rudies, and the Planets. Positivity exuded on 1980's *Alive and Well* (on Clappers, at 66 Greene Street) and 1981's *Jah Malla* (WEA). Jah C shocked the Malla by moving to Northern Vermont.

Allen Ginsberg with the Gluons—the poet's first rock foray since the Fugs—heard the part-time Coloradoan reciting an anti-Reagan ode, "Birdbrain," backed by Mike Chapell's Denver band the Gluons on a 1981 33 RPM 7″. The next year, Ginzo guest-starred on the Clash's NYC-created *Combat Rock* ("Ghetto Defendant"). **Snuky Tate** (Lionel White), a gay black, Hendrix-inspired guitar genius, moved to NYC in 1979. Chris Stein produced the reggae of 1982's *Babylon Under Pressure* for Blondie's Animal label. In '83, Island issued a 12″ reworking of Snuky's '79 funky 7″ "He's the Groove."

David Roter Method starred David Roter, who almost sang in Blue Öyster Cult, and wrote BÖC's 1981 hit "Joan Crawford (Has Risen from the Grave)." His label Unknown Tongues issued 1987's *Bambo* (with BÖC, Dictators, and Del-Lords vets), 1989's *Beauty of the Island*, and 1997's *Find Something Beautiful*. BÖC's Al Bouchard released 1999's *They Made Me*. **Bill Popp and the Tapes** consisted of members of the Tormentors, an act that lived up to its name. Popp passed his CBs audition when Hilly found out the College Point, Queens, singer worked as a plumber, and hired him—to fix the sinks and toilets.

Justin Trouble, a.k.a. **Justin Love**, a friend of Johnny Thunders who'd open for the Heartbreakers, played a stylish punk/rock with '60s harmonies. Johnny produced and cowrote 1981's Justin Trouble "Ponytail" b/w "No Love." **Richard X. Heyman**, a clever pop songwriter, did 1980's "Vacation" b/w "Takin' My Chances" aired on WNEW-FM and picked a *Billboard* "Pick Hit." Then came 1986's *Actual Size* cut in his Upper West Side apartment. He wrote about it all in *Boom Harangue*. **Trixie Sly** (Torquill Smith), a London scene friend of Jerry Nolan and Johnny Thunders, moved to NYC in 1978 to play as the Nothing (1979's "Scream 'n' Cry" b/w "Uniformz"). Trixie earned infamy playing the terribly unlucky band manager in Abel Ferrara's 1979 horror film *Driller Killer*.

Nasty secretary: Joy Ryder, Max's Kansas City, 1978.
Photo by Cathy Miller/Frank White Photo Agency.

THE FALL

It's the end of the '70s
It's the end of the century
—RAMONES, "ROCK AND ROLL RADIO"

By 1980, the terrain had changed. Blondie and Talking Heads exploded, playing radio-friendly "new wave"—a term taken from the French film movement by Seymour Stein at Sire Records to counter public resistance to punk. The Ramones went from Forest Hills to performing to thousands on theater stages. Mainliners in the Heartbreakers and Dead Boys crashed. Patti Smith did the unthinkable, quitting New York and moving to Detroit to raise a family! Television shut off. Most of these bands never played at CBGB again.

HANDSOME DICK MANITOBA (The Dictators): Scenes have a life span. It'd been a few years, then the drugs took more and more effect, and the records weren't selling. After that, came a new generation. So between the drugs and the non-sales and the era, it was time for a new bunch of kids to come in. (2003)

DANNY SAGE (D Generation): It was a weird time in New York, '79–'80. It was no longer punk, and it wasn't yet the new hardcore. You'd go to clubs and see bands that weren't great, but there was nothing else. We were hungry but unsatisfied. (2004)

TOO MANY CREEPS

POST–PUNK/NO WAVE

1977–1983: Teenage Jesus, The Contortions, Mars, DNA, Dark Day, *No New York,* Lust/Unlust, White Columns, Franklin Furnace, Artists Space

No New York: Harold Paris, Kristian Hoffman, Diego Cortez, Anya Phillips, Lydia Lunch, James Chance, Jim Sclavunos, Bradly Field, and Liz Seidman, Bowery, 1978. Photo by GODLIS.

POST-PUNK/NO WAVE

Suburban wealth and middle-class well-being
All it did was strip my feelings
—TEENAGE JESUS AND THE JERKS, "THE CLOSET"

THE RISE

"No wave" arose against the backdrop of a decaying New York, just as rock lost its last shreds of innocence with December 8, 1980's Manhattan murder of John Lennon. After years of spreading rock as an art form, here was its ruin. "No wave" was a savage reaction to "new wave," that radio-friendly dilution of punk. There was no appealing to the music biz, no trying to sign to Capitol. The severity was about disengaging from pop culture.

LYDIA LUNCH (Teenage Jesus and the Jerks): "No wave" was a journalistic tag for a movement of insane people trying to articulate their particular pain in a dissonant fashion. It had nothing in common with punk other than the general time frame. To me, punk was bad three-chord rock and roll, played fast and badly with a political intent, and had nothing to do with what was going on in New York at the time. (1993)

CYNTHIA SLEY (Bush Tetras): No wave was an arty backlash against the status quo, against chord progressions or anything like that. The bands were really out-there, a total spectacle. It was this cool spurt of weirdness. We all had this spirit of rebellion, coming from more of an art background, but with the spirit of punk. (2004)

TARO SUZUKI (Youth in Asia): We just didn't see any place for visual arts to go. So we expressed this rage with a band. We really didn't have any musical training. We were just making noise with a beat. (2010)

Punk still had a rock & roll side. No wave was barely music; it was angry artists jacked on punk's negativity, using rock to express discontent. They were escaping rock's prison but using the same tools. The intent was to rile: crowds run for the door, with a few who "got it" riveted. Teenage Jesus, Contortions, DNA, and Mars conveyed nothing more than "fuck you!"

GLENN BRANCA (composer): This kind of music started happening in New York about 1977. Although it's clear it was related to the punk scene, the music had almost nothing to do with pop music because pop was still derived from the blues. Punk was still using blues progressions and rock conventions, whereas the "noise" music, although it was using the instrumentation of rock, that's about as far as it went. (1981)

DAVID LINTON (Interference): A lot of the just-out-of-art-school Downtown kids at the time, for different reasons, were of the mind that playing in a band was the best way to do art. It's not that one, art or noise, influenced the other—we believed they were synonymous or maybe that being in a noise band was better than doing art. (2007)

JIM SCLAVUNOS (Teenage Jesus and the Jerks): It was the outright hostility and aloofness we'd show the audience. We weren't a popular band. In fact we were distinctly unpopular. It wasn't designed to be popular, it wasn't ever meant as an entertainment-like spectacle. It was meant as an affront. Not just to musical lovers, but to the punks because we out-punked the punks. It was a stark moment of anti-music. (2008)

MARK CUNNINGHAM (Mars): It was a transitional period when no rules felt worth respecting. The bands on *No New York* were all close socially but the common musical element was we did what we wanted without caring about fitting into any existing style. We had that freedom because of what came before. There was a direct evolution from the Velvets through the Mercer Arts Center scene, the new wave and punk to no wave. So of course we had to go further and be more radical than our predecessors. Part of this was the do-it-yourself idea, which came from Warhol, where we didn't have to be fucking pros, or even musicians, to get our fifteen minutes of fame. (2004)

ADELE BERTEI (The Contortions): There was all this cross-fertilization going on. It was all about experimentation and picking up your instruments and having them become an extension of your psyche. None of us were trained musically. We were just exorcizing our demons through performance. (2000)

I've got what it takes
To drive you insane
—THE CONTORTIONS, "CONTORT YOURSELF"

No wave reflected a distinctly '70s Downtown flavor. James Chance and Lydia Lunch were intense originals displaying their "post-punk angst" at Mudd Club and Max's and galleries like Artists Space and White Columns. It was all so intense, it could only last a sec, and that nihilism rarely translated in-studio. Heroin made the sound. Young artists devolved overnight into stoned junkies. Such extremism changed the course of rock music.

STUART ARGABRIGHT (Ike Yard): Within the quote-unquote "no wave" years, every year it changed a lot. But no one was walking around saying, "I'm into no wave"—they were quite possibly too busy living it. (2010)

LYDIA LUNCH: Fear is an important thing. I mean Mars were insane. This group gave you the fucking creeps. The Contortions, you thought you were gonna get punched in the fucking face. And before that was Suicide. It was the apocalypse happening. (2008)

THE SCENE

I hate you perfectly
Perfect perfection XYZ
—MARS, "PUERTO RICAN GHOST"

Lust/Unlust Records began in 1977 with music producer Charles Ball—described by writer Roy Trakin as an Alan Lomax type doing primitive field recordings. The label became synonymous with no wave, behind Teenage Jesus (their first 45 sold as "7 inches and a hole"), Mars, and DNA. Lust/Unlust's first LP, Martin Rev's solo debut, cut by Ball on 8-track, came out in February 1980. Releases included Peter Gordon, Dark Day, and Z'ev. In late 1980, Ball got into some kind of trouble and went AWOL, ruining a few promising bands.

ROBIN CRUTCHFIELD (DNA/Dark Day): Charles Ball was a relatively handsome, middle-class golden boy with an unadventurous wardrobe of tan and maroon sweaters and blazers, and a conservative haircut to match his gold wristwatch. His music interests leaned more towards Van Morrison and Bruce Springsteen than the no wave he became identified with. I never understood what appeal it had for him, but I'm glad it did. (2009)

JON TIVEN (Prix): Charles Ball was damaged. Aside from being messed-up on drugs, he was a malicious guy who saw himself as an entrepreneur. But he was really just a pain in the ass that liked music. He destroyed Alex Chilton and fucked with me. He was an industry scumbag with none of the positives. A Morris Levy made you a somebody and stole your money. Charles made you a nobody and stole your money. (2011)

No New York captured that fleeting moment. But nowhere on November '78's comp's cover does it say "no wave." Brian Eno got the idea while living in SoHo as he worked on Talking Heads' *More Songs about Buildings and Food,* after Judy Nylon brought him to a gig at Artists Space. *No New York* (Antilles/Island) was 44 minutes of Teenage Jesus, Contortions, DNA, and Mars. Theoretical Girls, Boris Policeband, Red Transistor, Tone Death, Terminal, and Gynecologists were considered. Richard C. Walls in *Creem* (4/79): "I haven't heard so much ugly avant-garde since Albert Ayler puked on my brain in '64. And like Ayler who jumped into the Hudson for a final swim, this music has no future."

> **BRIAN ENO (producer):** There's a certain quality of sound that's common to those people. For a start, things sound really messy, and it's a mess I've never heard before. It's a sort of jungle sound, really. And there's a peculiar perspective to it, so that everything's up-front, but there's this very wide space behind it. (1979)

> **RIK LETENDRE (Circle X):** In those days, we rehearsed in the same building as most of the no-wave groups. We were down the hall from DNA, and often passed each other in the halls. We were quite young— we were all moving so fast. There was so much going on, it's hard to recount. . . . (2009)

Artists Space (105 Hudson Street) opened in SoHo's "Fine Arts Building" in 1977. The underground lab of new ideas focusing on women artists sponsored events like May 2–6, 1978's festival fusing Super-8 film and new bands on $3 bills: such as Mars/Teenage Jesus; Contortions/DNA; Gynecologists/Theoretical Girls; Terminal/Communists; and Tone Death/Daily Life. (Years later, the location became the first Nobu restaurant.)

> **STEPHEN SPROUSE (designer):** We all went to clubs a lot in those days, and Robert Longo and Michael Zwack got a bunch of bands to play Artists Space. It was historic. Teenage Jesus & the Jerks was iconic. (1998)

White Columns (325 Spring Street) began in 1970 as 112 Workshop (112 Greene Street) and then moved in 1980, renamed for large white columns. Josh Baer (son of painter Jo Baer) and Thurston Moore hosted June 16–24, 1981's "Noise Fest" that debuted the new noise-rock. Over nine nights, sixty to seventy fans per night took in the twenty-six performers like Glenn Branca, Y Pants, Rhys Chatham, Red Decade, and Sonic Youth (with Anne DiMarinis and Richard Edson). On May 4–8, 1983, WC hosted the noted "Speed Trials" with the Fall.

BOB NICKAS (curator): On the bill was Sonic Youth, and a few nights later Swans and a still-hardcore Beastie Boys. These were the first times that I stepped foot into White Columns, but I couldn't have been the only one. A lot of people I met in the early '80s art world looked familiar to me when we first met. And why? Because it really wasn't the first time: I'd seen them years before at Max's or the Mudd Club or Tier 3 in the early hours of a day that became yet another in a long line of morning afters. . . . (2007)

THE MUSIC

You are my razor
I want to touch you
—TEENAGE JESUS AND THE JERKS, "I WOKE UP DREAMING"

Teenage Jesus and the Jerks, the crux of no wave, performed terrifying ten-minute shows. Tom Gardner in the *East Village Eye* called it "music to get people to leave your party." The Jerks started with Rochester teen runaway Lydia Lunch (Koch), immortalized in the Dead Boys' song "I Need Lunch," and sax fiend James Chance (Siegfried), as the Scabs. Four TJ cuts on *No New York* incited 1978's Robert Quine–produced "Orphans" / "Less of Me," 1979's *Baby Doll* 7″ EP, a *Teenage Jesus and the Jerks* seven-song 12″ with new Jerks Gordon Stevenson and Jim Sclavunos, and a *Preteenage Jesus* (Ze) pink-vinyl 12″.

LYDIA LUNCH (Teenage Jesus and the Jerks): My theory was to stick a thorn in every side that'd come before me. It was as if my job was to dispute the "alternative" that'd already been established. (1997)

JAMES CHANCE (The Contortions): Lydia was living with me, and I encouraged her to do music after she played a few songs for me, which was most of the Teenage Jesus songs. I think most people would've just told her to stop! So first it was Lydia, Jody Harris, the Japanese bassist Reck, and me. It just didn't gel. She more or less kicked me out. Her concept became more minimal as it went along—to the point where she didn't want the sax in there. That's when I started the Contortions. (2005)

The Contortions created an abusive punk/jazz/funk assault. Chance, a conservatory-trained Milwaukee saxophonist, came to SoHo in 1976. The first Contortions involved filmmaker James Nares on guitar. Chance knew drummer Don Christensen and Nares's replacement Jody Harris from a bar band, Loose Screws. Cleveland-reared original organist Adele Bertei played in Peter & the Wolves with a pre–Pere Ubu Peter Loughner. Contortions blew minds, with shows at Artists Space, and songs on *No New York*. In 1979 came the *Grutzi Elvis* 12″ (soundtrack to Mudd Club star Diego Cortez's unfinished film), and Contortions' *Buy* LP. Chance's James Brown–style rebranding as James White & the Blacks premiered on February 2, 1979, at Club 57, leading to 1979's *Off White* with Lydia (as "Stella Rico"), Anya ("Ginger Lee"), and Kristian Hoffman ("Tad Among"). In 1980, he reworked James Brown's "King Heroin" as James Chance & the Contortions.

JODY HARRIS (The Contortions): We had a gig at some place called Artists Space, and James went in the audience and punched out Robert Christgau of the *Village Voice*. Ever after that Christgau loved him. "James Chance is an asshole! But he's a genius!" That went on for several shows and James started getting really hurt. After a while we stopped saving him from these bloody incidents 'cause it was getting ridiculous. (2005)

BOB BLANK (producer): Well, I wouldn't be speaking out of turn if I told you James had a heroin addiction. He was always a gentleman, always focused, polite, and easy to work with. The problem with people on heroin is they can be a little unreliable. . . . He said to me, "You know, I can play legit saxophone." He never had to tell me, you could tell by his playing. Even if he was literally shooting up in the back room, he never lost it. (2006)

Mars began as China, named for bassist/singer Constance "China" Burg (a.k.a. Lucy Hamilton). The jarring quartet premiered at CBGB on January 14, 1977, and then twenty-five to thirty more times, the finale at Max's on December 10, 1978. Their 1978 Lenny Kaye–coproduced "3E" / "11,000 Volts" single brought about *No New York* songs and 1979's post-breakup five-song 12″. Singer Sumner Crane composed 1980's "no wave opera" *John Gavanti* (released on Mark Cunningham's Hyrax label), inspired by both *Don Giovanni* and bluesman Bukka White. Glenn Kenny in *Trouser Press* loathed "the most unlistenable record ever made."

MARK CUNNINGHAM: Mars wasn't negative for us; it was transcendental. And I think most of the bands were musically positive. Certainly there was that black nihilist mystique that came with underground New York, but we reached for something beyond simple protest or noise for its own sake. We found music in the noise. (2004)

DNA, named for a Mars song, typified no wave's "clear the room" aesthetic. Lydia Lunch introduced Brazilian-bred guitarist and Mars lyricist Arto Lindsay to Trenton State performance artist Robin Crutchfield, playing keyboards in his first band, and Tokyoan drummer Ikue Mori, who didn't speak English or own drums. After 1978's *No New York* tracks and the Robert Quine–produced "You & You" 45 (Lust/Unlust), Pere Ubu bassist Tim Wright tweaked the sound on 1981's last gnaw, *A Taste of DNA* (American Clavé).

ARTO LINDSAY (DNA): I had friends in this band Mars. Television's manager, Terry Ork, also booked Max's Kansas City. I was always there with Mars, helping them with equipment. He asked me if I had a band. "Oh sure," I said, even though I didn't have one. He asked me if I wanted to play the next week and I said, "How about next month?" True story. I went out and cobbled a band together. (1997)

Stained forever
Saint for never
—8 EYED SPY, "RAN AWAY DARK"

Beirut Slump expressed the era's danger and lunacy. After Teenage Jesus, Lydia tried guitar, while Bobby Swope—of the Eckerd College scene with Arto

Lindsay, China Burg, and Mark Cunningham—screamed crazy shit he heard bums yell. Sister-bassist Liz Swope, organist Vivienne Dick, and drummer Jim Sclavunos joined the mania. Diego Cortez booked their gigs, August 16, 1978, and April 29, 1979, at Max's, and June 1979 at Mudd Club. Lust/Unlust's Charles Ball produced March '79's "Try Me" b/w "Staircase" (as Bobby Berkowitz).

Dish it out: Flyer for Gynecologists, Theoretical Girls, and Arsenal, The Kitchen, 1979. Collection of the author.

8 Eyed Spy, Lydia's band between Beirut Slump and 1980's solo *Queen of Siam*, featured Contortions tough-guy George Scott III. With Lydia's wail over Scott's bass, drummer Sclavunos, and guitarists Pat Irwin and Michael Paumgarden, they made: 1980's 7″ mess of Manfred Mann's "Ditty Wah Diddy" (its B-side, "Get You Me B Side" live at Hurrah on August 3, 1980), 1981's *8-Eyed Spy* cut at Blank Studios, 1981's *Live* cassette "live between January and August 1980," plus tunes on her *Hysterie* comp.

Dark Day starred Robin Crutchfield after DNA. Participants included Jim Jarmusch (Del-Byzanteens), Nancy Arlen (Mars), Peter Principle (Tuxedomoon), and Nina Canal (Ut). They made 1979's "Hands in the Dark" 7″ and 1981's "Trapped" 12″ and the LPs 1980's *Exterminating Angel* and '82's *Window*.

Gray, blended by Jean-Michel Basquiat and Michael Holman, debuted on April 29, 1979. The unrecorded act included Nick Taylor (guitar/violin) and Wayne Clifford (bass/loops), first with Konk trumpeter Shannon Dawson, later with filmmaker-keyboardist Vincent Gallo. They gigged at Mudd Club, Max's, CBGB, Hurrah, and galleries, like for art guru Leo Castelli's b-day. Jean-Michel named the band for its steely sound and the book *Grey's Anatomy* that fueled his art. Glenn O'Brien saw in *Interview* (1/81): "an easy listening, bebop, industrial-sound-effects lounge ensemble."

Theoretical Girls, theater-trained composers Glenn Branca (guitar) and Jeffrey Lohn (vocals/guitar) with Margaret DeWys (bass/keyboards) and Wharton Tiers (drums), fused avant-garde and gutter punk. They began in November 1977 at Franklin Furnace, ended April 1979 at Max's, and played twenty or so late-night parties at Lohn's Thompson Street loft. The 1978 "U.S. Millie" 7″ defined rock/minimalism.

The Static started after Lohn left Branca to pursue theater in Paris. The trio of Branca, girlfriend-bassist Barbara Ess, and drummer Christine Hahn debuted at 1978's Franklin Furnace premiere of Glenn's sixth and final play, *Cognitive Dissonance*. Seventy-nine's Branca-composed "My Relationship" single introduced his influential three-octave tunings. Glenn went solo after debuting his multi-guitar *Instrumental for Six Guitars* at April 1979's Max's Kansas City Easter Festival.

Lizzy Mercier Descloux, a Parisian artist friendly with Patti Smith and Richard Hell, moved to NYC in 1976. Lizzy grabbed an axe (guitar) and played clubs and galleries in a duo with D.J. Barnes. That resulted in a 12″ for Ze under the *nom-de-rock* Rosa Yemen (*Live in N.Y.C. July 1978*), named for Jewish anarchist Rosa Luxemburg. *Press Color* coincided with her role in Amos Poe's 1979 film *Blank Generation*. Island's Chris Blackwell funded 1981's Caribbean-style *Mambo Nassau*, cut at Compass Studios in the Bahamas.

Love of Life Orchestra, composer Peter Gordon's troupe, debuted on 1977's *Star Jaws* LP, a warped piece with wry lyrics by Kathy Acker. Percussionist David Van Tieghem joined in 1979. Their 1980 *Extended Niceties* 12″ ("Cover Concept: Laurie Anderson") involved guitars by David Byrne, Arto Lindsay, Randy Gun, and Larry Saltzman. Arthur Russell and Rhys Chatham also partook. From 1980's *Geneve* to 1981's *Untitled*, LOLO grew from offbeat riddims to serious sounds, boosting academians Gordon and Van Tieghem.

> *Follow all of the rules, even-tempered and cool*
> *Keep it under my hat, well I can't do that*
> —THE GOLDEN PALOMINOS, "I'M NOT SORRY"

Golden Palominos, studio band of drummer Anton Fier, blended electric chops and ambient grooves, creating digital sounds sampled, looped, and sequenced. *Golden Palominos* of 1981 involved Arto Lindsay and John Zorn. Both 1985's *Visions of Excess* and 1986's *Blast of Silence* starred Syd Straw and Jody Harris; 1989's *A Dead Horse* and 1991's *Drunk with Passion* swapped Straw for Amanda Kramer (Information Society). Lori Carson sang on 1993's *This Is How It Feels* and 1994's *Pure*, Nicole Blackman on 1996's *Dead Inside.*

Lounge Lizards fused bebop and no wave, defining NYC cool. Sax-y John Lurie and pianist brother Evan moved to East 3rd Street in 1977 to film Super-8s. The act, first called Rotating Power Tools, grew of scant chops—the "fake jazz" of 1981's *Lounge Lizards* with Arto Lindsay and Anton Fier hailed by *Voice* critic Robert Christgau as "*Slaughter on Tenth Avenue* goes to the Mudd Club." They got sleeker over time with Marc Ribot and Dougie Bowne on 1987's *No Pain for Cakes* and '89's *Voice of Chunk.*

Kongress merged witchcraft, gore, and ritual sacrifice, with magician/singer Geoffrey Crozier breathing fire, twirling fiery batons, igniting explosions, and staging scary optical illusions. The five-piece included Otto Von Ruggins 666, a Crowley-trained warlock on synth, drummer Von LMO, guitarist Rudolph Grey, and Marilyn ("Sex Means Nothing When You're Dead"). Martin Kent wrote in *NY Daily Planet* (6/14/77): "If rock & roll is the new religion, Kongress is rock & roll hell." (Crozier died on May 17, 2001, found by his mother with a nylon cord around his neck.)

Red Transistor was Kongress's Von LMO and Rudolph Grey with drummer Mark "M" Edmands, replaced by Jim Sclavunos, with saxist Ken Simon. The Brooklynites claiming to be space aliens blended jazz blasts with pneumatic repetition. They often played fifteen-minute sets, ending with LMO trashing his gear while still playing, usually with a fire axe and chain. (Their "Not Bite" b/w "We're Not Crazy" single intended for Marty Thau's Red Star in 1977 came out in 1990 via Sonic Youth.)

Boris Policeband, a wacky star of Jonathan Demme's 1984 anthology *Alive from Off Center,* jumbled police scanner transmissions, electric violin, and verbal assault. His earsplitting shows in dark sunglasses cleared rooms from Mudd Club to the Kitchen. Dike Blair produced the 800 units of 1979's *Stereo/Mono* nine-song 45. The avowed "materialistic-socialist" moved on to classical viola.

Gynecologists arose from SoHo art circles, with future Kitchen music director Rhys Chatham, Rudolph Grey's ex-wife Nina Canal, and Nina's London art-school mate Robert Appleton. Jim Sclavunos replaced first drummer Heddy Van Dyke (Daile Kaplan). Robin Crutchfield briefly joined. A twenty-minute practice tape captured their din, as heard at May 1978's Artists Space Fest with Theoretical Girls.

Von LMO (Frankie Cavallo), an "intergalactic superstar," became a 1980-era solo star of Max's and CBs. His severity overran past bands: before Kongress and Red Transistor, psych-era Funeral of Art with Sal Maida (pre-Sparks) and Dan Hartman crony Charlie Midnight. Long before 1994's *Cosmic*

Interception and 1996's *Red Resistor* (riffing on Red Transistor) came 1981's *Future Language*. The *New York Times*' Ann Powers hailed Von "the Sun Ra of trashy guitar rock."

Chain Gang raged in the punk years (and later reunited). Bronx bad boys Ricky Luanda, Larry Gee, Ted Twist, and Phil Von Rome played objects like chairs and kitchen sinks. Their 1977 pro–David Berkowitz "Son of Sam" 45 begot bad vibes, as did 1987's *Mondo Manhattan* ("Kill the Bouncers at the Ritz") and 1990's *Kill for You* double-7". *Trouser Press*: "This is the real sound of the decline of Western civilization."

Blinding Headache, an aptly named quartet, began in NYU's Brittany dorm. They opened for Teenage Jesus, Contortions, DNA, and Mars at CBs, and 1980's "New Wave Vaudeville" at Irving Plaza. **Information** started with Minneapolis expats Chris Nelson and Phil Dray with Jim Sclavunos. When Jim left for Teenage Jesus, Blinding Headache's Rick Brown joined. Yo La Tengo, on their 1989 *New Wave Hot Dogs* LP, included Chris on a cover of Information's "Let's Compromise" off 1980's *Tape #1* compilation with Blinding Headache and Mofungo. Seventy-nine's *No Magazine #4* inserted a rare flexi-disc.

Mofungo, named for a Latin dish of plantains and innards, blended jazz beats, dissonant guitars, and militant politics. After Blinding Headache, Robert Sietsema and Willy Klein unnerved on 1980's *Elementary Particles* EP (with BH's Jim Posner) and 1981's *End of the World* cassette with Chris Stamey. Mofungo's juiciest morsel, *Frederick Douglass* (Twin/Tone), came out on April Fools' Day 1985, in a PBS special about the black leader. Black Flag's SST label released 1988's *Bugged* and 1989's *Work*. **The Scene Is Now** began with Mofungo's Chris Nelson, Jeff McGovern, and Philip Dray, and over time Pere Ubu's Tony Maimone and the dB's Will Rigby. Their Zappa-Beefheart blend of avant-garde and postmodern inspired Yo La Tengo (who covered "Yellow Sarong"). The very unsexy act spat left-of-liberalism like "Social Practice" with Chairman Mao quotes.

Futants—D.C.-bred drummer-singer Stuart Argabright, German keyboardist Martin Fischer, and NYC's bassist Danny Rosen—blared their funky noise with DNA and Lounge Lizards. After a fire in the band's East 11th Street apartment destroyed all their tapes, Fischer jammed with Defunkt and Nona Hendryx until April 7, 1980, when he died falling four stories from his girlfriend's window. **Circle X** (Tony Pinotti, Rik Letendre, and Wm. Bruce Witsiepe) came from Louisville in 1978 and spent the next year causing havoc in Dijon, France. The noise/rock heard on 1979's French-only *Untitled 12"* and 1983's *Prehistory* LP (as Circle X Internationale) predated the sound of Sonic Youth.

Leaving for the other side
Going to take a Holland Tunnel dive
—Implog, "Holland Tunnel Dive"

impLOG was Don Christensen (drums/music/vocals) with Jody Harris (guitar) on a four-track with a drum machine, from the Contortions' end through early Raybeats. "Holland Tunnel Dive" 12″ (Lust/Unlust) and "Breakfast" 7″ (Log) stand as 1980-era druggy dance anthems. **Arto/Neto**, a one-off project of Arto Lindsay's before Lounge Lizards and Ambitious Lovers, melded Arto's art-school voodoo rhythms with yelped lyrics by choreographer Seth "Neto" Tillett. The 1979 Bob Blank–produced "Pini Pini" b/w "Malú" (Ze) single connected with that disturbing no-wave ennui.

The Dance played sparse rhythms, with quirky funk, and poetic meter popular in the clubs. Model Citizens' Eugenie Diserio and Steven Alexander, with Robey Newsom and Thomas Doncker, stepped lively on 1980's *The Dance* EP. The Dance stumbled on 1981's *In Lust* for Polydor France and 1982's *Soul Force* on Germany's Static. They disbanded after Island refused to issue 1983's Mark Kamins–produced *Into the Future*. **The Bloods** oozed no wave–edged dance-rock. Adele Bertei drove her junkie lesbian band (dubbed "Adele & The Drells" by John Lurie) to February 1980's cover of *East Village Eye* and opening for the Clash at Bond's in June 1981. "Button Up" on Exit, UK label of Au Pairs, got named a 1981 *NME* "Single of the Week." The quintet recorded the Roulettes' "Bad Time" and Puccini's *Turandot* before disbanding on a hectic spring 1982 tour.

Y Pants, an offbeat girl act, played clubs and galleries. Artist Barbara Ess was in Daily Life and the Static with Glenn Branca. Ess then teamed with Gail Vachon and Virginia "Verge" Piersol. Instruments employed included Ess's dad's ukulele and toy piano. They did 1980's Branca-produced *Y Pants* EP (99 Records), "Magnetic Attraction" on 1981's *Tellus* tape, and 1982's *Beat It Down* (Neutral). **Ut**, a female troika united through Peter Gordon, consisted of Nina Canal (Robin Crutchfield's Dark Day, Rhys Chatham's *100 Guitars*), Jaqui Ham, and Sally Young; all three traded instruments (filmmaker Karen Achenbach also briefly joined). They "debUTed" in January 1979 at TR3 and their buzz-fueled 1980's *New Beat Music* (Lust/Unlust) never came out because Charles Ball disappeared after the release party. They moved to London to work with the Fall.

Quine/Harris, the experimental guitar union of Jody Harris (Contortions/Raybeats) and Robert Quine (Voidoids/Lou Reed), sounded like Robert Fripp but nastier. The 1981 *Escape* 12″ (Lust/Unlust) with tunes titled for Three Stooges films got made over eight months on Quine's 4-track. May 1981's *Musician* mused: "You can pick out a barbed-wire Quine lick or a classic Harris twang, or you can sit back and enjoy the scenery." **Sick Dick and the Volks-wagens**, named for an imaginary band in Thomas Pynchon's *The Crying of Lot 49*, begat Donald Miller (Borbetomagus), Brian Doherty (Lhasa Cement Plant), Doug Snyder (Doug Snyder & Bill Thompson), Mark Abbott (John Zorn), and for one gig, Lester Bangs. Charles Ball produced a lost 1981 LP (songs later heard on 1991's *Interference*). A 1980 *Slash* review derided them as "excruciatingly arty."

Come On compared to Talking Heads in preppy shirts. David Byrne once brought Brian Eno to see them. The angular five-piece of Jamie Kaufman, George Elliot, Elena Glasberg, Ralf Mann, and Page Wood self-released a 1978 single "Don't Walk on the Kitchen Floor," and Ron Johnsen (Wicked Lester/ Klaus Nomi) produced a 1980 demo.

Red Decade was equal parts no wave and film noir. The minimalist quintet based around Rhys Chatham guitarist Jules Baptiste and sax-y Fritz Van Or-den (alto) and Bill Obrecht (tenor), gigged from the Kitchen to Mudd Club. *Jules Baptiste Red Decade* (Neutral), 1982's two-song 12″, involved Laurie Anderson producer Roma Baran and Taro Suzuki artwork. *Billboard* (8/7/82) posited: "After a while one does have to ask: what's the point here?"

Don King wailed no-wave free jazz with Third World riddims. The quartet named for the boxing promoter debuted at 1981's Noise Festival with Mars' Mark Cunningham and Lucy Hamilton plus paroxysmal percussionists Arto and Duncan Lindsay. Pere Ubu's Tony Maimone laid the beat down on 1983's UK-only *One-Two Punch*. A 1986 tape, *On the Mediterranean* with Toni Nogueira, failed to land that knockout blow. **Interference** began at Noise Festival with Anne DiMarinas, Michael Brown, and David Linton. DiMarinas was in early Sonic Youth. Linton moved to NYC with college mate Lee Ranaldo, and attained fame with the Kitchen and Wooster Group. June '82's 22-minute double-LP for Neutral came out twenty-eight years later.

Borbetomagus, saxists Jim Sauter and Don Dietrich and WKCR's Donald Miller on guitar, grew from no-wave noise to Ornette/Ayler skronk. The Ny-ack troupe named for a Catholic treaty between the pope and a government put out annual albums, like 1988's *Snuff Jazz* live at ABC No Rio and 1992's *Experience the Magic* at CBGB. Don said in 1991 (*Seconds #14*): "Music is far more about artistic integrity than stylistic perception." **V-Effect** merged organ, saxophone, glockenspiel, and Marxism. The 1983 album *Stop Those Songs* featured "bits of guitar at crucial moments by Fred Frith." Robert Christgau

(*Voice*, 1/24/84) crowed of "They Can't Get It" on Elliott Sharp's *Peripheral Vision: Bands Of Loisaida:* "Either Ann Rupel's and David Zonzinsky's vocals and sax got squashed in the machinery or their onstage chutzpah concealed difficulties with breath production."

Massacre featured guitarist Fred Frith (off his 1979 split from Henry Cow), bassist Bill Laswell (before producing Mick Jagger), and drummer Fred Maher (Lou Reed, Material) blasting improv jams. In June '81 at Martin Bisi's studio, they cut *Killing Time*, released in January 1982 on Laswell's OAO label. Maher quit after a July 4, 1981, gig, so Anton Fier stepped in. **Z'ev** (Hebrew name of Stefan Weisser) played percussion with large metal objects. *Salts of Heavy Metal* (Lust/Unlust) grew from local 1980-era performances, before the industrial pioneer moved to Holland and then SF. *East Village Eye* (11/83): "Z'ev exemplifies contemporary performance art, as well as modern composition and theater."

Youth in Asia—Taro Suzuki, Steven Harvey, Frank Schroder, and Stephan Wischerth, and at times Lounge Lizards' Evan Lurie and Ordinaires' Fritz Van Orden—debuted with the Contortions at 66 East 4th Street, last in a "shock opera" at Danceteria. **TV Sex Star** did a self-titled 1981 LP through Lust/Unlust, the B-side live at CBGB. **Terminal**, Roy Trakin wrote in *SoHo Weekly News* (6/15/78) at 1978's Artists Space Fest, "had a woman synth player whose makeshift machine was set up on a roll-away table, propped up by phone books."

The Communists, female-led punks, played Artists Space with Terminal. **Arsenal** never recorded but guitarist Rhys Chatham wrote in his *Composers Notes 1990:* "It wasn't until after this 'field work' that I felt comfortable enough to make a composition in the classical sense." **Tone Death**, Rhys's 1977 Franklin Furnace piece, involved Peter Gordon, Robert Appleton, and Nina Canal. Radical feminists **Disband** featured Franklin Furnace owner Martha Wilson and late *Interview* editor Ingrid Sischy. **A Band**, a quintet with Paul McMahon and Wharton Tiers, played Max's, CBs, Hurrah, and Franklin Furnace and rehearsed at 135 Grand Street. **IMA** (Intense Molecular Activity) with Don Hunerberg and Andy Blinx made a 1980 four-song flexi via Ed Bahlman's 99 label and an unreleased 12-song LP. Robert Longo wrecked grungy galleries in **Built On Guilt**.

These are the days: Downtown club scene, Danceteria, 1983. Photo by Ted Barron.

POST-PUNK

1979–1984: POLYROCK, RAYBEATS, BUSH TETRAS, LIQUID LIQUID, ESG, HURRAH, MUDD CLUB, CLUB 57, DANCETERIA, SAVE THE ROBOTS, THE WORLD, *EAST VILLAGE EYE, ROCKPOOL*

Sexual intellectuals
Make love so ineffectual
—MODEL CITIZENS, "YOU ARE WHAT YOU WEAR"

THE RISE

By 1980, the punk groups broke up or moved on. A post-CBGB scene evolved, based on NYC's decadent nightcrawler lifestyle. This post-punk/post-disco era was into kitsch and nostalgia. That was very new, with rock's first revivalist scenes into ska, rockabilly, surf, and garage rock. It was the first spasms of the digital age with electro-pop. The attitude was artistic, strident, and affected—so advanced that it's just now understood.

MOBY (DJ): Musically, there's never been a period like the late '70s and early '80s in New York. The music that dominates the world today—alt rock, punk, dance music and hip-hop—all came out of New York in a seven-year period. None of that music would exist in its current form. All the progenitors of all those scenes come from here. (2004)

NINA CANAL (UT): New York was in a magical zone. It blew my mind being in a place where anything was creatively possible. The scene came about organically and spontaneously and burned out fast because it went against the "normal" grain. It was at once anarchic and inclusive: everyone was equal for the blink of an eye, so the field of possibilities went wide open. And just as suddenly there were other people of all disciplines starting bands to play what I call "weird loud music." It was very Village-like, with most living in the East Village or Downtown. (2006)

PARKER DULANY (Certain General): I'm proud of being part of that post-punk time in New York. There was punk, that 1975–78 era with Television and Ramones—and that's the focus on modern New York music history. But the post-punk time in the East Village was like 1979–1983. Whether you're talking about the Contortions or Swans or us, it was so cool and romantic to be part of that generation. It was a time of transition, melding disco and rock energy. That's not what punk was about. We were a bigger audience, a bit more intellectual, taking chances; and everyone had something to offer. There were no total slouches in the crowd. I loved New York's scene in those days. I don't go to my high school reunions but I played Danceteria and Mudd Club reunions. I couldn't believe there are such places where the worlds I loved collided. (2011)

The era's "rock discos" or "new-wave discos" were a cross-collision of punk, disco, and art, a redux of Studio 54 glitz but with punk attitude. Decadent "dance rock" dens including Hurrah, Mudd Club, Danceteria, and a reopened Peppermint Lounge—plus short-lived spots such as Berlin, Studio 10, Rocker Room, or Chase Park—would halt the dance-floor action with short sets by edgy bands, sex cabarets, and performance artists. Unlike pricey discos, working-class types could afford a night at Danceteria—when Studio 54 opened in 1977, they charged $150 for an annual membership that included $3 off the $10 cover, whereas the Smiths played Danceteria in 1984 for $5—so long as they got past a snarky door staff curating a crowd into art, music, and style.

DANNY CORNYETZ (VJ): It was a new genre, and it was really taking off. They'd rip out the seats; it was no longer about going to a concert hall. Unlike rock clubs before, it was a return to the '60s yeah-yeah discotheque. It wasn't like disco—it was a reaction to disco—the dancing wasn't formalized. It included any number of partners, not just couples. It was a great time. (2004)

RICHARD BARONE (The Bongos): I always loved dance music, and that's a moment where rock and punk and dance music merged in interesting ways. At that time, people were way more open-minded about dance music. There were remnants of the cool parts of disco. DJs didn't just play the same beats all night. There was an eclectic mix of sounds and visuals, and types of people. (2011)

RICHARD McGUIRE (Liquid Liquid): Our music evolved into what we referred to as "body music." We knew a song was a keeper if it made you wanna move. Living on the Lower East Side and being surrounded by Hispanic culture had an influence. We'd hear meringue and salsa out of radios. It all entered into what we were playing. (2000)

Clubs battled over which UK flavor-of-the-month to fly over. It was still the same money-laundering mobsters applying disco principles to underground rock, so crazy loot got spent on the U.S. debuts of up-and-coming new-wave acts. British bands funded entire tours off one or two late-night NYC shows. Club crowds posed with attitude, from sassy girls in colorful Fiorucci to dour dudes in trench coats. Hot guys wore eyeliner; the coolest chicks went out with makeup, diaphragm, cocaine, and a few joints.

MICHAEL MUSTO (journalist): It was a different era; it seems unfathomable now, when people went to clubs, based on word of mouth. It wasn't publicity-driven, and it wasn't about models and celebs. It was cool people tipping each other off that this was the place to go. It was for die-hard club people not ready to say die. (2004)

Bush Tetras ("Too Many Creeps") was the big Downtown band of 1980. DJs like Mark Kamins, Anita Sarko, Johnny Dynell, and Walter Durkacz rocked OMD's "Enola Gay" or Kraftwerk's "Pocket Calculator." Definitive moments included: DEVO's January 1980 "riot" at Hurrah; New Year's Eve 1980's Hurrah show with Gang of Four, Mekons, and Au Pairs; and May 15, 1981's near-wreckage of the Ritz by PiL. Those in the know hit after-hours clubs like the Jefferson or Save the Robots, and twenty-four-hour East Village eateries such as Veselka, Kiev, and Odessa, or Florent, the Meatpacking District's first hip spot.

Intense but innovative characters oversaw this subculture, be it Jim Fouratt (Danceteria, Pep Lounge), Arthur Weinstein (Hurrah/The World), Steven Lewis (The World, Limelight), Rudolf Pieper (Pravda, Danceteria), or Ruth Polsky (Hurrah, Danceteria).

> **RUDOLF PIEPER (club owner):** People have the impression every-thing is prepared for them to have a good time, but in reality the re-sponsibility is on the people, and they are the ones who are going to make a great night, by the way they dress, by the way they dance and by the way they are around, with the new fashions they come up with. I alone can't do very much. (1983)

Late night city ain't nothin' so pretty
Late night city ain't nothin' so smooth
—Comateens, "Late Night City"

The East Village arose from a hostile no-man's-land of shooting galleries, abandoned cars, and wild dogs. There were no cabs to hail or cops to call, just danger and crime. Avenue A had a bar or two, a pizza joint, a newsstand sell-ing nickel bags, and bodegas selling $10s of coke. Walking by Tompkins Square Park, hip kids dealt with junkie hustlers and drug dealers hawkin' "fresh works." The adage went: Avenue A ("all right"); B ("beware"); C ("crazy"); D ("dead"). The heroin culture impacted the art and music.

> **LYDIA LUNCH (Teenage Jesus and the Jerks):** New York was bankrupt, dirty, violent, drug-infested, sex-obsessed—delightful. In spite of that, we were all laughing because you laugh or you die. (2008)

DAVID LINTON (Interference): New York City's environment wasn't "on the point" of urban decay—it had already long been there by the time we got there in 1979. If anything "our" generation was the start of the gentrification trend that has continued to inflate at an exponential rate since. But looking back, things then were simpler, the contrasts more stark, and a sense of desperation kept things raw. (2012)

KEMBRA PFAHLER (The Voluptuous Horror of Karen Black): The Lower East Side was a place nobody wanted to go to or live. It was inexpensive because it was decaying. Nobody in my high school was moving to New York. It seemed so horrific here. The only impression I had of New York was from seeing *Panic in Needle Park* with Al Pacino and Kitty Winn. New York to me was about crime and drugs and little puppy dogs drowning off the Staten Island Ferry. So when I got here, that's what it was. It was like that scene in *Sid and Nancy* where they're buying drugs out of abandoned Lower East Side buildings. It felt like World War III where I lived. I was on Avenue D and 4th Street in 1979, across from the heroin store Excalibur. It was a fertile ground for my philosophical and artistic education. I couldn't sleep at night because I was afraid I'd be robbed or that rats would eat me alive. (2006)

The early '80s East Village arts explosion started with the rise of storefront galleries. It began in 1981 with Fun Gallery, a $175/month space (on East 11th Street but best known on East 10th) whose shows introduced Kenny Scharf, Keith Haring, and Jean-Michel Basquiat, and graffiti artists Fab 5 Freddy, Dondi, and Futura 2000. Limos came to the slums to get in on the action of seventy-plus galleries like Pat Hearn, M-13, P.P.O.W., and New Math. The art got identified with Downtown rock. David Wojnarowicz worked at Danceteria and gigged in 3 Teens Kill 4. Basquiat sang in Grey, briefly with filmmaker Vincent Gallo. Such "artistic" acts defied the status quo in a final pre-AIDS bacchanal.

JIM JARMUSCH (filmmaker): It was not a mass cultural thing but it was happening. The origins of hip-hop and graffiti were intermingling; it was all interconnected on the fringe of everything. There were little galleries starting in the East Village and that stuff wasn't mainstream because there wasn't money behind it. It was just a spirit behind it. It wasn't like the SoHo galleries that came later. That was about big money. (1996)

Romantic me: Danceteria, 1983. Photo by Ted Barron.

PARKER DULANY: I was privy to being on both ends of the art and music, and I think the music and art and film all spoke the same language. I don't care if you talk about us or Liquid Liquid or Jarmusch or Basquiat, we were all going angular and primitive, all trying to express this primitive experience. We were trying to strip everything away. We tried to make it herky-jerky like musical geometry. That's what was going on with the art world: stop and go, red light, green light, pins and needles, don't go there, don't go there either, and if you do, go quickly. (2011)

THE SCENE

Mudd Club, all the way downtown
Mudd Club, they ain't messin' around
—FRANK ZAPPA, "MUDD CLUB"

Mudd Club (77 White Street)—named for Dr. Samuel Mudd, who tended to Lincoln assassin John Wilkes Booth, and name-checked in songs by Talking Heads, Ramones, Nina Hagen, and Frank Zappa—altered all notions of nightlife. The first Downtown club with paparazzi opened Halloween 1978 at the end of a dark alley. Owner Steve Mass, and "curators at large" Anya Phillips and Diego Cortez, ran a "citadel of dilettantism" into severe art, music, film, and cabaret. Basquiat, Haring, Scharf, Stephen Sprouse, and Anna Sui anti-designed the space; Brian Eno did the sound system. Doorpersons like Chi Chi

Valente, Robert Molnar, and Richard Boch barred the uncool. John Rockwell wrote in the *New York Times* (8/8/80): "The small size and elitist attitude make it a rock equivalent of Studio 54, at least insofar as despairing crowds left standing in the street are concerned." Artist/landlord Ross Bleckner took back the space after the five-year lease.

CYNTHIA SLEY (Bush Tetras): Mudd Club was a real experience. It was very exclusive, more like a membership club. All this amazing video art was there, so many creative people during that era. You could go every night. (2004)

DAVID HERSHKOVITS (*Paper*): Mudd Club appealed to artists—the idea was to combine art with the music, and of course the sex and the drugs. It became a magnet and a meeting place for the Downtown scene. It was the prototype for today's parties and clubs: it was a dance club with nightly themes and interesting DJs. The first time I went was opening night, and William Burroughs was at the bar. It was that kind of place. It was probably the first new wave club. (2005)

JOEY ARIAS (Strange Party): I worked at Fiorucci and went to Studio 54. CBGB and Max's were Downtown. But they were dingy little clubs, not what you thought they'd be, and there was nothing else going on in the East Village. Kim Hastreiter at *Paper* told us about Mudd Club. She said we'd love it, and that the music there was fantastic. So we went down there and went crazy. It was fabulous and fun and funky. I was actually the first doorperson there. I lasted about a month and a half. (2012)

LYN BYRD (Comateens): It was more arty, more fashion, more glamour than CBGB or Max's. It was the heroin-chic place—it was packed with that drug. (2010)

Hurrah (36 West 62nd Street) opened in November 1976 as a discotheque that inspired Studio 54 with its jet-set crowd and disco excess. Arthur Weinstein, an ex–fashion photog and Le Jardin waiter, foresaw disco's demise and in June 1978 brought in Jim Fouratt to rebrand "The Rock Disco," with a punk-but-sexier feel, based on dancing and hot bands. Fouratt and Ruth Polsky booked DJs like Tom Savarese, Lary Sanders, and Sean Cassette with the U.S. debuts of bands like the Cure, the Specials, and Psychedelic Furs. Blondie unveiled *Eat* *to the Beat* there at a January 1980 press conference. Joy Division was to play three nights in May 1980 but Ian Curtis hanged himself days before that American tour. Hurrah closed in late 1981.

> **JIM FOURATT (club owner):** I turned Hurrah into the first rock disco, and it was very successful. I saw it as political work. I had all kinds of musicians and a mixed audience. We had a video installation. Eventually, I had all the hot crowds. I could have made a lot of money, but I didn't care about the money, and I made bad business decisions. (2008)

Peppermint Lounge (128 West 45th Street), the '60s twist club, reopened in November 1980 as a new-wave disco, bridging the city's avant-garde with the bridge-and-tunnel set. The 542-person room had edgy bands and DJs and a video lounge (a pre-MTV novelty) where the first VJs Michael Overn and Danny Cornyetz ran an intricate 3/4-inch editing system. As per New York State tax petitions, Herb Taylor for his retired stepfather, lessee Abe Gladstein, ran the bar. Bernie Kurtz ran the club for Benjamin Cohen and Matthew Ianniello. Kurtz hired his niece's husband, Frank Roccio, to run the operation with Mario Mannino. From July 1982 to May 1985 the club was New Peppermint Lounge (100 Fifth Avenue).

> **RICHARD BARONE (The Bongos):** At the Pep we'd go on at like 2 a.m. It was a very young scene—that's when the drinking age was eighteen not twenty-one—so we were the same age as the people in the audience. All the English bands ended up at the Pep—that's how the Bongos first played with Echo & the Bunnymen—and that confluence of ideas of people in the audience was very energizing. (2011)

Danceteria (252 West 37th Street), a cultural meeting ground for artists, tastemakers, and wannabes, was another prototype for future clubs. It debuted spring 1980 by Rudolf Pieper and Jim Fouratt. Their Garment District's unlicensed after-hours "private club" fast fell prey to its own success: VIPs and media coverage brought about its closure within six months by NYPD and SLA (State Liquor Authority). In 1982, Danceteria opened legally under the lease of John Argento's failed disco Interferon (30 West 21st Street). Fouratt and Rudolf fell out soon after, so Fouratt left. The bands, mostly booked by Ruth Polsky, hit the first-floor stage at 2–3 a.m., for twenty to thirty minutes. The second floor rocked with now-famous DJs. A third-floor video lounge meshed kitsch movies and stag films. Doorman Haoui Montaug hosted his "No

Entiendes" variety show from the fourth floor ("Congo Bill") or the VIP roof-top. Madonna debuted at No Entiendes and producer Mark Kamins premiered "Everybody" on the second floor on a reel-to-reel. Scenes in her *Desperately Seeking Susan* were also shot there. (In 1989, Argento tried a Danceteria in the homogeneous Hamptons, but that did not work out.)

MOBY (DJ): A night at Danceteria was a full-on experience. It was a sense of musical eclecticism. You'd see a rock band on one floor, a gay disco on another, a reggae DJ on another, a video lounge—and it all made perfect sense, it never seemed strange. That influenced the bands as well. (2004)

MARK KAMINS (DJ): Danceteria was a magical space like Warhol's Factory or Max's or CBGBs. Jim Fouratt and Rudolf had this amazing finesse to hire people they believed in. Why were the Beasties floor-sweepers at Danceteria? Why was Madonna one of the dancers? Why was Sade a bartender? That's crazy shit, man. So you're talking about a magical moment, where it was really the beginning of something. (2008)

RAFFAELE (Cycle Sluts from Hell): I started going to Danceteria, and then I got a job there. I try to explain it now but you can't. You were a member of a subculture. If you looked freaky, you had instant entrance into those places. I had no bartending experience and was really green and Rudolf put me behind the bar because of the way I looked. Not that it was so superficial of a scene but it was completely set up for us. . . . Danceteria was stressful because John Argento was an ass. He was nasty and coked-out and constantly giving these lie-detector tests to see who was stealing. I was pretty honest but I certainly gave away enough drinks to be considered stealing. We made hand-over-fist cash. (2006)

Club 57 (57 St. Marks Place), opened in 1979 in the basement of the Holy Cross Polish Church, was where Downtown shows took place, be it the Contortions' first gig, 8 Eyed Spy with Lydia Lunch, the start of Ann Magnuson's Pullsallama, or garage rockers the Fleshtones. The wild club run by Magnuson had art curated by Keith Haring (before his Mudd Club fame), Tuesday monster movies and B-movies curated by Susan Hannaford and Tom Scully, and DJs such as Johnny Dynell spinning new wave and retro sounds.

JOEY ARIAS: We found a little Ukrainian place where they had their Sunday coffee meetings. We started a monster movie club, once a week we'd congregate there. This was before video! We'd have beer and smoke pot and get crazy and see these films and pop popcorn. Then Ann Magnuson created a club, almost every night a party went on. Our own clubhouse! Everyone was discovering old stuff. (2009)

TR3 (a.k.a. **Tier 3**) (225 West Broadway) hosted post-punk bands, performance art, and experimental film from May 1979 to December 1980. Bush Tetras, Lounge Lizards, Polyrock, DNA, Raybeats, Bauhaus, and Madness all gigged there. Joy Division was to play June 1, 1980, but Ian Curtis died. The 300-capacity semilegal SoHo club, a narrow room with a tiny stage and three floors (thus its name) booked by twenty-two-year-old Hilary Jaeger, boasted a Basquiat-painted DJ booth, and Amy McMahon (later Amy Rigby) as coat-check girl.

HILARY JAEGER (TR3): I could say Tier 3 was never really a commercial venture. I made less than two hundred a week. The DJs made forty or fifty bucks; the bands made, whatever, three hundred. But the non-commerciality of it was a big part of what made Tier 3 unique. (2008)

Squat Theater (256 West 23rd Street) was a storefront performance space, opened in 1979, after Communist Hungary expelled a cadre of radical Jewish artists called Kassak Studio. Their mural-laden 200-capacity loft near the Chelsea Hotel booked offbeat music on off-nights from July 1979 to May 1981 (as "Squat: Rock, Blues, Jazz"), its ground-floor stage uplifted by the likes of Sun Ra and James Chance. Squat's founder, Istvan "Stephan" Balint's daughter Eszter, spun vinyl at the gigs, befriended John Lurie, dated Basquiat, and acted in Jim Jarmusch's *Stranger than Paradise* and Steve Buscemi's *Trees Lounge*.

JIM JARMUSCH (filmmaker): Squat Theater is hard to describe. Usually their plays begin with a film sequence that turns into live action onstage, and their performances almost always use random occurrences on the street. The audience faces a large window through which you can see the street, and the stage is between that window and the audience, so there are always people passing by that have no idea what's happening that sometimes get dragged into whatever's happening in the play itself. I got a lot of ideas seeing their stuff. (1985)

Bond's International Casino (45th & Broadway), the second floor of the old Bond's department store, opened in 1980 as the world's largest disco, a 9,000-square-foot, 3,500-person club. *Creem* hated the Times Square "shopping mall with bars and a dance floor, and telephones in the men's room." The Clash, touring *Sandinista!*, far oversold the room, leading to their noted seventeen-gig 1981 stint. Later Bond's gigs included Blondie, Plasmatics, and Blue Öyster Cult. The club closed after Studio 54's jailed Steve Rubell ratted out Bond's owners John Addison (Le Jardin) and Maurice Brahms (New York New York).

> **JOE STRUMMER (The Clash):** The Bond's gigs put the band on the map. There were lots of problems with the fire marshals and whatnot, but that attention took us from the underground to the mainstream. It was also the beginning of our end. (1999)

The Ritz (199 East 11th Street) hosted some of the most important shows of the '80s. The Art Deco Latin ballroom was reopened in 1980 by Jerry Brandt, a William Morris agent who owned the club the Electric Circus, managed Carly Simon and Jobriath, and produced "the first disco musical" (1979's *Got Tu Go Disco*). Brandt's raving radio spots rated memorable. The club was cutting edge, with a giant video screen run by a $120,000 projector. (In 1990, the Ritz moved to Studio 54's old site, so in moved Webster Hall.)

> **JERRY BRANDT (club owner):** My philosophy? Have fun, make a buck, and when the DA says "not guilty," don't applaud. (1979)

Heat (157 Hudson Street), a 2,400-capacity SoHo space run by Hurrah manager Henry Schissler, hired most of Mudd Club's staff for its July '79 opening; Johnny Thunders did some classic late-night gigs there. **Berlin**, a semilegal after-hours club, went on at a few places, like a 21st Street loft by Danceteria. Dead Kennedys played **Reggae Lounge** (285 West Broadway). **Chase Park** (Houston and Broadway) was where Heaven 17 gigged at 2 a.m. in March 1981. **The 80s** (on East 86th Street) hosted the dB's and X in May '81. **Milk Bar** (22 Seventh Avenue South) hosted great late-night depravity. **Heartbreak** (179 Varick Street), run from the blue-collar Varick Diner, offered steam tables by day with '50s rock 'n' soul by night by DJ Tom Finn (ex–The Left Bake). In 1984, Jerry Brandt and Patti Oja thought they had a winner with a rock & roll eatery, **Jerry's Bar and Mesquite Grill**, at the site of his former club, **Spo-Dee-O-Dee** (565 West 23rd Street).

Shaking our hair to the disco rap
AM/PM, Pyramid, Roxy, Mudd Club, Danceteria
The newest club is opening up
—Nina Hagen, "New York, New York"

New York always had a thriving after-hours scene, due to a convergence of shady mobsters and crooked cops. By 1980 came a new version, with intrepid artists creating after-hours scenes for hipsters and A-listers, to dance and get even more intoxicated.

ANTHONY HADEN-GUEST (journalist): A micro-culture was forming, an inner core addicted to clubbing harder, faster, but, with no particular place to go. (2004)

The Jefferson (214 East 14th Street), run from Arthur and Colleen Weinstein's loft above the old Jefferson Theater, began with a December 31, 1980, party by Arthur, model Paul Garcia, and Ritz bartender Scotty Taylor. Hundreds came every night they opened, and partied past dawn (most paid hefty $15 covers and bought $4 drinks). Wild action raged through 1981, when Arthur endured a dirty cop trying to murder him in a shakedown, followed by an NYPD Morals Squad raid with fire axes.

ARTHUR WEINSTEIN (owner, Hurrah/The World): We're selling liquor at five in the morning without a license. We've got cars double-parked in front. And we're catering to the sort of people where drugs proliferate. But we're not Mafia. We're in the entertainment business. And we've got no one to complain to when the police start hanging around looking for something. We've got to take care of them. (1983)

FBI inquests into Studio 54's Steve Rubell led to his friend Arthur wearing a wire. With $20K of government cash he opened **The Continental** (511 West 25th Street) from late 1981 till early 1983. *New York* (5/82) said: "The décor suggests what a Ramada Inn bomb shelter might look like. The crowd is heavy with celebs and drugs are everywhere." The wire took down the Tenth Precinct, but Arthur didn't get killed for it. Those efforts that made prosecutor Rudy Giuliani famous began the NYPD's taming and the end of after-hours clubs.

LINDSEY ANDERSON (New York scene): The Continental looked like a big garage. Maybe during the day they worked on cars. It was this big empty concrete space with ramps. I went there all the time. We'd get kicked out of the clubs at 4 a.m., then go to the Empire Diner and have hot fudge sundaes, then to the Continental or AM/PM. (2005)

The Cadillac (601 West 26th Street) hosted similar nefarious activity until February 5, 1983, when co-owner Victor Malinsky, a twenty-four-year-old cocaine-dealing Soviet émigré convicted of counterfeiting, got shot in the head execution-style out front—after he attended the opening of Weinstein and Paul Garcia's fleeting **Le Pop** on 27th and Eleventh. The incident brought about the closure of both clubs. **AM/PM**, run by Vito Bruno, ex–Brooklyn discotheque bouncer and Studio 54 manager, raged for years until a bloody shooting.

Save the Robots (25 Avenue B), Denis Pruvot's infamous Alphabet City after-hours spot (1983–1993), was where one went after a night on the town. Doormen included gay icon Dean Johnson and future TV host Craig Ferguson. DJs like Kip Lavinger and occasional bands rocked from 2:30 a.m. till 7:45 a.m. (to avoid police on the a.m. shift) as bartenders poured rotgut vodka from ammonia bottles.

LINDSEY ANDERSON: I remember the first time I went to Save the Robots. That was serious business. You didn't go to that neighborhood unless you were scoring drugs. Nobody went to that neighborhood. Nothing was going on over there. (2005)

The World (254 East 2nd Street) was likely the last outlaw club; the old wedding hall off Avenue C merits its own book. Shows spanned from Dead Kennedys to Neil Young. Techno dates back to DJs Frankie Knuckles and David Morales spinning in the ground-floor lounge or expansive ballroom dance floor. Arthur, after his FBI ordeal, teamed with Paul Garcia, signed a lease with landlord Jerry Blush, and began throwing parties. They brought in Pep Lounge's Frank Roccio and maritime lawyer Peter Frank and manager Steven Lewis for 1986's legal opening. The club shut in 1990 due to city violations, rent nonpayment, vendors' liens, and community board complaints (accusing the World of bringing crime and rats to Alphabet City!). John Gotti's limo driver Steve Venizelos tried to reopen the room in 1991 but got murdered before the grand opening. Weinstein's friend Peter Gatien named Arthur as Limelight lighting director before he died of throat cancer on July 9, 2009.

ARTHUR WEINSTEIN: We did great stuff there, but certain people got greedy. Certain of my people robbed it blind. There were problems, but it wasn't a big nut to crack to keep it going. I get sick every time I go by that building. (2005)

The Pyramid (101 Avenue A), an East Village institution named for a pyramid motif in the building's original tiling, opened in 1979. The deviant crowds matched the offbeat entertainment (first booked by Brian Butterick of 3 Teens Kill 4), hosting every crucial young rock band in its 100-capacity back room, from Nirvana to Red Hot Chili Peppers. The drag festival Wigstock began at the club. Kier and Dmitry of Deee-lite got known dancing on the bar. Antony Hegarty (Antony and the Johnsons) began in the bathroom's Blacklips Performance Cult. Security included Jimmy Gestapo (Murphy's Law) and Raybeez (Warzone), while doorman Bernard Crawford kept out the yuppies and junkies.

> **ANN MAGNUSON (Bongwater):** I'd go to the Pyramid and just walking by when the door was open in the middle of the day, was the smell of years of . . . waste. (1995)

8BC (337 East 8th Street) was an artistic outpost on 8th Street between Avenues B and C. The tenement townhouse–multimedia space of Dennis Gattra and Cornelius Conboy opened on October 31, 1983, and for two years hosted fifteen hundred performers (plays in afternoon, performance for dinner, bands at night) like Karen Finley and They Might Be Giants, and the NYC debuts of Butthole Surfers and Meat Puppets. The club gets name-checked in *Rent*.

> **CARLO McCORMICK (author/journalist):** 8BC wasn't a rock club, but strong for performance art: Ethyl Eichelberg, Karen Finley, Phoebe Legere, and Steve Buscemi's wife Jo Andres all did major work there. For music it has a dubious honor of being home for They Might Be Giants. More to my tastes were experimental musicians: Elliot Sharp, Christian Marclay, Mimi Goese, and John Zorn. It was a great time, when you could mix drugs, booze and horny people into a space where the entertainment was nuanced and challenging. (2011)

SoHo Weekly News blended investigative journalism with edgy art and rock. Music promoter-turned-publisher Michael Goldstein and *East Village Other* editor Jaakov Kohn launched *SWN* in October 1973 out of 59 Spring Street.

Future notable staffers included the *Voice*'s Michael Musto, *MTV News*' Michael Shore, *Hits*' Roy Trakin, *Details*' Annie Flanders and Stephen Saban, and *Paper*'s Kim Hastreiter and David Hershkovits. The publication shut in March 1982 after losing a vicious circulation war to the *Voice*.

DAVID HERSHKOVITS: *SoHo News* wasn't an underground paper. It wasn't started by people with community roots or high-principled ideas about politics and a utopian vision of how the world should run. Someone who thought they could make money off it started it. But even so, the energy came from punk rock, and we started covering that and giving it a fashion edge—that was the big difference between the *Voice* and us. They were still hippies. They never understood style. They still don't. (2005)

East Village Eye covered East Village subculture. The 'hood's first paper since *East Village Other*'s '60s radicalism included columnists Richard Hell, Cookie Mueller, and Glenn O'Brien, and writers Baird Jones, Richard Fantina, and Carlo McCormick. Publisher Leonard Abrams debuted it in May 1979, and put out seventy-two edgy issues—like the first-ever covers of David Byrne, Lounge Lizards, and Suicide—until January 1987.

LEONARD ABRAMS (*East Village Eye*): The punk scene was morphing into new wave and all these people were coming out of the woodwork—it was a great time. There were performances, there was art, there was rock and roll, and people were just showing up and meeting. These people who'd work together, party together, have sex or maybe be at each other's throats, were all forming the East Village scene. (2005)

Rockpool, the first new-wave promotions firm and record pool, impacted what was heard in clubs and on college radio. Mark Josephson and Danny Heaps began in 1979 with a pool of one hundred clubs, fifty radio stations, and club DJs like Mark Kamins and Afrika Bambaataa, receiving bimonthly vinyl supplied by labels. Josephson said of his DJs to *Billboard* (6/19/82): "Their special brilliance is they're genuinely avant-garde. They're searching for the new music." *Rockpool Newsletter*, the first "alt" trade paper—edited by Mark Fotiadis, Claudia Stanten, and Andy Dunkley, with contributors like Ivan Ivan, Iolo Carew, and Bebop—closed in 1993, at the height of the indie-rock boom.

MARK JOSEPHSON (Rockpool): For years, everybody has decried the lack of an American independent network that would allow for things to break. But after many years of complaining, here it is. And Rockpool is part of that system. (1982)

New Music Seminar, the original independent music trade show, presented panels, parties, showcases, and late-night revelry. Rockpool's Mark Josephson, Tommy Boy's Tommy Silverman, and A&R man Joel Webber launched the confab in 1981. Thousands came during its 1983–1988 apex at the Marriott Marquis. NMS' demise began with Joel's 1988 death at thirty-three. Tom left in 1992, and the annual event stumbled through 1995.

TOM SILVERMAN (New Music Seminar): Mark and I never made over $100,000 in a year, and that happened once. We were all stupid. For a while, the seminar grew at thirty or fifty percent. We kept building it up because we thought it'd keep growing. (1994)

99 Records (99 MacDougal Street) was a new-wave record and clothing store run by Ed Bahlman and his wife Gina. There Ed launched his 99 label that began with Glenn Branca's *Lesson No. 1,* which sold 10,000 units at the store alone, and Bush Tetras' cult hit "Too Many Creeps." Other 99 classics included ESG, Liquid Liquid, and Vivien Goldman's 1981 *Dirty Washing* EP with John Lydon, Keith Levene, and a young Adrian Sherwood. Grandmaster Flash's "White Lines" pilfered Liquid's "Cavern" but Ed lost the lawsuit, leading to his label's demise. Rick Rubin's Flipper-style Hose's 12″—wrecking Rick James's "Superfreak" and Black Sabbath's "Sweet Leaf"—came out through 99. Rubin self-released Hose's follow-up single "Mobo"—he called that label Def Jam.

CYNTHIA SLEY: Ed Bahlman put us all on the map. He had the right combination of bands, and some records actually charted. ESG had a huge effect on us all. At the time, Brits had the corner on the market, so the impact of his label was very important. (2004)

Rituals: Danceteria, 1983. Photo by Ted Barron.

TV Party, a Downtown riff on a late-night show, aired weekly-ish on Manhattan cable Channel J (1978–82). David Letterman hailed it "the greatest TV show ever." *Interview* editor host Glenn O'Brien was joined by his cohost Chris Stein and bandleader Walter Steding (Walter Steding & The Dragon People). Guests included David Byrne, Iggy Pop, and Debbie Harry. Amos Poe directed. Basquiat painted canvases; Fab 5 Freddy hung out. *TV Party* got shot live (at Mudd Club, in order to get paid as the entertainment), improvised, imbibed (puffin' joints on-air), and was prone to technical problems.

WALTER STEDING (artist/musician): Glenn O'Brien could've been a TV host but that wasn't to be, so we did our own show. It was avant-garde, like punk television. Long before YouTube was cable TV. And as there are no rules on cable, we felt, "Why not do what we were doing off camera?" *TV Party* was the meeting of Uptown and Downtown: Chris and Debbie were regulars, so was Fab 5 Freddy; and as all the early rap records used "Good Times" by Chic, Nile Rodgers was there. Jean-Michel did art as the show went on. It was a unifying center of what went on in the city. (2011)

THE MUSIC

I hope that no one's listening
Anticipating someone's there
—POLYROCK, "ROMANTIC ME"

Polyrock, a six-piece with skeletal proto-electro Kraftwerk grooves and arty Talking Heads–isms, defined 1980s-era post-punk. The six-piece with bassist Billy Robertson (ex–Model Citizens), brother Tommy, and Catherine Oblasney made inroads at Mudd Club and on Philip Glass–produced RCA albums, 1980's *Polyrock* and 1981's *Changing Hearts*. Gigs with the Cars and dates in towns like Moscow, Idaho, proved too futuristic. It ended after 1982's Billy-produced *Above the Fruited Plain* 12″ (PVC), according to *Billboard* (1/29/83), "well-stated but hardly mass appeal."

> **BILLY ROBERTSON (Polyrock):** In 1978, I'd just left Model Citizens and had the experience of working on an EP produced by John Cale. I moved into a ground-floor loft in Tribeca where we used an abandoned basement meat freezer for rehearsal space. Eight songs and six months later, we were playing Max's, TR3, Hurrah, CBGB and Mudd Club. One critic called us art-pop with Philip Glass–like wordless vocals. If there was anything Polyrock set out to do, it was to abandon R&B and traditional rock influences and embrace the likes of Philip Glass and Brian Eno. (1986)

Model Citizens, a Columbia MFA sextet, blurred rock, disco, and minimalism. A 1979 John Cale–produced 7″ EP (Spy) opened doors for 1980's "New Music for the 20th Century" concert at Carnegie Hall and a failed courtship with Warner Bros. (Citizens split into Billy Robertson's Polyrock, singer Eugenie Diserio and guitarist Steven Alexander's the Dance, and singer Gloria Richards and guitarist Tomek Lamprecht's 2Yous.)

Nervus Rex, a '60s-style post-pop quartet, got known for doing the Shocking Blue's "Venus," a club hit on par with "Rock Lobster." Shawn Brighton (Krushenick) met *Creem* writer Lauren Agnelli at CBGB in 1977. The 1978

45 "Don't Look" / "Love Affair" (on their Cleverly Named Record Co.) won *NME*'s "Independent Single of the Year." Blondie introduced them to *Parallel Lines* producer Mike Chapman, who changed them on 1980's *Nervus Rex* (Dreamland/MCA).

Student Teachers starred five punk-fan teens from suburban Larchmont, NY, led by sixteen-year-old Mumps Fan Club prez Bill Arning on keyboards. They debuted on Easter 1978 at Max's, and by 1979 headlined Saturday nights at CBs. Blondie's Jimmy Destri dated their drummer Laura K. Davis so he produced the band. They opened for Iggy Pop three times, and were slated to play *Midnight Special* but got cancelled. Destri brought Bowie to a rehearsal, and then Bowie brought Eno to see them at CBGB, where they by chance covered Roxy Music's "Remake/Remodel."

U.S. Ape featured Pep Lounge/Irving Plaza booker Tom Goodkind (bass/vocals) and keyboardist Shauna Laurie. The FBI seized all copies of 1978's "Hell on the West Side" in an unrelated pressing plant piracy raid. Seventy-nine's "Ignorance Is Bliss" got WPIX-FM play and VJ rotation for a Danny Cornyetz–produced video. Nineteen eighty's Stiff distributed "Animal Luxury" rates for its ad spot that ran at 2 a.m. during *Mary Tyler Moore*. Ape devolved after a part-finished album got stolen or erased.

The Erasers' Susan Springfield (Beschta), a striking Ohio-bred photographer who dated Richard Hell, led a Patti Smith/Television–style quartet (named for an Alain Robbe-Grillet novel) with Richie Lure, Jody Beach, and Jane Fire. A 1978 demo produced by Richard Lloyd included "(It Was So) Funny (That Song That They Hear)." Susan starred with Debbie Harry in Amos Poe's *The Foreigner*, in which the Erasers had a song ("Jumped"). In 1980, Fred Smith produced Susan Springfield Band's 7" EP, *The Tenant of the Room*.

The Necessaries played with Chris Spedding, who came from London in 1978 for a one-year gig as Robert Gordon's guitarist. After that, Chris replaced The N's Randy Gun, joining Ed Tomney (Harry Toledo & The Rockets), Ernie Brooks (Modern Lovers), and Jess Chamberlain (Red Crayola). The 1979 John Cale–produced "You Can Borrow My Car" came out before Spedding. Iowa-bred avant-garde theorist and future dance pioneer Arthur Russell replaced Spedding on 1981's *Big Sky* and 1982's *Event Horizon* for Sire UK.

Raybeats, Ventures-style instrumentalists, arose from no-wave circles. In 1979, George Scott III (Contortions/8 Eyed Spy) lived on Avenue C and worked at Bleecker Bob's. He loved Link Wray and Dick Dale and began such a band of ex-Midwesterners: Scott (from Iowa), Don Christensen (Nebraska), and Jody Harris and Pat Irwin (Kansas). Scott OD'd on August 5, 1980, at age twenty-seven, but they carried on with 1981's "Guitar Beat" 7″ and *Roping Wild Bears* EP that comprised 1982's *Guitar Beat* LP (Jem).

Outsets, with Ivan Julian (Voidoids) and Vinny DeNunzio (Feelies), rocked a quirky, sexy punk. They made 1980's "I'm Searchin for You" b/w Peggy Lee's "Fever" and 1983's Garland Jeffreys–produced *Outsets* 12″ EP. (Ivan joined wife Cynthia Sley as the Lovelies, on '88's *Mad Orphan*.)

Comateens, named for a *Post* headline, perfected an urbane synth new wave. It began with Ramona Jan (Janquinto) and Nicholas "Nic O. Teen" North (Dembling). Lyn Byrd (Billman) joined, and Nic's brother Oliver North replaced Jan. Seventy-nine's self-released "Cool Chick" 45, two songs on *Marty Thau's 2x5*, and 1981's *Comateens*, yielded Mercury releases: 1983's *Pictures on a String* and 1984's *Deal with It*.

Dizzy and the Romilars, named for a side effect of Romilar cough syrup, began when Ramona Jan quit Comateens and joined Val Star (Ghent), Angelo Zip (Zarrelli), and Joe Klemmer. Jimboco issued 1979's "Elizabeth's Lover" 45 in two sleeves, one with a cover of Bowie's "TVC 15." Chris Butler produced 1982's *Daily Dose*, diagnosed by *Billboard* (8/14/82): "In an age of bland, pompous music, their prescription for a good time is the medicine needed."

It was so funny: The Erasers, 1978. Photo © Eileen Polk.

You're going nowhere very fast
And I'm sure you'll get there last
—BLOODLESS PHARAOHS, "NOWHERE FAST"

Bloodless Pharaohs, an urbane Roxy Music–ish act on the Max's/CBs scene, launched Brian Setzer. It all began with Brian and drummer-brother Gary Setzer, sounding more Polyrock than pomade, like on 1980's *Marty Thau*

Presents 2x5. Brian bored of playing Long Island bars, and moved to London for fame in Stray Cats. (In 1996, Setzer's lawyers blocked keyboardist Ken Kinnally's plan to distribute the old tapes as *Brian Setzer & The Bloodless Pharaohs.*) **Revelons** rocked a '60s-style new wave. The band of Gregory Lee Pickard over time included Jimmy Wynbrandt (Miamis), Mark Suall (Alda Reserve), Fred Smith (Television), and Jay Daugherty (Patti Smith). They lived near CBGB so they filled in many nights, and headlined Danceteria, Mudd Club, and Max's. After 1979's "The Way (You Touch My Hand)" 45 (Ork) came *Marty Thau Presents 2x5* material. They disbanded in 1983 after a dreadful Bottom Line show.

The Swinging Madisons began with the Mumps' Kristian Hoffman jokingly singing Bobby Rydell's "Volare." Hoffman gathered Mumps bassist Kevin Kiely, drummer Paul Rutner, and guitarist Robert Mache to debut at TR3. They dressed in '50s lounge-act tuxes with a pompadoured Kristian and the others in turbans. *Billboard, Rockpool,* and *Cashbox* adored 1981's *Appearing Nightly* EP for dance-music label Select. **The Cosmopolitans** did 1981's ironic new wave hit "How to Keep Your Husband Happy," a B-52's-inspired tune based on Debbie Drake's 1964 happy-housewife exercise album. UNC dance grads Jamie K. Sims and Nel Moore moved to NYC and became Cosmopolitan Dance Troop, choreographing steps to boyfriends' bands like "The dB Drop" or "The Fleshtone Flank Step." Mitch Easter produced 1980's three-song demo, released as a 7″ on neighbor Alan Betrock's Shake imprint. But then Sims contracted the dreaded Epstein-Barr virus and retired.

The Waitresses served the scene after Chris Butler quit Akron band Tin Huey to work for Michael Zilkha's Ze label. He began the Waitresses on January 3, 1981, at Club 57. His pop act with brassy Akron party girl Patty Donahue, Television drummer Billy Ficca, and saxist Mars Williams created hits on 1982's *I Could Rule the World If I Could Only Get the Parts* ("Christmas Wrapping," *Square Pegs* theme) and *Wasn't Tomorrow Wonderful* ("I Know What Boys Like"). The next year's *Bruiseology* hurt so good till Patty departed (briefly replaced by Holly Beth Vincent); cancer took her life at age forty. **Major Thinkers** starred Pierce Turner and Larry Kirwan, who came from Wexford, Ireland, and stayed on expired visas. Kirwan recalled "punky new wave spiced by a dash of Irish attitude, and obligatory cool haircuts." After 1980's "Back in the 80s" 45 and 1981's Irish-only LP came 1983's *Major Thinkers* EP (Epic) with the Alphabet City anthem "Avenue B," before getting "royally screwed by the record label" (*New York*, 3/22/93).

Tom Tom Club began as the side project of Talking Heads' Tina Weymouth and Chris Frantz. *Tom Tom Club* (Sire), produced by Chris and Tina after Lee Scratch Perry failed to show, featured "Wordy Rappinghood" and the 1981 #1 "Genius of Love." Outselling TH's *Fear of Music* started a blood feud with David Byrne. After 1983's *Close to the Bone* (their *Soul Train* debut), they semi-retired in Cock Island, CT, where they at times record, such as 1988's *Boom Boom Chi Boom Boom* or 2000's *The Good, the Bad, and the Funky*. **Dinosaur L** starred Arthur Russell (The Necessaries). In 1978 he, with DJ Nicky Siano as Dinosaur, did the first dance 12" "Kiss Me Again" (Sire). "Is It All Over My Face" as Loose Joints in 1980 resulted in 1981's *24-24 Music* (Sleeping Bag) as Dinosaur L with the Paradise Garage anthems "Go Bang" and "#1 (You're Gonna Be Clean on Your Bean)."

Material began with future producers Bill Laswell, Michael Beinhorn, and Fred Maher. Their experimental funk group over time included Bootsy Collins, Sly & Robbie, David Byrne, John Zorn, Robert Quine, Niles Rogers, and William S. Burroughs. Deep grooves abounded on 1979's *Temporary Music 1* and 1982's *Temporary Music 2* 12" EPs. The 1981 club hit "Bustin' Out" with Nona Hendryx opened ZE Records' seminal *SeiZE the Beat* comp. **Defunkt** featured Joseph Bowie, younger brother of jazz star Lester Bowie. The brainy collective of horny horns and gritty guitars soared on 1980's *Defunkt* and 1982's *Thermo Nuclear Sweat* (with guitarist Vernon Reid), which inspired Red Hot Chili Peppers.

ESG (Emerald, Sapphire and Gold) was ghetto sisters Marie, Renee, Deborah, and Valerie Scroggins (with Leroy Glover). Ed Bahlman found them in 1980 while judging a South Bronx talent show. He'd manage/produce them on his 99 label: 1981's *ESG* and 1982's *ESG Says Dance to the Beat of Moody* are minimal funk classics. They opened for the Clash and for A Certain Ratio, who got them signed to Factory Records UK. **Liquid Liquid**, a percussion-based art/funk group, began as the punk band Liquid Idiot. Bassist Richard McGuire contacted Ed Bahlman, leading to 1981's *Liquid Liquid* and *Successive Reflexes* EPs on 99. But the "White Lines" lawsuit bankrupted Ed's business.

Konk created a soundtrack to East Village art, at galleries and semilegal spaces. Saxist Dana Vlcek, trumpeter Shannon Dawson (of Basquiat's Gray), and rhythmist Geordie Gillespie first wailed Latin-flavored alt funk with bassist Jonathan Schneider (DJ Johnny Sender) and Sonic Youth drummer Richard Edson on trumpet. (Donald Fagen of Steely Dan adored "Love Attack" and rereleased it as 1988's *Konk Jams*.) **Kid Creole & The Coconuts** starred Thomas Browder, a.k.a. August Darnell from Dr. Buzzard's Original Savannah Band. Kid Creole, from South Bronx via Canada, got his tag from Elvis's film *King Creole*. The punky Cab Calloway type oversaw a Havana-flavored quasi–big band with wife Taryn Hagey and vibraphonist Coati

Mundi. Highlights included 1981's *Fresh Fruit in Foreign Places* and 1985's *In Praise of Older Women and Other Crimes*.

Bush Tetras' funky post-punk was the sound of decadent Alphabet City. Contortions guitarist Pat Place and drummer Dee Pop, a *Creem* and *New York Rocker* writer, got with Cleveland Institute of Art dropouts singer Cynthia Sley (designer for Lydia Lunch and Judy Nylon) and Contortions roadie/bassist Laura Kennedy. They topped 1980's *Voice* "Pazz & Jop Poll" with "Too Many Creeps" (99)—Pat's vocals inspired by jerks she dealt with working the Bleecker Street Theater ticket booth. The Clash's Topper Headon produced 1981's *Rituals* (Stiff). That preceded 1983's *Wild Things* (ROIR) tape and various reunions. **Pulsallama** did 1982's "The Devil Lives in My Husband's Body" (Y Records). The percussive seven-to-twelve-piece of Downtown starlets led by Wendy Wild, Ann Magnuson, Jean Caffeine, and Lori "Bubbles" Montana evolved from Club 57's "Ladies' Auxiliary of the Lower East Side." They opened for the Clash in Asbury Park and then disbanded while recording an album with Mark Kamins at Blank Studios.

Certain General, "the missing link between Television and Sonic Youth," personified post-punk with dense guitars and offbeat rhythms. New Orleans painter Parker Dulany's EV act began at an Avenue B party with DNA and club debuted with Liquid Liquid at Hurrah. Both 1981's *Perry* and 1982's *Holiday of Love* EPs portended a 1984 UK tour and a Band of Outsiders/Certain General split LP, *Far Away in America*. Through manager Ruth Polsky, they opened for new bands like the Cure and New Order. CG got popular in France on LPs like 1986's *These Are the Days* (with Ivan Julian). **Ike Yard** perfected a dour post-punk with scrap metal rhythms. The band, named for an LP in the record shop in *A Clockwork Orange*, began with Mudd Club habitués bassist Kenneth Compton (who dated Madonna) and percussionist Stuart Argabright (Futants) at Kristian Hoffman's Chinatown loft. Michael Diekmann and Fred Szymanski, of Brown's McColl Studio of Electronic Music, joined on synth. "Night after Night" became a 1981 *Melody Maker* Single of the Week ("Ike Yard create violent urban landscapes"). That year's *A Fact a Second* was the first American group released on Factory Records.

Shox Lumania, self-described as "DEVO meets Ziggy Stardust as played by Bauhaus," were the hi-tech troupe in costumes and makeup of singer Lari Shox (Larry Hrynyk) and keyboardist Richard Bone, claiming to come from the pre-Atlantis world of Lumania. *Billboard* (12/12/81) hailed 1981's *Live at the Peppermint Lounge* ROIR tape and "(I Have) No Shoes" b/w "Signals" as "the closest thing New York has to a New Romantic synthesizer dance band." **3 Teens Kill 4**, a multimedia group, incorporated electronic grooves, film snippets, and electro beats. The East Villagers named for a *Post* headline ("3 Teens Kill 4, No Motive")—David Wojnarowicz, Brian Butterick, Jesse Hultberg, Doug Bressler, and Julie Hair (she in 1979 helped David drag a hundred fifty pounds of cow bones to Castelli Gallery)—made 1982's *No Motives* EP with shots of Wojnarowicz and his art.

Del Byzanteens included vocalist Phil Kline, bassist Philippe Hagen, keyboardist Jim Jarmusch, and percussionist brothers Dan and Josh Braun. Author Luc Sante wrote some lyrics; painter John Lurie would jam onstage. Their danceable art-rock attained acclaim from Mudd Club to Pep Lounge. Both 1981's *Del-Byzanteens* and 1982's *Lies to Live By*, with a rip on the Jaynetts' "Sally, Go Round the Roses," gained popularity in Yugoslavia. **Ambitious Lovers** with guitarist Arto Lindsay and keyboardist Peter Scherer featured Arto's vox bilingual or in Portuguese. Three LPs named for seven deadly sins, 1984's *Envy* (Editions EG), 1988's *Greed* (Virgin), and 1991's *Lust* (Elektra) felt like a twisted David Byrne.

> *From the Westside to the Eastside*
> *Everybody's up on the right side*
> —URBAN BLIGHT, "GET CLOSER"

Urban Blight, a ska/funk sextet with brassy dance beats, wowed crowds from CBGB to the Ritz. The wiseass city kids starred graffiti artist Nelson Keene Carse on vocals and his brother Jamie Carse on keys. Mark Kamins remixed 1983's "A Nite Out" and 1984's "Peacetrain" 12″s. Beastie Boys opened for them at the Ritz on October 26, 1985, and UB guys played on *Licensed to Ill*. Eighty-seven's *From the Westside to the Eastside* involved Cro-Mags drummer Mackie Jayson plus Ricky Powell photos. **The Toasters** featured British expat Robert "Buck" Hingley in his porkpie hat. "Beat Up," a 1983 45 of rude boy riddims, set in motion 1985's *Recriminations* produced by Joe Jackson (as Stanley Turpentine), 1987's *Skaboom* (for Celluloid), and 1992's *New York Fever* for Buck's prolific Moon Ska label.

The Nails came out of Boulder, CO, punks the Ravers (whose roadie Eric Boucher became Jello Biafra). Dave Kaufman (keys/guitar), his brother George (bass/trombone), and singer Marc Campbell formed a brassy six-piece in NYC with club appeal. The 1981 *Hotel for Women* EP (Jimboco) introduced the ska-style "44 Lines about 88 Women." The song became the Nails' calling card. RCA came in for 1984's *Mood Swing* with its MTV hit of "44 Lines." But 1986's metal-edged *Dangerous Dreams* turned into a nightmare. **Blue Angel** launched Cyndi Lauper. She, John Turi, and Arthur "Rockin' A" Neilson, wrote 1980's '50-style *Blue Angel* (Polydor). *Rolling Stone* said: "Imagine The Crystals with punk hair and Fender guitars, and you've got the picture." Cyndi hated it, from producer Roy Halee's mix to the airbrushed art that made her "look like Big Bird." Lauper's 1983 solo debut reworked the LP's "Witness"; her '86 follow-up redid "Maybe He'll Know."

The Now rocked a new-wave groove at clubs like Max's and Hurrah. Geoff "Lip" Danielik and Mamie Francis played in the punk bands Arthur's Dilemma and Peroxide (1979's "Heart Disease") before the Now with Bobby Orr and Robin Dee. Midsong International (the label behind Silver Convention's "Fly Robin Fly") sold 200,000 of 1980's *The Now* with "Can You Fix Me up with Her." The band began on a follow-up *Bad Publicity Is Better than No Publicity*, until the label shuttered its office. **The Cooties** spread when guitarist Aid MacSpade taught bass to CBGB door girl Vicky "Flaesh" Rose. The danceable new-wave pop act rehearsed at Jerry Williams's 171A. Wayne Kramer produced 1981's "Dinosaurs" single with Dave Parsons's cover graphics. Their 1982 "Patch It Up" 45, with John Holmstrom artwork and Ronnie Ardito (The Shirts) production, listed their mailing address c/o the Avenue A punk rock watering hole, the Park Inn.

Marilyn got known after Steve Mass saw her Miss America shtick at his Mudd Club. Her sonic sickness shone on 1980's club hit, "Sex Means Nothing When You're Dead." *So Disgraceful* with Tommy Victor (pre-Prong) and Harry Viderci (Comateens) dented the charts in 1982. *Billboard* said, "It sounds decadent but it's great." **Glorious Strangers** was drummer Wharton Tiers (Laurie Anderson, A Band, Theoretical Girls) and vocalist wife Carol. "Why Don't You Join the Army?" embodied 1980 no-wave ennui. *Glorious Strangers* with Wharton, David Brown, Magic Franklin, and Richard Peare came out in 1984 on Fun City, for Tiers' studio where he produced Swans, Sonic Youth, et cetera.

Breakfast Club involved a young Madonna (then called Emmy) on drums, her boyfriend singer Dan Gilroy, his brother guitarist Ed, and bassist Angie Schmit. Emmy quit to join Steve Bray, and sing new wave from 1981 to '82 as Emmenon, or Emmy & The Emmys. *Breakfast Club* with both Bray and Gilroy but no Madonna spun 1987 Top 40 hits in "Kiss and Tell" and "Right on Track." *Stereo Review* loved "Bray's Detroit funk and Gilroy's New York art-school rock." **Dancing Hoods** did FM-friendly new wave. Bob Bortnick traded $400 of cool vinyl from his LI record shop with Ed Tomney and Glenn Morrow to record 1984's *Dancing Hoods*. After '85's *Jealous Roses* and '88's

Hallelujah Anyway (with the MTV hit "Baby's Got Rockets") they split to L.A. and broke up. (Bob did A&R, signing Garbage. Guitarist Freddy Mark Linkous rocked as Sparklehorse until his 2010 suicide.)

Alan Vega (Boruch Bermowitz) made ten solo records like his work in Suicide; Ric Ocasek produced the first three. The Brooklyn College grad began doing light sculptures and in 1971 began "Project of Living Artists" through which he met pianist Martin Rev. The 1980 solo album *Alan Vega* featured the rockabilly-style "Jukebox Babe." Eighty-one's *Collision Drive* (Gene Vincent's "Be-Bop-A-Lula") and 1983's *Saturn Strip* (Hot Chocolate's "Every 1's a Winner") involved Magic Tramps' Larry Chaplan and Sesu Coleman. **Martin Rev** (Martin Reverby) did offbeat solo work—per David Fricke in *Rolling Stone* (11/13/08): "more radical than the chant-and-heartbeat music he does with Vega"—that suffered on labels: 1980's *Martin Rev* for Lust/Unlust, 1985's *Clouds of Glory* on New Rose France, 1991's *Cheyenne* on the Alice Cooper–linked Alive, 1995's *See Me Ridin'* ROIR cassette, and 2000's *Strangeworld* for Helsinki's Sähkö. Rev quit his secular pursuits to become an Orthodox Jew.

Walter Steding, a Warhol-linked Downtown star, fused punk and avant-garde. He awed audiences opening for Blondie, Suicide, and Ramones, yelling in his "bug suit" of blinking lights that distorted his bow scrapes into blips and squeaks through "pan diatonic biofeedback," spark machines, Tesla coils, and liquid smoke. Marty Thau's Red Star label issued 1979's 7" of Chris Stein–produced rips on "Get Ready" and "Hound Dog," and 1980's *Walter Steding* LP with Roberts Fripp and Quine. *Dancing in Heaven* came out in 1982 on Blondie's Animal/Chrysalis label. **Klaus Nomi** (Klaus Sperber) a kitschy queer Bavarian countertenor, mixed theater, disco, and punk, on wry covers like Lesley Gore's "You Don't Own Me" or *The Wizard of Oz*'s "Ding Dong (The Witch Is Dead)." Bowie saw Nomi and Joey Arias at Mudd Club and they backed him on *Saturday Night Live* (December 1979 on "TVC 15"). That brought about RCA albums, 1981's *Klaus Nomi* and 1982's *Simple Man*, and Nomi's cover on Kristian Hoffman's "Total Eclipse" in *Urgh! A Music War!* Nomi died an early AIDS victim on August 6, 1983.

Ned Sublette moved from New Mexico in 1976 to join La Monte Young. The quirky guitarist recorded as: Ned Sublette Band; Clandestine Featuring Ned Sublette (remixes by Arthur Russell and Nicky Siano); Ned Sublette & The Persuasions ('89's *Ever Widening Circles of Remorse*); Ned Sublette, Lawrence Weiner & The Persuasions ('93's *Ships at Sea, Sailors & Shoes*); and Ned Sublette & Lawrence Weiner ('97's *Monsters from the Deep*). The Cuban music scholar's 1999 *Cowboy Rhumba* melded C&W and Santeria. (In 2006, Willie Nelson did his "Cowboys Are Frequently, Secretly Fond of Each Other.")

Jill Kroesen, a Bay Area–bred composer, studied electroacoustics under Terry Riley at Mills College. Her Patti Smith–ish "I Really Want to Bomb You" (Lust/Unlust) single of 1980 involved Television bassist Fred Smith and Dolls-associated drummer Tony Machine. Kroesen's 1982 EP *Stop Vicious Cycles* showcased Peter Gordon, David Van Tieghem, Jody Harris, and Bill Laswell.

Karen Finley became notorious for performance art like smearing herself in chocolate or shoving yams up her ass. She first pushed limits in Kipper Kids, troupe of first spouse Brian Routh. She then worked at Danceteria and performed solo at the Kitchen. Her food thang resulted in dance vinyl: 1986's *Tales of Taboo* ("Yam Jam") and 1988's "Lick It" sandwiched 1987's *The Truth Is Hard to Swallow*. **Phoebe Legere**, both a chanteuse genius and nutcase, hailed in *Billboard* "the female Frank Zappa," played accordion or grand piano (like doing "I Get a Kick out of You" with legs wrapped behind her neck). The Vassar alum opened Bowie's *Glass Spiders* tour, starred in *Mondo New York* (strumming guitar with her vagina), and in *Toxic Avenger, Part II* and *Part III* (as TA's lady). She also wrote an all-girl musical of Tom Robbins's *Even Cowgirls Get the Blues*.

John Sex (John McLaughlin), a star of Club 57 and the Pyramid, said that he sculpted his blond pompadour by mixing Dippity-Do and cum. John and Wendy Wild moved to the Village as a straight couple in '75 from Northport, LI. He attended SVA with Haring and Basquiat, and hustled in a sailor suit on the corner of 53rd & Third. Rockers recall Sex from the Cars' 1984 Warhol-produced "Heartbeat City" video. He didn't record until 1988's *Mondo New York* soundtrack ("Hustle with My Muscle") and then died of AIDS. **RuPaul** (RuPaul Charles) got known at Pyramid "genderfuck" parties, Suzanne Bartsch Copa events, and public access TV. Ruth Polsky got the Atlanta queen her first NYC shows in 1988, before moving here with Larry Tee and Jon "Lady Bunny" Ingle. Her 1993 hit "Supermodel" won Ru a MAC Cosmetics deal as the first drag fashion model.

Went to work
But it wasn't workin'
—BAND OF OUTSIDERS, "NERVOUS"

Band of Outsiders starred Marc Jeffrey (Mikulich) of power-pop teens the Limit. BOO began on East 11th Street with 1981's "Done Away" 45 and 1984's

Far Away in America split album with Certain General. Ivan Kral produced 1985's *Everything Takes Forever* (L'Invitation au Suicide). Nikki Sudden guested on 1989's *Armistice Day*, live November 11, 1988, at CBGB. Art Black in *Trouser Press* hailed Marc's 1990 solo CD *Playtime* "this generation's Nick Drake." **The Corvairs** sped away from Boulder, CO. Phil Gammage's band involved John Cormany of the Ravers, who moved to NYC to be the Nails; so the Corvairs came too. Dave Kaufman produced 1983's *Temple Fire* EP; they recorded 1985's *Sad Hotel*. Fleshtone Keith Streng oversaw 1987's *Rio Blanco*, while Don Fury produced 1989's *Hitchhiker* (its "Ready to Burn" video starred Wendy Wild).

Hi Sheriffs of Blue rocked a bumpy blend of Delta blues, avant-garde, and punk. In 1979 slide guitarist/musicologist Mark Dagley quit his Boston cult band the Girls and moved to Alphabet City. Robert Palmer in the *New York Times* (1/23/83) extolled HSOB's first 12″ as "an intriguing kaleidoscope of whining slide guitars, fractured rhythms and electronic effects that are often bizarre but never inappropriate." **His Master's Voice** involved Hawaii art star Keiko Bonk and her surfer husband Mark Abramson, and briefly Patti Smith's Jay Dee Daugherty. The couple hosted Love Club parties, first at the World and then Lismar Lounge. The band's 1984 *Missionary* EP (PVC/Jem) of techie punk/rock faded when Jem folded.

Strange Party starred drag star Joey Arias, who moved from L.A. in the '70s to design costumes and work at Fiorucci. Arias's art/punk ensemble, like a gay Funkadelic, included over time Ann Magnuson, Fred Schneider, and Nona Hendryx. Strange Party made 1981's "Sleepwalking through Life" b/w "Jewels from Miami Beach" and recorded some gigs. **Adele Bertei** came to NYC in 1977 and joined the Contortions. After the Bloods, she scored Scott and Beth B's 1983 film *Vortex*. Adele, like Madonna (also in *Desperately Seeking Susan*) got deep into disco-pop; Thomas Dolby produced '83's "Build a Bridge" (Geffen) that preceded '85's Scritti Politti–produced "When It's Over" (Chrysalis UK).

Velveteen starred sexy Lisa Burns, "discovered" by producer Craig Leon and lawyer Jonathan Blank at CBGB. From that came 1978's *Lisa Burns* (MCA), produced by Leon and backed by Willie "Loco" Alexander's Boom Boom Band. Velveteen, her synth-pop band with Sal Maida (Milk N' Cookies) and drummer Richard Reinhardt (later Richie Ramone) did 1983's Maida-coproduced *After Hours* EP (Atlantic). They excelled from Danceteria to R.T. Firefly's as "Velveteen with Lisa Burns." **Crossfire Choir** wowed CBGB's Hilly Kristal, who managed and made them "house band." The quartet of Eddie Freeze and Jay Pounders signed to Geffen in 1984, toured with Siouxsie, and had a buzz with "What's It to Ya (Motherfucker)." But members dissed Geffen, so the label shelved their $200K Steve Lillywhite–produced album. On 1986's *Cross-fire Choir* (Passport) they tried to rework those tunes. Ira Robbins railed, "Choir's problem: more ambition than talent."

Dominatrix, with the breathy vocals of Dominique Davalos, daughter of actor Richard Davalos (*East of Eden*), whipped up interest after Joel Webber saw them at the Pyramid. Her 1983 smash "The Dominatrix Sleeps Tonight," produced by Stuart Argabright (Ike Yard) and Ken Lockie (Cowboys International), fused club beats and S&Misms. MTV nixed 1984's Beth B–directed video. **Book of Love** contained synth-pop new-wave hits in "Book of Love" and "I Touch Roses." Lauren Roselli, Jade Lee, and Susan Ottaviano with drummer Ted Ottaviano (no relation!), began at Philadelphia College of the Arts as the Bush Tetras–style Head Cheese, and moved to NYC to record for Ivan Ivan's label, I Square/Sire. Their 1984 debut *Book of Love* outsold 1988's *Lullabye*, '91's *Candy Carol*, and '93's *Lovebubble*.

Dean and the Weenies starred Dean Johnson, a 6′6″ queen in stilettos and shaved head, noted for his party "Rock & Roll Fag Bar." His song "Fuck You" was a hit in 1988's *Mondo New York* film, of which Island pressed but never released a Keith Masco–produced CD. (The queer icon died in September 2008 in a wealthy Saudi man's D.C. home.) **Deee-lite** transformed the dance floor with Downtown fabulosity; equal parts disco-pop and rap mixology. Ohio's Lady Miss Kier (Kirby) and USSR's Super DJ Dmitry (Brill) pole-danced at Pizza a Go-Go before encountering Tokyo's DJ Towa Tei in 1986 at the Pyramid. Nineteen ninety's *World Clique* included "Groove Is in the Heart" and "Power of Love."

THE FALL

We hear the drums again
And fall back in step again
—IKE YARD, "HALF A GOD"

Community activists decried the '80s gentrification begun under Mayor Koch, but the change had just barely begun. The '70s/'80s underground faded due to lifestyle: the effects of drugs and the ravages of AIDS killed a generation of nightlife denizens. Another change came in 1985, when the drinking age in New York rose from eighteen to twenty-one; without kids on the club scene, the energy changed. The final straw may have arrived on September 7, 1986, and the tragic death of Ruth Polsky at age thirty, when a cab careened into Limelight's front door where she stood speaking to the door staff.

PARKER DULANY (Certain General): The clubs are closing and gentrification is going on, meaning money's taking over the neighborhood and it's not feasible to run a club anymore. (1986)

BOB PFEIFER (Human Switchboard): The club scene is very difficult in New York right now. It used to be three or four years ago that you had clubs with music three/four nights a week, like Hurrah and those places. Now you're down to two nights a week in most rooms. The other thing is fewer and fewer people are going out to clubs. I think that has to do with the economic situation. It's harder and harder. You used to be able to get an apartment for $300 in New York; now you're lucky to find one for $600. (1986)

BLOOD, SWEAT & NO TEARS

NEW YORK HARDCORE

1980–present: Bad Brains, Cro-Mags, Murphy's Law, Agnostic Front, Warzone, Sick of It All, Madball, Rock Hotel, A7, 171A, ABC No Rio, fall of CBGB

United Blood: Roger Miret of Agnostic Front, CBGB all-ages matinee, 1989. Photo by Frank White.

NEW YORK HARDCORE

THE RISE

We gotta stick together
Support one another
—Agnostic Front, "United & Strong"

New York Hardcore was more than a trend or style. It was a radical music and antiauthoritarian scene based on an unseen level of violence and physicality brought to the rock realm. Alienated kids created a crude sound based on fast tempos and a disdain for all things pop. It was more than rowdy skinheads; it was an urban art form. Most everything in today's heavy music can be traced back to the misfits and runaways of the Lower East Side of the late twentieth century.

DON FURY (producer): New York Hardcore, it's almost mythic. It's like the Greek legends. People view New York as a mythic town. Where could this music be done better than in New York? We are a hard-ass town. That's never gonna change. (1998)

ROGER MIRET (Agnostic Front): Hardcore was a big turn in my life and will always be important to me. It made me more politically aware and more street-smart. I feel like I could do anything, I've been through everything. It made me a stronger man. (1996)

WALTER SCHREIFELS (Gorilla Biscuits/Quicksand): Hardcore taught me to make music how I've always wanted to do it. It definitely shaped the way I see music and the way I feel about it. The thing about hardcore is people are able to express themselves and bring it directly to the kids. And I like that, that's what I always wanted to do. (2008)

DANNY SAGE (Heart Attack): You felt part of something happening at the moment. The '50s was your parents' music. In '77 punk, there was a snubbing attitude. Here, we were making history. We knew we were making original music. I remember getting into shit with these older guys, those *New York Rocker* snobs. We were so proud to be this different animal that nobody ever saw before. At the Mudd Club, they wouldn't even let us into shows. The Ritz would rope off an area for hardcore, and treat you weird. (1996)

RICHARD KERN (filmmaker): I always felt Blondie was a girl band from the '50s and the Ramones were like doo-wop. I was into it, but for that reason I felt it was something being redone. Hardcore to me was what the Ramones were supposed to be. (2004)

DAVE INSURGENT (Reagan Youth): I found myself through New York Hardcore. It's something I'll always be proud of, no matter how long I live or die. (1988)

You and your crew would've never made it through
The days we hung out in 1982
—Judge, "New York Crew"

New York Hardcore was a product of its environment. The early-'80s East Village was a perilous, drugged-out slum—no police, no taxis, and no good reason to be there.

TODD YOUTH (Agnostic Front/Murphy's Law): Before the gentrification and drug crackdown, the East Village was a scary, crazy fucking place, a total no-man's-land. I'd walk around with a two-by-four. You'd see death all the time: murders, ODs everywhere. You couldn't walk two steps without hearing, "coke, dope" and "works, works." (2004)

HARLEY FLANAGAN (Cro-Mags): New York didn't have a benefit of picket fences and families that'd spot them money to record demos. A lot of bands formed from people with no money living in an apartment with twenty people and barely paying the rent. (1996)

JOHN JOSEPH (Cro-Mags): I didn't choose to live in squats; the way I was living down here, that's the way it was. I didn't have anything else; there were no other choices. There was no other way this whole thing could have happened. (1996)

NYHC took some time to define its style. It was never a pose. The scene's ferocity and intense lifestyle ensured its survival. Today, hardcore punk rock evokes images of the tattooed hooligans of Cro-Mags, Murphy's Law, and Agnostic Front.

PETE KOLLER (Sick of It All): People thought New York Hardcore was all gangs and tough guys. When we first got into the scene, it was the most unified scene ever. Every band sang, "We need unity." Then after all the nasty shit that went on afterward, you realize that we actually had unity. (1994)

PAUL BEARER (Sheer Terror): The misconception is everybody got along. You knew who your friends were, and that was it. Hardcore always had that "we're in this together, and we're gonna fight" shit. We were just as ignorant back then, just to different people. If a bunch of longhairs came around, that's the first people you'd fucking grab when you dove offstage: go right for the hair, boom, take 'em down to the floor. (1995)

DREW STONE (Antidote): Drugs proliferated in the New York scene. I have vivid memories of kids huffing glue and then going fag-bashing. I'm not mentioning any names but I had vivid memories of main guys with a bag over their mouth huffing glue and then with that fuckin' million-mile stare, going out to beat and rob people. Drugs were a big part of it. (2008)

New York thrash: The Stimulators button, 1979. Design by Nick Marden. Collection of the author.

You don't wanna support the scene
Why don't you get the fuck away from me
—Agnostic Front, "United Blood"

NYHC began with the Stimulators playing a rowdy '77 punk not yet HC. When the Bad Brains moved to New York, at first living with the Stimulators on East 12th Street, the scene began in earnest. BBs set a standard that everyone strived to attain.

JESSE MALIN (Heart Attack): The Stimulators brought together a lot of the kids like the Beasties, Jimmy Gestapo, Danny and me, and the Luscious Jackson girls. There was like seventy-five, a hundred people who'd always go see the Stimulators. I don't think the band was that good, but it was an event to be at. There was a lot of shit brewing. (1997)

SEAN TAGGART (artist): I grew up in SoHo; I was a SoHo brat. I'd skate with Adam Yauch of the Beastie Boys, back then he had long hair. The seeds were *Skateboarder Magazine* and the Sex Pistols. I started going to clubs late '79, early '80, like Max's Kansas City and CBGB and TR3. It was around that time I was going to Stimulators gigs at Max's. There was this great band from D.C. called the Bad Brains. I saw them open for the Stimulators, and that was amazing. It was the purest hardcore I'd ever heard. (1997)

H.R. (Bad Brains): The music that we play is very, very hard. People slam, people jump and scrape, they hurt, they punch, they scream and they bite. They act barbaric. And even myself, a man who came out of a civilized family, has become uncivilized. (1989)

Embryonic NYHC bands like Undead, Beastie Boys, and Even Worse were music nerds lacking that ass-kick that came with blue-collar Queens bands such as Kraut, Reagan Youth, Murphy's Law, and Urban Waste.

ADAM YAUCH (Beastie Boys): I wanted to start a hardcore band. Hardcore hadn't really come to New York yet. Reagan Youth gigged but they were more a punk band. We knew there was hardcore in D.C. and we thought, "Let's start a New York hardcore band." So we started writing faster punk songs. It was kind of a goof but then we talked Mike into singing and Kate played drums. We played a gig on my seventeenth birthday. (1998)

JACK RABID (Even Worse): There was an urban mentality, and most of the bands—Nihilistics, Heart Attack, and Undead—were from New York City. Reagan Youth was from Rego Park, Kraut from Astoria. It was a bunch of poor Queens kids. Obviously the Beastie Boys came from money. It's so funny to always see them portrayed as these street punks. But I feel we were a lot more authentic, in terms of urban and suburban. There was no violence at New York Hardcore gigs, until around '83. (1996)

BILLY PHILIPS (Urban Waste/Major Conflict): When the boys from Queens went out to a show we filled a whole train car or two! In my eyes, Astoria was responsible for keeping hardcore going. Back in the days it was falling apart. (2006)

NYHC began as a teen rebellion of limited means. New York boasted the world's finest recording studios, but none recorded hardcore. NYHC may've been the most primitive, lo-tech rock scene ever. But what these bands lacked in production, they more than made up for with passion.

JASON O'TOOLE (Life's Blood): I never thought about an LP record. Just putting out a demo made you feel like a rock star and the seven-inch record was king. (2009)

TOMMY RAT (Warzone/The Psychos): The music was strictly underground. There was no airplay. No major labels. It was a word-of-mouth thing. Not many people knew about it. You had to know somebody. You could say it was a family atmosphere. (2008)

JOHNNY WASTE (Urban Waste): Today NYHC is a legacy. But if I look back to when it was all happening, we needed more support. I remember how hard it was, we'd go around putting up flyers even in areas we knew no one would be interested in coming to see us. But all NYHC kids were hardworking in trying to spread the word. (2006)

> *Ain't really got nothing to say*
> *It all comes across in a negative way*
> —CRO-MAGS, "DO UNTO OTHERS"

Cro-Mags, Murphy's Law, Agnostic Front, and Warzone faced crushing survival issues—dispossessed teens living in LES squats without plumbing or running water. Avenue A became the NYHC 'hood; the pitbull the NYHC dog; and angel dust the NYHC drug.

ROGER MIRET: Angel dust was the drug. And glue. We were on drugs every day. You had to be. I remember on acid watching someone's head explode. That big roller thing went down the street; somebody jumped in front and their head popped like a pimple. We were street kids, anti–straight edge. Kids from D.C. and Boston didn't understand because they lived in suburbia with their mother and father. You can't come home bombed all the time when you're livin' at home. We were livin' in the street and were totally whacked. You hafta be drugged to be livin' in the streets. (1996)

The NYHC logo, tagged on bathroom stalls and blank walls, read like gang graffiti. Cro-Mags, spearheaded by Harley Flanagan and John Joseph (a.k.a. Bloodclot), foretold hardcore's future as a brutal antifashion. Crazy action went down within a tough-guy milieu. NYHC bands had a street-rat mentality that did not serve them well in the music biz. It was the most visceral music scene ever, which is why it still resonates so strongly.

RAYBEEZ (Warzone): Harley grew up down here, and he pretty much ruled the area as far as hardcore went. People don't realize that Harley made it a lot easier for kids today to be around here. Without Harley it wouldn't be the way it is today because he kept shit together with the scene back then. (1997)

HARLEY FLANAGAN: There was a lot of ill shit. There'd be bands that'd piss off me and my friends, so we'd kick the shit out of them on- stage. There's this band—I don't even want to say their name—but we beat the shit out of them. I did that more than a few times. I'm not gonna pretend I was a nice guy. I'd go to shows and if the band pissed me off, me and my friends would ruin their gig. (1996)

RAYBEEZ: Anybody who came to a show with a camera got fucked up. If we didn't know you and you started taking pictures—the camera, the shoes, the wallet, everything got taken. No cameras were allowed in the club unless you were down with us. Forget about a video camera, not even a still camera. (1996)

DONNA DAMAGE (No Thanks): We opened for the Bad Brains at CBGB in 1983. CBS News showed up to get some punk rock footage. My band was onstage when they came in, and we refused to let them film us. Jaime kicked the cameras. There was a lot of spitting at the news crew. (2007)

RAYBEEZ: Today when people go fag-bashing they may hit 'em for like a minute or two and take their money and run. Back then it was like get a pipe and a bat and really destroy the faggot. Not that I had any part of it. . . . (1987)

In reaction to skinheads came "peace punks"—street-crud dreadlocked or Mohican types into UK "anarcho" bands like Crass and old Discharge. Notable LES peace punk bands included Reagan Youth, A.P.P.L.E., and Nausea.

SEAN YSEULT (White Zombie): There were all these factions of hardcore, from skinheads to straight edge. Peace punks in New York were slightly political but all about dreadlocks and crazy-color hair—a fashion thing—and a little more laid back than some others in the scene. People into Reagan Youth and Crass. I knew all these people from hanging out on a St. Marks stoop with a brown paper bag and a forty-ouncer. (2011)

ALLEGRA ROSE (New York scene): We loved bands like Heart Attack and Nausea. I had a band called Direct Action. We were very political and always going to rallies. The government and Central America and nuclear power freaked us out in the '80s. We thought the Cold War would become a hot war. We didn't believe in landlords or real estate, and if there was an empty building, we should be able to take it over. (2006)

GEORGE TABB (journalist/musician): The peace punks represented squatters. They were dirty and smelly like hippies in ugly dreadlocks and black leather jackets. They looked like homeless people who were not taking showers. (2004)

If the world was flat I'd grind the edge
To the positive youth my heart I pledge
—Youth of Today, "Youth Crew"

NYHC posed spiritual questions, as seen in the mystical quests of Bad Brains and Cro-Mags; street toughs enlivened by Rastafarianism and Hare Krishna. Youth of Today, a Minor Threat–style, straight-edge "youth crew," took to the next level the "Krishna-core" created by Harley and John Joseph.

DJINJI E. BROWN (Absolution): Hardcore and punk rock had such an anti-government and even atheist attitudes. I was always spiritual and not deceived by the material. When I saw H.R. and what Bad Brains brought to the table, and then Bloodclot and Harley, and their emphasis on the spirit soul and bhakti yoga, I was pulled towards that energy. Those people became "spiritual masters from the street." (2008)

VIC DiCARA (108): I came into contact with subversive spirituality the first time I listened to "I Against I" by the Bad Brains. Next I became a fan of the Cro-Mags. The majority of my friends in the New York Hardcore scene at the time were connected to Krishna or Rasta or occultism in some way. Spirituality was a major ingredient in the NYHC that I grew up in, at least in my perception of it. (2007)

JIMMY YU (Judge): The first New York skinheads were street kids. No parents, no family. There were two things in their lives: Hardcore and Krishna. Krishna provided all of us free food. If you were living on the street, that's where you'd go. And New York Krishnas were all different, with tattoos all over because they were former skinheads or whatever. So Krishna, even if you didn't follow it, was a part of that early scene. (2008)

Back with a bong: Murphy's Law, outside CBGB, 1989. Photo by Frank White.

THE SCENE

It's the truth
We're doomed youth
—KRAUT, "DOOMED YOUTH"

A7 (112 Avenue A), across from the crime hub of Tompkins Square Park, served as the home of early NYHC. It was an illegal club hosting punk subculture bands. There was no real stage but a half dozen or so bands played a night, usually for $3. If fifty people came, the place was packed. Some gigs drew 250 kids. For an HC band, playing A7 in 1981 was like Madison Square Garden. On a good night, Raybeez was doorman; Jimmy Gestapo deejayed, and Doug Holland bartended. Gigs began at midnight, so most ended past daylight.

DREW STONE (Antidote): The first time the High and the Mighty played A7, we came from the Bronx. We were parked in front of A7 and all huddled in the van and this punk girl was crossing the street and a cab hit her. She had a quart of beer and she went flying over the hood, beer hit the ground, bam, and she got up and staggered away. We were shook up and didn't leave the van because where the fuck were you gonna go? (2008)

HOLLY RAMOS (New York scene): The girls' bathroom was up a step and there was no lock on the door, so you were directly across from the entrance of the club, so if anyone walked in when the door was open, you were in the bathroom at eye level for everyone to see. I remember one night going to see the Undead, and Natz was so fucked up that I got a black eye from his bass hitting me. (1996)

JIMMY GESTAPO (Murphy's Law): I'd take an A7 pit and drop it in the middle of a Roseland show and all those kids would be crying and bleeding. (1996)

171A (171 Avenue A), a rehearsal studio with a PA, fostered the East Village scene, from Richard Hell and Konk to the new HC bands. NYHC began with the rowdy kids who hung at the former glass shop. Jerry Williams opened in late 1980 and was in full swing by 1981. Five dollars an hour to record to a live mix by JW was a steal. It's where Bad Brains and Beasties recorded, and where Henry Rollins auditioned for Black Flag.

> **RAYBEEZ (Warzone):** 171A was our meeting point. That was our place, and the people that ran it were totally into what we were doing. When that was a studio, it was cool. It's where I met Dave Insurgent from Reagan Youth. He knew what was going on—he was a true punk. Back then it was so true, so street. (1996)

> **POPA CHUBBY (musician):** 171A was a squat with a stage, a whole other reality. Jerry Williams lived in the control booth. Dave Parsons lived under the stage. Dave Id brought the Bad Brains, and nobody saw that coming. 171A became important because it wasn't contrived or created—it was a natural phenomenon. I spent 24/7 with Jerry at 171A. In his inner circle you hung out all day listening to music and smoking weed. In many ways it was the best days of my life. He got me off heroin, and taught me everything about music. He never turned his back; he always had a joint and a kind word. I owe him so much. (2011)

Rat Cage Records began when Jerry Williams's pal Dave Parsons stopped selling punk records from a shopping cart and ran his Rat Cage shop from 171A's cellar (with no cash register). Teen punks hung out and got high; Nick Marden sold badges. Parsons's label's releases included the debuts by the Beasties (1982's *Polly Wog Stew* and 1983's *Cookie Puss*) and Agnostic Front (1983's *United Blood*). Dave moved to Zurich to be a Charlie Chaplin impersonator, where he lived as Donna Lee Parsons until colon cancer at fifty-eight.

> **NICK MARDEN (The Stimulators):** When Rat Cage Records opened in 171A, it was not quite the Brill Building but close. Bad Brains set up onstage, and we set up on the floor, and we both recorded at the same time. D.O.A. played and recorded there. I've been blessed with an accidental time and place. (2011)

> **ADAM YAUCH (Beastie Boys):** Dave Parsons sold punk vinyl on the street on Astor Place. Then he set up in the basement at 171. I guess

they let him stay for free. He'd open up the metal doors on the street and you'd walk down a ladder, and him and Cathy sold a few records there. Bad Brains lived upstairs and recorded there all the time. They inspired us so much. Everyone else was fucking around; it was cool to suck at your instruments. Bad Brains were so tight and powerful, some whole other shit. (1996)

Cro-Mags, Warzone, Murphy's Law,
Agnostic Front, Sick of It All
CBGBs where it all began
—AGNOSTIC FRONT, "TAKE ME BACK"

CBGB Matinees, all-ages Sunday shows, became the scene's focal point. From 1982 to 1989, and during the '90s, misfits of all substratas—punks, skinheads, straight-edgers, druggies, music geeks, and freaks—partook in this weekly subculture. If you ever went to one of those gigs, you'd never forget the "dancing"—the hardest "skanking" ever by kids like Harley Flanagan, Jimmy Gestapo, Vinnie Stigma, Keith CFA, Kevin Crowley, and Kenny Ahrens, stage-diving or in a "wall of death" blasting crowds with locked arms.

CHAKA MALIK (Burn/Orange 9mm): I look back to those days of Burn, Sick of It All, Killing Time, Krakdown and Gorilla Biscuits. You'd go every Sunday because there'd be at least one great band. For the scene to get back to that, it would have to undergo a heart transplant. (1998)

FRANK MARINO (Step2Far): CBs was a focal point. I'd know something was going on at CBs and just show up. There was no Internet to browse to see what's going on at CBs online. You just fuckin' showed up to the matinee. (2011)

ABC No Rio (156 Rivington Street), a Lower East Side cellar/storefront named for a broken sign across the street, was a seminal gallery, venue, and squat. When CBs ceased Sunday matinees on November 6, 1989, ABC's first Saturday matinee was November 9, run by *Bullshit Monthly* editor Mike Bullshit (Bromberg). "BSM Presents" upheld an ethic: three to four bands for $3 to $5, thirty to fifty paid, no violent, racist or antigay bands, and only one bouncer

(Gavin Van Vlack of Burn/Absolution). Burn, Rorschach, Bad Trip, Citizen's Arrest, Born Against, Yuppicide, Krakdown, and GO! were the key bands to that 1990s-era scene.

> **MIKE BULLSHIT (SFA/GO!):** I'm trying to put out bands that are not racist. That are not Brooklyn this or Jackson Heights that. Not "Fuck the immigrants" or "Fag bash this" or "Bitch, whore, slut." Bands that take a little more time to write their lyrics, take a little more time to think about what they're saying. . . . (1990)

Rock Hotel (113 Jane Street) staged the first major NYHC shows. Rock Hotel events with Bad Brains, Cro-Mags, Murphy's Law, and Agnostic Front elevated the scene. Chris Williamson, a Doug Henning–style former Juilliard pianist and dance troupe tour manager who hung at Max's, managed Studio 54, and lived at the 79th Street Boat Basin, organized it all. It began at 113 Jane Street, before relocating to the Ritz. Rock Hotel Records issued classics by Cro-Mags, Murphy's Law, and Leeway, who all say that they never got paid.

> **DREW STONE:** Rock Hotel was on the West Side of Manhattan in a small ballroom of a run-down sleazy hotel, run by Chris Williamson. He had a background in Lincoln Center ballet, and somehow got involved doing these shows. Rock Hotel was a great time for New York Hardcore. Before that, there were CBs and A7 and a few other crapholes. Rock Hotel was where big out-of-town bands played. It was a major gig. Most of the shows were friggin' packed. (2008)

R.A.P.P. Arts Center (220 East 4th Street), an acronym for Redeemer Arts Performance Project, in the Most Holy Redeemer School, dedicated itself to painting, theater, and dance. It attained infamy as a home to NYHC, like the *Squat or Rot* zine show with the likes of Underdog, Absolution, Krakdown, and Radicts. New York's Catholic Archdiocese hated it all and pulled the plug. **2+2**, at the corner of 2nd and Second, hosted early-'80s gigs. So did the **S.I.N. Club** (Safety in Numbers Club) that, when on Avenue B, gave out flyers asking patrons to come via Houston Street to avoid the heroin dealers. Beasties and Reagan Youth opened for Dead Kennedys at **Reggae Lounge** on July 6, 1983. By **Great Gildersleeves'** 1983–84 demise, the club hosted gigs booked by Alexander Hammer, like Black Flag, Minor Threat, Circle Jerks, Suicidal, D.O.A., Reagan Youth/Beastie Boys, and TSOL/SSD. The scene spread past Manhattan, like 1982's DKs fiasco at Staten Island's **Paramount Theater**

or Circle Jerks/Necros at **My Father's Place** in Roslyn, LI. In 1983–84, **The Subway,** a closed Queens subway station, booked the likes of Reagan Youth. **The Left Bank** in New Rochelle hosted Black Flack or Angelic Upstarts, and **February's** in Elmont, LI, did Sunday matinees with bands like Major Conflict and SFA.

The Big Takeover, published by Even Worse drummer Jack Rabid, led a wave of early NYHC fanzines with Misguided drummer Lyle Hysen's *Damaged Goods,* Savage Circle singer Javi Savage's **Big City,** and Wendy Eager's *Guillotine.* Then came *Schism* by Alex Brown (Gorilla Biscuits) and Porcell (Youth of Today) or *Plain Truth* by Jason O'Toole (Life's Blood) and Sam McPheeters (Born Against). Notable '90s zines included **Teach Me Violence, Village Noize, Bad Newz, Boiling Point, Just Lies,** and **Right Trash.**

One-man labels drove NYHC. Not just Rat Cage and ROIR but Jack Flanagan's **Mob Style** (The Mob, Urban Waste), Javi Savage's **Big City** (*Big City* comps), and Bob Sallese's **S.I.N.** (*NYC Rotten to the Core*). **Revelation** began with debuts by Warzone and Sick of It All and 1988's *New York Hardcore: The Way It Is* comp. Bill Wilson's **Blackout!** (Sheer Terror, Killing Time) began with 1989's *Where the Wild Things Are.* **SFT** (Striving for Togetherness) (V.O.D., 25 Ta Life) got hot, as did Fred Feldman's **Another Planet,** behind Steve Poss and Jimmy Gestapo's 1997 *Creepy Crawl Live.*

Park Inn, by A7 and 171A, strongly tied to NYHC as a tavern for the underage scene. We're describing a New York where bars served almost anyone who'd come through the door. The seedy bar offered cheap booze and a jukebox with great soul and R&B, and Bad Brains' "Pay to Cum." Bouncer "Ike the Dyke" ignored lots of illicit activity.

HARLEY FLANAGAN (Cro-Mags): It wasn't a club but was connected to the scene—a spot for the beer drinkers where we got stupid drunk. You'd be drinking and some shit would go down and in half a second, the entire place turned upside down. Everybody in the bar pounded whoever started shit to a pulp. (1996)

Dancing in the front lines: The Stimulators, Max's Kansas City, 1981. Courtesy of Denise Mercedes and Nick Marden.

THE MUSIC

1980–1986

I hate music
You hate music
—The Mad, "I Hate Music"

The Mad, the band of special-effects artist Screaming Mad George, awed punks with faux ritual sacrifice and a blood-spewing prosthetic penis. Members included fleeting Cramps member Julien "Griensnatch" Hechtlinger and future blues star Popa Chubby. Hisashi Ikeda died jumping out a window; he replaced original bassist Rick, who stabbed himself onstage! The Mad was best known for "I Hate Music" on *New York Thrash* (ROIR). **Th' Influence**, black punks from Queens, cut a fourteen-song demo at 171A with Jerry Williams, where they befriended the Bad Brains. Bassist-singer Donell Gibson drew the BBs' "Rasta lion" logo. Two of their 171A tunes were intended for the unissued BBs' *Hardcore 1982* comp. **Cracked Actor** predated NYHC but played in an HC style. The Stony Brook quartet, named for a David Bowie song, made 1981's antifascist "Nazi School." Jeff Bale bellowed in *Maximum RockNRoll* (#2, 1982): "You'll flunk unless you give it a listen."

The Stimulators portended New York Hardcore. In 1980, maybe thirty kids attended any of their shows at Max's or TR3 but those kids launched the scene. Punk guitarist Denise Mercedes teamed with poet Patrick Mack, and then she hired her eleven-year-old drumming nephew Harley Flanagan. Nick Marden, Avenue C–bred nephew of Joan Baez and Mimi Fariña, soon joined. Nineteen eighty's "Loud Fast Rules" 45 and 1981's "M.A.C.H.I.N.E." 7" EP preceded 1982's *Loud Fast Rules* (ROIR) tape. **Bad Brains** came from D.C., and a scene rose around them. The band crossed racial boundaries, merging HC and reggae, offering punk rock as sacred music. Their 1980 "Pay to Cum" single cut in the MONY building with Jimmi Quidd defined future HC. The BBs stayed with the Stimulators, who introduced them to 171A's Jerry Williams, producer of 1982's *Bad Brains* (ROIR). *I Against I* (SST) with disco producer Ron St. Germain fueled major label interest in 1986, until singer H.R.'s erratic behavior scared off offers.

Kraut, NYC's first big HC band, began in Astoria, Queens, with singer Davy Gunner and guitarist Doug Holland. They debuted opening for the Clash at Bond's on June 11, 1981. Their first singles, 1981's "Kill for Cash" and 1982's "Unemployed" 7"s set in motion 1983's *An Adjustment to Society* and 1984's *Whetting the Scythe* LPs. Their end came after Holland joined Cro-Mags, and his replacement Chris Smith (Battalion of Saints) OD'd and/or drowned in his tub. **False Prophets**, fronted by Stephan Ielpi, tied to the radical squatter scene. The cult popularity of 1981's "Blind Obedience" and 1982's "Good Clean Fun" 45s got them on *New York Thrash*. Fans included Jello Biafra, behind 1986's *False Prophets* and 1987's *Implosion*.

The Undead arose after Bobby Steele (Robert Kaufold) departed the Misfits. The first lineup with Jack Natz and Patrick Blanck debuted on January 30, 1981, at A7. The next year's *Nine Toes Later* denoted the removal of Steele's infected toe. He spent the '80s high on 'ludes, once so zonked, he puked on John Lennon; another time he forgot he booked a tour. It all ended after '84's *Act Your Rage* with Steve Zing and Brian Payne. **The Misguided** made 1982's *Bringing It Down* three-song 7" and 1983's four-song *Options*. Lyle Hysen, the *Damaged Goods* zine publisher and NYU kid who brought Rick Rubin into the scene, also did Damaged Goods Records, behind the very first NYHC record, Heart Attack's *God Is Dead* EP.

Heart Attack began after singer Jesse Malin's junior high school band Rocker played his Whitestone, Queens, talent show. First came the three hundred copies of Heart Attack's 1981's *God Is Dead* 7″ EP, 1982's songs on *New York Thrash*, 1983's *Keep Your Distance*, and 1984's *Subliminal Seduction.*

The Mob started as a Jackson Heights, Queens, high school Van Halen cover band. Ralph Gebbia, Jack Flanagan, Jose Gonzales, and Jamie Shanahan debuted on June 5, 1981, at BC Club opening for the Bad Brains. Jack started Mob Style Records, for the Mob's 1982's *Upset the System* and 1983's *Step Forward.* But 1986's *We Come to Crush* allegedly crossed a metal edge.

The Nihilistics came from the boredom of the LI burbs, making their FTW vibe even more intense. Ron Rancid (Valachi), a Nassau Community College dropout and Massapequa Hospital morgue attendant, assaulted fans ("Kill Yourself," "Misanthrope"). Wayne Robins wrote in *Newsday* (3/11/84): "This South Shore band is the best thing to happen to the fringe punk genre known as hardcore since Jello Biafra's Dead Kennedys." **Even Worse** began with Dave Stein and Paul "Jack Rabid" Corradi doing punk covers in Summit, NJ. Frontman John Pouradis bailed on a Tompkins Square Park show, so they found original Beastie John Berry (in both bands for a sec). Rebecca Korbet sang their songs on *New York Thrash*. Rabid's own band fired him in March '82, so he retorted with even worse musicians: guitarist Thurston Moore, bassist Tim Sommer, and singer Ken Tempkin on 1982's "Mouse or Rat" / "1984" and 1983's "Leaving" / "One Night Stand."

Beastie Boys evolved from an ordinary NYHC band to iconic rappers. Adam "MCA" Yauch, Michael "Mike D" Diamond, and Adam "Ad Rock" Horovitz began in the punk "bands" Young Aborigines and the Young and the Useless. Dave Parsons at Rat Cage dug their first show, releasing 1982's *Pollywog Stew* 7″ EP and 1983's prankster *Cookie Puss* 12″ (in between came their tracks on *New York Thrash*). The band met NYU student Rick Rubin; two of the first Def Jam 12″'s were 1985's "Rock Hard" and Adam Yauch's "MCA and Burzootie." The 1985 12″ "She's on It" (Columbia) predated 1986's *Licensed to Ill*. They moved to L.A. to do 1989's *Paul's Boutique* and returned home to renewed fame in 1991. **Reagan Youth** (a riff on Hitler Youth) never recorded in their prime, for financial and drug reasons. Dave Insurgent (Rubinstein) and guitarist Paul Cripple (Bakija) began at Forest Hills High. Years later, in 1991, heroin dealers beat Dave into a coma. In 1993, cops found his hooker girlfriend Tiffany Bresciani's body in the back of serial killer Joel Rifkin's pickup. Then his father accidentally ran over his mother in the driveway. Strung out and down, Dave killed himself on July 3, 1993. ("Degenerated," done by D Generation, was featured in the film *Airheads*.)

Ism starred Josef "Jism" Ismach, a Juilliard-trained pianist from Bayside—Ism was the first letters of "Ismach." His 1981 "Queen J.A.P." became a hit on *Dr. Demento* until it offended too many Jewish listeners. LI's new-wave station WLIR played their covers of Partridge Family's "I Think I Love You" and the 1972 campaign song "Nixon Now More than Ever." **Adrenalin O.D.** embodied "funny" HC. The Jersey crew of Paul Richard and Jack Steeples found fans in the city: on *New York Thrash* and WNYU's *Noise the Show*, and at wild gigs at A7 and CBGB. Buy Our Records' first releases were '83's *Let's Barbecue with Adrenalin O.D.* ("Trans Am") and '84's *The Wacky Hijinks of Adrenalin O.D.* They threw in the towel after they began to attract the same Jersey metalheads they derided.

Urban Waste and **Major Conflict** were basically the same band. Queens guitarist Johnny Kelly and drummer John Dancy started Urban Waste as thirteen-year-olds with singer Billy Philips. They debuted at Billy's parents' house in the Ravenswood Projects, where dusted-out locals took it in. For 1983's epic *Urban Waste* EP (Mob Style), Kenny Ahrens sang and the late Andy Apathy bassed. By their final show, with Minor Threat at CBGB, they still traveled by subway; gear crammed into shopping carts and paper bags. The 1983 *Major Conflict* EP starred Philips, Kelly, Dancy, and Orlandito "Dito" Montiel.

Savage Circle starred Bronx punk Javi Savage (John Souvadji) of *Big City* fanzine and Big City Records. Javi drew the artwork for 1982's *Kill Yourself* 7″ EP (backed by metal stars Anthony and Carlo Fragnito of Blacklace). They had two songs on 1983's *Big City Ain't So Pretty* comp, and Javi did one as Javi & the Bastards on 1985's *Big City One Big Crowd*. As per *Guillotine* (#6): "Sounds like Donald Duck if the song was long enough to detect it." Javi hailed Staten Island's **Bitter Uproar** "New York's Negative Approach." The 1983 LP *Live at CBGB's* (Big City) came off a board tape of their first show that February 26. Singing for the Psychos came next for frontman Big Rob, who'd quit the scene and get a job.

Ultra Violence, part of the Apartment X squat scene of Warzone and Agnostic Front, did a nine-song cassette with songs that appeared on six compilations (including all four *Big City* comps). Singer Tony T-Shirt (Anthony Meyers) screen-printed the first NYHC T-shirts. Bassist Keith "Zippy McPhee" McAdam went to Sheer Terror, Crawlpappy, and Trip 6. Charlie Rage's drumming résumé included Warzone, Reagan Youth, the Abused, the Psychos, and Trip 6. **The Psychos** were like a proving ground for NYHC frontmen, going through Roger Miret, Billy Milano, Carl Griffin, Tony T-Shirt, and Tommy "Rat Poison" DeRosa. Miret wrote "Fight" and "Discriminate Me" for them, but then he put those songs on AF's *United Blood*. Big Rob (Bitter Uproar) reverberated on 1984's *One Voice* demo but they only put out '85's "Before" on *Big City One Big Crowd*.

Crucial Truth, intense LES skinheads, began in Pompano Beach, FL. Alex "Garry Shaft" Mitchell, Mario Sorrentino, Derek Graham, and Mike Marer opened for the Bad Brains at CBGB and headlined Peppermint Lounge. Fellow Floridian Dave Parsons put out 1982's *Darkened Days*, as per MRR (#2, 1982): "'Male Domination' is a particularly outstanding cut, with its adrenaline kick and anti-chauvinist lyrics." **Counterforce**, a crude LES squatter group, involved Rob Kabula (pre–Cause for Alarm) on drums and Frenchy on bass. They began with two female singers, but both quit. Counterforce battled through a dozen or so gigs at CBs and A7, spewing raw NYHC like "Middle Age Delinquency" and "White Color Crime" (seen in Lyn Tiefenbacher's 1983 short film *Hardcore Punk*).

Borscht from Rockland County blared a gnarly early NYHC. The quartet named for beet soup with vocalist-guitarist Steve Veraja, bassist Adam Nodelman, guitarist Mike Oswald, and drummer Phil Franklin, got hot at CBGB and A7, and the Office in Nyack, particularly after 1982's *Primitive Borscht* cassette, and comp slots such as *Flipside Vinyl Fanzine* and *Thrasher Skate Rock Vol. 2*. **Armed Citizens**, Chris Colon's Queens quartet, rocked a heavy NYHC that predated the metal crossover. They cut forty-seven songs in their brief time, but only released 1983's *Make Sense* eight-song 7″ with Sean Taggart artwork, and songs on three *Big City* comps recorded at Tito Puente's PRI Studios.

Anger, frustration, locked in a cage
Gotta bust loose, I'm on a rage
—Murphy's Law, "Rage"

Murphy's Law, led by Jimmy Gestapo (Drescher) of Astoria—"the David Lee Roth of Hardcore"—remain NYHC's most enduring band, with a beer-'n'-weed-soaked, ska-tinged party vibe. They debuted at Giorgio Gomelsky's "Green Door" loft on New Year's Eve 1983 with MDC and Reagan Youth. Their 1984 Jerry Williams–produced *Bong Blast* tape brought on big gigs at CBGB, and an ill-fated deal with Rock Hotel Records. Their havoc-wreaking on the Beasties' breakthrough *Licensed to Ill* tour (exhibiting the first-ever arena stage-diving), resulted in 1986's Robert Musso–produced *Murphy's Law*, with their classic lineup of Alex "Uncle Al" Morris, Pete Martinez, and Petey Hines. Jimmy, guitarist Todd Youth, bassist Doug E. Beans, and drummer Chuck Valle (RIP) then partied/toured with the Chili Peppers, sparking 1989's self-produced *Back with a Bong!*

Don't tread on me: Harley Flanagan,
Cro-Mags, 1988. Photo by Frank
White.

Cro-Mags defined the look and feel of NYHC. Driven by the intensity of emerging HC and the skinheads he met on a Stimulators' '79 UK tour, Harley Flanagan started his own preteen hate gang. He played bass, but was so poor that he played with a chain for a strap and a bread clasp as a pick. Things came together with his literal partner in crime, frontman John Joseph (McGeown), a Navy deserter and Krishna devotee. In 1984 they joined hot metal guitarist Parris Mitchell Mayhew and Frontline drummer Mackie Jayson, followed by Kraut guitarist Doug Holland. The five-piece ruled the NYHC scene around the time of their 1986 opus *Age of Quarrel* (Rock Hotel). The first big punk/metal act toured with Motörhead and Metallica, but management allegedly never paid them. Said issues killed spirits and resulted in feuds and LPs without key members: 1989's *Best Wishes*, 1992's *Alpha Omega*, and 2000's *Revenge*. Expect no true reunion soon.

Agnostic Front began with Vinnie Stigma (Capuccio) from Little Italy, who fell in with the early punk scene and befriended Sid and Nancy. In 1980–81, he formed a band, the Eliminators (the roots of AF's "The Eliminator"), and published a fanzine called *Agnostic Front*. The band Agnostic Front (first called the Zoo Crew) began at the Norfolk Street squat Apartment X. Drummers included Raybeez (Warzone) and Robbie Cryptcrash (Cause for Alarm). Early AF singers included John Watson, James Kontra, and Keith Burkhardt until they struck gold with Union City, NJ, Cuban émigré Roger Miret. Their 1983 Don Fury–produced debut *United Blood* 7″ EP (Rat Cage) defined American skinhead glory.

Warzone began with Ray "Raybeez" Barbieri, who served on the USS *Yellowstone* with John Joseph. Back in NYC, Ray lived in Apartment X with an embryonic Agnostic Front. He drummed on AF's *United Blood,* but then fronted his own band (first called Rat Poison). Warzone began with 1986's *Lower East Side Crew* (Revelation), 1987's *Don't Forget the Struggle, Don't Forget the Streets* (Fist), and 1988's *Open Your Eyes* (coproduced by Dr. Know and Jerry Williams). Ray worked as a bouncer at Downtown clubs and the big NYHC gigs. In Warzone, he'd often sing in the crowd to break up fights before things got outta hand. The beloved Raybeez died on September 11, 1997, of pneumonia or AIDS.

Every person has a choice
You make yours and I'll make mine
—VIRUS, "PIECE OF MIND"

Virus infected with a slow, angry sludge from the stoops of St. Marks Place. Undead rhythm section bassist Jack Natz and drummer Patrick Blanck teamed with Soviet-bred skinhead singer James Kontra; No Thanks guitarist Jimi Human replaced Bad Brains producer Jerry Williams. Virus toured after 1984's *Dark Ages* (Rat Cage) but disbanded en route home. **Bloodclot!**—for a Rasta epithet the Bad Brains yelled—involved BBs roadies: future Cro-Mags singer John Joseph, Jerry Williams, Popa Chubby, and Alvin Robertson (Harley Flanagan once drummed, on acid, at 11/82's Rat Cage benefit). They broke up after recording for that unreleased 1982 BBs-organized compilation. **Cause for Alarm,** a primal LES skinhead crew, began in NJ as Hinckley Fan Club. Jerry Williams produced 1983's *Cause for Alarm* EP. MDC's R Radical label released that and 1984's *Time Will Tell* EP. But singer Keith Burkhardt's overbearing Krishna zeal killed the band.

The **Young and the Useless** played silly HC covers like "Grease" and "Billy, Don't Be a Hero" at Mudd Club, CBGB, and A7. In 1982, Rat Cage released 800 copies of *Real Men Don't Floss,* a six-song 45 cut at 171A. In 1983, guitarist Adam Horovitz left to join the Beasties. Dave Scilken, the band's clued-in singer, died on May 26, 1991: the Beasties dedicated 1992's *Check Your Head* to him. **Frontline** starred bassist Noah Evans (son of jazz star Gil Evans), guitarist Miles Kelly, and drummer Mackie Jayson (pre-Cro-Mags). The teen skaters who grew up in the West Village's Westbeth arts complex excelled live, like on November 22, 1982's Rat Cage benefit with Reagan Youth, the Young and the Useless, and the Beasties (whose "Time for Livin'" sampled the 1982 Frontline demo).

Hose, a noisy band like PiL or Flipper, featured Rick Rubin on guitar. In 1981, Rubin rolled out Hose in 1981 from his Weinstein Hall dorm. They debuted on 1982's *Mobo* EP (the first Def Jam record sold in a brown paper bag). Rik Rosen replaced singer Michael Espindle on 1983's *Hose* 12" with Mondrian art and obliterations of Rick James's "Super Freak," Ohio Players' "Fire," and Black Sabbath's "Sweet Leaf." **Brooklyn** was a project with Beastie Boy Adam Yauch, Bad Brain Darryl Jenifer, Murphy's Law drummer Doug E. Beans, and guitarist Tom Cushman after the Beasties' *Licensed to Ill* and Bad Brains' *I Against I*. Yauch funded a demo given to those in-the-know (25 Maxell XL-90s dubbed) before the Boys began work on *Paul's Boutique*.

The High & the Mighty (for a stoned interpretation of the John Wayne film of the same name) began after Drew Stone returned home from fronting Boston straight-edge pioneers the Mighty CO's. The Bronx five-piece rocked lo-tech from CBGB, 2+2, and A7 to loft parties, as on 1984's *Crunch* eight-song cassette. **Antidote** starred former Misfits drummer Arthur Googy. Jerry Williams produced 1983's eight-song *Thou Shalt Not Kill*, on which Puerto Rican singer Louie Bloodclot's "brotha" John Bloodclot (Cro-Mags) sang on "The Real Deal." The CBs' matinee idols first broke up in May 1984 after a bad show in D.C. with the High and the Mighty. Guitarist Robert "Nunzio" Ortiz then convinced Drew Stone to replace Louie, who sang at some big shows. In 1990, Nunzio shot back metal-style on *Return 2 Burn*.

The Abused delivered brutal straight-edge HC. They met at A7, and made 500 copies of 1983's *Loud and Clear* 7" EP. Guitarist Raf Astor, bassist Dave Colon, and drummer Brian Dundon joined Kevin Crowley, their Netanya, Israel–born skinheaded singer, the creator of the NYHC "cross" logo. Their big sing-along was "Blow Your Own Brains Out." **Krieg Kopf** was a crude Queens quartet fronted by Jason Deranged. "Warhead" appeared on 1985's *Big City One Big Crowd* and they made a seven-song 1986 tape that *MRR* loved. In 1988 they did an LP that never came out. Jason attained infamy for allegedly selling fake LSD, and quit the scene. Perry Pelonero (Clenched Fist) sang until Kopf went kaput.

NY Hoods included guys from Gilligan's Revenge, Breakdown, and Raw Deal. Two crude demos made the rounds, 1986's *Neutral* and 1987's *Built as One*. They played a lot: from CBGB and R.A.P.P. Arts Center to Sundance in Bay Shore, LI, with friends Token Entry. They and Krakdown contributed to a split LP, but nothing ever came of that. **Damage** played brutal no wave–edged NYHC. The five-piece's lineups included vocalist Steve "Boot" Hudacek, bassist Mike Kirkland (pre-Prong), and drummer Patrick Blanck (Virus/Undead). Two lost live-at-CBGB albums shared material: 1984's *Sins of the Father* (Gnarl) and 1987's *Live off the Board* cassette for CBGB/Celluloid.

Physically strong, morally straight, positive youth
We're the youth of today
—YOUTH OF TODAY, "YOUTH OF TODAY"

Youth of Today set the path of the late-'80s scene: straight-edge zealots and all-ages matinee idols into Krishna and veganism. Frontman Ray Cappo (Ray 2 Day), schooled in Mozart and Vivaldi, had drummed in the CT punk bands Reflex from Pain and Violent Children. VC's song "Youth of Today" inspired their band, which aimed to never "go metal" like AF. Eighty-six's *Break Down the Wall* featured a lineup with Richie Birkenhead (Underdog), Craig Setari (Straight Ahead), and Drew Thomas (Bold). YOT broke up in 1987 before *We're Not in This Alone* with Gorilla Biscuits' Walter Schreifels and Sam Siegler, and 1990's *Youth of Today* EP (or "Disengage," for its A-side) done by Ray and Porcell.

Sick of It All remains NYHC's most reliable band. Flushing-bred Koller brothers Lou (vocals) and Pete (guitar) started the group that came to form with bassist Craig Setari (Straight Ahead) and drummer Armand Majidi (Rest in Pieces). A 1986 nine-song demo resulted in 1987's *Sick of It All 7″* EP (Revelation) and vinyl on In Effect: 1989's *Blood Sweat and No Tears*, 1991's *We Stand Alone*, and 1992's *Just Look Around*. Atlantic's 1994's *Scratch the Surface* and 1997's *Built to Last* made them the first NYHC band to hit the Top 100. SOIA roadies included Toby Morse (H_2O), Danny Diablo (Crown of Thornz), and Tim Shaw (Ensign). **Rest in Pieces,** antisocial Queens matinee stars with a logo of a skinhead with a sledgehammer, made 1985's *Rest in Pieces 7″* EP and two LPs: 1987's *My Rage* (1,200 units on One Step Ahead) and '90's *Under My Skin* (Roadracer).

Straight Ahead began with bassist Craig Setari from Bayside. His older brother Scott's friend Dan Lilker (Anthrax) turned on the twelve-year-old to NYHC. A CBs matinee regular by thirteen, Craig joined Straight Ahead, which became **NYC Mayhem**—whose 1985 *We Stand* EP included Straight Ahead drummer Tommy Carrol singing with Rest in Pieces' Rob Echeverria and Armand Majidi. That band was so young they only played locally. "Craig Ahead" joined Youth of Today in '86, and remade Straight Ahead for '87's *Breakaway*.

Token Entry began with High School of Art and Design pupils as Gilligan's Revenge. They started on January 29, 1982, opening for their friend

Johnny Feedback's band Kraut, and then taped a ten-song demo off Davy Gunner's boom box. Anthony Comunale (pre–Raw Deal) replaced singer Eddie Sutton (pre-Leeway); guitarist Andy Gortler departed for the Devil Dogs. As Token Entry (a subway sign) came 1985's *Ready or Not Here We Come* EP and 1987's *From Beneath the Streets* before '88's *Jaybird* and '90's *Weight of the World* for Roadrunner. **Leeway** personified NYHC's second wave. Eddie Sutton and guitarist A. J. Novello fueled the b-boy punk/metal Astoria crew first called the Unruled. Promoter Chris Williams produced 1989's *Born to Expire* and '91's *Desperate Measures* for his Rock Hotel Records. Leeway lost out due to various business issues and Eddie's drug problem.

Breakdown, a hard-ass Yonkers crew named for Black Flag's "Nervous Breakdown," debuted at a Mamaroneck youth center, and made a 1987 demo issued posthumously on Bill Wilson's Blackout! label (1990's *'87 Demo*). Carl Porcaro, Rich McLoughlin, and Anthony Drago carried on as Raw Deal; Sean O'Brien alt-rocked in Come. **Raw Deal** was the very negative five-piece of Porcaro, McLoughlin, and Drago with Token Entry singer Anthony Comunale. After a 1988 demo, and a 1989 show at the Ritz, they signed to In Effect. A same-named heavy metal act sued, so they became **Killing Time**. Their 1989 debut *Brightside* felt bitterer than their Blackout! releases: 1991's *Happy Hour* EP, 1995's *Unavoidable* EP, and 1997's *The Method* LP. Drummer Anthony Drago became a cop.

Sheer Terror began December 1984 with Paul Bearer, the Don Rickles of NYHC. After two weeks, they cut two songs for 1985's *Big City One Big Crowd*. Blackout! put them on 1988's *Where the Wild Things Are* and issued 1989's *Live at CBGB* EP. *Thanks fer Nuthin* referred to an ill-fated Maze Records deal, for which they rerecorded *Ugly and Proud*, an LP Maze confusingly issued at the same time in 1992. Tommy Victor (Prong) produced 1995's *Love Songs for the Unloved* (Blackout!/MCA).

Bold began as rowdy fourteen-year-olds from upstate Katonah as Crippled Youth (1986's *Join the Fight*), part of Youth of Today's "Youth Crew." By age sixteen, they became matinee scene marvels. Bold launched Revelation Records, on 1987's *New York Hardcore: Together* and 1988's *New York Hardcore: The Way It Is* comps, plus 1988's *Speak Out* LP and 1989's *Bold* EP.

There's a drunk in the pit, and he's hurting my friends
But I'm gonna make it end
—PROJECT X, "DANCE FLOOR JUSTICE"

Project X, a Youth of Today side project, incited straight-edge militancy. Alex Brown and Porcell wanted to promote their *Schism* zine with a 7″ inserted in Issue #2. Their friends' bands had no music to offer, so Alex and Porcell wrote a few with YOT mates Walter Schreifels and Sammy Siegler. Three days, two rehearsals, and $100 at Don Fury's studio resulted in 1987's *Straight Edge Revenge*, five hundred pressed five-song 7″s with blank labels, most vinyl etched with antidrug messages.

Underdog, a Bad Brains–style band key to NYHC's second wave, began with Richie Birkenhead and Russ Wheeler (Iglay) in the Numbskulls (later True Blue). Birkenhead briefly left to play guitar in Youth of Today (on 1986's *Break Down the Walls*) so in came Icemen's Carl DeMola. Interest in 1986's *Underdog* EP and '88's *Over the Edge* tape brought about 1989's *The Vanishing Point* (Caroline) with Philly skater Chuck Treece.

Finish what you started: Gorilla Biscuits, CBGB, 1998.
Photo by Frank White.

Gorilla Biscuits, a "positive" straight-edge crew from Jackson Heights named for Quaaludes, wore flannel shirts, Vans, and X's on their hands. They shined on Revelation Records: 1988's *Gorilla Biscuits* 7″ EP and 1989's *Start Today* LP. Their first show was opening for Token Entry. Their second gig, a violent affair with Youth of Today, killed CBGB matinees and got them banned.

Side By Side, Jules Masse's Youth Crew quartet, began X-mas 1987. Alex Brown (*Schism*) replaced original guitarist Gavin Van Vlack. Don Fury produced songs for early Revelation comps. Their shows featured sing-alongs of Warzone and D.C. Youth Brigade. They met Nina Hagen at a Pyramid gig, but plans to join forces fizzled. The end was 1988's *You're Only Young Once . . . (Don't Fuck It Up)*.

Absolution was like NYHC's late-'80s answer to an early-'80s hardcore band. Djinji E. Brown grew up in the Bronx, son of Coltrane group saxist Marion Brown. Gavin Van Vlack defined his style in Side By Side. Alan Peters grew up fast in Agnostic Front. Their song "Never Ending Game" opened Freddy Alva and Chaka Malik's 1988 *New Breed* comp tape. Jerry Williams produced 1989's *Absolution* EP for Dave Stein's Combined Effort label. **Burn**, the closest thing to Bad Brains in 1989, reenergized NYHC live at the all-ages matinees but had just one official release—1990's *Burn* four-song 7″ (Revelation); 1991's *Live in New York* was a Euro bootleg, and 2002's *Last Great Sea* was a '92 demo. Chaka Malik (Harris) and Gavin Van Vlack's band propelled the scene.

Judge ruled with fiery antidrug attitude. After Youth of Today's 1986 *Break Down the Walls* tour, Porcell started Judge as a one-off with vocals by drummer Mike Judge (Ferraro). With Mike's former Death Before Dishonor's guitarist Jimmy Yu and Gorilla Biscuits drummer Luke Abbey, Judge made 1989's metal-edged classic *Bringin' It Down* LP.

Supertouch also included Mike Judge. Their 1987 debut "Searchin' for the Light" on *New York City Hardcore: Together* came out long before 1989's *What Did We Learn* or 1991's *The Earth Is Flat*. Nutley, NJ, singer Mark Ryan was one of NYHC's first real b-boys. Sami Reiss wrote: "At a Supertouch show in 1989 you'd see Adidas Ewings, flannel Stussy gear, Starter elbow pads on Ryan and a tie-dyed Gorilla Biscuits shirt. So cool."

The Icemen began after Frontline, with Marco Abularach, Noah Evans, and Mackie Jayson. They debuted at April 11, 1983's CBGB memorial for the Stimulators' Patrick Mack. In 1984 they cut an unreleased 45 with singer John Gamble. After other singers, things gelled in 1987 with Carl Griffin (DeMola) of the Psychos. Ninety-one's *Rest in Peace* EP (Blackout!) heard the Icemen at their coolest. They fired Carl, who later made a 7″ as the Icemen with no original members. **Beyond** spawned Quicksand's Tom Capone and Alan Cage and 108's Vic DiCara. The virulent straight-edge teens toured on weekends for 1988's five-song demo and 1989's *No Longer at Ease* LP. They disbanded after DiCara moved with his family to San Diego, where he cofounded Inside Out, with a young Zach de la Rocha.

School of Violence raged on the late-'80s scene. Brian Childers's stand-in Karl Agell (of Bridgeport, CT's Seizure) sang on 1988's *We, the People?* (Metal Blade). Childers later fronted Crawlpappy but died at age forty-two of alcohol abuse. Drummer Mark S. Evans went home to England in 2005, where he was killed and his body set afire. **Krakdown** began in 1985 but came to form in 1987. Richie Krakdown (Dowling) oversaw 1989's *Krakdown* EP and tunes on

New York Hardcore: The Way It Is and *Montreal/New York Connection* '85. Original singer Chris Notaro joined Crumbsuckers; other guys joined Murphy's Law and SFA. The Baldwin/Glen Cove quartet spewed in *Schism* (#6): "Our goal is to play as many places as possible and spread our word everywhere."

> *I'd like to punch your stupid face*
> *Grab you by your punk rock hair and bash your brains*
> —BORN AGAINST, "GO FUCK YOURSELF"

Life's Blood oozed brutal NYHC with a revolutionary flow. The New School of Social Research freshmen did twenty-six gigs, most at ABC No Rio and as far away as Ohio. The 1988 eight-song *Defiance 7"* opened with "Never Make a Change," a livid attack on Youth of Today who did "Make a Change," over which the two bands brawled at a CBs matinee. (Singer Jason O'Toole became an Atlanta sheriff and ranks highly in the Knights of Columbus.) **Born Against** was Life's Blood's Adam Nathanson and Neil Burke with frontman Sam McPheeters, behind 218 shows in thirty-seven states and fourteen countries with four bassists and seven drummers. They did 1991's *Nine Patriotic Hymns for Children* and 1993's *Battle Hymns of the Race War* on Sam's Vermiform label (plus two 45s, four split-7"s, and seven comps).

Rorschach fused metallic NYHC with art-noise, like latter Black Flag. The Paramus quintet played nothing melodious, as heard on 1990's *Remain Sedate*, written during, and while touring around, frontman Charles Maggio's lymphoma. Maggio founded his Gern Blansted label, with 1993's *Protestant*.

Citizens Arrest (for a Negative FX song) made tuneful thug NYHC. After their 1988 demo, Daryl Kahan replaced future alt-rock star Ted Leo on vocals. The five-piece that met at Some Records made 1989's self-produced *Light in the Darkness* and 1991's Don Fury–overseen *Colossus* (for Fred Alva's Wardance label).

S.F.A. ("Stands For Anything") coined "hatecore" to stand apart from "positive" antidrug HC. *Bullshit Monthly* editor Mike Bullshit, their tattooed queer frontman, began the band in 1985 but left in 1989. SFA then rejected "corporate" overtures from Caroline, Relativity, and Roadrunner. *The New Morality*, fronted by Brendan Rafferty, came out on DeMilo in 1991, weeks before *So What?* (Wreck-Age). We Bite America folded just as 1995's *Solace* came out. **Go!** was Mike Bullshit's next band. Their debut, 1989's *And the Time Is Now* 7" EP (on Mike's Noo Yawk Rehkids), featured "Holy Roller," assailing Bad Brains' mistreatment of gays and women; 1990's *Your Power Means Nothing* was likely their finest half hour; 1991's *There Is No Man* 7" EP ended with "Fear of a Gay Planet."

Nausea, "crusty" peace punk legends, wrote thrash songs about class war, vivisection, and gentrification. Their UK style stood out on 1988's *New York Hardcore: The Way It Is,* with two singers, Neil Robinson and Amy Miret (wife of AF's Roger). The group with Reagan Youth guitarist Victor Venom (Dominicis) and bassist John John Jesse (Guzman) made 1990's *Extinction* with a Crass-ish gatefold sleeve, and two 45s: 1991's "Cybergod" and 1992's *Lie Cycle* EP. **A.P.P.L.E.,** anarchist "peace punks" of the LES via blue-collar Brooklyn, was singer Jae Monroe and bassist/brother Vinny Vespole with guitarist Mike Millett and drummer Mickey Malignant. Shows for causes like apartheid, El Salvador, or animal rights promoted '87's *A Sensitive Fascist Is Very Rare* EP or '88's *Plutocracy* LP.

Youth Defense League was a skinhead crew based around Warzone's Rishi and Crazy Jay Skin (Vento). The 1988 Don Fury–produced *Skinheads 88* came out about the same time as their pro-cop "Blue Pride" on *New York City Hardcore: The Way It Is* (on which they thanked Skrewdriver's Ian Stuart). Music scribe Felix Von Havoc berated "The Voice of Brooklyn" in *MRR:* "There's no doubt YDL was a Nazi band mixed up with skinhead violence in NYC." **Trip 6,** squat scene supergroup of Tommy Rat (Warzone), Stu (Psychos), Zippy McPhee (Ultra Violence), and Charlie Rage (Warzone) did "Back with a Vengeance" on both *The Way It Is* and 1989's *Back with a Vengeance* demo; its credits read: "It doesn't matter whether you're a punk or a skinhead, or straight edge or not. All we wanna do is play our music." Don Fury produced 1990's *No Defeat! No Submission* (Inner Spirit).

Crawlpappy, a post-NYHC quartet predating grunge and stoner rock, were like urban mountain men from Red Hook. Guitarist Rick Roy's band did 1990's *Crawlpappy* six-song 12", 1991's "Temple Body" 45, and 1992's *Crawlpappy* LP, and over time included Brian Childers (School of Violence), Alan Peters (Absolution), Mike Sentkiewicz (Raw Deal), Stephen Moses (Alice Donut), Zippy McPhee (Trip Six), and John Stanier (Helmet). **Six and Violence,** a wry Queens quintet, employed two singers, smooth Kurt Stanzell and late growler Paulie G (Paul Gazzara), with shocking props and costumes. The 1989 LP *Lettuce Prey* (Fist) starred Jethro Tull's Ian Anderson! Of '95's *Petty Staycheck* (SFT) this writer opined (*Rip,* 8/95): "the reason to stay in the pit too long and catch a boot to the nose."

Outburst, Brian Donahue's angry Astoria five-piece, was one of the first to blend rap and NYHC. A 1988 demo and *New Breed* comp cuts brought about a Blackout! deal. In 1989 they opened *Where the Wild Things Are* and did Don Fury–produced *Miles to Go* EP. **Bad Trip**, the Douglaston, Queens, quintet fronted by singer Fred Muench, with Luke Montgomery, Marcos Siega, Brendan White, and Eric Matheu, rate for gigs with a trampoline. Of 1989's *Positively Bad*, two LPs, two EPs, and split-single over nine years, *Jersey Journal* recalled "one of the most energetic (if somewhat goofy) bands of the post-CBGB NYHC scene."

Burden of Proof began in Massapequa Park with Nihilistics bassist Good Old Mike (Nicolosi) and drummer Jon Wrecking Machine (Golden), a future NYPD cop involved in Slapshot's worst Boston mischief. Their 1988 *Burden of Proof* 12″ edged on head-crackin' Oi!—its DIY embodied by a typed lyric sheet with hand-scribbled edits. **Social Disorder** did three tapes of metallic HC: 1987's *Social Disorder*, 1988's *Agony*, and 1989's *Violent Times*. B'klyn's Saul "Soul C" Colon five-piece ended after 1992's *Media Lies* EP and 1994's *Goin' the Distance* LP. They returned in 2001, "looking for a guitarist—NYHC."

American Standard, named for the toilet, came from Hoboken but was down with D.C. emo acts like Swiz and Dag Nasty. Bill Dolan's quartet created melodic post-HC, first on 1989's *Wonderland* (cut at Chung King with Kevin "Red Light" Reynolds), 1991's split-7″ for *Suburban Voice*, and 1992's *Coming Up 3's* (Blackout!). **Turning Point**, equal parts tough-guy NYHC and emotive emo, raged on 1988's *Turning Point* six-song 7″ and 1990's *It's Always Darkest Before the Dawn* LP. By 1991, they disbanded for day jobs. Vigilant antidrug frontman Frank "Skip" Candelori overdosed on June 19, 2002.

We're not in this alone: CBGB matinee crowd, 1988. Photo by Frank White.

You want to tell me so bad who is on your guest list tonight
But I don't care
—QUICKSAND, "DELUSION"

Quicksand created a post-HC on par with Helmet or Fugazi. Walter Schreifels (Gorilla Biscuits/YOT), Tom Capone (Bold/Beyond), Sergio Vega (Absolution), and Alan Cage (Burn/Beyond) overtook the scene after debuting at ABC No Rio. The 1999 *Quicksand* EP (Revelation) and tours with White Zombie and Rage Against the Machine made them alt-rock darlings, but Quicksand cracked up after 1993's *Slip* (Polydor) and 1995's *Manic Compression* (Island).

Into Another fused HC brutality, metal skills, and humane lyrics. The Bad Brains-meets-Rush thrash of Underdog frontman Richie Birkenhead, Whiplash bassist Tony Bono, Bold drummer Drew Thomas, and guitar whiz Peter Moses recorded for Revelation 1991's *Into Another*, 1992's *Creepy Eepy*, 1994's *Ignaurus*, and 1995's *Poison Finger*. Disney's Hollywood label jumped in on 1996's fiasco *Seamless*. (Richie made news when he was briefly wed to billionairess Samantha Kluge. Tony died of a coronary at thirty-eight.)

Shelter showed Youth of Today's Porcell (Paramananda Das) and Ray Cappo in a new light. Their "Krishna-Core" promoted Vedic values: 1990's *Perfection of Desire* closed with "Interview with H.G. Satyaraja Prabhu." Both 1992's *Quest for Certainty* and 1993's *Attaining the Supreme* came out on the Krishna-core label Equal Vision. Roadrunner records like 1995's *Mantra* ("Message of the Bhagavat") and 1997's *Beyond Planet Earth* began a downward cycle as dharma faded. The band **108** made 1992's *Holyname 7"* EP and 1995's *Songs of Separation* LP for Equal Vision. Beyond's Vic DiCara returned after his West Coast stint in Inside Out to form a Krishna-core band with compatible singer Robert "Rasajara" Fish. (Slapshot assailed the group with their seething "108.")

Die 116—Gavin Van Vlack (Burn/Absolution), Andrew Gormley (Rorschach), Eric "Coop" Cooper (Sweet Diesel), and Manuel Carrera—made lost classics like 1995's *Damage Control* ("Thurston Moore Don't Tip") and 1996's *Dyna-Cool*, "recorded at gunpoint at B.C. Studios." Opined this writer (*Paper*, 4/95): "Die 116's the best thing to happen to HC since Void went metal." **Shift**— Joshua Loucka, Brandon Simpson, and Samantha Maloney—cranked atonal NYHC. The high school friends laid the proper groundwork: indie records, van tours, all-ages shows, and social activism. They started on Equal Vision: 1994's *Pathos* EP and 1995's *Spacesuit* LP. Columbia signed the Bond Street Café regulars for 1997's *Get In*, overproduced by Alan Winstanley and Clive Langer. The next year Maloney moved to L.A. to play drums in Hole.

Orange 9mm fused NYHC, rap, and metal. Chaka Malik (Burn) began with Chris Traynor (pre-Helmet), Eric Rice (pre-H₂O), and Larry Gorman. Their 1994 debut *Orange 9MM EP* (Revelation) yielded an Atlantic deal but 1995's *Driver Not Included* and 1996's *Tragic* flopped, as did 1998's *Ultraman vs. Godzilla* EP and 1999's *Pretend I'm Human* for the hedge-funded NG label. **CIV** starred Gorilla Biscuits' Anthony "Civ" Civorelli, Arthur Smilios, and Sammy Siegler. The 1994 single "Can't Wait One Minute More" (Revelation), rerecorded on Atlantic, soared on MTV. The next year's *Set Your Goals*, coproduced by GB alum Walter Schreifels, included the hit single with a B-side of Kraut's "All Twisted." *Trouser Press*: "CIV makes punk intensity palatable without sugarcoating it."

Dog Eat Dog came out of Bergenfield, NJ, rap/metallers Mucky Pup ("You Stink but I Love You"). Biohazard's Billy Graziadei gave their demo to Roadrunner, behind 1993's *Warrant* (a riff on Warrant's *Dog Eat Dog*). The MTV-approved 1994 *All Boro Kings* featured "No Fronts" produced by Run DMC's Jam Master Jay. Ronnie James Dio and Wu-Tang Clan guest-starred on 1996's *Play Games*. **Black Train Jack** rocked CBs matinees with that Astoria edge. The harsh/melodic band named for a Henry Rollins lyric starred Token Entry drummer Ernie Parada on guitar and his roadie-as-vocalist Rob "RoBorn" Vitale. Sadly, 1993's *No Reward* and 1994's *You're Not Alone* (with backing vocals by Queens friends Sick of It All) for Roadrunner got lost in the Green Door era.

Mind Over Matter, a manic Lindenhurst, LI, five-piece, left their mark on NYHC, with Wreck-Age vinyl: 1992's *Mind Over Matter*, 1993's "Hectic Thinking," 1994's *Security*, and 1995's *Automanipulation*. Future Thursday and Glassjaw members partook in their mosh pits. **Vision of Disorder** ruled the '90s scene with metal-core riffs and dark lyrics. The gnarly 1995 *Still 7"* EP (SFT) fueled 1996's *Vision of Disorder* (Roadrunner) and '97 Ozzfest dates. Irving Plaza banned the Merrick quintet for violent gigs circa 1998's *Imprint*. They quit after '99's *For the Bleeders* (Go Kart) and '01's *From Bliss to Devastation* (TVT).

Rival Schools was Walter Schreifels and Sammy Siegler with Cache Tolman (Iceburn), and Ian Love (Burn/Die 116). Schreifels pushed an EP series (on Some Records) for two bands to jam as one. After one EP with Jonah Mantraga of Far's Onelinedrawing (2000's *Rival Schools United by Onelinedrawing*), Rival Schools signed to Island and did 2001's *United by Fate*—Marcos

Siega (Bad Trip) directed its "Used For Glue" video. *Kerrang!* hailed it "the greatest rock album since Nirvana's *Nevermind.*" **Glassjaw** from Long Island socked a tuneful NYHC. Bad vibes with Roadrunner over 2000's *Everything You Ever Wanted to Know about Silence* resulted in 2002's *Worship and Tribute* (Warner Bros.) promoted by Warped Tour and Ozzfest dates.

> *I'm stayin' true to my ways*
> *Hardcore is my life, I'll carry the name*
> —MADBALL, "DEMONSTRATING MY STYLE"

Madball came out of a fun moment at AF gigs, when Roger Miret brought his preteen half-brother Freddy Cricien onstage to sing "It's My Life" by the Animals. AF's Miret, Vinnie Stigma, and Wil Shepler backed Madball's 1989 *Ball of Destruction* EP. Over time the fun turned deadly, seen in Madball's DMS gang loyalty on 1992's *Droppin' Many Suckas* (Wreck-Age) and 1996's *Demonstrating My Style* (Roadrunner). But they revived NYHC spirit with music like 2002's *NYHC* and "100% Hardcore Pride" on 2005's *Legacy.* **H₂O** starred SOIA's breakdancing roadie Toby Morse. Their 1996 debut *H₂O* (Blackout!) and 1997's *Thicker than Water* (Epitaph) portended a move to L.A. to join new friends in mall-punk glory. Things broke down on 2001's *Go* (MCA).

Maximum Penalty, a tough crew fronted by former Nausea drummer Jimmy Williams, blended NYHC with rap, jazz, and metal. They got known playing CBs matinees, and cut a 1989 demo with Type O Negative's Josh Silver, released as 1992's *Maximum Penalty* (Astor). Guitarist Rich McLoughlin (Breakdown, Killing Time) joined after 1994's *East Side Story* (Too Damn Hype) and 1996's *Superlife* (on Walter Yetnikoff's Vel Vel label). **Subzero** began when Richie Kennon and Lawrence Susi left Breakdown. The 1990 *Subzero* demo and 1991's "Ice Age" 45 burned with fury; 1996's *Happiness without Peace* included "Fuck MTV, I Want My NYHC." Lou DiBella survived lymphoma (tattooing "Cancer Killah" across his sternum) and returned to sing on 2003's *Necropolis City of the Damned.*

Merauder embody modern NYHC with loyalty to the scene and *la raza.* The Brooklyn gangster five-piece flying PR flags came together in 1995 with frontman Jorge Rosado (Ill Nino) infamous for his karate-chop mosh style. They excelled on metal-core for Century Media: 1995's *Master Killer*, 1999's *Five Deadly Venoms*, and 2003's *Bluetality.* **District 9,** a multiculti South Bronx crew spurred by "Puerto Rican Myke" Rivera, fused Uptown rap and Downtown HC; as heard on 1995's *Schoolahardknox* EP (SFT). Todd Hamilton (Warzone), Kevin Smith (Fahrenheit 451), and Pete LaRussa (No Redeeming Social Value) all served in D9. Myke joined Danny Diablo in the like-minded Skarhead.

Crown of Thornz came from the NYHC hotbed of Jackson Heights (Gorilla Biscuits, Raw Deal, The Mob). Sick of It All roadie Danny Diablo (Singer), son of a Jewish NYPD cop and Puerto Rican mom, fronted a thug-core group with guitarist Mike Dijan, bassist Steve O'Brien, and drummer Dimi on 1995's *Train Yard Blues* (Equal Vision) and 1996's *Mentally Vexed* (Another Planet). **Skarhead** was a "New York Hood Core" band with two singers, Lord Ezec (Danny Diablo) and Lou DiBella (of Subzero), Thornz's Mike Dijan, a DJ, and two bassists. *Drugs, Money and Sex* (Another Planet) in 1997 brought about a Victory deal and 1999's Warped Tour. Ezec expressed in 1998's *Kings at Crime* bio, "We don't give a shit what you think. If you don't like it get the fuck out of our way."

25 Ta Life started with AF roadie Rick Healey resolved to sing after Stigma and Miret told him he sucked. A '90s unifying character with tats and dreads helped chill out a scene with the crowd bringing too many guns and knives to gigs. Rick began his label Back Ta Basics but others put out his band: 1994's *25 Ta Life* (SFT), 1996's *Keepin' It Real* (We Bite America), and 1999's *Friendship Loyalty Commitment* (Triple Crown). After nearly dying in a 2006 beatdown, Rick shaved his head and tattooed "Victim in Pain" across his face. **Comin Correct**, his band with PA punks Krutch, recorded for Back Ta Basics and Triple Crown. The former issued 1995's *Resist to Exist Join the Fight* and 1996's *Knowledge Is Power*. Their follow-up, 1998's *One Scene Unity*, was recorded live at Wetlands at Raybeez's final gig with Warzone before he died. CC's drummer's suicide later that year motivated Rick to quit crack and dope.

Indecision, Catholic schoolboys from Bay Ridge, spewed deep antireligious views on 1996's *Unorthodox* and 1997's *Most Precious Blood*. After a 1996 set on her WNYU radio show *Crucial Chaos*, the band added nice Jewish girl guitarist Rachel Rosen to a lineup that ruled late-'90s NYHC. Fiery like SS Decontrol, Indecision did SSD's antidrug opus "Glue" (on 1998's split EP with Shai Hulud). Roger Miret produced 1999's *Release the Cure*. Dylan Klebold wore their T in the Columbine massacre. **Neglect** unleashed harsh NYHC from deep Long Island. With "Fuck Life" tattooed on his face, singer Brian Zoid sliced himself onstage. The hatecore of 1993's Don Fury–produced "Pull the

Plug" 7" (Wreck-Age) and 1994's *End It!* EP (We Bite) earned major gigs, from Sheer Terror to Hatebreed. (Expect no more Neglect as Zoid shredded his larynx after three gigs in 2006.)

> *Things as they are they cannot be*
> *We must resist the commonality*
> —Both Worlds, "Cornered"

Both Worlds was Leeway with Cro-Mags' John Joseph replacing Eddie Sutton. The Krishna crunch of 1996's four-song *Beyond Zero Gravity* (Another Planet), produced by A. J. Novello and Noah Evans, and 1998's *Memory Rendered Visible* (Roadrunner), with sitar and sarangi players, included bassist Eddie Coen and drummer Pokey. But Both Worlds failed to set the world afire. **Shutdown** was a drug-free quartet Raybeez hailed "the future of hardcore." Their Victory label bio read: "You'll never find singer Mark Scondotto preaching about anything other than 'get in the pit!'" Their 1998 Jimmy Gestapo–produced *Against All Odds* featured "We Won't Forget," in memory of Raybeez. The raging teens shut down after 1999's *Something to Prove* EP and 2000's *Few and Far Between* album.

 Ricanstruction, named for Ray Barretto's *Nuyorican* classic, fused Ramones riffs, Latin rhythms, and radicalism. Ponce, PR-born hothead Alano "Not4Prophet" Baez and his Harlem "Salsacore" crew briefly included Cro-Mags' John Joseph. Tower Records banned 1998's *Liberation Day* (CBGB Records) for artwork of Puerto Rican extremist group Machetero. Controversy arose over 1999's *Abu Jamal* that praised cop killer Mumia Abu Jamal. **Step2Far** melded NYHC and death metal. Their 1988 five-song *U Better Believe It* EP and various compilation tracks brought thug respect to the tough crew fronted by Harlem-bred CBGB bouncer Frank 2Far. The cover of 2006's *Hooligans* showed the title tattooed on the inside of one of their lips.

 Down Low, a popular '90s band, did a 1995 demo plus compilation tracks, like a rip on Reagan Youth's "U.S.A." and 1998's tunes on Jimmy G's *Creepy Crawl Live*. That brought about 2000's *Wall of Anger*, produced by Breakdown's Mike Dijan. Singer Joe V (a.k.a. Joey Downlow) released their catalog on *Drink Smoke Fight Fuck*. **Victim of Pain** began in Queens in 1986 as speed metallers Hell on Earth playing Cro-Mags and Slayer covers in their cellar. Bassist Andy Prezioso's five-piece came together in the '00s with Phil Reed, whose skinhead stance recalled Phil Anselmo or Roger Miret.

No Redeeming Social Value, a Queens quintet of drunken skinheads, attracted beer-soaked punks. Their rowdy tours got them banned in Italy and busted in Poland. Two thousand one's *40 Oz. of Hardcore* (Triple Crown) represented the decadent side of NYHC. **Blackout Shoppers** blared a raw thrash like the bad old days (opening for Effigies, Nihilistics, and Iron Cross). Ex-Daisycutter singer Seth Amphetamine (Fineburg), with Mike Moosehead, Blackout Matt, and Joey Methadone, let loose 2005's self-produced *Smash & Grab* EP.

Kill Your Idols, an '80s tough-guy NYHC throwback incited by singer Andy West and guitarist Gary Bennett, recorded topical songs like "Stop Comparing Us to Negative Approach" and "Only Dicks Don't Like Black Flag." Highlights include 2005's *Live at CBGB* and 2006's split-single with Poison Idea. In true HC fashion, cops shut their final gig, an oversold DIY affair at a Suffolk County VFW Hall in May 2007. **Most Precious Blood**, named for Indecision's 1997 album, began with that band's Rachel Rosen and Justin Brannan merging NYHC with Sisters of Mercy. The vegan, atheist, DIY Staten Islanders burned through drummers, from 2001's *Nothing in Vain* to 2005's *Merciless*.

Leftöver Crack (a drug oxymoron!) was a last gasp of NY nihilism. Stza Crack (Scott Sturgeon) and Alec Shaheed Mohamed (Al Baillie) from the ska/punk Choking Victim ruffled feathers on 2000's *Shoot the Kids at School* tape. "Crack City Rockers" spewed "intense hatred of white people and their pathetic Gap-wearing, R.E.M.-listening, 90210-watching culture with a healthy disdain for authority and the atrocities perpetrated by the US government." **Awkward Thought**, John Franko's gnarly five-piece, "bridged ABC No Rio and the rest of the NYHC scene" (*Slug and Lettuce*, 2001) on 2000's *Mayday* and 2001's *Fear Not* EP.

Hazen Street, named for the road to Riker's Island, starred Toby Morse (H$_2$O), Freddy Cricien and Hoya (Madball), and Mackie Jayson (Cro-Mags). Songwriting guitarist Chad Gilbert (New Found Glory) quit soon after. The punk/rap of *Hazen Street* with L.A. metal producer Howard Benson for DC Flag, label of Good Charlotte's Joel and Benji Madden, spawned the MTV-aired D.M.S. tribute "Fool the World." **Harley's War** was Harley Flanagan's early-'00s post-Cro-Mags band. The HC icon's gigs at Continental and CBs, doing his Cro-Mags and Stimulators songs, inspired 2003's self-made *Cro-Mag*, cocredited to "Hardcore All-Stars" including Vinnie Stigma (AF) and Micky Fitz (The Business). Harley's War, with Cro-Mags *Revenge* drummer Ryan Krieger and guitarists Sean Kilkenny (Dog Eat Dog) and Will "Caveman" Dahl, proved big in Japan.

Caught in a mosh: Crumsuckers, Long Island, 1988. Photo by Frank White.

THE FALL

Stomp, stomp, stomp,
The idiot convention
—ANTHRAX, "CAUGHT IN A MOSH"

The original NYHC scene faded with the punk/metal crossover. "Crossover" (the name of a DRI LP) was a major issue in HC circles. It was the logical result of both scenes' growth. Bands began experimenting, so the first cracks in the scene came with the influx of suburban "poodleheads" in tight jeans and bullet belts. Some NYHC participants embraced the possibilities; others reacted to this metal invasion as untenable.

HOLLY RAMOS (New York scene): I left the New York Hardcore scene after I graduated high school in 1984. Things were changing: bands were breaking up that I liked, like the Undead and Heart Attack, and metal came into it, which was a big no-no at one point. Then I heard Jerry Williams spinning the Black Sabbath record at a Reagan Youth gig, and it sounded amazing. People started getting into Motörhead and Venom then there were all these speed metal and thrash bands, and things just changed. (1996)

HOWIE ABRAMS (New York scene): Crossover started around 1985. There was a crossover more metal leaning, and one more non-metal. You had the Agnostic Front side, trying to fuse metal into punk, like on their second record. Then you had Murphy's Law touring with the Beasties and Fishbone; playing to very mainstream audiences, and went over well. Too bad their record situation didn't allow them to benefit from it all. They'd literally go to Dubuque, Iowa, and rock twenty thousand people who didn't know who they were. Because of all this, the original New York Hardcore concept disappeared. On the metal side, L'Amour in Brooklyn booked more hardcore bands with their metal bands; CBs booked a band like Carnivore with hardcore bands. It was a very different world. (1997)

From the metal side came kids from the outer boroughs and burbs lured by the speed and danger, like Anthrax, Carnivore, and Nuclear Assault—all way too intense for the era's corporate hair-metal. But the Anthrax guys went to CBs and got treated like interlopers. From the NYHC side came the crunch of Cro-Mags, Agnostic Front, and Leeway, who played gigs at L'Amour ("The Rock Capital of Brooklyn"), where the bathrooms smelled of Aqua-Net.

JIM WELCH (New York scene): Metal kids were into hardcore because it was heavy. They couldn't give a rat's ass about the politics. It did rub off and you had some socially conscious metal bands out there. . . . The punks wanted to think they were open-minded but they'd start trouble because they didn't like the way the metal kids looked. (1996)

MIKE SCHNAPP (New York scene): Moshing was the metal word for slam-dancing. It came from the S.O.D. crowd. It was a new term for a similar thing I knew from the punk world once removed from the original meaning. The bad thing was the crowd changing, to those that came to kill each other. I remember a show with Flotsam & Jetsam and like Leeway. A fucking disaster. It should've been good except that people jumped down and started punching other people 'cause they had long hair. "Grab the longhair and fucking punch 'em in the face." There was a lot of that shit. (2003)

PETE STEELE (Carnivore): I can't say there was total interaction. It was cliquish but everybody seemed to get along. The scene started to attract so much attention that the real hardcore kids got sick of it and bowed out. You'd have kids showing up that looked like skinheads but weren't really skinheads. It was just a style. I feel sorry for the hardcore scene founders because it quickly got exploited and became commercial. (1997)

TODD YOUTH (Agnostic Front/Murphy's Law): The crossover shit, I hated it. That Nuclear Assault guy was a clown: playing stupid music and wearing a headband, sweatbands and leather jacket. I stopped going to shows, unless it was the Bad Brains. It was time to do something new. (2004)

A crossover disaster was 1986's Rock Hotel show with Discharge. The noted UK anarcho-punks debuted a heavy metal style with soaring falsettos, so they dodged hurled beer bottles and trash cans thrown off the balcony. The nadir was probably December 18, 1994's Life of Agony show at L'Amour East, where bouncers killed stage-diver Christopher Mitchell.

SEAN TAGGART (artist): I was both for the metal crossover and against it. Concurrent to hardcore, I'd still listen to AC/DC. I thought the point was to listen to heavy music, be it Black Flag or Black Sabbath. The gig, I knew it was over was when Nuclear Assault was playing a CBs matinee with bodyguards onstage to protect 'em from the hardcore kids. It was so antithetical to what hardcore was all about. Nuclear Assault were of that "We're the band, and you're the audience" world. I also saw Kirk Hammett jump onstage with Crumbsuckers and do a very rock star guitar solo for which he got spit upon. (1997)

MIKE DIAMOND (Beastie Boys): The crossover? I have a good Slayer story. We all smoked a big joint with Tom the singer, right before they went onstage at L'Amour. He got really stoned and he spaced some of the words. We went backstage after, and Jeff Hanneman, the Nazi guy in the band, threw him against the wall and said, "Look, don't ever fucking smoke pot before a fucking show!" He was going off and we were dying laughing. (1994)

> *Mind your own business, do what you gotta do*
> *Don't look for trouble, sometimes trouble finds you*
> —MADBALL, "NEW YORK CITY"

By the '90s, NYHC transformed from a revolution of the mind to a revolution of the body. To those seeking political revolution, the scene lost relevance. But those seeking a sense of belonging found a lifestyle. It went from trailblazers and conceptualists to devotees and believers. But the intensely physical punk scene's violent underpinnings remained a lightning rod.

JASON O'TOOLE (Life's Blood): The scene was a weird mix of people who might've never been in the same room if it were not for a love of this music. Kids from politically connected families mingled with runaways from group homes. Rich kids into dope and straight-edge poor kids. Those of us who took it upon ourselves to organize gigs, produce fanzines and play in bands had strong personalities, so conflict was inevitable. (2009)

JOE MARTIN (Citizens Arrest): I'd made a promise to myself that I'd stop going to shows the day I got beat up. And then it happened to me at one of the matinees. Some skinhead picked a fight with me and I didn't get beat up, but I did get punched. So I said, that was it, no more, because I knew every time I'd go to a show from then on, I'd see this guy and panic and run away. (1996)

JOHN LAW (New York scene): I got my official hardcore beatdown at a CBs matinee. That Jersey band U.S. Chaos was playing. I was young and dumb, and stage-dived into Harley and his friends. That was a huge mistake—they really gave it to me. (2005)

DARYL KAHAN (Citizens Arrest): New York City had basically closed its doors to hardcore shows around '89–'90. Things had become increasingly violent at shows due to gangs from the Spanish sections of Brooklyn coming and stabbing people, moshing with hammers, fucking people up, and killing a few. It was fucking crazy. They basically ruined it all with this gang shit mentality. (2006)

NYHC remains a marginal subculture. Other than the Beasties' rap reinvention or the Bad Brains' musical influence, the scene's biggest successes were probably the Gorilla Biscuits guys' one-hit-wonder band, CIV ("Can't Wait One Minute More"). Unique NYC cultural exchanges include artist Matthew Barney's 2002 *Cremaster 3* film at the Guggenheim with Agnostic Front and Murphy's Law, and Jimmy Gestapo's role in *Grand Theft Auto IV* as "Liberty City Hardcore DJ." The city's hip-hop attitude upped the ante for antisocial behavior. The intimidating punk gang DMS (Doc Marten Skinheads) brought to the scene an unseen ultraviolence.

FREDDY CRICIEN (Madball): The scene in New York was dying out. We reignited the flame. Not just the music but the feeling itself. We got a lot of people to start bands. The older guys see us, they say, "Wow, I wanna get back into hardcore again." (1994)

LOU KOLLER (Sick of It All): The Hardcore scene has come full circle from when we got into it in '84, '85. Before, it was like a family; you didn't know everybody's name but it was a thriving scene with lots of young bands. The early '90s was what we call the Dark Ages of Hardcore, violence and clubs not wanting to touch it. People don't like to admit it, but the popular pop-punk sound of California brought back the scene. (1997)

New York Hardcore Tattoo (127 Stanton Street), the LES tattoo shop of Gestapo and Stigma, is like a punk rock barbershop. That's where the spirit lives on, with the boots of the late Raybeez on display. Such positivity conflicted with the negativity of July 6, 2012's attack on Harley Flanagan at a Cro-Mags gig at Webster Hall.

BRIAN CHILDERS (School of Violence): The scene is on such a downward spiral now that there's nowhere to go but up. This is zero. There are a lot of troublemakers and they're easily recognizable. Everyone knows the look troublemakers have, there's a look in their eyes, a smell to 'em. I know that'd never hold up in court but shit, there's a difference between prosecuting someone and fuckin' kickin' his ass. (1991)

WALTER SCHREIFELS (Gorilla Biscuits/Quicksand): I think a lot of kids just come to the shows like they're a football game. They think hardcore started with Raw Deal or something. These guys don't know anything about music. It's just gross! (1989)

JIMMY WILLIAMS (Maximum Penalty): The ignorance and stupidity of the tough-guy thing fucked up New York Hardcore, with the cliques and crews and all that shit. I mean, I have mad love for all these kids, but we don't associate with any of that. (1998)

RICHIE BIRKENHEAD (Underdog): Honestly, fighting and violence isn't something I want to romanticize; I was a bit of a hothead brawler. I had a short fuse. In all honesty, I don't think I ever beat up anybody who didn't deserve it, but there were a lot of situations I could've walked away from and didn't because of my pride and just stupid shit. (2005)

HOYA (Madball): A fistfight here and there is okay but sometimes you gotta go for yours. There have only been a few incidents, and we plan to keep it that way. (1994)

HARLEY FLANAGAN (Cro-Mags): Hardcore bands from New York now are living off fantasies because New York isn't that tough a place anymore. It's soft and you have to seek out the grittiness of the past. The scene's no longer a target to outside forces: we had to toughen up because Puerto Ricans, guidos, jocks and even metalheads would jump us. Things have changed so much, and we don't have to stick together to protect each other when we went out. Now it's a cut-and-paste of what they think it was. They have no real enemies so they jump each other. High school thug wannabe bullshit is what New York hardcore has turned into over the years. (2013)

> *We used to work together, band helped band*
> *But now it's different, it's out of hand*
> —ALONE IN THE CROWD, "IS ANYBODY THERE?"

Hardcore remains a self-contained universe, a form as reliable as jazz, blues, or reggae; you know exactly what you're gonna get. Each generation claims a validity that coincides with their salad days. And be it 1986, 1996, 2006, or 2016, you'll always find someone to say NYHC is "over." But thanks to a crew of committed NYHC bands, it carries on.

JUSTIN BRANNAN (Indecision/Most Precious Blood): That exciting fear of being at a show and not knowing what the fuck was going to happen, I think that was what was so productive, that underlying danger. Not enough danger that you were scared for your life, but enough that you knew this was some crazy shit, knowing that this isn't a club for everybody. That's very absent for me today, that whole element of danger. (2006)

SAM McPHEETERS (Born Against): I don't think hardcore's been innovative since 1986. Not my fault. I had the misfortune to be born in 1969 and missed the boat. I started going to shows in 1985, and that first year, all the people I hung out with talked about how Minor Threat had broken up and the whole thing was over. When I started doing bands, my friends and I were acting out of tradition as well, because we were saddled with this precedent. (2009)

MYKE RIVERA (District 9): New York Hardcore is huge in our lives. The scene's got our back and we've got theirs. We ain't fuckin' around. Down for life for real. (1996)

HEADKICK FACSIMILE

EAST VILLAGE NOISE ROCK, SCUM ROCK + ANTI-FOLK

1982–1992: Swans, Sonic Youth, Pussy Galore, Cop Shoot Cop, Missing Foundation, Helmet, The Pyramid, Operation Pressure Point, Tompkins Square Park Riots

Your property: East Village, 1985.
Photo by Ted Barron.

NOISE ROCK

Gorged on speed and bitter words
Found ourselves on B and 3rd
—Cop Shoot Cop, "It Only Hurts When I Breathe"

THE RISE

The late '80s was an exciting time in the East Village, with all the underground crosscurrents of rock, art, film, and performance. Economic hard times allowed for a significant last gasp of intense subculture before the encroaching business and real estate interests completely won out.

JIM THIRLWELL (Foetus): The scene that existed in New York in the late '80s and early '90s is a scene that hasn't been documented. It was a vibrant time. There's a core or nucleus of groups or thinkers that come together, and maybe there's a sort of collusion where there's like-mindedness, or people play on the same bill. Then it starts to disperse as the bands become more popular, or people go do different things, but for a snapshot of time you have this very vibrant thing going on. In that time, there was really interesting activity: Pussy Galore/Jon Spencer, Cop Shoot Cop, Unsane, Helmet, Surgery . . . (2004)

CARLO McCORMICK (author/journalist): This town was blessed in that time by a particular kind of anger. Smarter and more focused than the proverbial adolescent unrest of dopey rebel-without-a-cause teen ennui. It took its cues from the raucous performative absurdities of the Fugs and the Situationist-leaning antagonisms of punk and post-punk, honing their implicit dissent according to a righteous outrage we all felt with the smiling fascist face of Reagan's America. It was aggressive and nihilistic as befitted the times, though I'm not sure I'd care to listen to many of those records today. (2011)

PETER LANDAU (White Zombie/Da Willys): It was a transitional period before Nirvana and all that stuff got big, with still lots of freaks and misfits. It was an interesting time to be in the city, before everything solidified into regimented scenes. This was before Internet, so you had to seek things out. What attracted me was finding this underground community that gave creative people a chance to be autonomous and grow organically, and develop an individual point of view. It seemed creatively an asset to have that incubation. (2011)

SEAN YSEULT (White Zombie): There was a lot going on trying to survive in the East Village. There were scary bums and crazy people with knives on the streets. I remember Daniel Rakowitz cooking for the homeless in the park with his rooster, and later he cooked his girlfriend in those pots! There were so many characters; creative freaks. Hardcore was the prevalent music and that's what I was into; I went to every CBs matinee. We'd go to Richard Kern screenings in some room with folding chairs. The Pyramid was mainly gay, and I was so envious of Dean and the Weenies! And Jim Thirlwell was a huge instigator, making industrial music before anyone, a huge influence on Lower East Side and East Village bands and on all what came later. (2011)

I'm not scared, I'll take what I want
Something for nothing, I want what you've got
—SWANS, "FREAK"

In the '70s and '80s, there was a sense of the world unraveling in New York. The city was unfriendly, so a jaded disposition was all part of one's survival mechanism. This new scene was not punk, sneering, and belligerent. That "I've seen it all" attitude came off as "post-anger"—the reaction of young misfits resigned to their fate.

ADAM PEACOCK (Hugo Largo): There are problems with the New York scene now. It's very burned out. Everyone here is still living in the shadow of CBGB in 1977. Real estate is a huge problem because it dictates where and when and how people will operate a club. Coupled with the incessant need for people to "shake their booty," now people don't feel a need to promote live music. For people coming up, it seems bleak. (1989)

JESSE OBSTBAUM (The Thing): Music is generally dead. We're at the end of an era. New York sucks. Everybody in the New York scene sucks, generally, with a few exceptions, like Cop Shoot Cop. (1990)

People moved to the East Village because it was a magnet for what had been the punk generation. But the area wasn't for everyone. Heroin and crack ensured an air of despair, and a racially charged situation existed for those living on gentrification's frontline. But it was a great time for art because everything was so wide open, like a blank canvas. It was a dead time in that there were very few hits or stars. There was lots of dangerous and intense activity that may or may not make sense today.

STEVEN CERIO (Railroad Jerk/Drunk Tank): The scene was great back then. Cop Shoot Cop was in their prime, and early Unsane before Charlie [Ondras] passed away, and Honeymoon Killers and Dustdevils. There was a lot of thinking going on, which is what attracted me. It was a total fuck-you to mainstream attitude. There was a very aggressive edge to stuff back then. There was no expectation of what your role was. There was attitude about music but there wasn't attitude toward each other. (2004)

SCOTT WEIS (Ed Gein's Car/Iron Prostate): It was very cool but you weren't gonna make a living in music back then. There was a small network and everyone knew about every show and it was a scene. There were only a few places to play and you found out about gigs from all the wheat-pasted flyers. These days, I'm not gonna put down the fact that there are eighty thousand bands in the city and I can't spit on the L Train without hitting a guitarist. More power to kids doing it now, but before it was more of an outsider thing. But once you joined the scene, you no longer felt like an outsider. (2011)

PAGE HAMILTON (Helmet): There was a real competitive vibe then. It was kind of bitchy to tell you the truth, a lot of bands were afraid to admit anybody else was cool. There was also this weird thing as Sonic Youth was like the government; they were like mayors of Downtown, and you had to go get their stamp of approval. (2006)

JAMES KAVOUSSI (Fly Ashtray/Uncle Wiggly): We hate to talk about other bands, even though there are many bands we can't stand. My philosophy is if you don't have something nice to say, you shouldn't mention that you don't like Cop Shoot Cop. (1993)

TOD ASHLEY (Cop Shoot Cop): We're the only East Village band that's not funded by Grandma's trust fund. To my knowledge, every other underground band in New York is. You know the bands I'm talking about. They've got trust funds, so they can write songs about not being able to afford their drug habits. (1993)

It was a druggy era. The Alphabet City look and feel was of heroin; most musicians went down that road at one time. Cocaine also flowed in ample supply, and many partook. Quite a few took LSD, but not in a groovy way. Anyone could walk up to the weed window at 11th and A. All these drug-copping spots and drug users, within a small area, rubbed off on the rock sound. Bands still play that nodded-out drone and still try to attain that druggy affect.

STU SPASM (Lubricated Goat): There was still an element of danger here. Someone was always getting mugged. Avenue B was scary and going anything below there was unthinkable unless you were just going to get drugs, which we were. I compare it to the supermarkets: the avenues are the checkouts and the streets are the aisles. There was so much, it was hard not to do them. Hard drugs was our whole thing—all the ingredients constituted what we did, we were nasty evil drugged-out decadent bastards. (2013)

RICHARD KERN (filmmaker): The look is your outlook as a doper, a total nihilist. It's a bunch of pussy boys trying to look as tough as possible, which is what every rock look's been about: Elvis, Danzig, you name it. Posing by poseurs who hate poseurs. "Everyone's posing but me." I was way into that, too. (2004)

Lydia Lunch and Glenn Branca drove the sound and style. Lydia was the scene's star—her terrifying music and spoken-word set the bar for intensity. When one said "East Village Rock," they really meant "like Lydia Lunch." Glenn's compositional approach, heard in his guitar orchestras with young members of Sonic Youth and Helmet, and his release of the earliest vinyl by Swans and SY, paved the way for much of today's indie/alt sounds.

JIM THIRLWELL: Glenn Branca was a leitmotif through the whole thing. The legacy starts with him, then all of his "children." If you look at the people who have played in his ranks, and what they have gone on to: the Swans/Sonic Youth thing. I don't know how I fit into all that. But one of the first people I met in New York was Michael Gira. (2004)

PAGE HAMILTON: The center of my universe was Glenn Branca. His open-tuned, vertical thinking on the guitar, in a way like Ornette Coleman, was life changing. And it's well documented. Thurston and Lee from Sonic Youth did time with Glenn, so that was a big influence. Glenn wasn't classically trained. He didn't sit around studying sonata form. He had his own tuning, he invented his own guitar: the harmonic guitar was fifteen feet long and played with a slide. Working with Glenn was a religious experience. He was so possessed, so into the music, you couldn't help but be inspired by him as he conducted. He was the single-most inspirational guy I've ever been around. (2006)

I don't know why you wanna impress Christgau
Let that shit die and find out the new goal
—Sonic Youth, "Kill Yr. Idols"

"Noise Rock" was inspired by no wave, minimalism, industrial, and NYHC. It formalized Downtown rock from feeder schools like RISDI, Pace, and NYU. The sound was not "art rock" but Noise Rock was artists making rock. The music raged with angst, ennui, and cruelty. It was a huge FU to rock music, and to the listener. It was a Darwinian sorting-out to see how much a crowd could endure. The ideal result was all the "posers" and "sellouts" running for the door in horror. With that Nietzschean "what does not kill me makes me stronger"—if '70s prog-rockers read *The Hobbit*, '80s noise bands knew their Nietzsche—the intent was to rip the wheat from the chaff. They really wanted to hurt you.

THURSTON MOORE (Sonic Youth): There was a time in New York after no wave, there wasn't much exciting going on, just a lot of lame-ass pop bands. So we all just said, "fuck it" and got cheap guitars and screwdrivers and turned the amps up to ten. (1989)

SEAN YSEULT: We fit into this weird category of bands playing art-noise rock. We played with all them: Swans, Rat At Rat R, Honeymoon Killers, Live Skull, and Pussy Galore. They all lived in the East Village, a block or two from each other. It was not the friendliest scene. In fact it was odd, you'd play and nobody acted enthusiastic or into it. They'd cross their arms and study you like art on a wall. There was competition, each band was like, "Fuck you, we're gonna be more creative!" The crowd was made up of these bands checking out each other. I'm not sure they even had any fans. It was not fun; it was not good times. But we were all driven to make the noise that we did. (2011)

PAGE HAMILTON: Live Skull, Rat At Rat R, Sonic Youth and Swans were the big bands Downtown. All four of them came before us so you have to look at all of them as an influence. Their whole world of sonic exploration created some musical moments that were absolutely life changing. Every night could be magic or a train wreck. That's what music is about. That's certainly what the spirit of improvisation in jazz was. (2006)

VICTOR POISON-TETE (Rat At Rat R): The only thing the bands had in common was location. We didn't really influence each other. We were never the same politically, or in the way we approached what we were doing. For a while, some of the members of the bands might have thought that we had more to do with each other than we really did. They hear loud guitar and dissonance in a few Lower East Side bands, so they think they're alike. Of all these groups, some have become more successful than others. (1989)

Psycho-head blowout: White Zombie, 1987. Photo by Michael Lavine.

Noise rock achieved monumentality because of New York's monumentality—in this case, of something great gone to hell. After decades of building up rock as an art form, here came its destruction. It was a scene of smart, druggy headbangers, who instead of doing something sensible with their lives, got into art and this blaring music. Live Skull or Pussy Galore didn't have to be like Stradivarius to get attention. They had ideas and executed them so everyone got it when they heard it.

RICHARD KERN: Everything was negative; total nihilism. The drug abuse propelled the sound: New York cynicism taken to its furthest extreme. Musical heroin. (2004)

MICHAEL GIRA (Swans): It's not a flippant experience; it's not enjoyable. I'm trying not to cater to anyone's preconceptions. How it's perceived is the audience's business. Frankly, I could care less about the audience. (1995)

KEMBRA PFAHLER (The Voluptuous Horror of Karen Black): Not that the experience is painful; it's just demanding and severe. But when it's your own idea, your own conception, it's easy to do because there's all this voodoo attached to it. (1989)

JULIA CAFRITZ (Pussy Galore): The music itself is abusive. It's more that people like to be abused by it as opposed to identify with it. And they like the bad words. (1988)

CHRIS SPENCER (Unsane): We play the way we do—really loud and painful—because everything else in music is kind of a drag. (1991)

Taste of the month
Voice for the cause
—HELMET, "MAKE ROOM"

Cop Shoot Cop personified noise rock: industrial edged, drug abusing, piss-drunk, and that name! It's a junkie term: you cop, shoot up, and cop again. Police really hassled the band. Ads would list them as "CSC" or even "Cup Sloop Cup." Their lineup had no guitarists—just two basses (one low-end, one high), a keyboardist, a sampler, and a rhythmist playing sheet metal and trash cans. Most of them attended RISDI and, when they moved to the East Village, recruited street-rat bassist Jack Natz (Undead, Virus). Tod Ashley (bass/vocals) drew the band's unsettling artwork. In the same breath, many cite Missing Foundation: both EV acts intimidated audiences and irked authority.

RICHARD KERN: Missing Foundation was no wave to the max; noise rock meets political punk. The objective of every gig was to destroy the club. Wherever they got booked, the club got trashed and it was a big joke. It was a natural artistic progression. They were trying to do something new, and that was total destruction. (2004)

BOB BERT (Sonic Youth/Pussy Galore): Peter Missing could be the nicest guy, and then turn around and be a total asshole. One night after a gig at like 3 a.m., he was at his apartment showing us a new song. He was blasting his guitar at maximum volume and some lady downstairs complained, so Peter goes running upstairs and there's all this crashing and he's wrecking her apartment with a baseball bat! (1988)

By 1990 came LES bands like Helmet, Prong, Surgery, Railroad Jerk, Barkmarket, and Unsane, inspired by Swans and Sonic Youth, with earsplitting volume and affected ennui. Most dressed like white-trash truckers, and spread their fashion style as they toured.

Kill yr idols: *Seconds* Magazine event featuring the films of Richard Kern, Madame Rosa's, 1987. Artwork by the author.

PAGE HAMILTON: In retrospect, us and the bands we came up with were a transition because we were artistic and academic and doing something cutting-edge but we didn't really look or dress the part. At the end of the day, we were a bunch of dudes. (2006)

THE SCENE

Down on my luck, on the pavement
Oh what a predicament, but I was a participant
—Railroad Jerk, "Participant"

These bands came from a self-reliant realm with its own media and industry. So when the scene got known, it felt significant. Labor Records, begun by Susan Martin and Michael Gira, put out early Swans, UT, and Certain General. The Neutral label, begun by Glenn Branca and White Columns Gallery's Josh Baer, put out groundbreakers like Sonic Youth's 1982 *Sonic Youth* and 1983 *Confusion Is Sex*, and Swans' 1983 *Filth*. Circuit Records, Ernie Triccaro's label behind Cop Shoot Cop's 1990's *Consumer Revolt*, was supposed to put out Unsane's debut 7″ in 1988, but they claim that Ernie blew the money on blow and still owes them $200. Shockabilly's Mark Kramer began Shimmy Disc for his Noise New York studio. He said his "stepping-stone" label was meant for his bands Bongwater and B.A.L.L., not clients like Gwar, King Missile, and Lotion. The word spread through an explosion of fanzines (a term spanning short-run journals, adult comics, and a few slick mags), launched at Ted Gottfried's cellar shop See/Hear (59 East 7th Street).

The Pyramid, Ritz, and Cat Club all booked great shows. Cat Club's "Dead Cat Mondays" staged touring acts like Einsturzende Neubauten or Faith No More, with locals like Rhys Chatham or Christian Marclay. But the club went back to hair metal after GG Allin's October 6, 1986, show that ended with GG lathered in his own feces. The Village mainstay Folk City hosted proto-alt, three bands for $3, like Hüsker Dü, Soul Asylum, or DC3. The squalid Times Square dive bar Tin Pan Alley hosted bands from the Butthole Surfers to Ritual Tension. New York rockers imbibed late night at places like Deb Parker's No-Tell Motel, where the Fleshtones' Peter Zaremba held court. Cassettes got handed out like business cards. It was the last of the punk generation going toward grunge.

The Love Club, weekly party of artist couple Keiko Bonk and Mark Abramson, staged EV bands, from They Might Be Giants to the first gigs by White Zombie and Lunachicks. Love Club began in 1983 in the World's first-floor lounge, and lasted until 1985–1987 at Lismar Lounge (41 First Avenue). The club **428 Lafayette** (a.k.a. "Undochine," under the eatery Indochine) was very hip around 1987. Opened by noise-rocker Jon Sidel (Fudge Factory Inc.) after his L.A. club Power Tools, 428 was where grungy dudes mingled with stylish stars. Thursday night bands included Pussy Galore, White Zombie, and Throwing Muses. **The Knitting Factory** (47 East Houston) started with Michael Dorf and Bob Appel in 1987 as a performance-art space selling hummus and tahini. The 150-capacity room got known for breaking They Might Be Giants with a 1988 Wednesday residency. The Knit, never a spot for NYC's beautiful people, catered to offbeat rock and avant-garde, like Elliott Sharp, John Zorn, and Cecil Taylor (till Taylor derided it as "The Slave Factory").

Cinema of Transgression expressed the era's dope-fueled despair. *Underground Film Bulletin* publisher Nick Zedd upped the ante with 1985's "Manifesto of the Cinema of Transgression," proposing, "all film schools be blown up and all boring films never be made again." Zedd opened doors for other punk-related filmmakers inspired by Alphabet City's unhinged environs. He showed his films in the clubs, like 1985's *Go to Hell*, and wheat-pasted the EV with the bands. That paved the way in 1986 for Richard Kern's *Fingered* (with Lydia Lunch), Tommy Turner/David Wojnarowicz's *Where Evil Dwells* (about Long Island "Satan teen" Ricky Kasso), and Tessa Hughes-Freeland's *Rat Trap*.

NICK ZEDD (filmmaker): I met Richard Kern through Beth B, who took me to the Limelight. He introduced himself. Tommy Turncoat [Turner] worked as a bartender. We'd all be running into each other in 1984 in the Lower East Side, gravitating to Kern's apartment where heroin was injected and movies were made. Sometimes there'd be a party somewhere, and if somebody lived there who was lovers with someone or a band was playing, we'd all end up there, usually high, or to get high. (2011)

DAVID HERSHKOVITS (*Paper*): That Cinema of Transgression was a great East Village moment. Very drugged, people behaving in a way they'd never behave unless they were totally fucked up. But they captured a moment. (2005)

Psychedelic Solution (33 West 8th Street), in the heart of the Village by Electric Lady Studios, was a psychedelic poster shop with a gallery that foretold modern interest in "rock art." Owner Jacaeber Kastor legitimized lowbrow artists with major shows for the likes of Robert Williams, Rick Griffith, Joe Coleman, Mark Mothersbaugh, and Pushead.

STEVEN CERIO (Railroad Jerk): A very important place. It was basically the only alternative gallery. I got my first job in New York there; it was a real education for me. It was a headquarters for incredible people to stop by, a real destination. There were shows with R. Crumb and Robert Williams and Mark Mothersbaugh and Rick Griffin. Jacaeber's a legend. (2004)

JOE COLEMAN (artist): Psychedelic Solution was a place for other kinds of art. I had some big one-man shows in the East Village, but I never felt connected to that intellectual primitive stuff done intentionally bad. When I do something, I want to be the absolute best. When Jacaeber came in, he showed a deep interest in draftsmanship, so I liked that. My first important show was there. It was a special time. He only did maybe fifteen shows but it was a significant place, in the way CBGB was. There was something important, and it revitalized me, to be more about serious art but not as serious as Uptown. (2011)

THE MUSIC

I am an island in the cesspool called history
I inhabit the crippled remains of a place that once was
—LYDIA LUNCH, "CESSPOOL CALLED HISTORY"

Lydia Lunch (Lydia Koch) was the era's ultimate character. Her stark, unforgiving persona—dressed in black, exuding negativity, never mellowing or mutating—inspired much to come. Her résumé reads like New York Rock history, from her bands (Teenage Jesus and the Jerks, 8-Eyed Spy, Beirut Slump) to solo (*Queen of Siam, 13.13, In Limbo*), spoken word (*The Uncensored Lydia Lunch, Conspiracy of Women*), and collaborations (Clint Ruin/Lydia Lunch Stinkfist "Don't Fear the Reaper," Lydia Lunch/Sonic Youth "Death Valley 69"), films (for directors Scott and Beth B., Vivienne Dick, Richard Kern, Nick Zedd), and books (*Incriminating Evidence, Adulterers Anonymous*).

Glenn Branca, from Harrisburg, studied at Boston's Emerson College. In 1975 he and John Rehberger founded the Bastard Theater and played as the Musical Ensemble (with up to twenty-five instruments). In 1976 he moved to SoHo and applied avant-garde composition to punk rock in his punk bands Theoretical Girls, the Static, and Y Pants. He premiered his first multi-guitar orchestra *Instrumental for Six Guitars* at 1981's Max's Kansas City Easter Festival. Glenn's guitar symphonies launched the likes of Rhys Chatham, Ned Sublette, Thurston Moore, Lee Ranaldo, and Page Hamilton.

Jim Thirlwell (J.G. Thirlwell, Clint Ruin), the big daddy of industrial noise-rock, moved to London from Australia in 1978. He came to the East Village on Halloween 1983, playing in the Immaculate Consumptive with

Marc Almond, Lydia Lunch, and Nick Cave. The next year Jim moved here to live with Lydia. He has made more than fifty records under monikers such as Foetus (Scraping Foetus off the Wheel, You've Got Foetus on Your Breath), Wiseblood, with Roli Mosimann (*Dirtdish* featuring Robert Quine), Stinkfist (with Lydia), his orchestra Steroid Maximus, and project Manorexia.

Swans set the bar for much slow, brutal, visceral musical intensity for music to come. They came from such a deep place, there's a genre based on their early records. Michael Gira grew up in L.A. but ran away as a teen, hitchhiking across Europe, and serving time in an Israeli prison on drug charges. He moved to NYC in 1979, among the first of the new EV artists. Gira lived on East 6th Street and, in his rear-storefront, set up a studio for his first band Circus Mort. Swans' 1983 *Filth* EP and 1984 *Cop* LP came to define sonic sadism. *The Burning World* (MCA) of 1989 resulted in a return to the indie ranks. Lineups included Norman Westberg, Roli Mosimann, Algis Kizys, and Jane "Jarboe" Jarobe.

Sonic Youth spread from the LES to define modern rock. They embodied urban noise but grew far beyond. They weren't druggies, so they survived, while their nihilistic peer bands were doomed to die or fail. SY's strengths, along with their music, were fandom and savvy—friends with Lydia, Nirvana, and Beastie Boys. It all began on Ludlow Street with Kim Gordon and Thurston Moore: she an L.A.-bred art critic, he a CT rocker. Moore, after brief gigs in the Coachmen and Even Worse, met guitarist Lee Ranaldo in early '81 in Branca's guitar orchestra at Hurrah. SY's gigs with drummer Richard Edson included CBGB, Great Gildersleeves, and White Columns. Steve Shelley, drummer of Lansing, MI's Crucifucks, replaced Bob Bert, who replaced Edson. Records like 1983's *Kill Yr. Idols*, '84's "Death Valley 69" (with Lydia), and '86's *Evol* cemented them in rock circles. They also excelled as Geffen's "magnet band," luring Kurt Cobain and others. (SY ended in the couple's divorce; thirty years of cool killed by the guitarist's sins of the flesh.)

Live Skull treaded a similar fuck-you noise rock. The LES quartet started in 1982 as Body. Things began with 1983's "Corpse" on the *Tellus* #1 tape, and 1984's *Live Skull* EP. Marnie Greenholz on bass/vocals, guitarists Tom Paine (Lance Goldenberg) and Mark C., and drummer James Lo created the grind of 1986's *Cloud One* (with a cover of Curtis Mayfield's "Pusherman") that brought Martin Bisi's BC Studios to attention. Eighty-seven's *Don't Get Any on You* was recorded live at CBs on November 8, 1986. They hired Thalia Zedek (of Boston's Uzi) on 1987's *Dusted*, after which Marni left, and drummer Rich Hutchins (of Ruin) replaced Lo. The roots of alt-rock are evident on 1988's *Snuffer* and 1989's *Positraction*.

Rat At Rat R moved from Philly to the EV in 1982 to leave their stain on the scene. Singer/guitarist Victor Poison-Tete, bassist Sondra Andersson (Glenn Branca's cousin), guitarist John Myers (later Glenn's conductor), and monster drummer David Tritt made a din that unlike Swans or Sonic Youth, crossed a metal edge. There were no hit records among 1985's *Rock & Roll Is Dead, Long Live Rat At Rat R* (Neutral), 1988's *Stainless Steel/Free Dope for Cops & Kids* (Purge) and 1991's *Rat At Rat R* (Sound League). Carlo McCormick wrote (*Seconds #8*): "As Rat At Rat R has made a conscious decision to situate itself outside the industry machinery, longevity becomes a concept sketchier and even more limited in scope."

> *When everything is so dark you cannot see*
> *Wallowing in the mire of misery*
> —PUSSY GALORE, "KILL YOURSELF"

Pussy Galore, named for the female protagonist in James Bond's *Goldfinger*, embodied noise rock with scruffy clothes, noisy grooves, and FU attitude. Ivy League outcasts Julia Cafritz and Jon Spencer moved to NYC after two lo-tech self-releases: 1985's *Feel Good about Your Body* and 1986's *Groovy Hate Fuck*. Next came a destruction of the Stones' *Exile on Main Street*, on cassette only. They discharged cruelties for the Caroline label: 1987's *Right Now*, 1988's *Sugarshit Sharp*, and 1989's *Dial M for Motherfucker*. PGers included Bob Bert (Sonic Youth), Neil Haggerty (Royal Trux), Kurt Wolf (Loudspeaker), and Jon's wife Cristina Martinez. Julia quit to be a soccer mom after 1990's *Historia De La Musica Rock*.

Honeymoon Killers, named for Leonard Kastle's 1969 gore classic, defined EV noise rock but never moved beyond the 'hood. Jerry Teel and Lisa Wells cut 1984's *Honeymoon Killers from Mars* on a 4-track at Sixth Street Butcher Shop. Sally Edroso drummed on 1985's *Love American Style*. Kramer produced 1986's *Let It Breed*. Pussy Galore's Cristina Martinez played on 1988's *Turn Me On*, while 1991's *Hung Far Low* included Jon Spencer and Russell Simins.

Cop Shoot Cop blurred political radicalism, punk antagonism, and no wave nihilism. The East Village band (from the ashes of RISDI act Dig Dat Hole) came to form on 1988's *Headkick Facsimile* cassette (produced by Wharton Tiers), 1989's *Piece Man* EP (1,000 "blood-splattered" covers), and 1990's *Consumer Revolt* (cut with Martin Bisi). The 1991 record *White Noise* (Big Cat UK) resulted in an unlikely Interscope deal that ended the band after 1993's *Ask Questions Later* and 1995's *Release*.

Missing Foundation was one of the most dangerous bands ever. Peter Missing (Colangelo) from the Bronx and the CBGB punk band Drunk Driving led the shadowy LES noise mob that incited with anti-gentrification graffiti (an upside-down martini glass with a caption, "The Party's Over" or "1988=1933"), and live antics like blowing up roman candles, setting oil drums afire, and spray-painting yuppie patrons. WCBS-TV's Mike Taibbi attacked MF as satanic squatters. Jim Waters's production of MF's trash-can vibe excelled on 1988's *1933 (Your House Is Mine)* and 1990's *Ignore the White Culture*, before ego feuds and dope abuse.

Big Stick, art-schoolers John Gill and Yanna Trance, were the original White Stripes, wearing Batman masks and big wigs and issuing lo-fi opuses like 1985's "Drag Racing" with hot-rod sounds from Raceway Park in Englishtown, NJ, and 1987's un-PC *Crack Attack*. Stick punked *Spin* into a full-page obituary on "the death of singer Trevor White."

Bewitched featured Bob Bert (Bertelli), in between drumming in Sonic Youth and Pussy Galore. Wharton Tiers produced 1986's solo *Bewitched 12"* for PG's label after SY's rejected it. Bob then made it a band, with Thurston Moore, Mark Cunningham (Mars), and Dave Rick (Phantom Tollbooth). Terry Tolken's No. 6 label released 1990's *Brain Eraser* and 1992's *Harshing My Mellow*. Jason Pettigrew purred in *Alternative Press*: "Say no to drugs because Bewitched is the best trip you've never taken."

Less of me: Black Snakes, 1988. Photo by Michael Lavine.

Black Snakes starred the bleakest scenesters. NYHC vets Jack Natz and Patrick Blanck joined filmmaker Richard Kern and Texan Darin Lin Wood. Shows with Pussy Galore, Raging Slab, and Sonic Youth came through Kern. A 1987 nine-song demo got released in Sweden as 1988's *Crawl* (Radium)—David

Wojnarowicz drew their logo and Michael Lavine shot their photos. But the lifestyle proved costly: Kern quit; Lin went home ('68 Comeback, Red Devils); Natz joined Cop Shoot Cop; while Blanck checked out in a 2001 car crash in the Dominican Republic.

Boss Hog, the punk/blues band of Cristina Martinez, begun after she played in Pussy Galore and Honeymoon Killers. Martinez won alt fame for onstage nudity, seen in Lavine photos. The 1989 disc *Drinkin', Letchin' & Lyin'* featured Jerry Teel, Kurt Wolf, and drummer Charlie Ondras; Pete Shore was on 1991's *Cold Hands*. A major label effort, 1995's *Boss Hog* (Geffen), employed drummer Hollis Queens. Jim Thirlwell produced '00's coda, *Whiteout*.

Alice Donut, a punk/rock act with a dark poetic edge, arose from the twisted mind of Tomas Antona, originally with Dave Giffen, Ted Houghton, and Stephen Moses. Their 1988 *Donut Comes Alive* was a play on Peter Frampton. The B-side of 1990's "Demonology" wrecked the Angels' malt-shop classic "My Boyfriend's Back." *Option* (10/93) railed: "Alice Donut is so dumb and talentless you can picture Tomas Antona musing, 'Gee, what can I write that'll make my mom mad?'"

King Missile was the first NYC alt-rock band with a hit. It began as King Missile (Dog Fly Religion) with Stuyvesant High grad John S. Hall and guitarist Stephen "Dogbowl" Tunney. Dogbowl went solo, so Hall sang with Dave Rick on three Shimmy Disc albums cut at Noise New York: 1987's *Fluting on the Hump*, 1988's *They*, and 1990's *Mystical Shit*. The latter spawned the radio hit "Jesus Was Way Cool." Their biggest moment was 1992's *Happy Hour* (Atlantic) that penetrated MTV on "Detachable Penis."

Helmet, the first noise-rockers to attain chart success, offered a blue-collar LES vibe. Their "thinking man's metal" with machinated rhythms and down-tuned riffs became a modern rock formula. Helmet debuted at Lauterbach's in Park Slope (booked by the Shirts' Bob Racioppa), second at the Pyramid, and third at CBs, where they'd play monthly. The buzz over 1989's "Born Annoying" 7"—with their classic lineup of Page Hamilton, Peter Mengede, Harry Bogdan, and John Stanier—got Atlantic to pick up 1990's *Strap It On*. That, 1992's *Meantime*, and 1994's *Betty* sold two million total.

Surgery operated with a similar Ludlow Street art-bent din. As per this writer (*Kerrang!*, 12/3/93), "Imagine Metallica marooned at Sonic Youth's house, and you've got a good idea of the musical terrain." The quartet moved from Syracuse frat parties to the LES to live their VU dream. Kim Gordon told Atlantic about 1989's *Souleater*, 1991's *Nationwide*, and 1993's *Trim, 9th Ward High Roller* 10", so Atlantic released 1994's striking *Shimmer*. By then, they so loved dope their A&R man needed rehab. Singer Sean McDonnell died at twenty-seven, in January 1995.

Unsane began with Chris Spencer and Pete Shore, who created gore effects for Richard Kern's film. Unsane embodied LES skater/trucker style with a coarse noise assault. After 1991's *Unsane*, Swans drummer Vinnie Signorelli supplanted Charlie Ondras, who died at a 1992 New Music Seminar show, accidentally injecting an air bubble. Things looked promising after 1994's *Total Destruction*, 1995's *Scattered, Smothered and Covered*, and 1998's *Occupational Hazard*. But in 1999 Spencer nearly died in a beatdown in Vienna over the American flag on his jacket.

Railroad Jerk rocked urban noise with a tweaked backwoods style, pissing up a similar stream as Blues Explosion. The quartet, centered on Twin Cities–bred artist Marcellus Hall with New Jersey bassist Tony Lee, began on 1990's *Railroad Jerk* (cut in two days with Wharton Tiers). "Cartoon rocker" Steven Cerio drummed on 1991's "The Ballad of Jim White" and 1992's *Raise the Plow*. Hall jerked the brakes after 1995's *One Track Mind* and 1996's *The Third Rail*, and tabled 1997's *Masterpiecemeal*.

Barkmarket blended punk, industrial, and metal: in the vein of Helmet or Unsane but funkier. Their 1988 *1-800-GODHOUSE* demo set in motion 1989's *Easy Listening* and 1990's *Vegas Throat* for L.A.'s Triple X. Aspiring producer Dave Sardy engineered sessions that struck Rick Rubin, who signed Sardy's trio with John Nowlin and drummer Rock Savage to his American Recordings, behind 1993's *Gimmick* and 1995's *Lardroom*.

Lubricated Goat, Australian punks led by Stu Spasm (Gray), came to infamy on Aussie TV in 1988, playing naked in just instruments. Stu spent a month in a Berlin hospital in 1990 after getting stabbed on tour in a drug deal gone awry (allegedly infected by a knife dipped in dog shit). Amphetamine Reptile reissued Goats records Stateside like *Paddock of Love* and *Psychedelicatessen*, so Stu moved to Seattle and then NYC. He'd jam in Crunt with wife Kate Bjelland (7 Year Bitch) and Russell Simins (Blues Explosion). Stu then bred LES Goat lineups, as heard on 1994's *Forces You Don't Understand* with Richard Kern shots.

Alienation's for the rich
And I'm getting poorer every day
—They Might Be Giants, "Don't Let's Start"

They Might Be Giants is the quirky duo of "Two Johns," Brooklyn-bred childhood chums John Linnell (organ/accordion) and John Flansburgh (guitar/vocals). They debuted at a 1982 Sandinista Rally in Central Park, and honed their proto-alt at 8BC, Darinka, and Love Club. TMBG self-promoted with *Voice* ads, "Dial-A-Song," and flexi-discs tacked to telephone poles. A twenty-song demo in 1985 excited Bar/None Records, behind 1986's *They Might Be Giants* and 1988's *Lincoln*. Elektra issued 1990's *Flood* ("Istanbul Not Constantinople") and 1992's *Apollo 18* (with a full band). **Skeleton Crew**, a prog-punk quartet pared to a duo (hence the name) was Fred Frith (Henry Cow) and Tom Cora (Curlew). Zeena Parkins and Dave Newhouse played on 1984's *Learn to Talk* and 1986's *The Country of Blinds*. *Spin* said their songs on 1986's *Passed Normal* compilation felt "like root canal without anesthesia." Frith quit when they began sounding like the slick rock they once reacted to.

Workdogs—the inebriated rhythm section of punk vets Rob Kennedy, bassist of D.C.'s the Chumps, and Beasties-linked drummer Scott Jarvis—created a punky blues. Eighty-six's "Funny $" b/w "Last Friend's Gone" 45 featured Mark Dagley and Rudy Protrudi. Eighty-eight's *Roberta* hired Ted "Popa Chubby" Horowitz and Greg Strzempka. Ninety-three's "rock opera" *Workdogs in Hell* involved Mo Tucker and Lydia Lunch. Jon Spencer and Jerry Teel rocked 1996's *One Night Only*. **Saqqara Dogs** jammed a psychedelic new age. Bond Bergland, of SF industrial pioneers Factrix, along with Hearn Gadbois (dumbek), Chris "Sync 66" Cunningham (stick/cello), and projectionist Ruby Ray, recorded 1986's *World Crunch* EP, 1987's *Thirst*, and Bergland's 1986 solo *Unearth* for Douglas Lichterman's Pathfinder label. Carlo McCormick crowed (*Seconds* #3): "Saqqara Dogs' shamanistic self-expression is a complex labyrinth of four metaphysical paths to Nirvana."

Band of Susans blared angular, abrasive, and academic art-noise. Robert Poss studied guitar with Rhys Chatham and nixed offers to replace Keith Levene in PiL. Avant-garde flautist Susan Stenger strummed with Glenn Branca. Named for 1986's first lineup with three Susans (Stenger, Tallman, and Lyall), *Melody Maker* picked 1987's *Blessing and Curse* EP (on Poss's Trace Elements) as "Single of the Week." Their 1988 *Hope Against Hope* LP included the EP's tunes. Page Hamilton played on 1989's *Love Agenda* and 1990's *Peel Sessions*. **Hugo Largo**, from the same harsh environs, rocked with "echoes of folk song, minimalism and the rich, pulsing drone of Lou Reed's *Street Hassle*" (*Times*, 11/13/86). The drummer-less quartet (two basses, guitar, violin, and vocals) featuring Mimi Goese's breathy vox included Branca vets Hahn Rowe, Tim Sommer, and Adam Peacock. Michael Stipe coproduced 1988's nine-song *Drum* (Warner Bros.) with songs off 1987's seven-song *Hugo Largo* (Relativity). (Sommer later signed Hootie & The Blowfish.)

Hope, Jesse Malin and Danny Sage's band after Heart Attack and before D Generation, played a proto-grunge/punk. A 1986 demo at Hi-Five Studios with Jerry Williams included an early take on D Gen's "She Stands There." They got gigs through Malin's work as "man with a van," moving band gear or people's boxes by the hour. **Das Damen** had Heart Attack's friends from the Misguided, Lyle Hysen and Alex Totino. The punky longhairs fronted by Jim Walters rocked like Redd Kross, but not as pop. *Marshmallow Conspiracy* (SST), 1988's *Mousetrap* (Twin/Tone), 1989's "Sad Mile" 45 (Sub Pop), and 1990's live-at-CBGB *Entertaining Friends* (City Slang) inspired a young Kurt Cobain.

Bongwater began at Club 57, where Kramer mixed sound for Ann Magnuson's band Pulsallama. With Dave Rick (Phantom Tollbooth) and David Licht (Shockabilly) they became a cult sensation. Eighty-seven's *Breaking No New Ground* featured Fred Frith on guitar. Eighty-eight's *Double Bummer* double-LP included "Dazed and Chinese," Led Zep in Mandarin. The Playboy Channel was big into the title track to 1991's *The Power of Pussy*. Like all great bands, Bongwater spilled into lawsuits after Kramer put out 1992's *The Big Sell-Out*. **B.A.L.L.** got rolling with Kramer and Don Fleming and their drummers, David Licht and Jay Spiegel (Velvet Monkeys). Eighty-seven's *Period* featured Cheryl Dyer artwork, wrecked John Lennon ("Always"), and Pretty Things ("I Can Never Say"). Eighty-eight's *Bird* trashed George Harrison ("Bangla Desh") and Ringo ("It Don't Come Easy"). Eighty-nine's *Trouble Doll* featured troubling cover art in blackface. Nineteen ninety's *Four* included *Period* pieces.

The Voluptuous Horror of Karen Black offer a theatrical spectacle at once alluring and revolting. Kembra Pfahler embodied the American Dream gone awry, damaged by her L.A. upbringing. The singer got a rep in performance and porno circles for antics like shooting eggs from her vagina. She and Hiroshima native guitarist Samoa debuted with 1990's "Alaska" 45, 1993's *A National Healthcare*, and 1998's *Black Date*. Kembra was in Matthew Barney's 1999 film *Cremaster 2* and 2008's Whitney Biennial. **Purple Geezus** arose from similar East Village vice. Singing conceptual artist Mike Osterhaut "ministered" Church of the Little Green Man—a tongue-in-cheek Sunday convening of performers, musicians, and other EV fuckups. From this mess came 1989's three-song single released by the CT punk club the Anthrax, with cover artwork by Alex Grey and George Petros. Rumors proved false of their ties to "Preppy Murderer" Robert Chambers.

The anti-naturalist: Kembra Pfahler,
The Voluptuous Horror of Karen
Black, 1999. Photo by Frank White.

Flip, flip, flip your lid
That's what she did
—PHANTOM TOLLBOOTH, "FLIP YOUR LID"

Phantom Tollbooth, a lo-fi trio inspired by East Village noise rock and post-HC like Hüsker Dü, began with 1985's three-song "Valley of the Gwangi"—as per John Leland, "it speaks to you in ejaculations, blurted-out bits of info or flat-out sprints"—then did three LPs: 1986's *Phantom Tollbooth*, 1987's *One Way Conversation*, and 1988's *Power Toy*. **Fish & Roses** was no-wave drummer Rick Brown (Blind Headache, Information, V-Effect) and wife-bassist Sue Gardner (C&W-style Last Roundup) making jangly proto-alt. Chris Nelson produced 1987's *Fish & Roses* with stuffed-animal art, Wharton Tiers oversaw 1989's *We Are Happy to Serve You*, and Gene Holder turned the knobs on '90's *Dear John* (with Chris Stamey).

Of Cabbages and Kings (a Lewis Carroll allusion) featured Algis Kizys and Carolyn Master of Chicago post-punks Bag People, and guitarists for Glenn Branca's *Symphony No. 6*. They began at Pyramid and Limbo Lounge. Ted Parsons (Swans/Prong) drummed on 1987's *Of Cabbages and Kings*. Rich Hutchins drummed on 1988's *Face* and 1990's *Basic Pain, Basic Pleasure*. *Hunter's Moon* of 1992 included Cop Shoot Cop's David Ouimet and Unsane's

Vinnie Signorelli. Wharton Tiers produced them all. **Ritual Tension** delivered LES drone with tribal beats. Singer Ivan Nahem (Swans drummer, with a solo 7″ as Ivan X) and guitarist-brother Andrew (sons of Brooklyn Dodgers pitcher Sam Nahem) joined Marc Sloan and Michael Shockley to forge fiery art-metal like 1986's *I Live Here* EP, 1987's *Hotel California*, and 1988's *Blood of the Kid*. Ninety-one's *Expelled* spelled the end.

The Ordinaires, an LES nonet (six men, three women) of art-punk vets, began with alto saxist Fritz Van Orden after his stint with Jules Baptiste's Red Decade. First called Off-Beach, they debuted on "Ordinaires" for Elliott Sharp's 1982 comp *Peripheral Vision: Bands Of Loisaida, New York City*. The Jamie Kitman–managed peers of the Scene Is Now and Mofungo got press for stringy reductions of Zep's "Kashmir" and the Stones' "She's a Rainbow" on 1985's *The Ordinaires* (Dossier) and 1989's *One* (Bar/None). **Blind Idiot God** began in St. Louis with a 1987 LP on Black Flag's SST label. Then the "math rock" pioneers came here to work with John Zorn and play with Helmet. After 1988's *Undertow* and 1992's *Cyclotron*, guitarist Andy Hawkins recorded solo with Bill Laswell on 1994's *Sacrifist*. Andy's intense instro project Azonic made 1994's *Halo* with BIG's Gabe Katz, and 1995's *Skinner's Black Labs* with Godflesh's Justin Broadrick.

Fly Ashtray began with Fordham students John Beekman, Mike Anzalone, and James Kavoussi mixing warbling melodies and offbeat rhythms. Their 1987 "The Day I Turned into Jim Morrison" 45 predated 1990's *Nothing Left to Spill* cassette and "President Stoned" 7″, 1991's *Clumps Takes a Ride*, and 1993's *Tone Sensations of the Wondermen*. **When People Were Shorter and Lived Near the Water,** Kim Rancourt's eccentric ensemble that began at Lauterbach's and Maxwell's, deconstructed pop hits. An eponymous 1987 EP defiled Wayne Newton's "Danke Schöen," Herman's Hermit's "Dandy," and Lincoln's *Gettysburg Address*. The 1988 *Uncle Ben* EP butchered Burt Bacharach's "This Guy's in Love with You." In 1989, *Bobby* reworked Bobby Goldsboro hits. Two years later, *Porgy* tweaked *Porgy and Bess*.

¡VIVA CARLO! ¡VIVA LIBERTAD!

A Benefit for Carlo McCormick's Legal Expenses

$12 In Advance

$15 At The Door

Raging Slab
Arto Lindsay
Deee-Lite
Richard Hell
Alien Comic
Mike Osterhout & Work Dogs M.C.'s
& Surprise Guests

Thursday - July 26, Irving Plaza - 17 Irving Place

6:00 Art Viewing 7:00 Art Auction 8:30 Poetry/Performance 10:00 Music
Tickets Available at Max Fish, 178 Ludlow St. Or Call (212) 226-4405

Don't dog me: Legal benefit for Carlo McCormick with Raging Slab, Arto Lindsay, and Deee-lite. Irving Plaza, 1993. Collection of the author.

THE FALL

Films make things look black and white
A thing of the past can't fight back
—Barkmarket, "Poverty"

Tompkins Square Park Riots, the final battle in the war of gentrification, signified the end of the "Loisada." On August 6, 1988, Mayor Koch decried a "cesspool soiled with feces and urine" and sicced the NYPD on "anarchist activists" (yippies, punks, and other radicals) homesteading in a squatter camp. Things came to a head when the cops moved in with the riot squad. Members of Missing Foundation and Letch Patrol began throwing bottles. NYPD retaliated by hiding their badges and busting heads. There were dozens of arrests and over a hundred brutality complaints. A *Times* (8/26/88) editorial blared: "Yes, a Police Riot." The city closed the park for more than a year to prevent such a situation from ever happening again.

GEORGE TABB (journalist/musician): I was there. It was clearly a setup; the cops instigated the violence. It was atrocious, the second-worst thing to happen in New York after the Towers. It became clear the East Village was changing. That was the beginning of the war. (2004)

NICK MARDEN (The Stimulators): The riots were a weird convergence. It was a full moon, with lots of energy on a hot summer night, and that's when they decided to close the park. Now, it was not a nice place, with all these homeless psychos in the park, all these drugs, and the loonies let out of mental hospitals. Clayton's video began with Peter Missing's weak toss of a bottle at cops. That's no way to start a riot! So the cops stormed. It was insane; it was like a war. It was the turning point of the boot coming down on the artist. (2011)

DREW STONE (Antidote): The Lower East Side became a magnet for people around the country. Probably like San Francisco was in the '60s, people came to the Lower East Side in the '80s for the punk scene, the hardcore scene and the dope, and at one point they had people living in Tompkins Square Park in absolute fucking squalor. You'd walk through needles everywhere. It was disgusting. They had to get violent to get these people out. Keep in mind also that AIDS came into play too. People using dirty needles, it just became a health hazard. It took a while to clean it out, but they finally did. (2008)

DAVID HERSHKOVITS (*Paper*): Over time the homeless people, anarchists, whatever, were people that decided they'd just live in the park. They made tents and it was not a safe situation for anybody, rats all over the place, it was avoided by anybody who lived in the area, so people like myself couldn't help but think that's going to be a good thing but at the same time you didn't like how they did it. Once the police started beating people up and going off on their police trip not listening to what anybody had to say or making distinctions between different people, then obviously that was not a good thing. (2005)

CLAYTON PATTERSON (artist): In August 1988, I was going to the Pyramid to document what was happening that night, but there was this huge police gathering in and around Tompkins Square. People were starting to protest, so I decided to film what was going on. The really critical shot is the ten seconds where the white shirts are trying to stop the blue shirts from running down the street—so the police had no control over the other police, and that turned into a police riot. One of the people who showed up was [club owner] Rudolf, and he got his head cracked—there was blood everywhere. (2009)

PETER MISSING (Missing Foundation): The FBI raided my house because they tried to say that I started the riot in 1988. But in the end they realized they were dealing with an entire angry neighborhood, which fought gentrification, homelessness and for homesteading rights on city-owned abandoned property falling into deterioration. And a government that was and is not working for the people. The FBI investigation fell back on the 9th Precinct police department, which found no criminal actions against Missing Foundation. Basically, they would have to arrest the entire Lower East Side. (2009)

> *Get out, some people live in the place*
> *My block, can you guess my race?*
> —Unsane, "Alleged"

The late '80s and early '90s proved to be a difficult transitional era. Following Mayor Koch came 1990's election of David Dinkins, and four years of racial tension and street crime, highlighted by the shameful Korean Deli Boycott and Crown Heights Riot.

KEMBRA PFAHLER (The Voluptuous Horror of Karen Black): The first change in the neighborhood was like '87, after the first group of friends started dying quickly of AIDS. There was a panic with people fleeing the neighborhood because there was so much death. That was a big transition. I remember going through my Rolodex and tearing out the cards. Everybody died or got off drugs in the late '80s. There was a shift in lifestyle. Hence there was an infiltration of new people. That's when Korean deli people came to Alphabet City. And the first restaurants. (2006)

LYNNE VON SCHLICHTING (Da Willys/Trick Babys): Late '80s New York was still dangerous and not yet gentrified. East of Avenue A was still a wasteland. There was the Pyramid, where us bands played, and the Wigstock scene that made the club famous. The rock scene died out, that vibe was waning, and there was nothing to take its place. It was the start of alt-rock and college radio, and the way people made music changed. (2011)

Scum anthem: Prong, Damage, Ritual Tension, Ed Gein's Car, CBGB, 1986. Artwork by Scot Weis.

SCUM ROCK

You're looking at the clock, the seconds pass
You're all alone, your fame has passed
—Reverb Motherfuckers, "Nowhere Nothing Fuckup"

"Scum Rock" was ugly music for an ugly time, blending noise, blues, grunge, and gutter punk. The term came from 1989's *New York Scum Rock Live at CBGB* (ROIR) tape—twenty bands produced by *Maximum RockNRoll* writer and self-avowed "commie faggot" Mykel Board—that captured the era's attitude. Scum-era hits included Letch Patrol's "Love Is Blind," Iron Prostate's "Give Me the Head of Jerry Garcia," Reverb Motherfuckers' *Route 666* LP, and *Urban Rag*'s *On the Rag* comp. Scum rock became the soundtrack to the Tompkins Riots, as squatters screamed "Die Yuppie Scum!"

SCOTT WEIS (Ed Gein's Car/Iron Prostate): We were the third generation of New York punk rock at that point, but we couldn't define ourselves as punk rock. I don't know who came up with it, maybe Hilly or Mykel Board. I was hanging out at CBs doing grungy stuff and drinking 40s on a stoop. Seemed like as good an appellation as any. (2011)

ROY EDROSO (Reverb Motherfuckers): It took a lot to be too much for the Lower East Side. We slagged bands like Sonic Youth, whose oeuvre was, by our standards overly precious. We were hanging with, playing with, and for, people even more excluded and maddened than us—the squatters, runaways, and antis of every stripe. They'd covered the 'hood in angry graffiti. They were turning Tompkins Square Park into some berserk, Mad Max version of a KOA; and they stood like a ragged phalanx in front of the yuppies—remember that word?—infiltrating the neighborhood. (2002)

> *If you want to see rock & roll*
> *Rock with Letch Patrol!*
> —LETCH PATROL, "HOW WE ROCK"

Letch Patrol, vehicle of street person Harris Pankin, over time included George Tabb (Furious George), Pete "Damien" Marshall (Samhain), and 2007 SF mayoral candidate "Chicken" John Ranaldi. At the Tompkins Square Park Riots, Harris displayed his battle scars to TV news in his Letch T. Jim Testa wrote in *Jersey Beat* (6/89): "Letch Patrol embodies what scum rock's all about: making do at the bottom rung of rock & roll's ladder, coping with a dying club scene and an indifferent public." **Sharky's Machine**—named after singer Jim Schuermann saw the Bert Reynolds film on LSD—came out of the NYHC band Killdozer or Killdozer 85 (1984's *There's No Mistaking Quality*). They changed again over the Wisconsin Killdozer, for 1987's *Let's Be Friends* LP and 1988's *A Little Chin Music* EP. Expect no reunion after Schuermann threatened violence to drummer Mike Edison over comments in his 2009 book, *I Have Fun Everywhere I Go.*

Artless featured the shocking Mykel Board. They self-made 1980's *The Only Record in the World*, 1983's *You'll Hate This Record* comp (with plastic vomit on the cover), and '84's *Artless/GG Allin split-7"* ("How Much Punk Rock Do You Hear in Russia?"). Nineteen ninety's *Beer Is Better than Girls Are* spoke to Mykel's true ambitions. Ninety-two's "Harass" included a creepy B-side of the Divinyls' "I Touch Myself." **You Suck!,** John S. Hall's grating group before King Missile, attained infamy for 1983's Board-produced "You Suck Chant" b/w "Get the Fuck off the Stage" with an X-rated blowjob cover shot. You Suck! included various nonmusicians playing chess, juggling, and doing sign language; Board got credited for "nails on the blackboard." More than a hundred participants over time included a pre-Missile Steve Dansiger and future anti-folkist Roger Manning.

Reverb Motherfuckers, begun by AA dropouts Roy Edroso and Big John Terhorst, personified degenerate psycho-delic scum rock. It started as a punk band the Deadbeats playing Nightingale's and Neither/Nor bookstore at 6th and D. RMF defiled CBGB, Pyramid, Love Club, and Limelight with a proclivity for disrobing and lathering in BBQ sauce. Eighty-eight's *Route 666* possessed day-glo art, and the best/worst Elvis cover ("Suspicious Minds"). Of 1989's *Twelve Swinging Signs of the Zodiac*, Jeff-O opined in *Flesh & Bones*: "It sounds like retarded boy scouts doing duck calls thru electrified vacuum cleaner hoses." **Sloth**, the five-man electrical band of Jed Parker, Mike Hoffman, Paul Cook, Greg Ginter, and Chris Raymond, rocked from LES clubs to Pratt parties. Neither 1987's Belgian-only *Sloth* nor 1990's *Spin*-approved "Fetch the Wedge" 45 (Baylor) resembled their boozy, earsplitting performances.

Ed Gein's Car played wry NYHC with a noise-rock edge. It all began at SUNY–New Paltz with Eric Hedin and Tim Carroll of the anti-hippie punks Deadhead Assassins, who moved to Brooklyn and teamed with offbeat singer Scott Weis (plus a *Spinal Tap* array of drummers). Eighty-five's *Making Dick Dance* spewed slop like "R.A.P.E." and "Go Down on My Dog." Eighty-seven's *You Light Up My Liver* (live at CBGB on April 17 and May 14, 1986, for CBGB Records) featured the anti–Live Aid anthem, "We're Not the World." **Rats of Unusual Size** attacked with a sardonic drone. Jim Fourniadis's CBGB regulars unleashed 1990's "Can't Call You" 45, 1992's *Elephant Man* EP (with Chris Spedding), 1993's *Id, Ego, Superego & Burns Ltd.*, 1994's *Yes I Can*, and 1996's *The Prime Directive Cannot Be Denied* (with "Barry White's Big Balls" and a raw delivery of "Proud Mary").

Iron Prostate, a heavy metal spoof, included rock critics Charles M. Young, George Tabb, and Steve Wishnia, with Mike Linn and Ed Gein's Car's Scott Weis. Ninety-one's *Loud, Fast and Aging Rapidly* blasted geriatric opuses like "Rock 'n' Roll Nursing Home." Meatloaf producer Jim Steinman funded 1992's "Bring Me the Head of Jerry Garcia" with a B-side of Jefferson Airplane's "Volunteers." Prostate imploded while trying to do an album, so Tabb tried to carry on with Japanese singer Minoru Niihara (Loudness). **Hammerbrain**, a nasty LES quartet, revolved around snarly Al Landess. George Tabb in *New York Press* picked them "New York's Best Unsigned Band" and wrote: "They're so damn good it's not funny." Joey Ramone raved, "They'll blow your brains out." The kings of *New York Scum Rock* partook of '88's *Urban Rag* and '95's *Picklemania NYC* comps.

Angel Rot set in when White Zombie fired guitarist Tom Five (Guay). His loud return with bassist Mike Davis and drummer Steve Kleiner debuted in March 1989 with Antiseen and the Thing. Two singles, 1990's "Screw Drive" and 1991's "Necrostrangle" 7"s, came out on Fuck Records, and Fuck You Records. Rot cut an LP in 1993 but the studio owner went to jail. Those lost tapes got discovered in the storage room of Nanuet Mall and got released as 1999's *Unlistenable Hymns of Unlistenable Damage* (Man's Ruin). **The Thing** was into noise, smoke bombs, and firecrackers. As per George Petros (*Seconds #13*): "The Thing enters through numerous channels: psychedelia, heavy metal, science fiction, jazz, horror, even primitive pop." Jesse Obstbaum, Sal Canzonieri, Jake Otterman, Sean Bolivar, and Andy Nelson self-released 1986's *Bobo46* tape, leading to 1989's *Blu4U* 7" EP, 1990's *From Another World* LP, 1991's *Peel Sessions*, and 1992's *Austere Precautions* 10".

Low Meato shocked Downtown with wild gigs and "cock rock" stickers showing their logo of a penis in a black leather jacket. The 1989 *Low Meato* EP included "Ben Wa Balls," "Penis Power," and "Easygirl," subjects explored on 1991's "Dopey Love" 45. (Armando J. Macchiavello went by the *nom-de-putz* Thruster HW. Felix Sebacious left to run Blue Grape Marketing. Todd "Meato" Irwin drummed in Murphy's Law.) **Falafel Mafia** featured irate vocalist Heavy Duty, an NYHC hero and junkie weed dealer. Their 1995 *You Love Us* included insolent punk/metal paeans like "Satan Drank My Piss," "Dump in Her Drawers," and the pro-heroin "Drivin' on H." (Heavy Duty later did spoken word on *Howard Stern* and *Jon Stewart* with guitarist Head G, until forsaking his past to become a street evangelist.)

Bad Tuna Experience included NYHC females from Killer Instinct and No Thanks. Even Worse bassist Eric Kyle led **Spineless Yesmen**, who did a demo produced by Jerry Williams. **Porno Dracula** with Stimulators bassist Nick Marden rocked Hank's Crystal Palace, a skid-row Bowery bar selling bottles of Thunderbird. **Traci Lords' Ex-Lovers** starred Chad Pillieri (whose "We're Not Gonna Make It" got covered by one-hit wonders Presidents of the United States of America) before his alt-rock fame in All About Chad. **Bloodsuckers from Outer Space, Bloodsisters, Holy Crow**, and **Ghetto Dogs** were on *New York Scum Rock*. Mykel Board wrote of **Roadkill** in *MRR*: "Chris, the singer, looks like a hetero Joan Jett. Kind of makes it hard to sit down. Kind of makes it hard, period."

Scum together: *Downtown* Magazine cover story by Mykel Board, 1991. Courtesy of Mykel Board.

ANTI-FOLK

Years seem to drop like flies in that mud
You wake up younger, dumber, and not in love
—Brenda Kahn, "She's in Love"

"Anti-folk," an acoustic realm equal parts beatnik poet and punk squatter, was born of the punk clubs, not folk cafés. Anti-folk's star, Lach, built a scene that lasted years, first in his 1984-era Rivington Street loft the Fort (for Kurosawa's *The Hidden Fortress*), and briefly at Sophie's Bar on East 5th Street, before establishing itself at the Sidewalk Cafe (94 Avenue A) where he'd MC "Anti-Hootenanny" open-mic nights, billed as "The Fort at the Sidewalk." Fort stars included Paleface, Roger Manning, Brenda Kahn, Kirk Kelly, Zane Campbell, Moldy Peaches, and Cyndi Lee Berryhill. Most played on 1996's *Lach's Anti-hoot: Live from the Fort at Sidewalk Cafe*. During the Tompkins Square Park Riots, the Fort served as the safe house, with Lach as media spokesman.

The industry took notice: Khan made an album for Columbia, Kelly and Manning for Black Flag's SST. Tom Goodkind (Washington Squares) produced Lach for Danny Goldberg's Gold Castle. Danny Fields managed Paleface. The Moldy Peaches launched Adam Green and Kimya Dawson. But anti-folk's biggest hit was L.A.'s Beck, who learned the ropes staying with Pale-face. The California Scientologist presented a palatable answer to LES scum. (Anti-folk carried on, more "knerdy" slacker than twisted druggie.)

LACH (musician): When I arrived to the West Village folk clubs, there was no path for me the way there is one today. There was no MTV Unplugged, no Violent Femmes, no Springsteen's Nebraska. It was un-charted territory; a bunch of us just knew there had to be something more than where "folk" had landed. We dug Phil Ochs and Woody but also loved Rotten and Strummer. Dylan and Woody would've fit right into the scene at the Fort. (2002)

PALEFACE (musician): Anti-folk started as this thing by punk rock kids with acoustic guitars who couldn't get gigs in those Village '60s clubs, so they had to play in the Lower East Side in art spaces and dive bars and whatnot. Nobody wanted to be the next Joan Baez—it was about playing as hard and fast and loud as you could. But it was also very lyrical with all these freaky poets and performance artists before the gentrification and the riots. It was a volatile scene: anarchists and Missing Foundation were all part of anti-folk. (2011)

CINDY LEE BERRYHILL (musician): Kirk Kelly, Lach and I met in summer 1985 outside Folk City. After a few weeks of hanging out, the three of us arranged a meeting to talk about us outsiders. Lach had a little folk fest he ran out of his place on the Lower East Side that was retaliation against the folk establishment. The established clubs like Folk City hated our attitude. We were scruffs and didn't sound like James Taylor. I just liked the sound of "anti-folk." Lach eventually called his fest "The Anti-Folk Fest" where all of us scraggly acoustic types with a love of the Pistols and Woody Guthrie played for each other. (2002)

Don't make me fight, I don't want to fight you
Don't make me love, I don't want to love you
—LACH, "THE CONTENDER"

Lach ("rhymes with snatch") straddled Village bohemia and LES street punk. Tom Goodkind produced the SUNY-Purchase dropout's 1990 *The Contender* that *Spin* said, "arrives with the kind of mythmaking that announced the young Dylan at Folk City or Hendrix's debut in London." Too bad the label folded. Richard Barone produced 1999's *Blang!* and 2001's *Kids Fly Free.*

Kirk Kelly differed from his pal Lach by not looking homeless. As Folk Brothers, the two made 1985's *All Folked up with Nowhere to Go* tape. The Long Island–bred troubadour released 1988's *Go Man Go* (SST) of union protest music with a requisite singer-songwriter subway shot (by filmmaker Beth B.) and appeared on 1989's *Broome Closet Anti Folk Sessions* tape with Paleface and Cindy Lee Berryhill. ("The Billy Bragg of New York" still at times performs at picket lines.)

Roger Manning learned the ropes playing on the streets and subways, and in Missing Foundation. Credits to 1988's *Roger Manning* (SST) read: "Dedicated to my father who never heard these songs, and to the riders of the NYC MTA who heard it 1st." Most of his titles had "Blues" ("Radical Blues," "Tompkins Square Blues," "East 5th St. Blues").

Brenda Kahn began at the Anti-Hoots with Lach, Kirk Kelly, and her ex Roger Manning. Indie recordings, 1990's *Goldfish Don't Talk Back* for Albert Garzon's Comm3 and 1992's *Life in the Drug War Trenches* EP, portended a Sony deal. Her 1992 David Kahne–produced *Epiphany in Brooklyn* yielded tours with the Kinks and Bob Dylan. *Interview* called her "the girl in high school whose braininess was sexier than the whole cheerleading squad."

Paleface, the original lo-fi slacker, learned music at age twenty in the LES from a down-and-out Daniel Johnston. Next roommate Beck soaked it in, as did Moldy Peaches, who slept on his couch. His 1991 *Paleface* (Polydor) came about after Danny Fields saw him play at Lach's Antihoot. But the CD flopped and 'Face got dropped. Kramer accidentally erased 1994's follow-up *Generic America*; they reconciled and recut it as 1995's *Raw* (Shimmy-Disc). And then 1996's Andy Paley–produced *Get Off* (Sire) came out the same time as Beck's *Odelay.*

DRUMS ALONG THE HUDSON

PROTO—ALT/GARAGE REVIVAL

1980–1987: Fuzztones, Fleshtones, Feelies, Bongos, Individuals, Raunch Hands, Maxwell's, Club 57, The Dive, Pier Platters, Midnight Records, Bar/None, WFMU

We're outta place: The Outta Place, 1984. Photo by
Sherry Mincello. Courtesy of Andrea Matthews Kusten.

GARAGE REVIVAL

THE RISE

In the dark you hear a sound
From my basement underground
—THE FUZZTONES, "CELLAR DWELLER"

The '80s garage-rock revival of a '60s sound arose from young fans of the pop
sides of punk bands like the Ramones, Dictators, and Cramps. The Fuzztones,
Fleshtones, A-Bones, Zantees, Rousers, Cheepskates, Vipers, Mosquitos, Mad
Violets, Raunch Hands, Senders, and others oozed Downtown attitude as
they entertained teenagers high on booze, 'shrooms, and acid, at semilegal
clubs and spaces. In 1986, the city's drinking age rose to twenty-one, but

eighteen-year-olds and above got grandfathered in, ensuring a few more years of underage energy.

JON WEISS (The Vipers): I think the one thing all the garage bands have in common today is they admit to their influences. The upholding of an American tradition from the '60s, when rock and roll was aggressive. (1985)

PAUL MARTIN (The Vipers): The garage-rock scene of the '80s was like a Hollywood version or the impressions your little brother or sister had of what it was like in the '60s, rather than from an understanding of why the stuff actually occurred. In other words, it was made up of people too young to have experienced the first go-round. Not to denigrate the scene, which was perfectly valid and was a great happening. (2004)

The Fuzztones and Fleshtones were the key bands. The media even stoked a semi-imaginary "Fleshtones vs. Fuzztones" rift. Fuzztones' first gigs at Club 57 inspired the Cramps' trash-culture obscurae. Fleshtones spurred a scene, starting with gigs at Club 57. Things looked great when Fleshtones singer Peter Zaremba hosted MTV's *Cutting Edge* from 1984 to 1987.

RUDI PROTRUDI (The Fuzztones): When The Fuzztones formed in 1980 there weren't any bands around in New York City doing what we were doing with that '60s psychedelic edge like we have. So we were ahead of everybody. (2007)

DEB O'NAIR (The Fuzztones): We hung out together at Club 57. I go-go danced for them at Irving Plaza for the "Club 57 New Wave Vaudeville Show," when Henry Jones projected his Soul City film on top of them. I personally never felt rivalry with them. We were very different musically. I think they're a good band and they have their own *Spinal Tap* stuff going on, which I got to see a lot of too. Personally I was always a fan. (2012)

THE SCENE

Have you heard the American sound?
Don't want to hear you put it down
—THE FLESHTONES, "AMERICAN BEAT"

The garage revival was about nightlife and live shows. The Fuzztones-organized "FuzzFest '84" included the Mosquitos, Tryfles, Cheepskates, Outta Place, and Vipers. The show, June 30, 1984, at the Upper West Side club 240 West, was the first time those bands met. The "Mind's Eye" series run by Mad Violets' Dino Sorbello made the cover of *High Times*. Shows occurred at: the Strip, booked by Deb Parker and Gary Balaban; McGoverns, a 14th Street saloon; Southern Funk Café by Port Authority, iffy spaces like No Se No, Charas Hall, or the Asylum; or Maxwell's in Hoboken. Notable compilations included *Battle of the Garage Bands*, a *Goldmine*-sponsored ROIR tape with local bands, and the more nationally minded ROIR cassette *Goldmine Presents Garage Sale*, launched by a March 1985 Fuzztones/Mosquitos/Cheepskates show at Irving Plaza. The zine **99th Floor**, begun in 1982 by Ron Rimsite, Dawn Eden, and John Hanrattie, did two issues that included 10″ flexi-discs, notably 1984's *New York Freakout!* with Fuzztones and Vipers. Long Island zine editor Blair Buscareno (*Teen Scene*) coined '83 "The Summer of Fuzz." Unlike L.A.'s "Paisley Underground," NYC garage groups had urban grit and FU attitude.

No Se No (42 Rivington Street), a scary graffiti-strewn storefront Puerto Rican social-club-turned-gallery/performance space (No Se No and nearby Nada Gallery were the first such LES spots), had a doorman with a baseball bat to keep out junkies and bums. You'd step down five steps into chaos; all drinks were $1. It's where many of these bands played. Ray Kelly and other "Rivington School" artists welded thirty-foot scrap metal sculptures in the adjacent lot at Rivington and Forsythe (razed by developers in '87). It shut in late 1985.

MIKE MARICONDA (Raunch Hands): We enjoyed No Se No—a real den of sin after-hours dump on Rivington Street. A totally illegal social club, bands started playing at 3:30 a.m. It was really dark in there and people were always fucking or taking drugs in the bathroom or just inside the club most of the time, 'cause the wait for the bathroom was too long because people were in there fucking or taking drugs or both! (2001)

The Dive (257 West 29th Street), a former belly-dancing club with candlelit tables and mirrored tiles, offered tarot card readings, comedians, and magicians. Opened in 1982 by mentalist Glenn Gazin, it featured art by his wife Tani Conrad like a nine-foot skeleton marionette. The Dive became the garage scene's epicenter from 1983 to 1987, first with gigs by Cheepskates, Fuzztones, and Fleshtones (as the Hextones). Gazin paid the talent 100 percent of the door, so others wanted to play. Rick Sullivan's *Gore Gazette* hosted retro bands and B-movies. Mad Violets' Wendy Wild and Dino Sorbelli held their wedding party there.

RUDI PROTRUDI (The Fuzztones): The Dive was a small club, but it was our club, where all the '60s freaks would hang. Everyone was into dressing the part: bowl haircuts, '60s clothes, the whole bit. Lots of people tripped, many more drank like fish. Everyone was fucking everyone else. All the bands were there: Mosquitos, Mad Violets, Outta Place, Tryfles, Vipers. It was an incredible time. I doubt anything like it'll happen again. (2010)

DEB O'NAIR (The Fuzztones): Shows at the Dive were real fun. Club 57 was drawing to a close, and the Dive became the New York garage scene den—the hangout place, a place to have fun and be seen. . . . I'm not sure how it faded out. (2012)

MICHAEL STARK (New York scene): At the Dive, the bands were fans and the fans were bands. Everyone came out to see everybody else. The scene was made up of some real music lovers, and zealots, impeccably dressed, and some could really dance. (2004)

BLAIR BUSCARENO (*Teen Scene*): I remember that a bunch of mod kids, who'd go to the Dive, would scale a wall if they didn't think they would get in. Guys had a harder time being underage than girls did. (2004)

JOHN FAY (The Tryfles/The Outta Place): New York City clubs remained lax in their carding. I changed my birthdate on my paper New

York driver's license. Easy to do for me, I just wet the "1" in front of the "3" until it disappeared. Then put it in a window wallet. (2004)

LYNNE VON SCHLICHTING (Da Willys): The Dive in Chelsea had a cheesy decor, real '60s looking, so it was right for all those bands. It was fashion-oriented. . . . All that '60s fetishism looked cool but it could be a bit limiting. (2011)

Midnight Records (148 West 23rd Street) was the brainchild of enigmatic Frenchman J. D. Martignon, who'd sung for the French prog band Dagon and wrote for Paris's *Parapluie*. In 1973 he came to cover the new punk scene in NYC, where he began a '60s-music mail-order firm, then in 1978 opened a record shop, and in 1984, a label: A-Bones, Fuzztones, Outta Place, Senders, Tryfles, Vipers, and Zantees all made Midnight records. (In 2004 J.D. got indicted for selling live bootlegs, charges later dropped in U.S. District Court.)

JOHN FAY: Despite questionable practices, Midnight documented the New York garage scene, so in hindsight, hats off to 'em. We'd not be here if they had not done so. There were also one or two bands that were able to use them as a stepping-stone. (2004)

Kicks began in 1978 with *New York Rocker* writers Billy Miller, a Long Island–reared high school chum of Joe Satriani, and Miriam Linna, drummer in the Cramps and Nervus Rex. The couple put out a manically musicological zine devoted to pre-'70s rock, soul, rockabilly, B-movies, and other now de rigueur kitsch Americana. Chris Morris wrote in *Billboard* (5/30/92): "*Kicks* is a wacked-out treat for fans of the outer limits of musical life." **Norton Records** came from *Kicks'* Billy and Miriam, a label similar to Bomp! but dedicated to unheard/unhinged outsider music. Their first releases came from in-depth *Kicks* features, such as 1986's 500 copies of hillbilly cat Hasil Adkins's *Out to Hunch*.

MIRIAM LINNA (*Kicks*): Bomp! Records for us was like the Bible, but after a certain point I wasn't interested in the modern bands they were pushing. That's why we started *Kicks* in 1979, because we were into older stuff. Old records that were new to us. (2011)

The summer of fuzz: Mad Violets, Swamp Goblyns, and Secret Syde, The Dive, 1984. Artwork by Lynne Von Schlichting.

THE MUSIC

Don't get left behind
Just let me blow your mind
—THE FUZZTONES, "HIGHWAY 69"

The Fuzztones came out of a Harrisburg, PA, garage band, Tina Peel, based around singer Rudi Protrudi (Glen Dalpis) and keyboardist Deb O'Nair (Carol Krautheim). In 1977 they moved to East 10th Street, after Vin Scelsa chose their "Weekend Geek" as his WPIX-FM theme song. In 1980, named for the FuzzTone guitar pedal, they'd excel at CBs, Pep Lounge, and Mudd Club. Fuzztones led the revival: dressed like 1966, playing psych nuggets and similar originals. They introduced Screamin' Jay Hawkins to hipsters, coheadlining Irving Plaza in 1984 and 1985. Their 1984 "Bad News Travels Fast" single starred Elan Portnoy on "lead grunge." Both 1984's *Leave Your Mind at Home* and 1985's *Lysergic Emanations* stand as NYC garage classics. (Protrudi moved to L.A. in 1986.)

RUDI PROTRUDI (The Fuzztones): The press hated the garage revival in the beginning, I don't know why. There's always been something about the Fuzztones that threatens people. (2007)

DEB O'NAIR (The Fuzztones): There were conflicts between Rudi and I with other members over songwriting. Rudi would go behind our back and cut shady deals. Rudi and I lived together but he was dogging around, he can't keep his wang in his pants. He likes to be kept; he's a kept man. (2012)

> *I got a different fascination*
> *To satisfy my needs*
> —THE FLESHTONES, "F-F-FASCINATION"

The Fleshtones played '60s party-rock with Farfisa, tambourine, and harmonica. Peter Zaremba was the paisley-crazed pied piper of the garage revival. Marty Thau released 1979's "American Beat" 45 and 1980's *Marty Thau Presents 2x5* comp on his Red Star label, and produced 1979's ROIR cassette *Blast Off.* Fleshtones starred in the 1981 film *Urgh! A Music War* shot at CBGB (where they debuted in 1976). They cracked the charts with 1981's *Roman Gods* (IRS), and over time did more than a dozen albums. (Ben Sterbakov stole Peter's prized *Roman Gods* jacket at City Gardens before dying of cancer.)

PETER ZAREMBA (The Fleshtones): We've never been heavily identified with being a New York band—egghead guys and girls, ugly haircuts and some guy who's really skinny and wears glasses and plays an out-of-tune guitar. I like that stuff. We represent American rock and roll at large, the whole thing. We're an American band. (1983)

> *I'm not a pretty boy, I'm not a lonely boy*
> *I'm just a party boy*
> —THE ROUSERS, "PARTY BOY"

The Rousers (named for Duane Eddy's Rebel Rousers) blared a punky roots-rock. The Rousers Clubhouse (4 St. Marks Place) became a late-night terminus after their gigs at Hurrah, Max's, or the Rocker Room (on East 48th). *New York Rocker*'s Andy Schwartz managed them for a sec. They'd also fall out with Nancy Jeffries, Andy Somers, Bob Rowland, Danny Heeps, and Polydor's Jerry Schoenbaum (calling Schoenbaum's girlfriend a "whore"). Their only release would be 1981's Wayne Kramer–produced "Party Boy" 45 (Jimboco).

The Senders, led by Parisian émigré/Heartbreakers roadie Philippe "Flipper" Marcadé, cranked sexy '50s throwback rock in sharkskin suits. Johnny Thunders filled in on guitar in 1978 (three times at Max's, twice at Hurrah), but one lineup had Robert Gordon guitarist Wild Bill Thompson, Victims drummer Marc Bourset, and Walter Lure's brother Richie on bass (replacing Steve Shevlin who went deaf!). Their early catalog consisted of 1978's "The Living End" 7″, 1980's *Seven Song Super Single* 10″ on Max's Kansas City's label, and 1981's *Retour A L'Envoyeur* LP (Skydog). Marcadé then formed **The Backbones,** a flashy revue doing a sax-y mix of rare soul covers and old-school originals heard on 1986's *The Backbones* (Midnight). The Senders' 1988 Monday residency at the Continental lasted for years.

The Outta Place, NYC's garage rock "Cave Teens," starred Maine expat singer Mike Chandler, roommate guitarist Jordan Tarlow, bassist Orin Portnoy (brother of Fuzztones' Elan Portnoy), drummer Andrea Matthews, and Rudi Protrudi–associated organist Shari Mirojnik. The Dive regulars, like most of these bands, rehearsed at the Music Building. *We're Outta Place* (Midnight) got cut after Mike left to do Raunch Hands, but got lured to record in 1984 with booze, et cetera. *Outta Too,* cut under similar promises in 1987, rocked too.

Raunch Hands, an inebriated garage/R&B act, first gigged at No Se No and then left their stain at Maxwell's and CBGB. It began with Outta Place frontman Mike Chandler, guitarists Mike Tchang and Mike Mariconda, bassist George Sulley, and drummer Vince Brnicevic. Their 1984 debut *Stomp It* EP (cover shot of them stepping in cow shit) came out on Egon Records, the one-off label of a pre–Yo La Tengo Ira Kaplan and Georgia Hubley (named for their cat). Of 1985's *El Learn to Whap-a-Dang with the Raunch Hands* (Relativity), *Spin* enthused: "Watching the band onstage is like getting lassoed into honkytonk heaven, where the tap never runs dry and there are plenty of cowgirls to go around."

The Zantees, punkabilly pioneers named for the aliens in an *Outer Limits* episode, featured Billy Miller and Miriam Linna of *Kicks* magazine. They jammed swamp-drained blues, first with 1979's one-song *Goldmine* flexi ("Francene"), then with 1980's *Out for Kicks* LP and Peter Holsapple–produced "Rockin' in the House" single. Billy and Miriam broke it up in 1983, and shot back in a similar vein as the A-Bones. **The A-Bones** (a hot-rodding term for a 1929 Model A Ford) were begun by Linna and Miller and joined by saxophonist Lars Espensen, guitarist Bruce Bennett, and bassist Marcus "The Carcass" Natale. Efforts like 1988's *Free Beer for Life!* (artwork by Vacant Lot's Pete Ciccone) or 1992's *I Was a Teenage Mummy* (Christopher Frieri's film they were in) conveyed trash culture mania.

The Vipers (a jazz term for the hiss of smoking marijuana), personified the revival. Jon Weiss grew up listening to the oldies on WCBS-FM. He learned of punk bands doing '60s songs and Lenny Kaye's *Nuggets* comp. "We're Outta Here!" on a *New York Freakout!* 10″ flexi preceded 1983's "Never Alone" 45. *Outta the Nest* sold 20,000 units in 1984. Fewer sold of 1987's *How about Somemore?*

The Cheepskates, led by Shane Faubert on Farfisa and vocals, thrived on the Dive scene. Both 1983's "Run Better Run" 45 and 1984's *Run Better Run* LP (Midnight) offered shades of the Zombies or the Seeds. A 1986 follow-up, *Second and Last,* included original bassist Tony Low and drummer Van Kieth Morrow. (Guitarist David John Herrera recorded solo as Herrera & the Handouts; Shane carried on with different lineups into the '90s.)

Mad Violets, a garage/psych band led by late Downtown star Wendy Wild (Andreiev) with Harrisburg-bred guitarist Dino Sorbello, began at Private's, where Wendy emceed and Dino bussed tables. At their first gig at Lucky Strike gallery, with Fleshtone Keith Streng on drums, they tossed 'shrooms into the crowd and played four hours, as the band and fans tripped. "Psilocybe" on 1984's *Battle of the Garages (Vol. 2)* predated 1986's *World of LSD.* **Blacklight Chameleons** with a psych stage show was Dino Sorbello's next band. After Dive gigs came March 1985's six-song EP (for Voxx). June 1985's *Vanity Fair* ran two pages on the band, shot at their Avenue B apartment. The acid-laced ensemble peaked in '86 with model/singer Sharon Middendorf. *High Times* knew enough to put her on their cover.

The Tryfles, a high-energy, half-female quartet, starred vocalist-guitarists John Fay and Lesya Karpilov. Towering bassist Peter Stuart stood center stage, making for a distinct look. The paisley group gigged at the Dive, Maxwell's, or Irving Plaza, their promo enhanced by Karpilov's groovy posters. They released 1985's "(Had Enough of) Your Lies" 7″ and 1986's self-titled LP (Midnight). **The Optic Nerve** began with wild gigs at the Dive and Brooklyn house parties, and two C&W-tinged Cryptovision 7″s, 1986's *Ain't That a Man* EP and 1987's "Leaving Yesterday Behind." Mike Stark wrote in *Jersey Beat* (#23, 11/85): "They're as unpredictable as the drugs they'll have you thinking you're on."

The Mosquitos (for a band on *Gilligan's Island*) were a Northport, LI, quintet with British Invasion style. They debuted with "Darn Well" opening 1985's *Presents Garage Sale*. The popularity of 1985's *That Was Then, This Is Now!* (Valhalla) yielded a *Teen Beat* profile, and Ritz and Irving Plaza shows. The title cut went Top 10 when redone by the Monkees on their 1986 comeback. The Secret Service, a Who/Animals-style mod quartet friends with the Mosquitos, did 1988's self-released, Chris Xefos–produced *It's All Happening Here* EP meant to come out on Celluloid in 1986. The Stepford Husbands began with Gary Thomas and Dave Amels bonding at Peppermint Lounge over '60s psych-rock. They did five 7″s and an LP, all for Cryptovision, but only six gigs. In 1985 they split to SF to record 1985's "I'm Rode Out" with hippie guitarist Bill Harper (of Savage Resurrection).

The Maneaters, an all-girl act named for Herschell Gordon Lewis's B-movie of hellish female bikers, impressed in their short time. Shari Mirojnik and Andrea Matthews came outta the Outta Place. Ellen O'Neill drummed in the Tryfles; Tara McMunn bassed in the Ultra V; late guitarist Linda Lutz was in the Pods. They ended after a 1986 four-song demo produced by Peter Holsapple (paid in pot). Das Fürlines, praised by *People* as "the Polka pride of the Lower East Side," began as a drunken idea to cover German rockers the Monks. Wendy Wild, Deb O'Nair, Rachel Amodeo, Holly George, and Elizabeth Gall awed in Tyrolean dresses, Attila the Hun helmets, pretzel crowns, and studded lederhosen, be it at the Pyramid, Love Club, or Wigstock. The Pussywillows were a Ronettes/Crystals-style girl group formed by Raunch Hands singer Mike Chandler for his young girlfriend Elinor Blake, and her friends Lisa Dembling and Lisa Genio. Todd Abramson (Telstar label rep and Maxwell's booker) got them gigs, leading to 1988's *Spring Fever* EP and "Vindaloo" in the film *Kill the Moonlight*. (Blake became the chanteuse April March.)

The Rat Bastards played obscure garage rock gems (like the Remains' "Don't Look Back" and the Count Five's "Double Decker Bus") but left behind no recordings. They broke up in 1988 after trying to make an album with Billy Childish (Thee Headcoats) and split into Vacant Lot (singer Pete Ciccone and drummer Paul Corio) and Devil Dogs (guitarist Andy Gortler and bassist Steve Baise). World Famous Blue Jays, a Brooklyn bar band, played trucker-friendly swing with punk veracity. *Vending Times* editor Jeremy Tupper and Jay Sherman-Godfrey began Diesel Only Records, releasing 7″s produced by Del Lords' Eric Ambel like 1988's "Ten Pin Boogie," 1991's "Good Morning Mr. Trucker," and 1993's "Do It for Hank," for which they began a jukebox network. The Headless Horsemen, with Fuzztone Elan Portnoy and Tryfle Peter

Stuart, released 1987's *Can't Help but Shake* and 1988's *Gotta Be Cool*. Their final session of covers got issued as **Chris Such & His Savages** (1989's *Leave My Kitty Alone*). **Soul Assassins**, the band of *High Times* staffers Flick Ford and Steve Hagar with Fleshtones' Brian Spaeth, did a 1988 four-song 45 that got DJ play at Carmelita's and Pyramid.

Wait too long
And the moment's gone
—EASTERN BLOC, "WAIT TOO LONG"

Eastern Bloc—Holly and the Italians guitarist/vocalist Mark Sidgwick, Patti Smith bassist Ivan Kral, and David Johansen drummer Frankie LaRocka— rocked a new wave–edged pop. They covered Patti's "Dancing Barefoot" on 1987's Neil Giraldo–produced *Eastern Bloc* (Jem), sold as "a study in musical contrasts." **The Washington Squares**—Lauren Agnelli (Nervus Rex), Tom Goodkind (U.S. Ape), and Bruce Jay Paskow (The Invaders)—began Peter, Paul and Mary–style in berets, goatees, and sunglasses. In total, 1987's Grammy-winning *The Washington Squares* and 1989's *Fair and Square* sold 250,000 copies. Dave Van Ronk conferred artistic blessings, but most folkies saw them as a novelty.

Del Lords played rootsy Americana rock with punk cred and greaser cool. The quartet came from Dictators circles with Scott "Top Ten" Kempner and Eric "Roscoe" Ambel on guitar, Manny Caiati on bass, and Frank Funaro on drums; all four sang. *Frontier Days* played on MTV in 1984 with "Burning in the Flame of Love" and a rave-up of Blind Alfred Reed's "How Can a Poor Man Stand Such Times and Live." Ensuing recordings suffered similar fates: too soft for metal, too punk for pop, and predating alt country. **Alter Boys** got known for 1986's 7″ "Piles," a lo-tech VU-ish "hit" on WFMU, cited in *Spin*. The buzz generated the five twenty-year-old Catholic high school grads a big-time deal. But 1987's Andy Shernoff–produced *Soul Desire* (Big Time) ended when the label went bankrupt.

THE FALL

In the end, minimal interest from the rock press and record business crushed most of these bands. Jon Weiss of the Vipers went on to produce the Cavestomp festival and label that caters to '60s bands and fetishists. Little Steven (Van Zandt) promotes garage rock through his radio networks. Some of these players created indie rock, the roots of Yo La Tengo or Nada Surf. Others partook in the '90s punk revival at Coney Island High. A few diehards still have a mod-ish spirit.

SAMMY JAMES JUNIOR (The Mooney Suzuki): The '60s garage rock audience are passionate and musically literate, and are great to talk music with and can really let it all hang down at a show—but believe me, it is a small, finite gang. We've had the privilege of meeting almost all of them! (2001)

Drums along the Hudson: The Bongos, Hoboken Train Station, 1981. Rob Norris, Richard Barone, Frank Giannini. Photo by John Friedlander.

HOBOKEN PROTO-ALT

THE RISE

Don't think I can ever sing that song
Little secrets we bring along
—Yo La Tengo, "Today Is the Day"

Hoboken—a fourteen-block, mile-square town across the Hudson from Manhattan—arose as a tough waterfront pier of stevedores and longshoremen, as well as a railroad hub. The home to the nation's first brewery in 1642 boomed with fifty saloons, and served as an embarking point for U.S. troops in WWI. Amid Prohibition, its cabarets and speakeasies a ferry away beckoned as "Greenwich Village West" or as per Christopher Morley "the last seacoast of bohemia." In the '30s, seventy-five thousand Italian-American immigrants lived there. The town hit the skids after 1966, when the Hoboken Terminal stopped running the ferries and trains. Sinatra's home, famous for the aroma of the Maxwell House factory by the river, became a land that time forgot, a sleepy municipality rife with '70s poverty, crime, and corruption.

Hoboken's first palpable scene coalesced around a group of late-'60s artists and the hippie freak band the Insect Trust living in the Hoboken Power and Light Company building at 39 Second Street. In the '80s, the town became a cheap real estate option for those seeking proximity to NYC. That's how Hoboken grew into a rock epicenter. The story starts in 1977 when Glenn Morrow, an NYU grad and *New York Rocker* ad rep, found a six-bedroom $65 apartment on 11th and Hudson, and his band members moved in. Morrow's band "a" (named for *a*, Warhol's only novel) was the first group to play Maxwell's, and became a magnet for the new scene. Morrow brought to Maxwell's edgy NYC bands such as the dB's, Fleshtones, and Necessaries. Members of "a" formed the Bongos and the Individuals.

GLENN MORROW (The Individuals): When I moved to Hoboken, it was a bombed-out city; the building and apartments were falling apart. There was the white flight and riots of the late '60s, when everyone left for safety in Secaucus or something. There was a dangerous junkie Lower East Side element, with gangs and knife fights. Soon after us, it got nicer and landlords started burning down their buildings to build new condos. (2011)

RICHARD BARONE (The Bongos): The musical difference from the East Village and Hoboken suited the geography. Before I was going to CBGB every night absorbing punk, but that ground was covered. Hoboken bands were more pop-oriented and less distorted. I feel just as aggressive but more melodic. The way we dressed and played had a sense of an earlier rock, very '60s-ish. Being next to Manhattan made it easy for us to get press yet we were physically detached by the Hudson River. It was an amazingly unique energy; we were able to create our music in a place not totally dominated by commerce. (2011)

The Bongos' Rob Norris attended the first Feelies show, at CBGB. The Feelies, an NJ group big in the city and on the seminal Stiff label, inspired many locals. Norris turned on his singer, Richard Barone, who was equally awed. Thus began the Bongos/Feelies bills that defined Hoboken's proto-alternative sound.

GLENN MORROW: We all loved the Feelies because they were from Jersey but they made it in New York. The Feelies inspired people with a homegrown sound. They weren't trying to be punk or new romantic. There was a shared aesthetic; we were all into the VU and Eno and oblique lyrics. Suddenly there was the Bongos; my the Individuals; Fast Car with James Mastro later of the Bongos; Red Buckets; Phosphenes . . . (2011)

RICHARD BARONE: The Feelies predated and influenced us. We loved what they did, even though they didn't play often; like four times a year. We ended up friends and worked well together. The Bongos, we were more conscious of songwriting, while the Feelies developed one-chord hypnotizing drone sections like the VU. As much as we were into the VU—Rob Norris played in that band's last lineup— we were more melodic. The analogy would be the Bongos were more the "banana" album, and the Feelies were more *White Light/White Heat.* The Feelies were like our slightly older brothers. Their influence was as if they were family rather than an outside force. (2011)

Some people called Feelies, Bongos, and Individuals "agit-pop": quirky white dance rhythms to leave one happily agitated. The sound tied to two scenes: Downtown's art-damaged no wave, and the jangly, jittery American power-pop explosion (from the Raspberries and Cheap Trick to the Knack and the Romantics). The town's pleasant environs made for a scene similar to Athens, GA (R.E.M., Pylon), or Minneapolis (Replacements, Soul Asylum). The Hoboken scene included the dB's from North Carolina, Human Switchboard from Ohio, New Jersey's Smithereens, Long Island's Dancing Hoods, and full-on NYers like Del Lords, or Sonic Youth, who rehearsed and recorded in Hoboken.

GLENN MORROW: "a" had a song, "Hoboken Party." The Bongos called it "The New Liverpool." We were kids from burbs into this new music but a bit intimidated by the city. The Lower East Side was intense, after 3 a.m. past Avenue A you'd get mugged. We wanted a friendlier environment, to be a part of something not so dark and scary. There was a sense of exuberance and enthusiasm. We'd jump around onstage, not withdrawn like New York. There were dark undercurrents but it was celebratory positive. Lots of transcendental guitars, a strong Tom Verlaine influence; trebly guitars like Strats and Rickenbackers and Telecasters. It was pre–jangly alternative rock, created by people from all over—like the South with the dB's and Amy Rigby. New York bands had things that made them more like Ramones. This was the burbs finding their sound. (2011)

GEORGIA HUBLEY (Yo La Tengo): I think the PATH train makes a difference. It kind of chills you out after a night of angry New York bands. So I guess when we get back home, it comes out in the music. Some people like it, some people don't. (1989)

Luxury condos coming to your neighborhood soon: The Bongos and Human Switchboard, Maxwell's, New Year's Eve, 1980. Artwork by Guy Ewald.

Maxwell's (1039 Washington Street), a former blue-collar tavern for Maxwell House Coffee factory workers, was opened in August 1978 by Steve Fallon with his sisters and brother-in-law (Kathryn Jackson Fallon, Anne Fallon Mazzola, and Mario Mazzola) as not another dingy 'Boken bar with Sinatra on the jukebox or some CBGB-ish punk club, but a brunch spot catering to the new yuppies and nearby students of Stevens Tech. The eatery had a hip jukebox and local artists' works on the walls. The 200-capacity back room served as Jersey's first underground rock club and helped build the national alt-rock scene. Touring acts loved to play there because they got treated well and fed a hot meal. Press compared the venue's demise to CBGB's closure, but that was an overreach.

GLENN MORROW: Steve Fallon was the architect of this whole thing. Maxwell's was a mix of New York rockers and schoolteachers, the underground gay community, and various Hoboken drug cultures. Whatever music you made—garage rock, new romantic, English punk—you felt comfortable. His gift was he gave so many people a shot. I was the first person in the door with a band. When "a" first played Maxwell's, we brought a PA. The back room was in disarray with old beer signs and junk. That's where we rehearsed. I booked one or two nights a week: Nervus Rex, Necessaries, the dB's, Come On, and got paid dinner once a week. It all happened fast, bands began moving to Hoboken. (2011)

Pier Platters (56 Newark Street) was a great American independent record shop; alt-rock was literally born from its bins. The 400-square-foot shop near the PATH train reeked of stale cigs and Chinese takeout, offered 7″s, LPs, CDs, cassettes, fanzines, in-store shows, and Maxwell's tickets. Steve Fallon opened it in 1982 with Irishmen Bill Ryan and Tom Prendergast, and then left to focus on Maxwell's and his Coyote label. Prendergast spent most of his time on his Bar/None label and Tomorrow Management. Musicians Donna Croughn and Otis Ball worked the counter. *Billboard* (5/8/93) said they made $500,000 in 1992. In 1995, Bill and Tom closed shop; around that time the Fallons sold Maxwell's.

GLENN MORROW: There was a point where Pier Platters became the first place to get new alternative music. It catered to a new crowd of listeners suddenly coming to Hoboken, and conversely people went there on their way to Maxwell's. It was like the prototype for what you see in Williamsburg. But then a Sam Goody opened across the street, and you had stores in the city like Kim's doing what they were doing. I guess they overexpanded, got in over their heads. It was like a *High Fidelity* situation, you really had to earn their friendliness. Bar/None started in the back room of Pier Platters. (2011)

Coyote Records put Hoboken on the map. The first two releases of Steve Fallon's label (with Chris Stamey's contacts) came in 1982, with Fallon's sister's boyfriend's band Phosphenes EP and the first Beat Rodeo 12″. A big moment was November 20, 1985's release of *Luxury Condos Coming to Your Neighborhood Soon*, a Hoboken compilation with Rage to Live, the Wygals, Yo La Tengo, Syd Straw, and Raunch Hands. Coyote put out forty records, mostly distributed by A&M. Fallon, with Hüsker Dü's Bob Mould, also formed the Singles Only Label, their 7″ imprint run by former WFMU DJ Nick Hill.

Bar/None Records began in 1986 at Pier Platters. Tom Prendergast's first release was the debut by Rage to Live, whose singer Glenn Morrow became his business partner. Next came 1986's hit debut by They Might Be Giants that sold six figures. After 1994's creative apex with Freedy Johnson and Esquivel,

Tom returned to Dublin and sold the business to Morrow, behind a catalog of more than 100 releases at the time of this writing.

WFMU (91.1 FM), among America's top noncommercial stations, tied to the Hoboken explosion and the rise of alt rock. The student-run station of East Orange, NJ's Upsala College came to infamy in 1968 when Vin Scelsa (host of a bold show, *The Closet,* from midnight to 6 a.m.) and a few other radical students seized the station. The college shut it in 1969, and then reopened in 1970. In 1994 FMU became listener-supported and free of Upsala (which shut in 1995) and in 1997 became one of the first stations to broadcast on the Web.

Water Music was launched in 1982 at 201 Grand Street by Robert Miller and Rob Grenoble of the upstate pop/rockers Cries. Steve Fallon heard of their new studio, where they cut the first Chris Stamey 7" on a 4-track. The Feelies, Yo La Tengo, dB's, Bongos, Freedy Johnston, Bob Mould, Marshall Crenshaw, and Mitch Easter all worked there in the '80s.

A band called "a": The roots of Hoboken rock, 1118 Hudson Street, Hoboken, 1980. Photo by Rob Norris with tripod and timer.

THE MUSIC

The band **"a"** (often billed as "A Band") was vocalist Glenn Morrow, guitarist Richard Barone, bassist Rob Norris, and drummer Frank Giannini. The Roxy Music–style NJ group first played in Glenn's hometown at Glen Ridge Congregational Church, and the Showplace in Dover (with Richard Hell's

Voidoids). After those shows as the first group to play Maxwell's, they disbanded over musical direction while recording a demo.

GLENN MORROW (The Individuals): It was impossible to find anyone in New Jersey with any idea of CBGB or Eno or the VU. It wasn't like now with eight million indie-rockers. There was no indie anything, you signed to a major or you did covers. We took a *Voice* ad but used a friend's "212" number because we knew a "201" wouldn't be taken seriously. Richard moved into my place, then the whole band. My friend told me about a bar around the corner that wanted bands. Before that we played the Showplace, the center of the Jersey music scene. We were trying to get the courage to play Max's or CBs. (2011)

RICHARD BARONE (The Bongos): I really didn't know the Warhol novel. "a" was the simplest name we could think of, and alphabetically it'd be the first record in stores. Glenn wrote the music, with lots of ornate arrangements, and anthemic choruses and lyrical concepts, sometime topical. My input was a few lyrics, choruses and refrains. The other guys gravitated to my bassline, the groove-oriented songs. That became the Bongos. (2011)

> *I want to row back home*
> *I want to go back home*
> —THE BONGOS, "IN THE CONGO"

The Bongos embodied "The Hoboken Sound." Richard Barone was first known at age seven as "The Littlest DJ" spinning rock & roll Sundays on WALT-AM in Tampa. He attended NYU when he answered the *Voice* ad to join "a." The original Bongos trio of Richard Barone, Rob Norris, and future Maxwell's chef Frank Giannini honed their sound on the UK label Fetish, when its owner Rod Pearce signed them after their second-ever show, at Maxwell's. They added Fast Car guitarist James Mastro and charted with a UK-only cover of T. Rex's "Mambo Sun." Those new tunes, "Telephoto Lens," "Bullrushes," and "In the Congo," came out Stateside on 1982's cult *Drums along the Hudson.* Nancy Jeffries (of The Insect Trust) signed them to RCA. But both 1983's Richard Gottehrer–produced *Numbers with Wings* and 1985's

Beat Hotel (made at five studios) flopped. Mastro quit in frustration; so they tried with Ivan Julian and then Steve Almaas.

ROB NORRIS (The Bongos): In 1979 the band really clicked, and things took off. We had all the right things happening: the single on Fetish, the label connected to Throbbing Gristle; all this great press; and Vin Scelsa as a big champion on the radio. That mix of power-pop and insane avant-garde craziness—great songs with tremendous rhythms and trademark harmonies—was all there on *Drums along the Hudson.* (2011)

RICHARD BARONE: After *Drums* we signed to RCA. We did two very good records that sold copies, but it was a very different environment for us. We did the best we could but it was always a battle. We could never be the hit-machine they wanted. (2011)

ROB NORRIS: My parents lent us their mobile home to save money on tour. We were drivin' down the PCH and I said to the guys, "These are the good ol' days, they won't get any better than this," and I was right. We signed to RCA and made great records but . . . Our friends R.E.M. stuck to grassroots in-the-van working, but there was a part of us into the '80s glamour thing with all the trappings; it was a poor direction for us. Like with Beat Motel we did three gigs in New York, Boston and D.C. and grossed like $10,000, and we each ended up with like $50 each after tour bus, road crew, lawyers and managers. It started so organic, and over time it turned to compost. Look at the photo on *Beat Hotel*—it's embarrassing. It was a great band that didn't sound like that album. (2011)

> *Can't relax when there's things to do*
> *Big plans stay while the little ones fade*
> —THE FEELIES, "CRAZY RHYTHMS"

The Feelies, proto-alt-rockers of the punk era, perfected nerdy pop with jagged guitar. Glenn Mercer and Bill Million met in junior high school in Haledon, NJ, playing in the Stooges-style Dogfood Killer Band. Mercer and drummer Dave Weckerman then did the OutKids that in August 1976 became the Feelies (a *Brave New World* allusion). They auditioned at CBGB in December 1976 at 2:30 a.m., and got booked two weeks later. Terry Ork put them in Trod Nossel Studios with Prix's Jon Tiven in April 1977 to cut a single ("Forces at Work") for Ork Records that never came out. So 1979's "Fa Cé La" 7″ came on Rough Trade UK, and 1980's *Crazy Rhythms* on Stiff UK. After stoking Hoboken's scene, the Feelies went on hiatus, until 1986's *The Good Earth* and 1991's *Time for a Witness*.

GLENN MERCER (The Feelies): Our sound is very city-oriented, but there is a touch of suburban blues. We only live thirty minutes from Manhattan—there's lots of New York bands that live further away than that. I feel our perspective of the New York Rock scene is very different from someone always surrounded by musicians and music types. (1977)

JON TIVEN (Prix): The Feelies, it was their first time in the studio, and were primitive in terms of technical abilities. They heard the playbacks and it shocked them to be not as good as they thought; at first they didn't think it was them! Mercer and Million, they'd treat the rhythm section badly, make fun of them and treat them like idiots. I never understood why they were that way until I learned one of them worked in a mental institution, and that's how he dealt with people. It was all very strange. (2011)

> *It may not be love, but it might be magic*
> *So girl, don't you act so tragic*
> —The Individuals, "Our World"

The Individuals played melodic pop with a Downtown tilt. "a" singer Glenn Morrow began the Individuals with drummer John Klett. A *Voice* ad got them guitarist Jon Light Klages (scion of easy-listening icon Enoch Light) and bassist Janet Wygal, whose brother Doug replaced Klett. The band rehearsed at Maxwell's, where they wrote 1981's Gene Holder–produced *Aquamarine* (Lust/Unlust), picked EP of the Year in the *New York Times*, and 1982's Mitch Easter–produced *Fields* LP (Plexus) with "Dancing with My 80 Wives."

GLENN MORROW: We were combining dance grooves with transcendental Television guitars, trying to come up with new musical forms.

We really felt we were reinventing the wheel but also trying to be accessible. We came out of the TR3 scene, just as that New York club thing began to fragment. We toured the country playing with a young R.E.M., but it just ran its course for me. I left Hoboken for the city and got married. I saw my talents were more in recognizing talent than being the talent. (2011)

Young and dancing: The Individuals, 1982. Photographer unknown. Courtesy of Glenn Morrow.

I am in the air, I don't have a care
I thought you wanted to know
—CHRIS STAMEY AND THE DB'S, "(I THOUGHT) YOU WANTED TO KNOW"

The dB's featured Chris Stamey from Winston-Salem, NC, who attended NYU and rose on the Downtown scene with Alex Chilton. He made a Chilton-produced solo single, 1977's "The Summer Sun" (Ork) with W-S pals Will Rigby and Gene Holder. In 1978, Chris's next single—the Richard Lloyd–penned "(I Thought) You Wanted to Know"—came out as Chris Stamey and the dB's. Stamey invited North Carolina friend Peter Holsapple to come join the dB's. Albion UK issued two 1981 jangly classics: *Stands for DeciBels* and *Repercussion*.

Beat Rodeo began as the one-off project of Steve Almaas of Minneapolis punk gods Suicide Commandos. The *Beat Rodeo* EP (Coyote) of 1982 was produced by Richard Barone and recorded by Mitch Easter. Their "cowpunk," equal parts C&W and pop/punk, shined brightly on 1985's *Staying out Late with Beat Rodeo* and 1986's *Home in the Heart of the Beat* for IRS Records. *New York* hailed them "the perfect bar band."

Human Switchboard—part of the Ohio punk pipeline that brought the Dead Boys, Waitresses, et cetera—became popular at CBGB, Danceteria, and Maxwell's. But they had issues: Rough Trade cancelled an LP and Polydor fired their A&R man after hearing their 1983 demo. Singer Bob Pfeifer got into the biz, rising to Hollywood Records prez. That all ended after events involving allegedly underage girls and an irate Sharon Osbourne, plus harassment charges by a female employee involving wiretaps by P.I. Anthony Pellicano.

Phosphenes made Coyote Records' first release, 1982's five-song *Phosphenes* EP of jagged art-noise with punk snarl produced by Richard Barone and James Mastro. *Jersey Beat* (#2) wrote of March 1982's Maxwell's gig: "Phosphenes (Tim Sherry, vocals; Bob Pezzola, guitar; Ben Espo, bass; and drummer Stanley Demeski) did not look like they were having fun onstage, and the feeling was mutual."

Red Buckets rocked a dark urban folk replete with Nick Drake and Sandy Denny covers. Mass.-bred singer Richard Mason's band included Kristen Yiengst, Michael Carlucci, and Stanley Demeski. Mason kicked the Buckets to become Maxwell's' resident junkie busboy. (His 2004 memorial at Maxwell's included Feelies, Yo La Tengo, and Luna members.) **The Cyclones**—named for '60s instrumentalists Johnny & the Hurricanes, not for the Coney Island roller coaster—was Donna Esposito's trio behind 1981's "You're so Cool" b/w "RSVP" (produced by Andy Shernoff for Chris Capece's Little Ricky label) and 1983's *Out in the Cold* 12″ EP on Plexus (with Mitch Easter on bass). **The Cucumbers** starred husband and wife Jon Fried and Deena Shoshkes, creators of kinda cute dark-edged pop with nerdy Talking Heads flavor and creepy Lolita vocals. The end of the original band was signing to rap label Profile; 1987's *The Cucumbers* reworked 1983's "My Boyfriend" for MTV play.

Rage to Live began as Glenn Morrow's project with Necessaries guitarist Ed Tomney for 1985's Coyote comp *Luxury Condos*. Of 1986's *Rage to Live*, Robert Palmer wrote in the *New York Times* (4/9/86): "This is music that was made to last." *Blame the Victims*, 1990's C&W-ish third-ever session at Water Music, included a redux of CSNY's "Suite: Judy Blue Eyes." Peter Holsapple, Chris Butler, and Richard Lloyd all served in RTL. **The Wygals** began with Individuals guitarist/vocalist Janet Wygal and drummer Doug Wygal. They wiggled on with guitarist Eric Peterson and bassists Faye Hunter (Let's Active), Dug Allen (Rubber Rodeo), and brother Jeff Wygal, until Gene Holder (the dB's) bassed on 1987's UK-only *Passion* EP. It ended after 1989's *Honyocks in the Whithersoever* for Rough Trade.

The Last Roundup, "cowpunk" pioneers—co-guitarists Amelia "Amy" McMahon Rigby and brother Michael McMahon, lisping singer Angel Dean, and bassist-banjoist Garth Powell—debuted on 1985's *Luxury Condos*. But 1987's

Twister! (Rounder) would be their first/last. A highlight was playing in Nashville on *The Ernest Tubbs Show.* (Amy divorced the dB's Will Rigby in 1996, to record with the Shams and solo.) **The Silos,** led by urbane cowboy Walter Salas-Humara, fused punk angst with strings and pedal steel. After 1985's *About Her Steps* EP, meant to be a one-off, 1987's *Cuba* (nation of his conception) opened with the MTV hit "Tennessee Fire"; *Rolling Stone* picked them "Best New American Band." *The Silos* (RCA) flopped in 1990, so WSH split to Austin.

Gutbank, Hoboken's first girl-power band—singer Karyn Kuhl, bassist Alice Genese, and drummer Tia Palmisano with guitarist Mike Korman—played in the city at CBGB and Love Club, at Maxwell's or New Brunswick's Court Tavern. They made 1986's *The Dark Ages* (Coyote), produced by Roger Miller (Mission Of Burma) and "Dreamworld" on *Luxury Condos.* **Tiny Lights,** led by vocalist/violinist Donna Croughn, guitarist John Hamilton, and cellist Jane Scarpantoni perfected swirling hippie-esque melodies. Their 1986 *Prayer for the Halcyon Fear* possessed a dark side Psychic TV saw fit for their Temple label. Lights faded by 1995's best-of *The Young Person's Guide to Tiny Lights* and '97's *The Smaller the Grape, the Sweeter the Wine.*

Antietam began at Louisville School of Art with Tara Key and Tim Harris of the punk act Babylon Dance Band. They moved East and debuted June 1984 at CBs with Human Switchboard, and made jarring pop for the Homestead and Triple X labels. *Spin* hailed Key, "Patti Smith with a stuffy nose." Their 1992 opus *Antietam Comes Alive!* (riffing Frampton) was "recorded at CBGB July 10, 1991 from 8:40 to 9:30 p.m." **Winter Hours** from Lyndhurst, NJ, became college radio heroes with five indie releases like 1985's *Churches* covering "All Along the Watchtower" and 1986's *Wait Till the Morning* with "Hyacinth Girl." A Chrysalis deal for 1989's Lenny Kaye–produced *Winter Hours* killed the band.

Syd Straw, daughter of '50s actor Jack Straw (*The Pajama Game*), was an early indie-rock star. She came to NYC in 1978 at age nineteen to be an actress and stayed twenty years. After work for Pat Benatar and Van Dyke Parks, Anton Fier hired her in Golden Palominos as vocalist on 1985's *Visions of Excess* and 1986's *Blast of Silence.* Syd then went solo: 1989's *Surprise* (with Michael Stipe, Richard Thompson, and Jody Harris) and 1996's *War and Peace* (backed by The Skeletons, hailed by *Rolling Stone* "the greatest bar band ever").

The Smithereens, a revered NJ quartet, became NY scene stars. On 1980's *Girls about Town* EP, each title had "Girls" (like Brian Wilson's "Girls Don't Tell Me"). Alan Betrock produced 1983's *Beauty and Sadness* at the Record Plant, leading to 1986's Don Dixon–produced *Especially for You* with "Blood and Roses" and "A Girl Like You" on 1989's Ed Stasium–produced *11* that went Top 40.

RAGE TO LIVE

Blame the victim: Rage To Live, Hoboken waterfront, 1987. Photo by Monica Dee.

Yo La Tengo embodies indie rock, unsexy geeks sans machismo. Kinky-haired Ira Kaplan and his love Georgia Hubley began as Georgia and Those Guys, backing Jon Light Klages (The Individuals) on his 1985 *In a Dream* EP. YLT tackle unique covers and subjects, like covering Information's "Let's Compromise" or "Yellow Sarong" by The Scene Is Now, and writing "The Ballad of Red Buckets" about the Hoboken band or "Pass the Hatchet, I Think I'm Goodkind" on Tom Goodkind. Their trio with bassist James McNew at times plays as Condo Fucks.

THE FALL

Break the silence with a screaming head
Break the scream with a silent void
—THE FEELIES, "FA CÉ-LA"

Modern-day Hoboken as a family-oriented commuter colony of pricey bistros and Jell-O shot bars bears little likeness to that '80s rock heyday. But most modern rock sounds—like Brooklyn-tweaked indie rock—trace back to kings of the Hoboken Sound.

GLENN MORROW (The Individuals): I had a fantasy I'd be creating a scene and inviting all my friends—and it happened. It reached a level, from dream to real, with articles in the *Times* and *Musician* about the Hoboken sound. With all our friends jangling along, it was a cool thing. There was so much activity here in the '80s: the Replacements hung out, so did Husker Du and R.E.M. For such a little town it was such a center of activity, as good as Minneapolis or D.C. or New York as a music center. But then the rents got too hard for musicians. No one could afford to be there. That's what killed it. (2011)

ROB NORRIS (The Bongos): I felt Hoboken was a location more than coherence of community or sound. All our friends had similar scenes in other parts of the country, be it Athens with R.E.M. and Pylon, or Minneapolis. There was a lot of diversity in the Hoboken scene. There were great bands we were friends with, but it's not necessarily shared sensibilities. Cheap real estate fueled the scene, and then of course it gets flooded and ruined. Hoboken became such a zoo it became unbearable. (2011)

IRA KAPLAN (Yo La Tengo): Hoboken is Hoboken. We're definitely not in the thick of it. I'm so uncomfortable even thinking about that. (2005)

PYSCHO-HEAD BLOWOUT

EAST VILLAGE BIKER ROCK, JAM BANDS, BLACK ROCK COALITION, GOTH/INDUSTRIAL

1985–1992: Hell's Angels, Cycle Sluts from Hell, Raging Slab, Circus of Power, White Zombie, Lismar Lounge, Cat Club, Limelight, Scrap Bar, alt rock

Metal from the slums. Blitzspeer, East Village, 1989.
Photo by Frank White.

EAST VILLAGE BIKER ROCK

THE RISE

Calling all children of the velvet night
Get your motor down to the city of light
—Circus of Power, "Call of the Wild"

"East Village Biker Rock" was different from the same era's Sunset Strip glam metal. This gnarly scene, inspired by the New York Dolls, NYHC, and Downtown clubland, was a realm of lapsed punks, old-school rockers, and art-schoolers into Motörhead or AC/DC, cultivating an ironic (and now ubiquitous) blue-collar thrift-shop style. Most of these groups were too weird for the mainstream. Because of their proximity to, and interaction with, the music business, many of these bands released major label records.

JOEY RAMONE (The Ramones): I can count the bands on my hands that to me really have anything to say or are unique or innovative, of the contemporary bands. The thing I like about Circus of Power and Cycle Sluts from Hell are that they know what they're about, and they're rock and roll. They're the guts of rock and roll. (1989)

SEAN YSEULT (White Zombie): This whole other scene started at the same time as the art/noise world: a super heavy Southern rock thing going on in the East Village, led by Raging Slab, Circus of Power and Cycle Sluts. We played and were friends with those bands, and straddled both worlds. But this was not redneck backwoods. It was not L.A. Rock with girls in lacy bustiers and teased hair, and guys in spandex. It was smart educated punk kids into Motörhead and down with the Hell's Angels. (2011)

THE SCENE

Love don't come easy, it sure ain't for free
God only knows if you'll get it from me
—BLITZSPEER, "CAN'T LOSE WHAT YOU'VE NEVER HAD"

That decadent hard rock scene went down side by side below 14th Street with other Downtown punk and art subcultures, spanning the rising alt rock to the first jam bands. Relatively few bands from the conservative suburbs regularly partook in the madness.

LINDSEY ANDERSON (New York scene): Circus of Power, Cycle Sluts and these bands were too raw and gritty. They were never gonna be made over into something palatable and mainstream, for fourteen-year-old girls and mothers, like Bon Jovi were. (2006)

Circus of Power was one of the first fully tattooed rock bands (tattoos were illegal in NYC from 1961 to 1997). They weren't bikers, but NYHC vets with a Steppenwolf roar. Raging Slab, brainy ex-punk longhairs, fused speed metal and

Skynyrd. White Zombie blended a similar vibe into their alt/noise, before moving to L.A. for fame. Scene highlights include: Guns N' Roses' first acoustic gig, October 30, 1987, at CBGB Gallery; Joey Ramone's fall 1988 "Grand Inquisition Tour" with Richie Stotts, Raging Slab, and Cycle Sluts From Hell; and December 14, 1988's Cat Club gig with Cycle Sluts and Jane's Addiction. Big press included December 1988's *Details* spread on the scene with Bob Gruen photos, and Lisa Robinson's column in the *Post*.

Biker bands performed for the Hell's Angels at Lismar Lounge, right by their 3rd Street clubhouse. Such groups also played at Limelight, Cat Club, and Pyramid's Metalbar, and hung out at Scrap Bar, Alcatraz, or King Tut's Wah Wah Hut. But in the end, the biker-rockers couldn't hang with the real bikers because most rockers are fake tough guys.

TONY MANN (New York scene): It was still dangerous back then—burned-out buildings and empty lots. We'd spent our daytimes at cool stores like Live Shop Die, Love Saves the Day, Little Ricky, Manic Panic and See/Hear. I'd go see White Zombie at Cat Club then stumble into Lismar Lounge and drink with the Cult or Hell's Angels. It was rock-and-roll Sodom and Gomorrah, at any hour. The after-hours clubs Save the Robots on Avenue B had a sandbox you stood in to hide your stash if cops came. (2013)

RAFFAELE (Cycle Sluts from Hell): When we all started, everybody wanted to hear early Aerosmith and Montrose and all that '70s-energy rock. That's where the big hair came from. But most of the bands in our scene at the Lismar were a more cartoony biker-rock thing. Circus of Power and Raging Slab and us; it was a fertile rock scene. We'd play the Cult's *Electric* over and over. We had that mind-warp. The glam in New York was more ironic and gritty than L.A., especially with Hell's Angels always around. (2006)

LINDSEY ANDERSON: The Guns N' Roses thing, the whole nation went crazy for. But there were few hair-metal fans here, it's not something that rose out of New York. The New York stuff was tougher and rawer and not so polished. It was a great scene. (2005)

RAFFAELE: For us girls it was tight jeans or stretch Lycra pants, tights, thigh-high boots. The jackets were really short. We'd wear a denim vest over it with our "colors" on the back. We'd wear like five belts and spurs on your boots that you'd get from Trash and Vaudeville. Crimped our hair. I didn't realize how hard-looking I was. I was into being a badass. So everything had a real element of roughness: very biker, lots of leather. (2006)

Call of the wild: Lismar Lounge, 1986. Photo by Wayne Allan Brown. Courtesy of Raffaele.

Lismar Lounge (41 First Avenue) was the home of the era's scene. The 150-capacity Puerto Rican dive bar was always packed with big-haired women, Hell's Angels, and other shaggy dudes whacked on booze and blow and whatnot. Raging Slab, Circus of Power, Cycle Sluts, and Warrior Soul got signed to major labels out of the Lismar. GG Allin defiled the room on November 4, 1987. The Lismar's demise coincided with the rise of Nirvana.

> **RAFFAELE:** This hairdresser Glen Benson said some people were doing the Love Club at the Lismar Lounge. He wanted to make it a rock bar, and asked us to work there. This Chinese mafia guy that also owned Nightingale's and Wah Wah Hut owned it. He watered down the alcohol. He had a back room he wouldn't let us in, and every morning the bottles would be full. But from the minute it started, it was a success. The basement had shitty sound in a crappy room with water dripping but it was great. It was the start of a scene, though I don't know what you'd call it 'cause it wasn't really hair bands. (2006)

> **DONNA LUPIE (Cycle Sluts from Hell):** Lismar Lounge was exciting, different than any other East Village dive—full of gorgeous women and cute guys in bands who were always drunk, mostly on themselves! White Zombie, Circus of Power, Warrior Soul, Raging Slab, and us were all spawned at the Lismar. Joey Ramone hung there. It wasn't long before every A&R guy in town was drinking there, looking for a "Next

Big Thing." If your band hung at the Lismar and didn't get signed, it must've really sucked. (2010)

PAM GRANDE (New York scene): Every night you could go there and see awesome motorcycle-rock bands. I'd tease my hair. Really tight pants. That was the look. Cowboy boots tucked into pants. It was more about the bars and parties than the bands. (2006)

ALEX MITCHELL (Circus of Power): Lismar Lounge was the hub for all us bands, this little dive where we all hung out and played. It was a helluva time to be in New York. I've never been able to quite get it out of my head or put it to rest. It was so good it haunts me. That city was something else back then. (2007)

GLENN-MAX (Naked Sun): We opened for Warrior Soul at the Lismar, which was the great New York Rock spot at the time. We had a famous show there where at the end of the set, at the climax of our epic song, this crazy bleach-blond chick gets onstage and starts dancing with me. By the end of the song she'd stripped down, and was kind of like a prop wrapped around me as I sang. Then I looked and this naked girl was now shooting up on the bass drum case. That kinda shit happened there. Not that I condone it but it ain't gonna get any more rock and roll than that. I don't think it ever did actually. (2013)

Scrap Bar (116 MacDougal Street) promoted late-night metal debauchery. The site of the '60s cellar folk club the Gaslight, with a scrap-metal façade, hosted wild action fulla booze, blow, dope, piss, blood, sweat, vomit, and fistfights. If a big band like Metallica, Black Crowes, or Alice in Chains played town, they'd inevitably end up there. GNR held court; porn star Savannah once blew Slash at the bar. Hell's Angels worked as security. They had a Breathalyzer machine, and the goal was to get the highest score.

MIKE SCHNAPP (New York scene): Scrap Bar wasn't a music venue, but after any big show everyone hung out there. It wasn't pretending to change the world. It was a fucking bar. It was on MacDougal between West Third and Bleecker. It was the magic of sex and drugs and rock and roll. It's now the Wreck Room. Believe me we got wrecked down there. (2003)

TONY MANN: A typical night started at Scrap Bar, then to Alcatraz to Wah Wah Hut and ended up in Tompkins Square Park till dawn. Two Cycle Sluts worked at Alcatraz and two at Wah Wah Hut. I lost a hundred-dollar bill at Alcatraz one night and found one there another, that's how hectic it was. You could barely move to drink in there. (2013)

Badass mama: Cycle Sluts from Hell flyer, The Pyramid, 1988. Artwork by Dava Nasr.

THE MUSIC

It don't take no melody
To make some music history
—Manitoba's Wild Kingdom, "Haircut and Attitude"

Manitoba's Wild Kingdom began in 1986 when Dictators frontman Handsome Dick Manitoba got sober. He teamed with ex-mates bassist Andy Shernoff and guitarist Ross the Boss (fresh off Manowar), drummer J. P. Patterson, and "fifth Ramone" Daniel Rey. After popularity at CBs and Cat Club came two Shernoff-produced efforts: their song "New York, New York" in 1988's *Mondo New York* film, and 1990's *. . . And You* LP (MCA). But their metal-edged wry punk never translated beyond the tristate area.

ANDY SHERNOFF (The Dictators): We formed Wild Kingdom in the '80s; I got inspired after hearing speed-metal bands like Metallica, Slayer and Anthrax. After the '70s, punk rock was relegated to the trash pile of history. These bands revived the punk spirit by playing with ferocity. Wild Kingdom was the first record I made with mainstream acceptance, even MTV played the video. I used Andy Wallace to mix that record before he broke huge with Nirvana. (2011)

> *I took a powder to the river and drank*
> *I tried to float the boat but the damn thing sank*
> —Raging Slab, "Don't Dog Me"

Raging Slab blared hard rock in long hair and trucker threads straight outta Black Oak Arkansas. Their Skynyrd-infused triple-guitar blitz blended slide guitar and thrash. They came out strong with 1987's *Assmaster* (the first album with a band-as-superhero comic book) and 1988's *True Death*. Greg Strzempka, Elyse Steinman, and Alec Morton burned through a *Spinal Tap*–like string of drummers. *Raging Slab*, 1989's Daniel Rey–produced for RCA, ended badly, fueling live covers of Skynyrd's "Workin' for MCA" as "Workin' for RCA." Rick Rubin was a fan, and signed them to his Def American label, but 1993's *Dynamite Monster Boogie Concert* and 1996's *Sing Monkey Sing* were among his lowest-sellers ever. Tours with admirers Guns N' Roses, Mötley Crüe, and Lenny Kravitz bore no fruit. Greg and Elyse left the EV for the *Deliverance*-like woods of rural Pennsylvania before Elyse succumbed to health issues.

GREG STRZEMPKA (Raging Slab): I don't mean to wax Rodney Dangerfield but we never got any respect for what we do. We have yet, to this day, ever been mentioned in the *Village Voice*. I don't know if it's just habitually ignoring people or not getting it on the level we mean it but it's annoying. In my mind, we were the ideal New York band. (1993)

LAURIE ES (New York scene): Raging Slab was one of my all-time favorites, and remains so. So many people after them tried to do what they did, and nobody's ever come close. They got so much shit because back then, Pussy Galore was the big thing, and those people ragged on Slab for being these biker-rock sellouts. The fact was, Slab was incredible and nobody could figure out what the hell they were doing. (2011)

All the guys gonna treat her good 'cause she's bad
Ups and downs like a seesaw sucker, best ride you ever had
—CYCLE SLUTS FROM HELL, "BADASS MAMA"

Cycle Sluts from Hell got into gear in 1986 when bartenders Jenny Staska (She-Fire of Ice) and Mary Raffaele (Queen Vixen) worked at Lismar Lounge with Betty Kallas (Venus Penis Crusher) and Donna Lupie (Honey 1%er). Party-throwing Lismar manager Glen Benson coined "Cycle Slut Thursdays," where all four poured drinks as "Cycle Sluts." Someone tagged "From Hell" when they decided to do a show. The ladies—like the Ronettes meets the Runaways—partied with Motörhead and Metallica and other rock stars. Their name caused problems (feuding with A&M Records' Herb Alpert for trying to change it) before signing to Epic. But 1991's *Cycle Sluts from Hell*—with its twice-aired $80,000 MTV *Headbanger's Ball* video for "I Wish You Were a Beer"—featured homoerotic David LaChapelle artwork!

RAFFAELE (Cycle Sluts from Hell): We wrote a few songs and booked a gig at the Pyramid, which was easy because we knew everybody. So it was packed, purely on the name. Joey Ramone was there and loved it. So our second gig was opening for the Ramones at the Ritz! Joey brought us for a show in D.C. and there began a bidding war to sign us. But we made terrible decisions every step of the way, so it was a short-lived success. (2006)

DONNA LUPIE (Cycle Sluts from Hell): Our stint at stardom was a brief, bitter cocktail. What resulted was: an album none of us could agree upon; an obscenely expensive and god-awful album cover; a cool video played on *Beavis & Butthead,* a Motörhead tour, copious amounts of free alcohol, and tons of sexual and nonsexual adulation—all while being jerked around, ripped off and mismanaged by garden-variety, jive motherfuckers from days gone by. We were soon kicked back to the same gutter we arose from. (2009)

By the balls: Cycle Sluts from Hell, 1988. Photo by Jeff Tisman. Courtesy of Raffaele.

I'm no angel, I ain't made of gold
I'll tell you baby, I ain't selling my soul
—CIRCUS OF POWER, "NEEDLES"

Circus of Power was the unofficial house band for the Hell's Angels, whose bikers dug their tough look and heavy sound. Vocalist Alex Mitchell's résumé included work as a Miami disco singer and fronting NYHC thugs Crucial Truth. Guitarist Ricky Mahler knew Alex from the Florida punk scene; the two reconnected in 1985 at Alex's Bond Street apartment, fueled by Zodiac Mindwarp vinyl and cocaine. Daniel Rey produced for RCA 1988's *Circus of Power*, 1989's *Still Alive*, and 1990's *Vices*. They were last seen leaving to L.A. for stardom (1993's *Magic & Madness* for Columbia).

ALEX MITCHELL (Circus of Power): There's no line between our music and our lifestyle cuz the music is the lifestyle and the life-style is the music. It comes through in the way we play and the words I write. It's an art form inspired by ideas and sounds and visions. (1988)

RAFFAELE: They were into the biker thing; their big song went "She's got a motor." We were tight because they were in the Lismar every night and Alex was hitting on all the girls. They were our brother band. (2006)

Join the resurrection
Rave on in my direction
—WHITE ZOMBIE, "FAST JUNGLE"

White Zombie before fame was another art/noise band of street scum with dreaded hair and tribal body art. Lucky to draw twenty people, they played with bands like Pussy Galore and Raging Slab. Bassist Sean Yseult (Shauna Reynolds), on scholarship to Parsons, was in the NYHC peace-punk band Life with Ena Kostabi (brother of artist Mark Kostabi) and future Zombie drummer Ivan DePrume. In 1985, she met Rob Zombie (Cummings). Rob, Sean, Ena, and drummer Peter Landau made the 300 copies of 1985's "Gods on Voodoo Moon" 45. This writer booked their first gig, January 24, 1987, with Dinosaur, Jr. at Love Club. A 1987 12″, *Psycho-Head Blowout*, included DePrume and guitarist Tom Five (Guay). Jay Younger and John Ricci replaced them on 1988's Bill Laswell–produced *Make Them Die Slowly* and 1989's Kiss cover *God of Thunder*. The band moved to L.A. after Geffen's Michael Alago signed 'em for 1992's *La Sexorcisto: Devil Music, Vol. 1.*

ROB ZOMBIE (White Zombie): Unlike other Downtown bands, we're into the rock star thing. We want to set the record straight, and then no one could ever say we "sold out" because we're always in it for the money. We don't want any little punkers telling us we "sold out" or "went rock star" because that's our intention. (1986)

PETER LANDAU (White Zombie/Da Willys): I was in the first White Zombie with Sean and Rob and Ena Kostabi. I went to school at Parsons with Sean, and played on the first single but no shows. I wasn't into the music but Rob impressed me. He was into cartoons and horror movies, but unlike the drunks and addicts I knew, was very focused. I dropped out, and they became huge. If I just stayed in that band . . . they would've thrown me out. (2011)

SEAN YSEULT (White Zombie): Payback is when we put out *Psycho-Head Blowout* or *Soul Crusher*. People thought it was fucking horrible. Now people offer us tons of money for all those supposedly genius albums, which were once considered unlistenable. (1992)

ALLEGRA ROSE (New York scene): White Zombie struggled for a long time. Four or five years of playing before they started getting anywhere. They'd go around the East Village and hand you tapes they made. You were like, "What the fuck is this?" (2006)

Sticking with some sick ideal
While others sell out fast
—Prong, "Denial"

Prong began with CBGB soundman, guitarist Tommy Victor; Swans drummer Ted Parsons; and Damage bassist Mike Kirkland. Raw recordings like 1987's *Primitive Origins* and 1988's *Force Fed* portended industrial/metal classics on Epic with MTV *Headbanger's Ball* videos for the title tracks to 1990's *Beg to Differ* and 1991's *Prove You Wrong* with Flotsam & Jetsam bassist Troy Gregory. Killing Joke's Paul Raven bassed on 1994's *Cleansing* and 1996's *Rude Awakening*. They'd open for Black Sabbath with Ronnie James Dio at the Beacon Theater in 1992, and for Ozzy Osborne on 1995's first Ozzfest.

TOMMY VICTOR (Prong): Prong was a realization of the finality of, the death of the New York noise scene. It was time for something else. There were suddenly all these bands doing it. There were too many Kim Gordons—that's what disgusted me. (1990)

I get sick when I walk in New York City
See the human garbage just rotting in the street
—Da Willys, "NY Stomp"

Da Willys—named for their bassist, Cramps roadie Willy Kerr, and for the alcoholic DTs—played a mess of punk and Delta blues. Vocalist Lynn Von Schlichting and first White Zombie drummer Peter Landau came from the Cramps-style Swamp Goblyns; Peter and guitarist Leon Ross (Rossbach) came from the Kretins. In 1990 they released a split-single with Alice Donut, the German-only *Saturday Night Palsy* LP, and songs on Mykel Board's *New*

York Scum Rock comp. Soon after, Kerr moved home to Pennsylvania to get sober at home. Ross jumped out a window in 1992.

LYNNE VON SCHLICHTING (Da Willys/Trick Babys): Da Willys was a real Lower East Side band. We played our first show in 1986 at Charas Hall. We played loft parties, raw spaces in Alphabet City, and Williamsburg when nobody lived there. It took us two years to play CBGB and Continental Divide. Then we made our first album. By the time we recorded again, our guitarist was a heroin addict and it was too late. We were an obscure band, but enough people heard it. We were in the wrong place at the right time. (2011)

> *I am the child of the new generation*
> *The product of total frustration*
> —WARRIOR SOUL, "I SEE THE RUINS"

Warrior Soul fused theater, arena rock, and political punk; vocalist Kory Clarke called it "the embodiment of a fighter with the righteousness of a holy person" (*Seconds*, 1990). In 1983, the Detroit kid became Warrior Soul doing percussion over video projections at the Kitchen and Danceteria. Then he began his metal band Warrior Soul, with numerous lineups. With Metallica's management came Geffen albums, sans Metallica's success: 1990's *Last Decade Dead Century*, 1991's *Drugs, God and the New Republic*, 1992's *Salutations from the Ghetto Nation*, and 1993's *Chill Pill*.

Lunachicks—Brooklyn ladies Theo Kogan, Gina Volpe, Benezra "Sindi B" Valsamis, Sydney "Squid" Silver, and Susan "Becky Wreck" Lloyd—were prototypes for women in rock. They debuted after graduating High School of Music & Art in 1988, opening for Da Willys at Love Club. They got signed after their third gig at CBGB to Blast First UK, label of Sonic Youth, leading to 1989's *Lunachicks* double-7″ and 1990's *Babysitters on Acid*. Recordings for others like 1992's *Binge and Purge*, 1995's *Jerk of All Trades*, and 1997's *Pretty Ugly* should've fared better. Theo became the first sleeved tattooed supermodel (Calvin Klein, Burberry, Courvoisier) with Richard Avedon shots on buses and billboards; Wreck became the star of Howard Stern's "Lesbian Dating Game." Kate Schellenbach (Luscious Jackson) stood in for drummer Becky, and then handed her stool to Helen Destroy (of Lez Zeppelin).

Blitzspeer, a Motörhead-meets-Ramones street-metal group, began after

Raging Slab fired bassist Curt Fleck, and came to form when guitarist Scott Lano brought in vocalist-guitarist Phil Caivano (ex-Shrapnel). That synergy generated Epic Records: 1990's *Live* EP (live at Limelight, 7/89) with Pushead artwork, and 1991's *Saved* with guests Lydia Lunch and Joey Ramone. Drummers included Louie Gasparro (Murphy's Law), David Tritt (Rat At Rat R), Mackie Jayson (Cro-Mags), and Brian Essing (on *Saved*). They drew well at Pyramid's "Metalbar" and Limelight's "Rock N Roll Church," and cavorted at Lismar, Scrap Bar, Wah Wah Hut, and Billy's Topless.

Richie Stotts redefined guitar playing in Plasmatics. After a spot on Average White Band's *Cupid's in Fashion* and a cameo in *9½ Weeks*, he returned to fronting his own band, Stotts. By 1985 Stotts became King Flux with drummer Marky Ramone and Tommy Hilfiger's bros Billy and Andy on guitar and bass. At Flux's last gig, New Year's Eve 1988 opening for Ramones at Irving Plaza, Wendy O. Williams joined on Plasmatics' "Masterplan." Richie then graduated summa cum laude from Hunter College, and earned an M.S. in geology from Indiana. In '92, he cut Flux's "Man with the X-Ray Eyes" as a solo 7″ single with drummer Al Bouchard.

Full metal jacket: King Flux, Cat Club, 1985. Marky Ramone and Richie Stotts with Tommy Hilfiger's brothers Billy and Andy. Photo by Frank White.

Freaks fused '70s fashion and punk attitude, like a grungy Stooges. Bassist Howie Pyro (The Blessed) began the band named for the 1932 B-movie classic with his wife Andrea Matthews (ex–The Outta Place), her cousin Eric Eckley, and John Fay (The Tryfles/The Outta Place), which faded after 1987's quasi-rock-opera *Pippi Skelter*, 1988's 7″ (live on WFMU) and 1989's *Freaks in Sensurround* LP. **Skulls**, a Johnny Thunders–style trio led by singer-guitarist Charly Pip (The Colors, David Johansen) and bassist Mike "Mindless" Frigerio, released 1986's *Dress up and Die* EP, 1987's *Blacklight 13* (with Genocide/Misfits drummer Brian "Damage" Keats), and 1988's "Graveyard Signal." **Kretins**, also with Keats, was a leather-jacketed pop quartet, à la the Romantics. They self-released 1984's "Mercy of the Lord" 7″ before guitarist Leon Mang's (Rossbach) alcoholism finished off the band.

P.M.S., a fierce female five-piece, began playing with intense NYHC bands like the Bad Brains and Cro-Mags. Their 1987 album *Pre-Metal Syndrome* with Sean Taggart cover art starred Kiev-born singer Yana Chupenko bellowing "Ave Maria." "Living on the Outside (Fucked up World)," produced by Blondie's Chris Stein, came out on John Giornio's infamous 1989 compilation, *Like a Girl, I Want You to Keep Coming*. P.M.S. became **Wench**, for a while with drummer Kate Schellenbach.

Krave, a lusty lady band with a male drummer, opened for Soundgarden, White Zombie, and Helmet. WFMU DJ Laurie Es and belly-dancing singer Sarah Cook gave up after making a 1989 demo, a cut on a Shonen Knife tribute LP, and 1990's never-issued 7″. **Missdemeanor**, four big-haired Staten Island gals named for UFO's "Misdemeanor," opened for the Plasmatics and Cycle Sluts.

Nevermore, a Sabbath-style denim-and-leather five-piece from blue-collar Gravesend, sizzled on the scene. Rick Rubin, off Slayer's *Reign in Blood,* saw them at the Pyramid's Metalbar in 1987 and signed them, but 1989's *Nevermore* EP for Rubin's ill-fated Ill Records flopped. **Battalion**, a multiculti Ridgewood, Queens, mix of Judas Priest and hair metal in tight pants and silvery jewelry, shone live. But the quartet's 1988 demo for Russell Simmons's Rush Management languished. **Broom Hellda**, a GN'R-ish group from the same Queens scene as Battalion and **Hell's Kitchen NYC**, starred the Piñas: singer Roland, bassist Laz, and drummer Ric in leather jackets, ripped jeans, and kinky 'fros. Guitarist Leo Susana went back to Santo Domingo after 1987's *Something Wicked This Way Comes* with the misspelled "Initmacy Lunacy (The Seduction of Gretal)."

Love Tribe, Downtown's Aerosmith-style party-rock stars from Baltimore, never made a record. But peroxide blond Tommy Nordahl's act's gigs at Limelight and Cat Club, and late-night parties at their Pitt Street "Love Hut" rang as iconic. (Tommy went to L.A. for stardom, and became a Hollywood tour bus driver.) **Angels in Vain**, Dolls-style with poufy hair, scarves, and lipstick, cut three demos but never a record. Stiv Bators was to produce an album before he died (Kelly Nickles found fame in L.A. Guns; Nordahl's brother Danny Nordahl tried with the Throbs and N.Y. Loose). **Princess Pang** began with Angels in Vain's singer Jeni Foster, bassist Ronnie Roze (Johannson), and drummer Brian Keats. *Princess Pang* (Metal Blade) with hit producer Ron

St. Germain spawned a 1989 MTV video for "Trouble in Paradise" with the cowboy-metallers running past NYPD and LES squats. After brutal tours with Ace Frehley and Wolfsbane, Jeni got into techno.

The Throbs, NYC Rock's Next Big Thing circa 1990, began at Limelight's "Rock N Roll Church." Ronnie Sweetheart's sexy quartet signed to Geffen after three gigs—no demo or manager, just late-night partying with A&R ladies. January 1991's *Language of Vagabonds and Thieves* (Geffen) came out amid the cultural swing to Nirvana. Jimi K. Bones (ex-Kix) formed **Skin & Bones**, behind 1990's *Not a Pretty Sight* (Equinox UK) produced by Duran Duran's Andy Taylor. (Baltimore PD killed bassist Steve Mach under iffy circumstances on October 3, 2011. No one was ever charged.) **RU Ready**, a glam/metal band equal parts Jane's Addiction and Poison, made a 1991 six-song demo. A 1992 eponymous album hyped in *Billboard* never came out because their label's RCA deal dissolved. Singer Pat Briggs, a Cat Club bartender, was wrongly reported in metal mags to replace Jani Lane in Warrant.

Naked Sun blazed too arty for metal, too heavy for alt rock. Glen "Max Vanderwolf" Rechler on sax/vox evoked an evil Ian Anderson. *Naked Sun* (Noise) offered an offbeat metal/prog: the 1991 anti-grunge opus shared Nirvana photographer Michael Lavine. This writer hailed 1994's *Wonderdrug* in *RIP* (3/94): "Imagine *2112*-era Rush on Lollapalooza's side stage or a punk Jethro Tull, and you've got an idea about the grimy shit goin' on." (Drummer Anthony Scarpa, now Angie Scarpa, made 2003's doc *Betty Blowtorch and Her Amazing True Life Adventures* on the late Bianca Butthole.) **King of Kings** featured Kenny Young, a childhood friend of and influence on actor Fred Armisen. Tesla's Frank Hannon saw King of Kings at Limelight and turned on his Geffen A&R man Tom Zutaut. *King of Kings*, a 1991 classic-rock opus with Queen producer Roy Thomas Baker and Hannon on guitar, crashed with Nirvanamania.

Deans of Discipline, a beer-soaked punk party band with wild stage shows and rockabilly/metal tones fronted by Andrew "Flash Cooney" Benepe, rocked the Downtown clubs. *Horror Glitter Transvesto Billy* (CBGB/Celluloid), produced by the Shirts' Ron Ardito, sold meekly in 1987. They also lost a few master tapes. Ex-Deans included Callum Benepe and Nick Marden (ex-Stimulators), Ira Elliot (Fuzztones), Steve Missal (Billy Idol), and vocalist Vince Metzo.

The Beautiful—Waldos bassist Perry Bottke, Nasty Habits guitarist Jonathan Hale Lacey, and drummer Frank Ferrer—cut a demo and played a 63-date tour that attracted Warner Bros. to release 1990's *The Beautiful* EP and 1991's *Storybook* LP (with eight minutes of John Lennon's "Cold Turkey").

Post writer Lisa Robinson discovered **The Lost**. Husband Richard Robinson produced 1991's *The Lost* (Epic) album with guests like Joan Jett, Dan Zanes, and Raging Slab. Shaggy singer Lucas Janklow shot back on Sire in Darlahood (1996's *Big Fine Thing*) before quitting music in 1999 for literary fame, running his father's literary agency, Janklow & Nesbit. **Sea Monster** played CBs more than anyone. They began in blue-collar Freeport, LI, with guys from the Danceteria-era group Flak: Arthur Stevenson with Fred and Barney Wagner (muse for Fred and Barney in *The Flintstones*).

New York stomp: Da Willys, outside The Pyramid, 1988. Photo © Marti Wilkerson.

THE FALL

Can't breathe with all this Aqua-Net
I wish you were a beer!
—Cycle Sluts from Hell, "I Wish You Were a Beer"

LAURIE ES (New York scene): What I loved was a unity in the scene at the time: from Raging Slab to Honeymoon Killers, everyone got along, and were all in it for the rock. The vibe was like a Factory scene in the '80s, you could go to the show and everyone was a celebrity of a certain ilk. You'd see Hell's Angels next to Sonic Youth; it was the first of that kind in the East Village, where you had punks, freaks, metalheads, bikers, and drag queens all at the bar. For all who played there was an instant audience plugged in for it. Even with all the alcohol and drugs, it was a peaceful time. No one was fighting. (2011)

RAFFAELE (Cycle Sluts from Hell): The shift happened, and all these things we were into overnight became uncool. It was like, boom, this isn't cool anymore. That Nirvana video was the death knell for that scene. And all of a sudden Marc Jacobs did that grunge collection, and it became this whole other thing that I never connected to because I was into glamorous rock-and-roll energy. It was kinda like the party was over. (2006)

Dropping some NYC: Spin Doctors,
Wetlands, 1993. Photo by Frank White.

JAM BANDS

Take a little taste and tell me, what do you see
'Cause tonight we're gonna drop a little NYC
—BLUES TRAVELER, "DROPPING SOME NYC"

The jam band scene also traces to the East Village. Chris Barron of Spin
Doctors and his friends from Blues Traveler moved from Princeton, NJ, to
attend the New School's fledgling jazz program. At their first Downtown gigs at
Nightingale's and Wetlands Preserve, these acts befriended Joan Osborne and
God Street Wine and others inspired by the Grateful Dead but playing funky
like the Meters. This urban punk–fueled scene included participants who lived
as East Village street-scum. They commingled with the biker-rock and alt-rock
scenes. These bands broke with 1993's H.O.R.D.E. Festival, devised Downtown
by Blues Traveler's John Popper.

BOBBY SHEEHAN (Blues Traveler): In '87 we all moved to New
York. That's where we began jamming in bars down in the Village and
Lower East Side. We all played five, seven nights a week between
Houston and 14th, everywhere along that strip. (1999)

FRANKIE LaROCKA (Epic Records): I saw Spin Doctors at Nightingale's on Second Avenue playing to twenty people. But all of these people had grins on their faces that were contagious. They were all dancing and having a great time. (1991)

WALTER DURKACZ (Wetlands Preserve): The old club people don't understand this is history in the making. These kids are doing the '60s in their own way, for the '90s, and it's like nothing that happened before. It's not retro bands. (1990)

CHRIS BARRON (Spin Doctors): In the '80s, everyone hated music. So we were trying to make this new kind of old rock and roll. That whole genius '60s aesthetic had been lost. Everything sounded like fake drummers and synthesized bullshit, and we wanted to make something real. We wanted to bake some pumpernickel, not that presliced stuff. (1994)

Joey Miserable and the Worms—the first "jam band"—was a grungy six-piece that launched Simon Chardiet (Simon & The Bar Sinisters), guitarist Jono Manson, drummer Milo Z (Zwirling), and pianist Mark Ettinger (Flying Karamazov Brothers). Cree McCree crowed in *High Times*: "If not for Jono Manson, Blues Traveler, Spin Doctors and Joan Osborne and the NYC jam-band scene may've never happened. Jono showed these whippersnappers how to turn a blasé bar crowd into believers at the now-iconic hole-in-the-wall, Nightingales."

Spin Doctors started as Trucking Company, with John Popper on harmonica. Ninety's *Up for Grabs* live-at-Wetlands EP paved the way for five hundred gigs supporting 1991's triple-platinum *Pocketful of Kryptonite* ("Two Princes").

Blues Traveler gigs Wednesdays at Wetlands Preserve or weekends at Nightingale's resulted in A&M LPs with local themes such as 1990's *Blues Traveler* ("Dropping Some NYC") or 1993's *Save His Soul* ("NY Prophecy," "Manhattan Bridge"). But they never overcame bassist Bobby Sheehan's tragic 1999 overdose on cocaine, heroin, and Valium.

Joan Osborne from Kentucky got known selling self-made Etta James–ish CDs like 1991's *Soul Show*, live at the LES R&B bar Delta 88, and 1992's *Blue Million Miles* live at Brooklyn's St. Ann's Church. She got signed out of Wetlands to make 1995's triple-platinum *Relish*, cut in Katonah ("One of Us").

God Street Wine, Manhattan School of Music students led by Lo Faber and Aaron Maxwell (Lieberman), made a dollar-bin classic in 1995's *$1.99*

Romances (Geffen). **Cycomotogoat**, the Hoboken trio of Crugie Riccio, Dave Ares, and Tom Costagliola, bridged grunge and revivalism as Bah Gah Brothers (1990's *Is There a Doctor in This Fish*) before 1992's *Cycomotogoat*, 1994's *Alkaline*, and 1996's *Braille*. *Alternative Press* (8/94) proclaimed: "On a slacker's scale of one to 10, it's an 11." **Xanax 25**, **The Authority**, **First House**, **Walking Bird**, **Dreyer Brothers**, and **Arnie Lawrence** were other post-hippies playing blues bars like Dan Lynch's, Manny's Car Wash, Chicago B.L.U.E.S., Mondo Cané, and Lone Star Café.

Nightingale's (213 Second Avenue) was the East Village dive where Deadheads and *High Times* types hung out. There was a long bar on one side, a small stage a foot off the floor on the other, and a pool table in back. The likes of Blues Traveler, Spin Doctors, and Joan Osborne blared nightly, with a cover charge of $5 max.

> **JOHN POPPER (Blues Traveler):** When Blues Traveler first came to New York, there was a scene at Nightingale's. It was a hole-in-the-wall but great bands played there. You could get blow inside by the pool table or weed outside on the corner. The cabaret laws were in effect and no more than three musicians could be onstage at a time. It wasn't really a hippie scene; it was the bridge-and-tunnel crowd. (2011)

Wetlands Preserve (161 Hudson Street) served Deadhead culture and the nascent jam band scene, as a venue and political center. The weed-reekin' spot was opened February 1989 by the late Larry Bloch in an old Chinese eatery by the Holland Tunnel. The springboard for Blues Traveler, Phish, Spin Doctors, etc. hosted the first NYC gigs by Pearl Jam, Cypress Hill, and many NYHC matinees. Wetlands' last show was the night before 9/11.

> **LARRY BLOCH (Wetlands Preserve):** I wanted to work in the environmental field, but I didn't want to be a lobbyist. I wanted to have a place people would enjoy but also would take a stance on a range of issues. I couldn't compare it to any other venture. So I decided to take this raw space and turn it into an inviting nightclub. (1998)

> **JOHN POPPER:** When our bands broke nationally, it took the Wetlands scene to a new level. I'm not into the term "jam band," but that whole musical movement began with all our bands playing Downtown. It's undeniable, that's where it all started. (1994)

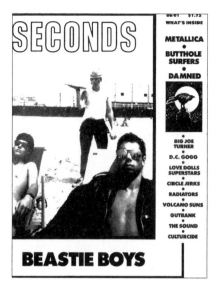

Slow and low: Beastie Boys' first cover story, *Seconds* Magazine #1, 1986. Photo by Josh Cheuse. Published by the author.

BLACK ROCK COALITION

Time ain't on your side, don't sit idly by
You've just got to try
—LIVING COLOUR, "TIME'S UP"

Black Rock Coalition was formed in 1985 by NY-based African-American musicians and writers to challenge stereotypes and create outlets for black rock bands. Their motto tried to reclaim rock's birthright: "Rock & roll is black, and we are its heirs." The *Voice* tried to promote the cause. The problem was, those bands got no love in the black world. BRC's flagship group, Living Colour, showed great promise but their metal-rock failed to endure. Others like 24-7 Spyz, Faith, Sophia's Toy, and Eye & I never overcame stigmas.

VERNON REID (Living Colour): BRC started when I went to see Melvin Gibbs' band Eye & I, with D. K. Dyson. It was great! And there was hardly anyone in the crowd. I said, "There's gotta be a reason why this is happening. We can't go on like this!" (1988)

GREG TATE (Black Rock Coalition): We started to air gripes people had about the "glass ceiling" for black musicians. Particularly instrumentalists who wanted to stretch out, and were being told by the R&B side of the industry, "Black folks don't wanna hear loud guitars," and the feeling from the rock side was that "niggers can't play rock and roll." What began as a bitch session became more about a proactive approach to the issue, which was, instead of talking about how we're locked out of the master's house, why don't we just build our own? (2001)

Living Colour starred Vernon Reid, a London-born jazz guitarist who honed his chops with Defunkt and Ronald Shannon Jackson before seeing Bad Brains. In 1985, Reid and *Voice* writer Greg Tate began Black Rock Coalition to push black rock acts, like Living Colour. Mick Jagger saw Colour at CBs and funded the 1987 demos that swayed Epic to release 1988's *Vivid* with the MTV hit "Cult of Personality" and 1990's *Time's Up,* which both won Grammys for Best Hard Rock Performance.

24-7 Spyz fused Motown and metal. Bassist Rick Skatore and guitarist Jimi Hazel (his moniker a nod to Hendrix and P-Funk's Eddie Hazel) led the South Bronx quartet behind 1988's *Harder Than You* and 1989's *Gumbo Millennium.* Singer Peter Fluid (Forest) and drummer Anthony Johnson quit the band after 24-7 opened Jane's Addiction's *Ritual de lo Habitual* tour. **Shootyz Groove,** Donny Rock (Radeljic)'s interracial rap/metal act from Washington Heights and Belmont, Bronx, recorded for Mercury (1994's *Respect* EP live from Astoria and *Jammin' in Vicious Environments*), Roadrunner (1997's *Hipnosis*), and Reprise (1999's *High Definition*) and did a live-at-CBGB split-7" with Downset. **Chain Angel,** Harlem's answer to the Crüe, were big-haired bruthas found late-night at Scrap Bar or Wah Wah Hut. *Paper* (2/94) extolled Ancel Starr's "powerful case for miscegenation."

Faith featured Felice Rosser, a CBGB scene fixture who sang on Brian Brain's 1989 version of "I Heard It Through the Grapevine" and acted in Jim Jarmusch's *Permanent Vacation.* Greg Tate in the *Voice* hailed the "tribal grunge" of 1994's "Like Springtime" b/w "Lost." **Sophia's Toy,** vehicle of Sophia Ramos, signed to Epic through New Kids on the Block manager Dick Scott, but the label dropped them after recording an album. The *New Yorker*

(9/96) wrote: "A man seeing Sophia onstage, strutting in a leather bustier, one hand gripping her crotch, her head bobbing and her tongue making snaky movements with her lips, is apt to conclude she's more strenuous fun than he feels comfortable with."

Jean Beauvoir attained infamy with shock-rockers Plasmatics. After a stint with Little Steven, Sly Stallone chose Jean's "Feel the Heat" as the theme to *Cobra*, fueling $1.5 million in sales of 1986's *Drums along the Mohawk*. He'd write and produce for Ramones, Pretenders, and Kiss, and boasts of partaking in $20 million in sales. **Lenny Kravitz**, son of jazz promoter Sy Kravitz and TV actress Roxie Roker (*The Jeffersons*), grew up around Ella Fitzgerald and Duke Ellington. He cut Prince-ish mid-'80s demos as "Romeo Blue" before 1989's *Let Love Rule*. On his first big tour, he chose as his opening act Raging Slab.

Dee Dee King was the moniker of Dee Dee Ramone after he got into rap music while in rehab with minorities. He assumed the King alias because Johnny Ramone disallowed him to denigrate the punk brand. His "Funky Man" 12″ on Profile (Run-DMC, Rob Base) shocked the rock world in 1987. Neither musical input by Chris Stein and Deborah Harry nor photos by Bob Gruen could save 1989's *Standing in the Spotlight* (Sire). Dee Dee never did another Ramones gig.

DEE DEE RAMONE (The Ramones): I just went rap crazy! I guess I just fell into the rap craze, and I got crazy too! (1987)

Demonic electronic: Bile, 1997. Photo by Frank White.

GOTH/INDUSTRIAL

Monday, time for Alchemy
I'm buried behind the Gallery
—Voltaire, "Alchemy Mondays"

As the vanguard of new wave, post-punk, industrial, and synth-pop, NYC hipsters had limited interest in the '90s goth/industrial revival. Most of the bands and crowds came from local high schools and art schools; in trench coats, capes, and black lipstick with clove cigs and patchouli oil. On the industrial side were devotees of Swans and Foetus in bands like Hanzel Ünd Gretyl and Bile. There was no credible NYC answer to Trent Reznor but young fans included Antony Hegarty, Regina Spektor, and the Yeah Yeah Yeahs.

NEVILLE WELLS (promoter): Most of the kids in the scene are very intelligent and go to Columbia or NYU. The vampire theme is more on the commercial level. But a lot of these kids tend to be pale-skinned anyway and don't get out much into the sun. (1994)

Communion, Tuesdays at the Limelight, named for the Catholic rite at this defiled church, became the major goth scene party. It began in February 1990 with British expat roommates Neville Wells and DJ Tony Fletcher. With MTV *120 Minutes* VJ Dave Kendall spinning in the Chapel, their long-running Anglophile party within a year drew more than a thousand a night (booking the likes of Morrissey, Christian Death, and Nitzer Ebb). Neville promoted years more depraved "Industrial, Goth & New Wave" parties at the Bank (225 East Houston) and Downtime (251 West 30th Street), a.k.a. Albion/ Batcave.

> **JASON LEDYARD (DJ/promoter):** Communion at the Limelight was a central place that had a lot to do with the English people in power at the time, and a big percentage of that music was goth. The Limelight as a church with those stairwells made for a perfect goth spot. I'm not sure why it folded but then Neville did his Batcave events at Downtime, and joined forces with the successful Albion parties from the Bank, and carried on as Albion/Batcave until 2004, when Neville landed in jail. (2013)

Alchemy, Monday nights at CBGB 313 Gallery, served the city's die-hard fin de siècle goth/fetish scene. Stylish hosts Althea Morin and DJ Jason Ledyard (specializing in dark-wave and death rock) began the long-running party in 1996, with a $3 cover, lots of dancing/posing in black, and events like "Gothic Easter Egg Hunt," "Miss Gothic NYC Pageant," or one of Voltaire's twenty-three shows. The club endured until CBGB's 2006 demise. **Absolution**, the first Saturday of the month at the Bank, began in 1998 with DJs Jason and Xtine. **Censored**, Dante Maure's Fridays club at the Building (at 26th and Sixth), also hosted **Damnation**, with DJs Craig Curiosity and Vanessa Miasma. **Equilibrium** was Neville Wells's Saturday party at Tilt with DJ Jason Consoli. **London Dungeon** went down Wednesdays at the S&M-ish club Zone DK. **Mission** rocked at a storefront bar on 5th and B. **Prophecy** was a fleeting weekly event at the Tunnel. **Purgatory**, at the Meatpacking District space that became Mother, had DJ Vanessa and DJ Reese; Mother also housed **Long Black Veil**. **Salvation** starred DJ Saint James Gallus. **Shadowplay** was a multi-DJ mobile event. **Stigmata** occurred Fridays at Pyramid and then at the Bank. There was **Wasteland** at Coney Island High, **Troublemaker**, Thursdays at Jackie 60 with DJ Reese, and **Ward 6** parties presided over by DJ Father Jeff at the Bank and then Palladium.

I think I'm stuck
Makin' no excuses and passin' the buck
—PSYCHOTICA, "ICE PLANET HELL"

Psychotica got dubbed the next Marilyn Manson at Lollapalooza. After their first rehearsal, manager Amanda Scheer-Demme signed the gender-benders, equal parts Klaus Nomi and Kabuki theater, to Rick Rubin's American Recordings. It began at Don Hill's with singer Pat Briggs (reinventing himself after singing hair metal in RU Ready), bassist Tommy Salmorin, and guitarist Paul "Ena" Kostabi. But Rubin hated *Psychotica*, 1996's Don Fury–produced, Stephen Sprouse–designed-logo debut. *Espina* (Zero Hour), overseen by Doug DiAngeles (NIN, Love and Rockets) in 1988, included a redux of "MacArthur Park." *Pandemic* (Red Ant), a techno-ish jam Ena cut in an English castle, held major 1999 listening parties in New York and L.A. before the label went bust.

> **PAT BRIGGS (Psychotica):** I've gone through many phases of creating this sexless image. It goes way beyond androgyny. I had so much of that stuff when I was younger and workin' the streets—I had to look like this or that to get laid and get money, or get a job—that I'd had enough of it by the time I was older. So I thought it'd be an interesting psychological experiment to take the sex out of rock and roll. (1999)

Sister Machine Gun, with Chris Randall and Chris Kelly, began playing for Neville Wells at Limelight and Downtime. Randall toured as a roadie for KMFDM, whose Sascha Knonietzko got their demo to Wax Trax!, so Randall moved to Chicago after 1992's *Sins of the Flesh* to carry on SMG. **Chemlab**, D.C. expats Jared Lousch (Hendrickson) and Dylan Thomas More, unleashed 1993's *Burn out at the Hydrogen Bar* and 1996's *East Side Militia*. **Thorn**—John John Jesse and Roy Mayorga of LES punks Nausea, with Stephen Flam of Long Island thrashers Winter—fused punk angst, metal chops, and industrial grind. Their 1994 *Pacing* EP cut at Electric Lady was a sampler of 1995's *Bitter Potion* (Roadrunner). The band performed "Martyr" in the Troma film *Tromeo & Juliet*. (JJJ became a top painter; Roy drummed on in Soulfly and Stone Sour.)

Hanzel Ünd Gretyl honed a European fan base with industrial stylings and Axis Power fetishism. Betty "Vas" Kallas (Cycle Sluts) and Rob "Kaizer Von Loopy" Lupie (brother of her Sluts mate Donna Lupie) began with 1994's *Kindermusik* tape sold at Bleecker Bob's. *Ausgeflippt* in five guttural languages yielded 1995 tours with Marilyn Manson, and 1997's *Transmissions from*

Uranus yielded dates with Prong and Rammstein. Ryan Bird in *Kerrang!* (4/26/07) dug a "breeding Ministry's shitstorm with White Zombie's hard rock stomp." **Bile**, vehicle of Long Island metal star Chris "Krztoff" Liggio, embodied pierced-and-inked electronica. **The Empire Hideous** starred Myke Hideous, future singer in a post-Danzig Misfits.

> *I can't afford this sinful pride*
> *I might as well be crucified*
> —Sister Machine Gun, "Sins of the Flesh"

JASON LEDYARD: In the '90s the goth scene was amazing in terms of the clubs and parties and DJs and touring bands from around the world. I know it will be controversial to say this, but most New York goth wasn't very good. The bands were all kind of flawed. Either not the right singer or not the right musicians, lots of great bands that needed someone to come in and change things. They all seemed to have problems. (2013)

The scene devolved on June 14, 2004, when Neville Wells killed the thirty-seven-year-old mother of three Judith Gubernikoff in an LES drunk-driving incident: his third DWI, with a blood alcohol level over three times the limit. He got convicted on May 21, 2005, of second-degree murder. Reporter Hoda Kotb blasted Wells on "The Worst Kind of Drunk Drivers."

NOW I GOT WORRY

INDIE ROCK

1991–2001: Mayor Giuliani, Luscious Jackson, Blues Explosion, Cat Power, Soul Coughing, Grand Royal, Matador, Max Fish, Mercury Lounge, Brownie's, 9/11

Now I got worry: Jon Spencer Blues Explosion, 1994. Photo by Frank White.

INDIE ROCK

THE RISE

I got that bad feelin'
But right now, we're gonna feel so good
—Blues Explosion, "Damage"

By 1990, the city could've gone either way. Soaring crime and racial rifts defined the one term of the city's first black mayor, David Dinkins. Downtown's bohemian slums still offered rock and art subcultures. But in the end, the artists and the minorities lost the gentrification war. Tenements became multimillion-dollar assets. Drugs gave way to booze, "superclubs" to bars. Finances exploded and the arts scenes splintered.

Downtown struggled to remain culturally alive. "Grunge"—the Seattle scene that produced Nirvana, Pearl Jam, Soundgarden, and Alice in Chains—took most NYC rockers by surprise because New York Rock was the embodiment of grunge. Record labels scoured Downtown for "the next Nirvana," a band inspired by Downtown punk and noise rock. The city boomed with major-label business. Geffen stars Sonic Youth (costars with Nirvana in *1991: The Year Punk Broke*) and the label Matador (Jon Spencer, Cat Power, et cetera) embodied a slacker noise-pop that kept going into the twenty-first century.

GLENN MORROW (The Individuals): In 1988–89 there was a sense of it all dying. Our distributors went out of business. The *Times* ran an article, "Is Rock Dead?" Then Nirvana came along and changed everything. It went from feeling like it was gonna go under, to all this money with alternative marketing departments. There was a total rush of activity, so the scene got reinvigorated, upstreaming to major labels and trickling down to indies. But there was no scene left in New York; the grunge bands came from elsewhere. I recall a gig at Brownies, and everyone was dressed identically in ironic T-shirts. (2011)

SEAN YSEULT (White Zombie): When we signed to Geffen we were their next record after *Nevermind*. Before that, it was cool to like rock and Guns N' Roses, and after that it was Sonic Youth and more alternative pop than straight-ahead rock. Within a year, it all changed, from spandex and big hair to wearing flannels and hair down. It was very fast, all because of that Nirvana record. (2011)

MATT SWEENEY (Chavez): I remember my bandmate Clay Tarver referred to indie rock as "America's fastest-growing sport." All these unbelievably square people I knew from high school or college were suddenly hip on the scene with a band. The bands I like, I want them to look like they're gonna steal your hubcaps, so this was all disconcerting to me. You wanted your music to be liked by people you thought were cool, or you wanted to alienate those you didn't think were cool. So it was wild to see our New York peer bands blow up—even though they began with no intention of that—of which we were all kind of horrified. All of a sudden with Nirvana that was an option. You had to be blind to see there wasn't this big cultural moment. (2013)

GABBY GLASER (Luscious Jackson): Things changed in the '90s, way different from the '70s and '80s. It used to be a scene for a scene's sake, not a scene for money. (1993)

Giuliani, he's such a fucking jerk
Shut down all the strip bars
Workfare does not work
—LE TIGRE, "MY MY METROCARD"

Modern New York began with the 1993 election of Rudolph Giuliani as a Republican mayor of the legendarily liberal city. The former prosecutor challenged the status quo of crime and depravity. He emphasized enforcement of "quality of life" issues, the idea being that minor crimes lead to major ones. Giuliani defeated them all: squeegee men, noise polluters, club owners, pot smokers, and community activists.

CARLO McCORMICK (author/journalist): Giuliani's hypocritical intolerance had such a detrimental effect on the New York scene's vitality. As much as he takes credit for many things he doesn't deserve—like the city's gentrification—he probably can't take all the blame as well. Much of what happened would've probably occurred without him, and the pricing out of marginal lifestyles is to my mind the worst blow we took in that time, along with the devastating depopulation of freaks caused by AIDS. Giuliani's worst assault on our community was his war on the social scene that bound us. Empowering the bitter old ladies who ran our community boards, he did all he could to shutter a nightlife that fiscally fed and spiritually sustained us. (2011)

DAVID HERSHKOVITS (*Paper*): It was all an image thing. They tried to clean up the graffiti because graffiti gave people a sense of anarchy that anybody could do anything they wanted. That wasn't the message the city wanted. They wanted people to think the city is safe and people can walk around and not be confronted by lawbreakers, so that really changed behavior in New York. Things became way more uptight. We smoked pot in the street, in the cab, in the movies, and nobody cared, so that totally changed. (2005)

MATT SWEENEY: I remember saying to my stepfather that a guy like Giuliani doesn't like a guy like me. There was no sympathy for the artist. In the '90s, everything got expensive, especially with the Internet boom. All of a sudden there were all these douche-y people in the 'hood—though nothing as bad as today. Having a part-time job and dedicating yourself to reading books and listening to records and making music was no longer an option. CBGB became like a pay-to-play thing. Then the AIDS epidemic killed half the great musicians. That gave more elbow room for bands like Sonic Youth, and for all the suburban types coming in. (2013)

Giuliani signified a city at war with its nightlife. Clubs got fined or shuttered by robust enforcement of drug, noise, and petty-crime laws. Another way to prevent dancing was to prosecute "cabaret laws" (an old relic of anti-miscegenation) that prevented patrons from dancing. In the '90s, clubs got shut on the spot for the mildest of rump shaking.

JESSE MALIN (D Generation): This is New York, people come from all over the world to experience decadence and culture and art and music, and to be free. It's so not free anymore. All the blue laws are being enforced for jaywalking or having a beer in a brown paper bag. It's hard to go out on a Saturday night with the invasion of all these people you don't wanna see. And if you do anything fun, you might get busted for smoking a joint on the corner. New York was supposed to be 24/7, and now it's Giuliani hell. You really feel it. (1999)

New bands with new values reflected the new demographic. The Jewish Lower East Side became the alt-rock LES. Blazing new bands had little in common with past junkie punk nihilism. Radical politics took a backseat to career aims. It was the demise of New York Rock's hegemony, and the roots of modern "post-rock." There were great groups, some known, most forgotten. For every Jon Spencer (Blues Explosion) was a more severe Stu Spasm (Lubricated Goat). Luscious Jackson and Soul Coughing far outsold the Bogmen or Jonathan Fire*Eater. Such groups socialized on Ludlow Street at Max Fish and the Pink Pony, or Aaron Rose's Alleged Gallery, where Shepard Fairey (artist of the "Obama Hope" poster) did his first big art show.

CHRIS SANCHEZ (The Fever): I don't think there were a lot of great New York indie-rock bands—though I loved Babe the Blue Ox. The exciting indie-rockers were like Southern or in California or Boston, and not New York at all. Indie rock wasn't sexy. It was like your arms folded and stand there, and I always found it uninteresting from the point of view of both the performer and the audience. (2005)

Business got handled via fax, mail, and landlines. New CD technology made music the realm of digital files: seventies vinyl collectors didn't have access to vast archives at their fingertips like '90s kids with CD reissues, retrospectives, and compilations. Most '90s acts drew upon wider stimuli, so musicians were less "purist" and their eclecticism sounded like a stew. It all fueled a surge of new bands, labels, and fanzines. Many artists were artificial constructs, with naive buildups and/or lack of interest.

MATT SWEENEY: I worked at a PR company, and we had to send out records, and half our time was opening boxes of CDs and stuffing them in envelopes—and being slaves to the mail system just for people to hear cool music. That's changed entirely; the physical nature of what it took to put music in someone's earhole was entirely different. You mailed someone a cool personalized package, and you then spent time following up. But the waste was insane, lugging down bags and bags of mailer envelopes filled with CDs. When I look back on that aspect of promoting music, all I see are me dragging around big yellow envelopes up to my knees in 50-packs. That no longer exists. (2013)

THE SCENE

The clubs have all shut down
And I have been dressed down
—LUNA, "GOODBYE"

Matador Records, like the alt-rock Motown, launched Pavement, Yo La Tengo, Jon Spencer Blues Explosion, Cat Power, Liz Phair, and Interpol. The label started in 1989 with Chris Lombardi in his LES apartment on a debut record by Swiss expats H. P. Zinker. Gerard Cosloy, of Dutch East India's Homestead label, joined the following year.

MATT SWEENEY (Chavez): I remember being very happy when I signed to Matador. I was very interested in what they were doing. Over time they developed a sound, so to speak, but their first ten-fifteen records you could not categorize, they were all over the map. What the bands all had in common was that they all hung out at Max Fish. (2013)

STEVEN CERIO (Railroad Jerk): Things at Matador got commercial real quickly. We still had that DIY punk attitude, and I remember someone at the label telling us, "Just think of touring as having a job," a real business attitude. Who needs that shit? Look at the underground roots those guys come from: Who wants to be a punk businessmen? It's sad and creepy. (2004)

Grand Royal Records, a spin-off of the Beasties' *Grand Royal* magazine, put out CDs by Luscious Jackson and Sean Lennon, and Ween and Cibo Matto projects. After fleeing to L.A. for 1989's *Paul's Boutique*, the Beasties retook the city. Mike D (Diamond) saw himself as a record mogul and ran the label (into the ground). According to Bid4assets.com, Grand Royal LLC sold its assets and licenses in a bankruptcy auction for $65,000. NPR reported (6/13/05) that the Beastie Boys' lawyers battled to the Supreme Court, which "refused to consider whether a 1992 Beastie Boys song infringed on the copyright of a recording by jazz flutist James Newton, who said the act's 'Pass the Mic' sampled his 1978 'Choir.'"

ADAM HOROVITZ (Beastie Boys): Initially, it was a goof and we had boots and shaved heads. Then it was a goof and we had ski outfits. Then it was a goof and we had the do-rags on. Now it's a goof and we don't have any of that. (1989)

Brownie's (169 Avenue A), opened in 1989 by Laura McCarthy (of the dive bar 2A), became where record label execs searched for the next Kurt Cobain. Dee Pop, Joe Hurley, and Chumley Twist all booked the 150-capacity room, four bands a night, seven nights a week. Elliott Smith, Sugar Ray, Interpol, and the Liars did big shows there, before 2000's dwindling crowds and 2002's closure. Their competitor **Mercury Lounge** (217 East Houston Street) opened in 1993. The 250-capacity industry-friendly space with clean loos and nice acoustics hosting major label showcases signified a departure from the previous anything-goes LES clubs. The Merc, part of "The Bowery Presents" empire at the 600-capacity Bowery Ballroom, came to form with Delsener/Slater booker Theresa Chambers.

GERARD GARONE (Radio 4): Brownie's was the CBGB of the 1990s. I used to work there in the heyday. Everybody played Brownie's at some point in their careers. (2004)

Max Fish (178 Ludlow Street), a dive bar named for the dry goods shop once there, catered to underground musicians and incognito VIPs, during the first taming of the 'hood. Ulli Rimkus's artistic outpost opened in 1989 with artist Harry Druzd bartending, Dustdevils members barbacking, and Carlo McCormick hosting. You'd find Johnny Depp there with Jim Jarmusch at 4 a.m., or limos idling outside looking to cop dope down the block. **Pink Pony**, Rimkis's next-door café, hosted early gigs by Helmet, Surgery, and Unsane. Yeah Yeah Yeahs and TV on the Radio members worked at both locations.

PAGE HAMILTON (Helmet): All these bands would be on the jukebox at Max Fish, where a lot of us would hang out and do drugs. Yeah, those nights of debauchery in the bathroom there . . . That's where I'd hang out with Casper Brötzmann and Jim Thirlwell and Todd from Cop Shoot Cop, and make our little runs up to 2nd Street to slide our money under the bulletproof glass. (2006)

LIZZIE BOUGATSOS (Gang Gang Dance): My guitarist used to work at Pink Pony, a coffee shop next to Max Fish. It was a bohemian, beatnik hangout. Taylor Mead was always there, and a lot of rare, free-jazz music. It was a really intense poetry and music hangout. (2008)

ULLI RIMKUS (Max Fish): Gentrification was always big on this block. I moved here before I opened the bar. It was all Hispanic families and whoever used to be here, and they moved because more white people moved in. And now we're being kicked out. . . . I do think the alternative culture is being forced out, but I don't think we should go. (2010)

THE MUSIC

Insane and unknown is my only creed
Enjoy, destroy, then set you free
—LUSCIOUS JACKSON, "DAUGHTERS OF THE KAOS"

Luscious Jackson (named for a joking mispronunciation of NBA star Lucious Jackson) came out of the NYHC scene. Kate Schellenbach drummed in the original Beastie Boys; Jill Cunniff was in the pre-Beasties Young Aborigines and knew Vivian Trimble. They all knew Gabrielle "Gabby" Glaser. Luscious began at the tail end of the Danceteria scene inspired by ESG and Bush Tetras. They gave their 1991 demo to the Beasties, who made 1993's *In Search of Manny* EP the debut on Grand Royal. "Here," off 1994's *Natural Ingredients*, was in the film *Clueless.* That year they rocked Lollapalooza and *Saturday Night Live.* Then *Fever In, Fever Out* yielded the 1996 Top 40 "Naked Eye." In 1998, they appeared in a Christmas ad for the Gap, doing "Let It Snow! Let It Snow! Let It Snow!"

GABBY GLASER (Luscious Jackson): We really packed a lot into those early years. We were exposed to so much stimuli that by the time we were seventeen we were jaded. (1999)

JILL CUNNIFF (Luscious Jackson): Having a hit is scary in that *People* magazine, Céline Dion way, and that's not what we've aspired to. We're kind of snobs. (1999)

Fuck shit up, do it punk
Take a stand, fuck the man
—BLUES EXPLOSION, "FUCK SHIT UP"

The Jon Spencer Blues Explosion turned black music into white noise, like a modern R&B minstrel show. Jon grew up in the Ivy League ghetto of Hanover, NH, son of a Dartmouth professor. He migrated to D.C. to join Julia Cafritz in

Pussy Galore, before they moved to the East Village in 1985. Amped on the punk-blues he jammed with the Workdogs at Max Fish. Spencer quit the hate-fuck to form a bass-less trio with guitarist Judah Bauer and drummer Russell Simins. First came 1991's self-made *A Reverse Willie Horton* and 1992's *Crypt Style* (Crypt). Ninety-two's *Jon Spencer Blues Explosion* was hailed in *Penthouse* (10/97): "Amped-up blues-tinged stompers recorded live in all their noisy glory as a '90s update on Alan Lomax's Southern field recordings." Well-received efforts include 1993's *Extra Width*, '96's *Now I Got Worry*, and '97's *The Controversial Negro*.

JON SPENCER (Blues Explosion): I love early rock and roll. I love rockabilly. I love raw and greasy soul and blues. But I don't think I moved towards those records and sounds as a reaction to something going on in the indie-rock scene or kicking against anything in the modern world that I'm aware of. (1996)

I could be condemned to Hell for every sin but littering
I could slip on the East River and crash into Queens all skittering
—SOUL COUGHING, "THE IDIOT KINGS"

Soul Coughing defined '90s Downtown with their "deep slacker jazz," a cross-collision of alt rock, bebop, hip-hop, drum 'n' bass, Beat poetry, and spoken word. Mike Doughty was a *New York Press* writer and Knitting Factory doorman (where the band named for a poem he wrote about Neil Young vomiting, debuted June 15, 1992). The quartet—with fiddler Sebastian Steinberg, drummer Yuval Gabay, and pianist Mark De Gli Antoni—signed to Slash/Warner Bros. Ninety-four's *Ruby Vroom* used baby rattles, whistles, car muffler, and bullhorn. Ninety-six's *Irresistible Bliss* spawned "The Bug" (in *Batman and Robin*) and "Super Bon Bon" (bumper music for Rush Limbaugh's radio show). Doughty quit the band (as well as heroin) in a never-healed 2000 rift over publishing money and songwriting credit.

SEBASTIAN STEINBERG (Soul Coughing): Soul Coughing is kind of like a Ouija board. It's this territory that exists between the four of us, and if any one monkey grabs the wheel, boom!—the TV goes off, the lights go on, the phone rings, and the spell is broken. Everything is a result of equal participation. (1996)

MIKE DOUGHTY (Soul Coughing): Soul Coughing was a weird universe; sort of a Dante's Inferno, where I was the Devil's asshole, and there was the band, the management, the record company, and everybody hated me. (2009)

I can't stand to let you down
I can't stand to have you around
—COME, "IN/OUT"

Come began with Boston cult star Thalia Zedek, who came to NYC in 1987 to replace Marnie Greenholz in Live Skull (on 1988's *Dusted*). Her next band was gonna call itself the Marshall Fucker Band before choosing Come. During this era she grew a nasty habit, and critics hailed them urban junkie blues. Robert Palmer wrote in *Rolling Stone* (4/93): "There's a kind of nervy, embattled grace that can be like manna from heaven." **Dim Stars** unretired Richard Hell for his first music since 1982. Don Fleming (Gumball) and Sonic Youth's Thurston Moore and Steve Shelley backed Hell on 1991's *Dim Stars* EP and 1992's *Dim Stars* LP lauded by some as SY's finest work. Palmer raved in *Stone* (9/92): "Dim Stars still shine brightly in the Lower East Side quadrant of rock and roll heaven."

Free Kitten, a Kim Gordon–Julia Cafritz project, gelled with Pavement bassist Mark Ibold and Boredoms drummer Yoshimi P-We. Their 1993 *Call Now* 12″ and 1994's *Unboxed* (covering X-Ray Spex and Minutemen) portended 1995's *Nice Ass* with "Alan Licked Has Ruined Music for an Entire Generation" and 1997's "Free Kitten with Me" with a DJ Spooky remix. **Blonde Redhead**, named for a DNA song, began with two Japanese art students and twin brothers from Milan via Berklee. Kazu Makino evoked Kim Gordon, and the noise/pop of 1993's EP (in English, Japanese, and Italian) inspired SY's Steve Shelley to produce and release their 1994–95 records. The band went on hiatus in 2003 after Kazu fell off a horse that stepped on her face and shattered her jaw.

Luna began when New Zealand's Dean Wareham left his Boston alt-rock act Galaxie 500. In NYC he launched Luna 2, with Justin Harwood of NZ's the Chills on bass, and Feelies drummer Stanley Demeski. Elektra signed them after a demo with Mercury Rev's David Fridmann. As Luna, their "dream pop" so evoked the VU (sans the nihilism) they opened VU's '93 tour. **Gumball**

starred Jay Spiegel and Don Fleming (B.A.L.L., Velvet Monkeys). J. Mascis joined 'em, and as Gumball, they rode the grunge wave to Columbia Records. Butch Vig (Nirvana) produced 1992's *Wisconsin Hayride* EP and 1993's *Super Tasty*. In Blue Öyster Cult fetishism, 1994's *Revolution on Ice* (riffing BÖC's *Revolution by Night*) featured BÖC drummer Albert Bouchard on "She's as Beautiful as a Foot."

Cat Power is the stage name of Charlyn "Chan" Marshall, a folkie with punk attitude, who moved to the East Village from Atlanta in 1992 at age twenty. She played with God Is My Co-Pilot, who put out her first Cat Power 45, 1994's "Headlights." That, 1995's *Dear Sir* 10″ (with Steve Shelley), and 1996's *Myra Lee* (for Shelley's Smells Like label) paved the way for cult fame. (In 2006, she got sent to a Miami mental hospital before recovering and returning to work.) **Madder Rose** evoked the doped-out sounds of Nico-era VU. Max Fish regulars vocalist Mary Lorson, guitarist Billy Coté, and bassist Matt Verta-Ray did 1993's *Bring It Down*, 1994's *Panic On*, 1997's *Tragic Magic*, and 1999's trip-hop-tinged *Hello June Fool*.

H.P. Zinker included Austrian Europop semi-stars Hans Platzgummer and Frank Puempel. In NYC, they began a power trio weaned on prog/punk SST Records acts like Minutemen and Gone. Matador Records' first release was 1989's debut . . . *And There Was Light* EP, with a drum machine and a cover of Led Zeppelin's "Dancing Days." That brought about 1990's *Beyond It All* and 1995's *Mountains of Madness*. **Loudspeaker** began on the LES with Matt Borruso and Christopher Faith (Douglas) of Bay Area punk legends Crucifix. With art-school dropout Pussy Galore guitarist Kurt Wolf they rocked a soulful noise, from 1990's "Pray" and 1991's "King" 45s, cut at Baby Monster, to 1996's *Re-Verberate*.

Codeine got known for a 1989 demo with a space jam on Harry Nillson's "Without You." Bitch Magnet were friends with guitarist John Engle and bassist-vocalist Stephen Immerwahr, and told their German label Glitterhouse, who in turn told Sub Pop. So at grunge's apex came 1991's *Frigid Stars* of "slowcore." They left to Louisville after 1992's *Barely Real* with a cover on MX-80 Sound's "Promise of Love." **Springhouse** gushed UK-style alt pop. Mitch Friedland, Larry Heinemann, and Jack Rabid did 1990's "Menagerie Keeper" for Bob Mould's Singles Only Label and four Caroline records. *Land Falls* spawned the video "Layers" (shot by Michael Stipe's partner Jim McKay at Flushing Meadows' geodesic dome) that in 1991 aired twice on *120 Minutes*, and once on USA's *Up All Night*.

God Is My Co-Pilot, the "queercore" act of Craig Flanagin and Sharon

Topper, made at least a lo-fi album a year focused on Jewish/lesbian issues with lyrics in English, Yiddish, French, German, and Finnish. *Stay Free* wrote: "Godco's unwieldy genderfucking skronk con-fusion is certainly the shit in the post-Lounge Lizard fake jazz/no wave scene and if they can keep up this avalanche of tuneage they might even make it on *Conan O'Brien*." **Babe the Blue Ox**, the Brooklyn trio of Brown grads Tim Thomas and Rose Thomson with Hanna Fox, in photos kissing, holding hands, or touching tongues, mixed upbeat alt rock with offbeat jazz. Their 1991 debut "There's Always Room for One More, Honey" 45 and 1993's *(BOX)* foretold a future of razor-laced pop. Streisand-mania inspired album titles: 1993's *Je M'Appelle Babe*, 1994's *Color Me Babe*, 1996's *People*, and '98's *The Way We Were*.

Piss Factory (for Patti Smith's first single) unleashed pre–Riot Grrl East Village noise rock. *Seconds* (#23) saluted 1993's Godfrey Diamond–produced *Piss Factory*, with its female crotch cover shot, as "the sound of Kim Gordon's Free Kitten mercifully put to sleep." Bassist/vocalist Lizzie Avondet, guitarists Harri Kapianian, and Paul Eng and drummer Andy Markham also unleashed 1994's *I Melt* EP. **Dustdevils** starred Michael Duane and Jaqi Dulaney (Cohen), a colorful British couple living above Max Fish and working there. A pre-Pavement Mark Ibold played on 1990's *Struggling Electric and Chemical*. Michael and Jaqi broke up in 1993 after she beat his ass and left the country. His song, "Receiver," told of the scabs on his face from that Ludlow Street beatdown.

Cibo Matto, Japanese ladies key to alt rock's rise, got their name from a mistranslation of *Seso Matto*, a '70s Italian movie. Singer Yuka Honda grew up in Tokyo, studied in Aix en-Provence, France, and came to NYC in 1986. Cibo's recipe, tasty grooves about food, debuted on 1995's *Cibo Matto* EP. Matto mixed Yoko Ono's "Talking to the Universe." Yuka then dated Sean Lennon, whom she introduced to the Beasties and Grand Royal, label behind Butter 08 with Yuka and Miho Hatori, and Buffalo Daughter with Yumiko Ohno. **Sean Lennon**, only child of John and Yoko, was five in 1980 when his father was murdered. Both 1998's Honda-produced *Into the Sun* (Grand Royal) and 2006's *Friendly Fire* (Capitol), inspired by his next love Bijou Phillips's affair with his late best friend Max LeRoy, tanked.

Talking to the universe: Sean Lennon, New York, 1997. Photo by Frank White.

The Murmurs started with Heather Grody and Leisha Hailey at American Academy of Dramatic Arts. Ninety-two's self-made *Who Are We* resulted in MCA releases: 1994's *The Murmurs* (with three producers) and 1995's *White Rabbit* (covering Jefferson Airplane). By 1997's *Pristine Smut* and 1998's *Blender* (both produced by Hailey's lover k.d. lang) they added Sheri Ozeka and Sherri Solinger. Critics likened them to the Go-Gos, and *Blender* featured "Smash" written by Go-Gos Jane Wiedlin and Charlotte Caffey. **The Aquanettas**, a foursome named for Aqua-Net hairspray, played a stinging punk/pop, like X or the Bangles. Singer Deborah Schwartz knew guitarist Jill Richmond from the L.A. punk scene and began a band in '87 with bassist Claudine Troies and drummer Stephanie Seymour. They broke up dejected by 1993's *Roadhaüs* EP.

Cake Like, a post-punk female trio akin to Bush Tetras, began at NYU's Experimental Theater division with Kerri Kenney, Nina Hellman, and Jody Seifert. What they lacked in training, they made up for in energy. John Zorn released 1994's *Delicious*. Ric Ocasek produced 1995's *Mr. Fireman* EP; he told Neil Young, who issued on his Vapor/Warner Bros. label 1997's *Bruiser Queen* and 1999's *Goodbye, So What*. **Rasputina**, a no-guitar act of three cellists in Victorian corsets—Melora Creager, Julia Kent, and Carpella Parvo—played tweaked strings on rock hits (Led Zep, Pink Floyd). They played at Downtown goth clubs until opening for Nirvana. Columbia jumped in on 1996's *Thanks for the Ether* and 1998's *How We Quit the Forest*, leading to Helmet and Marilyn Manson tours.

Black 47 (an Irish allusion to 1847, worst year of the potato famine) offer a whiskey-soaked *Riverdance* with a wry twist. Larry Kirwan came from Ireland in 1979 with Pierce Turner seeking new-wave glory as Major Thinkers. Larry's Black 47 packed weekly gigs at Paddy O'Reilly's on Second Avenue. Ric Ocasek produced and helped them self-release 1991's CD and do 1992's *Black 47 EP* for SPK, making 'em Irish-American stars. *Live in New York* was recorded live at Wetlands in 1999. David Johansen sang on "Staten Island Baby" on '04's *New York Town*. **Pierce Turner**, after Major Thinkers with Larry Kirwin, became a Celtic singer-songwriter, signed after 1985 residencies at Kenny's Castaways and Cat Club. Philip Glass produced 1986's *It's Only a Long Way Across* with "Wicklow Hills," voted to the *Today FM* list of Top 25 Irish Songs of All Time. Both 1989's *The Sky and the Ground* and 1991's *Now Is Heaven* proved to be too Erse for pop consumption.

> *Hold me and love me*
> *Tie me up and drug me*
> —Matthew Sweet, "Someone to Pull the Trigger"

Matthew Sweet moved to NY from Athens, GA (a member of Michael Stipe's sister's band Oh-OK), and signed to Columbia. *Inside*, his 1986 solo LP with Fred Maher, Chris Stamey, and Anton Fier, won press. Sweet then played on the Palominos' *Blast of Silence* (*Axed My Baby for a Nickel*). Maher produced solo 1988's *Earth* with Richard Lloyd (Television), Robert Quine (Voidoids), and Lloyd Cole (Commotions). Sweet left for L.A. after 1991's hit "Girlfriend." **Chris Whitley**, a dark-soul guitar-slinger raised in Houston, came to the city in 1977, busking on Village street corners. He spent time in Belgium with wife Hélène Gevaert before returning to record for Columbia for producer Daniel Lanois. Tours with Dylan and Petty came of *Living with the Law*, *Rolling Stone*'s "Best Debut of 1991." Drugs and divorce fueled his records, 1995's Lou Reed–style *Din of Ecstasy* and 1997's *Terra Incognito*. Whitley died of cancer in 2005 at age forty-five after *Soft Dangerous Shores*.

Jeff Buckley never knew his father, Tim Buckley, who OD'd in June 1975 at age twenty-eight, before Jeff turned nine. In fact, Jeff's mom raised him as "Scott Moorhead" to fend off his deadbeat dad. Taking his real name, Jeff moved to the LES in 1991 to play in Gary Lucas's Gods and Monsters and with Nusrat Fateh Ali Khan. After a 1992 bidding war and 1993's *Live at Sin-é* EP, Columbia issued '94's *Grace* with "Hallelujah" (one of *Rolling Stone*'s "500 Greatest Songs of All Time"). Buckley started on a new album in Memphis with Tom Verlaine. In May 1997, the thirty-year-old fell into the Mississippi and drowned: like his dad, legendary in death. **David Poe** came from Dayton, OH, in 1991 and mixed sound at CB's 313 Gallery. A 1994 self-produced six-track EP of dark folk (with Rollins Band drummer Simeon Cain) yielded an Epic deal in 1996. The 1996 *David Poe* involved avant-garde guitarist Marc Ribot. T-Bone Burnett produced the album, and then Poe cowrote music with T-Bone for *The Tooth of Crime*, a Sam Shepard play at Public Theater.

Dogbowl (Steve Tunney) began King Missile with John Hall but quit before their hit "Jesus Was Way Cool." With producer Kramer came far-out, quasi-concept solo LPs on Shimmy-Disc, like 1989's *Tit: An Opera*, 1991's *Cyclops Nuclear Submarine Captain*, and 1992's 21-song *Flan* (the latter title the same as Tunney's novel, hailed in *New York Press* as "Dr. Seuss gone psycho"), followed by queasy listening pseudo-C&W like 1994's *Hot Day in Waco*, 1995's *Gunsmoke*, or 1996's *Live on WFMU*. **Reid Paley** pens brutally honest Tom Waits–ish songs. The Brooklyn kid attended college in Pittsburgh, where he played punk in the Five. That band went to Boston, where Reid befriended fellow starving artist Frank Black, of the Five's opening act, the Pixies. Reid came home in the '90s, honing his busker style, as Reid Paley and then Reid Paley Trio.

Popa Chubby (Ted Horowitz) dropped out of high school in Forest Hills and moved to the LES, where he joined Screaming Mad George's punk band Disgusted, and then Jerry Williams's NYHC band Bloodclot! Popa kicked heroin to jam roots music, playing purist blues bars like Dan Lynch's and Manny's Car Wash, where he honed his persona. Fame began on 1995's Tom Dowd–produced debut *Booty and the Beast*. **Maggie Estep** ruled Nuyorican Café poetry slams with a fiery style (Lydia Lunch sans the nymphomania). She parlayed a 1994 *Voice* cover story into fleeting MTV fame and a rock career. I Love Everybody backed her on 1994's *No More Mr. Nice Girl* (for Nu Yo). A 1997 album, *Love Is a Dog from Hell* (Mercury), included guitarist Knox Chandler and drummer Paul Garisto. Rockers despised her poetic mash-ups, so she mutated into mystery writer Ruby Murphy.

Floating down Houston Street and the furies are after me
It's the type of night where I don't give a damn if the rent is paid
—GRAND MAL, "FLYIN' HIGH"

Grand Mal began when Bill Whitten quit his Hartford, CT, band St. Johnny, after two Sonic Youth–style albums for Geffen. After 1995's tour on Lollapalooza's side stage, the guitarist/singer came to NYC to form a drug-groove band, equal parts Heartbreakers and Spaceman 3. A highlight was 1998's *Maledictions* (London). The 2006 record *Love Is the Best Con in Town* included "From Hartford to Times Square." **Nada Surf** arose at Lycée Français de New York with Daniel Lorca and Matthew Caws; Fuzztones drummer Ira Elliot replaced Aaron Conte. A 1994 single, "The Plan," portended 1995's *Karmic* EP (No. 6). Ric Ocasek produced 1996's *High/Low* (Elektra) with the slacker smash "Popular." Elektra dumped the group after 1998's Fred Maher–produced *The Proximity Effect.*

Lotion played cheeky, offbeat R.E.M.-style pop. Kramer produced 1992's *Lotion* EP, in which time *Sassy* picked them in a "Cute Band Alert." *Full Isaac* (cited "Album of the Year" for 1994 in the *Voice*) featured "Dock Ellis," about the MLB pitcher who threw a no-hitter on LSD, and allusions to Robert Downey, Sr.'s film *Putney Swope*. Thomas Pynchon wrote liner notes to 1996's *Nobody's Cool.* **The Bogmen**, a Long Island alt-rock sextet, fell short of stardom. Clive Davis at Arista could not deliver a hit, despite 1995's Jerry Harrison–produced *Life Begins at 40 Million*, and 1998's Bill Laswell–overseen *Closed Caption Radio*. (Adam Sandler even wore their cap at the MTV Video Music Awards.)

The Rake's Progress (for William Hogarth's etchings that inspired Igor Stravinsky's opera) drew well Downtown (often with The Bogmen). Singer Tim Cloherty and bassist Bob Donlon oversaw 1994's six-song *Cheese Food Prostitute* EP with "You Must Be on Drugs" and a KROQ-FM hit, "I'll Talk My Way out of This One." Herb Alpert's Almo Sounds won a bidding war to put out 1995's *Altitude,* but glory eluded the group. **Ruth Ruth** (for a character in *The Incredible Shrinking Woman*) did many sweaty East Village gigs. Manager Amanda Scheer-Demme (filmmaker Ted Demme's widow) set up Chris Kennedy, Mike Lustig, and Dave Snyder to do 1995's *Laughing Gallery* for Rick Rubin's American Recordings, hailed in *Q* (1/96) "fiercely neurotic, shamelessly tuneful power pop." The title of 1998's *Are You My Friend?* (RCA) alluded to their Rubin fiasco.

Ivy began in the LES with Williams College grads Adam Schlesinger and Andy Chase with Chase's Parisian wife Dominique Durand. March 1994's Nico-like "Get Enough" got picked *Melody Maker* "Single of the Week." Then came 1994's *Lately* EP and 1995's *Realistic* LP. Positive feedback to 1997's *Apartment Life* (Atlantic) resulted in Durand's breathy vox and Ivy's music on TV, like *Alias, Roswell,* and *Felicity.* **Fountains of Wayne** got their name from a fountain store on Route 46 near Ivy's Adam Schlesinger's hometown of Montclair, NJ. Ninety-six's demo of Beatlesque pop yielded an Atlantic deal.

Ninety-six's *Fountains of Wayne* and 1999's *Utopia Parkway* (for the ironically named Queens road) made waves but the band got dropped and broke up in 1999. A 2002 reunion reaped the monster hit "Stacy's Mom."

Space Needle featured Jud Ehrbar, after drumming for Scarce, Providence, RI's almost alt-rock stars. His trio with guitarist Jeff Gatland and Varnaline's Anders Parker began on 1995's *Voyager* with its prog-flavored puerile jams, and 1997's *The Moray Eels Eat the Space Needle* (a riff on *The Moray Eels Eat the Holy Modal Rounders*) had cover art by Yes artist Roger Dean. **Skeleton Key** began with Lounge Lizards bassist Erik Sanko and Knitting Factory booker, guitarist Chris Maxwell. Their cerebral mix of jazz skronk, funk freak-out, and found sounds (that Eric called "a freight train filled with flowers") resulted in 1995's *In My Mind* (Dedicated UK) and 1996's *Skeleton Key* (Motel). *Fantastic Spikes Through Balloon* (Capitol) won a 1997 Grammy nomination, for its artwork.

The Spitters took their name from the methadone clinic practice of swallowing a dose and spitting it into a cup to re-sell. Wisconsin state swimming champ Mark Ashwill (ex–Missing Foundation) and Sonic Youth producer Jim Waters began the fiery LES quartet that over time included Bill Bronson, Judah Bauer, and Tim Bradlee. Their 1996 Roy Mayorga–produced *Sin to Sun* captured the chaos better than 1993's *The Spitters* EP or '94's *Give*. **Blue Humans**, Rudolph Grey's no-wave/free jazz act, over time involved Jim Sauter (Borbetomagus), Alan Licht (Love Child), Beaver Harris (Albert Ayler), Charles Gayle, Tom Surgal, and Rashied Ali. *Mask of Light*, released in 1991, is a skronk opus, as are 1993's *Clear to Higher Times*, live at CBGB in 1990, 1995's *Incandescence* at CBs in 1988, and '95's *Live NY 1980*. Grey's book *Nightmare of Ecstasy* inspired Johnny Depp's film *Ed Wood*.

Motherhead Bug melded industrial grind, circus-calliope music, and Zappa-isms. Cop Shoot Cop's David Ouimet's jarring, up to 17-piece ensemble included Swans' Norman Westberg, Railroad Jerk's Tony Lee, and Rasputina's Julia Kent augmenting his boozy Tom Waits wail. They rose on 1991's "My Sweet Milstar" and 1992's "Age of Dwarfs," and fell on 1993's *Zambodia* on the '80s dance label Pow Wow. **Sulfur** shared stages with Motherhead Bug. Head Bug David Ouimet's wife-to-be, Michelle Amar, did MIDI programming for producer Roli Mossiman with New Order and Young Gods. She began Sulfur (first called Virus, and confused for the NYHC band) with drummer Yuval Gabay. Ninety-six's *Delirium Tremens* involved twenty contributors on gear like accordion and glockenspiel.

Chrome Cranks, the Gun Club–style band of Cincinnati's Peter Aaron (Wegele) and William Gilmore Weber, in the LES with Jerry Teel (Honeymoon Killers) and drummer Bob Bert. Their PCP label punk-blues included 1994's

Vice Squad Dick EP and *Chrome Cranks* LP and 1995's *Dead Cool. RIP* (7/94): "These space truckin' warriors take the Branca/Helmet noize formula and shove it through the meat grinder of yr mind." **Speedball Baby**, a rockabilly-ish noise band with a druggy moniker, started as a drunken jam at singer Ron Ward's first wedding. Ward, Madder Rose guitarist Matt Verta-Ray, Kelly Township bassist Ali Smith, and various drummers rocked in a Blues Explosion style with Iggy-ish fire. Two 1995 efforts, a self-titled 7" and the *Get Straight for the Last Supper* 10" yielded 1996's *Speedball Petite* EP and *Cinema* LP for MCA that failed despite promo at tat parlors and skate shops.

Chavez featured guitarist-vocalist Matt Sweeney (ex-Skunk), guitarist Clay Tarver (Bullet LaVolta), drummer James Lo (Live Skull), and bassist Scott Marshall (Penny Marshall's nephew). They made indie-rock classics in 1995's *Gone Glittering* and *Pentagram Ring* EPs and 1996's *Ride the Fader* LP. **Bailter Space** (or **Bailterspace**), New Zealand's leading alt-rockers (two records for N.Z.'s Flying Nun label), came to the LES in 1990 for a Matador deal. Alister Parker, John Halvorsen, and Brent McLachlan made 1992's *The Aim* EP, 1993's *Robot World* LP, and 1994's *B.E.I.P.* EP. They carried on for a while after a 2003 feud, where Matador deleted all BS music from its catalog.

Firewater was the post-rock band of Cop Shoot Cop's Tod Ashley. Carlo McCormick hailed it (*Seconds #46*) "an Eastern European stew of gypsy curses, tango eroticisms, cabaret brawls and klezmatic frenzies." Firewater did six albums like 1997's *Get off the Cross . . . We Need the Wood for the Fire*, and 2001's *Psychopharmacology* with Yuval Gabay (Soul Coughing), Britta Phillips (Luna), and Jennifer Charles (Elysian Fields). **White Hassle** (a riff on White Castle) began when Marcellus Hall and Dave Varenka quit Railroad Jerk. Their guitar-percussion duo perfected a "back porch funk" (*Blender*, 6/98) launched on 1997's *Let Me Drive Your Car* EP and 1998's *National Chain* LP.

Jonathan Fire*Eater personified that VU "coolest band you've never heard" vibe. Yeah Yeah Yeahs cite JF*E as inspiration. The Albans Prep (D.C.) grads of 1993 by late 1994 lived in a Suffolk Street walk-up. *Tremble under Boomlights* for Kevin Patrick's Medicine label in 1996 triggered a *New York Times Magazine* piece, and a Dreamworks deal involving artistic control and a dental plan. By 1997's *Wolf Songs for Lambs*, singer Stewart Lupton was too high to try. **Congo Norvell** featured "Mexican, homosexual, rock & roll freak" Kid Congo Powers (Gun Club) and Texan actress/chanteuse Sally Norvell. The two met via director Wim Wenders; she played a nurse in *Paris, Texas*, he was in Nick Cave's band in *Wings of Desire*. They did a 1996 CD for rap label Priority, which wouldn't release *The Dope, The Lies, The Vaseline*. Kid left to the LES to do 1998's *Abnormals Anonymous*.

Knoxville Girls (for the Nick Cave–recorded hillbilly hymn "Knoxville Girl") began when Bob Bert and Jerry Teel quit Chrome Cranks for Kid Congo Powers, Jack Martin of Congo Norvell and Stab City keyboardist Barry London. They made fans with their "no wave country" (redneck blues with Downtown grime), heard on 1999's *Knoxville Girls*, 2000's *In the Woodshed*, and 2001's *In a Paper Suit*. **Heroine Sheiks**, a play on "heroin chic," began with noise-rock animals Cows singer Shannon Selberg and Swans guitarist Norman Westberg. Ill shit like 1999's *(We Are the) Heroine Sheiks* EP, 2001's *Rape on the Installment Plan*, and 2002's *Siamese Pipes* drew attention. Yeah Yeah Yeahs, Gogol Bordello, Fiery Furnaces, and Interpol opened for them before Selberg went back to Minneapolis.

Gunga Din merged noir cabaret, Southern rock, and no wave. Twelve-step guitarist Bill Bronson (Swans/Spitters) and Vienna-bred keyboardist Maria Zastrow (Stereo Total) met at an Avenue A video shop. Jim Sclavunos produced 1998's *Introducing the Gunga Din*, with Richard Kern cover shots. Jim joined on drums, so drummer Siobhan Duffy stepped up front on 2000's *Glitterati*, which sounded like an estrogenic Birthday Party. **Flux Information Sciences**, French art-schoolers Sebastien Brault and Tristan Bechet, moved to Brooklyn to make no wave–edged music: 1997's *Dedicated to Volt*, 1999's *Services*, 2000's *Summer*, and 2001's *Public/Private* for Swans' Michael Gira's label. Gira likened Flux to "being beaten by a sexually enraged clown." Jim Thirlwell extolled: "Like Cop Shoot Cop they burned so fucking brightly, it was gone by the time you blinked."

Gogol Bordello began as a "gypsy punk cabaret" of Ukraine-born Eugene Hütz, whose family left Kiev after Chernobyl. He came to the LES and found fame as a DJ at Bulgarian Bar on Canal Street, mixing Eastern Bloc punk on cassette, leading to modeling work for Marc Jacobs and Donna Karan. Jim Sclavunos produced 1999's *Voi-La Intruder*, after which they grew past Russian weddings to CBGB and beyond. **Fossil**, clever pop stylists managed by CBGB's Hilly Kristal, came out of NJ punks the Clowns. Bob O'Gureck's band gained Hilly's interest after their second gig, at his club. Seymour Stein signed them to Sire/Warner Bros., and Ivan Ivan produced 1994's *The Crumb* EP and 1995's *Fossil* with the college radio hit "Moon," before Fossil got buried deep in a corporate shake-up.

Smack Dab starred Appalachian-bred guitarist/vocalist Linda Hagood, whose Melanie-meets–Minnie Riperton wail edged on creepy. Their 1992 "Lucky" single and 1993 *Queen Crab* album made the B'klyn lo-fi trio critics' darlings. Bassist Alec Stephens quit before 1994's twisted *Majestic Root* to ramble on in Railroad Jerk. Coproducer J. Z. Barrell (ex–Alter Boys) joined to make it sound better. **Uncle Wiggly** wailed uneasy listening devoid of gnarly stage action. WFMU DJ Wm. Berger (ex–Smack Dab) coined the term "lo-fi"; James Kavoussi played in Fly Ashtray and as pHoaming Edison; Mike Anzalone was in Fly Ashtray. It all began with 1990's Maxell tape *He Went There so Why Don't We Go*.

Confederacy of Dunces—named for the John Kennedy Toole bestseller (published in 1980, after his 1969 suicide)—perfected British Invasion pop with warped chords and lyrics. *Trouser Press* called Queens-bred multi-instrumentalist tenor John Dunbar "an American Glenn Tilbrook" after 1989's *Tsk Tsk Tsk* and 1991's *Dunces with Wolves* (the latter for John's nominal likeness to Kevin Costner's *Dances with Wolves* role). After solo records came 1999's rebirth with his Kinks-like the Kunks. **Love Camp 7** (for the women-in-prison film) played off-kilter noise-pop, hailed in *Flipside* (6/27/96) as "Neil Young on dust." Dann Baker (guitar/vocals), bassist Bruce Hathaway, and drummer Dave Campbell self-released 7″s, 12″s, and LPs, including 1994's MTV video "Me & Arthur Brown."

Love Spit Love, Richard Butler's NYC band after Psychedelic Furs (named for a 1991 Ronnie Cutrone art show), fused Butler's droll vocals with phat grooves he absorbed Downtown. Imago released 1994's *Love Spit Love* then went bankrupt. *Trysome Eatone* died in 1997 on Madonna's Maverick label. Their lone hit was a cover of the Smiths' "How Soon Is Now?" for *Charmed*. **Space-hog** offered UK glam-pop with rock star image. Brothers Royston and Antony Langdon came from Leeds in 1993 and wowed Downtown from the onset, signed by Seymour Stein to Sire/Elektra. *Resident Alien* with "In the Meantime" was almost huge in 1995. *The Chinese Album* allegedly died of a 1998 ego clash between manager David Sonnenberg and Elektra prexy Sylvia Rhone. *The Hogyssey* of 2001 merited more interest. (Royston found media fame after spawning with actress Liv Tyler.)

Fun Lovin' Criminals starred Huey Morgan, an LES-bred Puerto Rican–Irish street tough. He barbacked at the Limelight, where his trio with Brian "Fast" Leiser debuted and then signed with EMI's Mike Schnapp. *Original Soundtrack for Hi-Fi Living* set in motion 1996's breakout *Come Find Yourself* and beyond. **Mindless Self Indulgence**, the coed electro/punk crew of ADD-gen legend Little Jimmy Urine (Euringer), began as a NIN-style project that grew into a band with guitarist Steve, Righ? (Montano). *Tight*, cut on an Atari PC in 1999, covered Method Man's "Bring the Pain." The next year's *Franken-stein Girls Will Seem Strangely Sexy* included thirty cuts like "I Hate Jimmy Page." The sleeve read: "If you're a piece of shit bigot, return this album, don't wear our T-shirts. Fuck off."

You'll rebel to anything: Mindless Self Indulgence, promotional street protest, 1999. Photo by Frank White.

Love Child began at Vassar. Alan Licht, a film studies major into La Monte Young and Tony Conrad, teamed with Rebecca Odes and Will Baum who all sang and wrote. Licht wrote a 1988 feature on Theatre of Eternal Music for *Forced Exposure*. The zine issued their 1990 EP of Moondog covers, *Love Child Plays Moondog*. Critics extolled the alt-noise of 1991's *Okay?* and 1992's *Witchcraft*. **Run On** roared a similar pop/noise, with Alan Licht, Fish & Roses drummer Rick Brown, and bassist Sue Garner, and WFMU's David Newgarden on trumpet/keyboards. Distorted harmonics flowed from 1995's Gene Holder–produced *On/Off* EP to 1997's Rod Hui–overseen *No Way*.

Drink Me, the offbeat Brooklyn duo of Mark Amft and Wynne Evans comparable to their friends They Might Be Giants, perfected slightly deranged alt-rock grooves. Ninety-two's *Drink Me* with "Grant's Tomb" displayed Amft on ukulele, slide guitar, and Fanta bottle. Ninety-three's "Cherry Pie" / "I Feel Good" reworked Warrant and James Brown. Ninety-four's *NYC* EP explored urban themes ("42nd St.," "NYC," "Penthouse to Pavement"). **Drunk Tank**, a needling Beefheart-inspired trio begun in Chicago by singer-bassist Julian Mills and guitarist David "Alex" Barker, gelled in NYC with drummer Steven Cerio. That brought about two grating Radial singles: 1989's "Leadfoot" / "Scissors" and 1990's "Hayride" / "Mary Worth." They last recorded 1992's *Drunk Tank* in March 1991 with Steve Albini.

Wider, led by Dave Reid—with Matt Sweeney (pre-Chavez), James Lo (Live Skull), and Eric Hubel (Of Cabbages and Kings)—shared bills with Foetus, Dustdevils, and Helmet (the latter to whom they often got compared). Richmond, VA's Peter McGuigan replaced Matt after the first of two 45s. (Reid rocked on with Foetus, Prong, and Don Caballero.) **Pony**, a Pixies-style Brooklyn alt-rock trio with offbeat lyrics, launched drummer James Murphy, later of

LCD Soundsystem. Pony, one of the first DUMBO bands, did a 1993 double-7″ (a "14‴") and two Homestead CDs: 1994's *Cosmovalidator* and 1995's *El Dorado*. Personal enmities made for intense gigs, but killed the band.

> *I like to inflict pain on others*
> *I'll kick the shit out of all you brothers*
> —Thrust, "Dominatrix Blues"

Thrust, a female punk tribe (Theresa Westerdahl, Sheyli Johnstone, Kelly Webb, Eileen Connelly, Ami Bonacre, Ilona Fabian, Paulina Braham, and Julia Kent) delivered a post-feminist sex-club vibe. David Aaron Clark in *Seconds #26* described their CBGB stage show after 1992's *She Who Must Be Obeyed* EP "with large male dancers, huge animated vaginas, demolished mannequins and bizarre slide and film show." **Mold** paid the price for jibing at alt rock's sacred cows. Kramer produced 1994's *Sonic Youth at Disneyworld* with the title track and "Bob Mould Hates Me"—a scene faux pas despite WFMU play and praise from *Voice* critic Robert Christgau. Steve Scavuzzo and Christy Davis made 1996's *Reject*, 1997's *The Hook*, and 1998's *Honey Lava* before Christy got pregnant.

Die Monster Die, a heavy-duty alt-metal group named for a Boris Karloff film, began when singer Alice DeSoto (Cohen) of Philly new-wavers the Vels moved to the LES to team with guitarist Evan Player. A buzz at CBGB and Continental set in motion 1992's *Chrome Molly* and 1993's "Barknuckle" 45. That resulted in 1994's *Withdrawal Method* (Roadrunner). **W.O.O.** ("Whole Other Orbit"), band of Philly scholar Bonnie Kane on sax, vox, and electronics, fused jazz, noise rock, and alt rock. W.O.O. (later W.O.O. Revelator with Chris Forsyth and Ray Sage) did ten releases, mostly self-made cassettes like 1989's *Should've Might as Well* (live at CBs 1988) or '00's *Notes on What's What* (at ABC No Rio, 1999).

Thin Lizard Dawn was a junkie-chic LES post-grunge quartet with Beatle-esque vocals named for a line in Tom Robbins's *Skinny Legs and All*. The Skidmore-formed quartet led by the James Taylor–ish Greg Lattimer and guitarist Howie Statland did a handful of records lost during Nirvanamania, two for RCA/BMG. **My Favorite** perfected a VU-ish drone with a hint of Portishead, with singer Andrea Vaughn. Michael Grace, Jr.'s LI pop saboteurs debuted with 100 tapes of 1992's *Brighton Riot* and 2,000 copies of 1994's *The Last New Wave Record* EP before 1999's *Love at Absolute Zero* LP.

Marcy Playground featured John "Woz" Wozniak, a Minneapolis native who attended the Seattle hippie haven Evergreen State, then split to NYC. Ninety-seven's double-platinum *Marcy Playground* had folky hits in "Sex and Candy" and "Saint Joe on the Bus." Ninety-nine's *Shapeshifter*, with Mark Ryden cover art—cited in *Billboard* "to affirm its position as core modern rock band"—flopped, as did 2004's Woz-produced *MP3*. **Rye Coalition**—Justin Angelo Morey, Jon Gonnelli, Herb Joseph Wiley V, Scott Thomas Bolasci, and Ralph Gregory Cuseglio from Jersey City's Greenville section—played cool punk rock & roll. After zine-worthy indie LPs, EPs, and 7″s they signed to Dreamworks, which folded. Dave Grohl produced what'd be 2006's *Curses* for original label Gern Blansted.

Hall of Fame played lo-fi, avant-garde, post-classical trance with groaning strings and jagged rhythms. Filmmaker/keyboardist Theo Angell joined Dan Brown (ex–God Is My Co-Pilot) and violinist Samara Lubelski (of Sonora Pine) for 1997's *Hall of Fame*. Of 1999's *First Came Love . . .* , *Spin* (5/99) said, "Hall of Fame is capable of turning even its rowdiest music into tempting audio anesthesia." **Azalia Snail** (her real name) made acid-dosed lo-fi records, like 1992's *Burnt Sienna*, 1995's *Swiss Bliss 7″* EP, and 1993's *How to Live with a Tiger* as Hail/Snail with Susanna Lewis of Hail. *Option* (6/97) panned: "Azalia Snail has managed to churn out another album, much to this reviewer's regret."

THE FALL

All the lies aside
I believe I am the luckiest person alive
—CAT POWER, "WE ALL DIE"

The end of the twentieth century—Y2K and the first technology bubble, followed by the carnage of 9/11—loomed large on the NYC psyche. The horror of 9/11 scarred many people, yet not nearly as many as one may expect. Unlike previous eras rife with a generational dialect or reactive movements, "hipsters" settled into an established alternative lifestyle. So '90s indie rock really never died. It manifested in the Brooklyn explosion, as the soundtrack for a new generation relatively unaware of the life-and-death struggles of the old-school Big Apple.

DEGENERATED

'00s PUNK REVIVAL + '00s NEW YORK CITY ROCK & ROLL REVIVAL

1989–1999: D Generation, Green Door, Coney Island High, The Continental, Squeezebox, Meow Mix, Manitoba's, Niagara, gentrification

No way out: D Generation, 1990. Photo ©
Marti Wilkerson.

PUNK REVIVAL

THE RISE

I've seen the movies and the groovies
And I'm searching for a ruby
—D GENERATION, "NO WAY OUT"

The '90s was the twilight of the East Village. Though ever more gentrified,
the 'hood remained a destination for creative types. The '90s punk revival—a
return to stylish NYC punk and glitter-rock—began in the East Village in opposition to the encroaching conservatism represented by newly elected mayor
Rudolph Giuliani. The scene arose at the same time as, and in reaction to, the
grunge and indie rock that eventually overtook pop culture.

Just the way glitter rock was based on New York Dolls and punk focused on Ramones, D Generation fueled the punk revival. Jesse Malin and Howie Pyro threw "rent parties"—first at Giorgio Gomelsky's "Green Door" loft and then at their own St. Marks Place club, Coney Island High—that brought their band to prominence. The fans created a studied look (junkie-rock with little heroin). The '90s was a tough time for rock music, and here were twentysome-things having sexy fun amid a decidedly no-fun era.

> **JESSE MALIN (D Generation):** With D Generation, New York City meant a lot to us, and we wanted to bring back a certain scene we fan-tasized and only read about, a certain decadent Max's Kansas City, CBGB, Studio 54 type of New York. So I put my energy into Coney Island and Green Door, making it the place I'd dreamed about or heard of in those Ramones and Lou Reed songs. I wanted to create that world. We wanted to represent New York to what we thought was its truest. (2004)

> **RICHARD BACCHUS (D Generation):** We were conscious of New York, and of what wasn't there at the moment. We thought things through. The music scene was a bunch of long-haired slobs, and we wanted to get away from that. We stuck out like a sore thumb, spiky and scruffy with loud colors. The previous generation recognized the Dolls in us, so we filled a gap for some people. We wanted to be sexu-ally ambiguous, and we had lots of gender-bending friends. There was a real workaholic side to it, and we'd go out and make things happen all the time. (2011)

> **DANNY SAGE (D Generation):** We were fans of the legacy, not ca-sual rock listeners but obsessed with it. It was the focus of our lives. Because we were born and raised here, which is a dying breed, the history of the city and its music is a big deal. To people older than us, from the Max's and CBs era, we also filled a void. But that was uninten-tional; I didn't know these people before D Generation. They had nothing to do with us in any other way—we just played rock and roll for people in our crowd. (2011)

> **HOWIE PYRO (D Generation):** That whole Cat Club–Guns N' Roses phase, we could not get with that. We loved rock and roll but hated it at that moment. We wanted our own thing that people could relate to. (2004)

TRIGGER (The Continental): D Generation always impressed me. I appreciated their professionalism and how they'd check in weeks before the show and really make it an event. Their music had a sense of urgency, and lots of people believed in them. (2004)

EDDIE TRUNK (DJ): I really felt D Generation was gonna be the next Guns N' Roses. I was a big believer. They had many opportunities, on a few different labels, but it just didn't happen. That was the one band to me that I heard and saw greatness. (2013)

GEORGE TABB (journalist/musician): D Generation was the corporate version of trashy New York Rock. They were packaged and ridiculous. But to be fair, if they didn't do D Generation, someone else would have. (2004)

THE SCENE

Down in the Village, with all the shades of blue
I finally found somethin' I wanna do
—THE NEW YORK LOOSE, "TRASH THE GIVEN CHANCE"

Green Door (140 West 24th Street), a punk revival club named for the green front door of former Yardbirds producer Giorgio Gomelsky's Chelsea loft, began with D Gen's Jesse Malin and Howie Pyro and Jesse's ex Holly Ramos. Their Saturday night party big on punk, glitter, and kitsch, inspired by Max's and CBs but updated, was a den of iniquity for misfit urban punks and bridge-and-tunnellers. Giorgio's former fashion store with mannequins lining the walls became a key scene club and rehearsal studio.

GIORGIO GOMELSKY (Green Door): I fell out with my landlord at 21 West 16th Street. The landlord lived there, and being in the music business we were up till two, three in the morning, and he couldn't sleep. I said, "This is ridiculous. We gotta find a place where to make noise." I walked around and found this place. Early 1978. (2000)

HOWIE PYRO (D Generation): New Year's Eve 1990 we threw a party at Giorgio's, and lots of people came. It was the right idea at the right moment. So we did it once a month, for years. It was true old-school madness: no rules, lots of drugs and alcohol, and dancing to rock and roll, which wasn't happening at all back then. We'd spin Stooges and Ronettes and anything in between. Through Green Door we started D Generation—that's where we played our first show, and where we rehearsed our entire existence. (2004)

DANNY SAGE (D Generation): We didn't have money to pay the bills, so we'd get cheap booze and invite people and play music, and that'd be our rent money. I worked on it early on, I'd pick up sixty-four cases of beer but I just wanted to play guitar. At Giorgio's were some of the best parties ever, from 1991 to '93 was genius: great bands, great music and hot people. It was sexual and fun and everyone seemed on the same page. (2011)

RICHARD BACCHUS (D Generation): Green Door was the high-light. It was a party with lots of other fun crazy people, very hedonistic and free, very pure and innocent; that weird innocence that any-thing can happen with no judgments. Giorgio was nurturing and loved the idea. People showed up 2 a.m. and left 11 a.m. the next day. Marti Wilkerson took photos. People were dying of AIDS, so there was nihil-ism to it, a last hurrah for Downtown. Green Door kept us alive when we weren't signed and generated money to keep us going. Green Door was integral to our day-to-day living. (2011)

LINDSEY ANDERSON (New York scene): It wasn't about D Gen-eration specifically. It was about all these people who felt similarly, and this band represented what they were feeling. We had nowhere to go to hear the danceable rock and roll we grew up with. We were totally alien-ated from the club scene of techno or hip-hop or whatever that was going on then. Now we had a reason to go out and rock out and be fabu-lous again. (2005)

HOLLY RAMOS (New York scene): We were kids at the end of the punk scene, and we cut our teeth in the hardcore days. I met Jesse at a Black Flag show in New Rochelle, back in Henry's long-haired period. By the late '80s the music world was Guns N' Roses and Metallica, and we wanted to get back to what we loved. Howie and Rick and I became the Green Door DJs, and in many ways we sparked a revival. (1996)

Coney Island High (15 St. Marks Place) arose from Green Door's popularity. In 1995 Jesse Malin, with Dean Richards and Lindsey Anderson, opened a Max's/CBs-style club inside the former Boy Bar on St. Marks Place owned by '60s "shag" hairstylist Paul McGregor. Coney Island High hosted No Doubt's first NYC gig and one of Ramones' many last gigs. But policies like free booze to any band members doomed the enterprise. Similar laxness with bill paying, plus Mayor Giuliani's club crackdown, spelled the end. The place got padlocked on July 2, 1999, for nonpayment of $250,000 in rent and taxes.

ALLEGRA ROSE (New York scene): Jesse told me he wanted to open a club but he didn't know how to, so I ran it with him. That was Coney Island High, around 1995. The place became pivotal. So many now-big bands came through there. We had such a scene because Jesse was smart, hiring only old-school hardcore people from the East Village. It was the first time a club was run by kids for the kids. It was like a little family. (2006)

PALEFACE (musician): I hung out in that Coney Island High scene. The club was 24/7 punk and fabulous rock and roll. Ramones and Blondie and all those people hung out, and it was so cool to see Iggy at this small club. The problem that I had was there were a lot of carbon copies of old punk. I felt it wasn't very inspired. That crew wanted to be just like their heroes, but brought nothing new to it. And a lot of those bands didn't make it. (2011)

LINDSEY ANDERSON: I co-owned Coney Island High, which was full-on punk rock, underage drinking, all-ages mayhem, girls dancing on bars, sex acts in dark corners and after-hours debauchery. I can say that now because the city shut us down: for the dancing part! The police told me we were on a list to be shut down by any means necessary. I said, "Why don't we work it out? If you have problems, let's see what we can do." That's what happens when there are complaints about your business. The cops said, "No, you're on the list." I asked, "Okay, how do I get off the list?" They said, "You don't." So I'm like, "Okay, so I guess this conversation is over." And that was it. They'd come on a Saturday night at 12:30, turn off the music, turn on the lights, conduct a two-hour inspection and then be like, "Okay, go about your business." So with legal fees and this and that, one day they showed up with a padlock, and that was the end. (2005)

The Continental (25 Third Avenue) opened at the old blues bar the Continental Divide near CBGB and the future Coney Island High. The 100-capacity room dedicated to New York Rock had walls covered in flyers and stickers. The Ramones adopted the club as a hangout—Joey played solo (like "Joey Ramone and Friends" on July 19, 1995, or at his last gig, December 11, 2000). Guns N' Roses and Iggy Pop played there. D Generation signed to EMI in the bathroom. "Stoner rock" came to form at Laurie Es's Tuesday night Dosage parties. Owner Steve "Trigger" Triggadov, a door presence in his Vietnamese peasant hat, probably shouldn't have told all the major labels to fuck off, but it was that kind of club. The Continental's last show was on September 20, 2006; the final song was Walter Lure, C. J. Ramone, and Daniel Rey doing the Rolling Stones' "The Last Time."

> **TRIGGER (The Continental):** In 1990, I had an idea for a club. After looking at forty, fifty spots, we moved in the old Continental Divide and opened October 1991. Iggy played that year. I felt like we carried on the tradition of Max's and CBs. With Joey Ramone and Lenny Kaye and all them hanging out and staying up with the local bands, there was a lot of encouragement and support, and passing of the torch. (2004)

> **DANNY SAGE:** Trigger got the Continental Divide and called it the Continental. We quickly started hanging out. One of the first nights I ever drank there was until ten in the morning. The place became our home; they really took care of us. Trigger was like our dad; it was he being lenient and/or not being there at all. They loved our band and liked us as people and understood our humor; they'd even play our mixtapes. Trigger would ask us to play and I'd ask crazy amounts of money, and he'd pay us. That really helped us out. Once we did two nights and packed the place and got like $2,500. These things kept us going through some tough times. (2011)

Gonna take the A train, gonna hop a jet plane
Gonna feel no pain, Squeezebox baby
—Toilet Boys, "Squeezebox Baby"

Squeezebox, a trashy gay party for rock & roll drag queens and straight on-lookers, took place Friday nights at Don Hill's, 1994–99. It started with gender-bending Psychotica singer Pat Briggs and Michael Schmidt, a designer for Cher and Michael Hutchence. Their party, similar to Dean Johnson's "Rock & Roll Fag Bar," reacted to Chelsea tank-top gym culture. Cherry Currie and Angela Bowie played at Squeezebox. Scissor Sisters' Jake Shears and artist Mike Diana began as go-go boys writhing on the poles. Bartender Ronnie G kept it all together. *Hedwig and the Angry Inch* was born of the Squeezebox experience.

DON HILL (club owner): Pat Briggs worked at Cat Club and was the bartender when I opened my place. He was starting Psychotica. Then Pat and Michael Schmidt had an idea to do a gay rock party, welcoming everyone. Not a disco or normal gay party or hetero rock show. It was a new concept, flamboyant and androgynous but total rock and roll. (2004)

MISS GUY (Toilet Boys): The basis was a gay rock party but everyone was welcome. It had nothing to do with sexuality; it was more to keep the assholes out; anyone cool enough wouldn't care if you were gay or straight. It was just about the music. (2004)

PAT BRIGGS (Psychotica): The Squeezebox following is not necessarily a gay following; it's more of an ambiguous following. I don't like to be exclusive one way or the other. I like everyone to feel welcome. But I am trying to make the gay community more into rock and roll. (1999)

JAKE SHEARS (Scissor Sisters): I was broke so a friend suggested I start stripping. So I started go-going at Squeezebox. One night I was on break in my dressing room, and Jayne County burst in the door and started doing lines on my dressing table. I was so star-struck—she was mythical to me. (2004)

TODD HAYNES (filmmaker): The '70s glam era was about not having a fixed sexual orientation. You could do anything—dress up, try this drug, try this sexual experience—it was all permitted. That was the last time rock and gay culture met until Squeezebox. When I moved to New York, the gay scene was at the Pyramid, where guys still lip-synched to Nancy Sinatra. At Squeezebox, those drag queens had loud electric guitars. (1998)

Meow Mix (269 East Houston Street), a seedy rock club "lesbian-owned, women-run, queer friendly, and welcoming to all," ran at the dingy Puerto Rican bar Vasmay Lounge. Brooke Webster lured lipstick-killers, while *High Times* cover girl Allegra Rose booked gnarly bands. The club's pop culture second was in '97's Ben Affleck film *Chasing Amy*.

> **ALLEGRA ROSE:** Meow Mix started in 1995 by Brooke as a weekly party. Her concept was rock-and-roll lesbian. The idea was an alternative for women who wanted to listen to rock and also provided a venue for women in bands to play. It wasn't a gay thing or a straight thing for me, it was just music—for women by women. (2006)

Niagara (112 Avenue A) opened in 1997 at the former site of A7 and King Tut's Wah Wah Hut. The trendy bar of D Gen's Jesse Malin and Johnny T (Clowns for Progress)—known for its wall mural by graffiti legend Dr. Revolt of Joe Strummer (crediting the Clash's role in New York Rock)—hosted seminal shows in the downstairs Tiki Bar.

> **JESSE MALIN (D Generation):** I love to rock and roll and make music and all that, but it's nice to just run a nice bar where you get to relax and just hang out or maybe get a little wild. I know that we left our mark on Avenue A. (2012)

Manitoba's (99 Avenue B), the watering hole of Dictators frontman Handsome Dick Manitoba, became a late-night New York Rock terminus. Dick's dive bar based on Jack Dempsey's in Midtown (with Dictators mementos on the walls) opened on January 14, 1999, with pro wrestling legend Classy Freddie Blassie insulting patrons at the door. One can still see the sober barkeep there with pals like Little Steven, David Jo, or one of *The Sopranos*.

> **HANDSOME DICK MANITOBA (The Dictators):** I'm a shopkeeper, an innkeeper. I run a tavern in town. It's my living room away from home, a hole-in-the-wall for locals who don't give a fuck, mixed with tourists. It's not a big bar with velvet ropes, more of a *Cheers* setup. It's comfortable, it's old-fashion, and it's rock and roll. (2003)

Live at Continental, Best of NYC, Vol.1 compilation:
Artwork by Dr. Revolt, 1999. Courtesy of Trigger.

THE MUSIC

Our minds are vegetated
And our act is imitated
—D GENERATION, "DEGENERATED" [BY REAGAN YOUTH]

D Generation fueled the '90s punk revival. Jesse Malin sang NYHC in Heart Attack and Hope. Danny Sage played guitar in both bands. Bassist Howie Pyro (Blessed, Freaks) was Malin's Green Door partner. D Gen debuted on December 7, 1991, at Green Door with guitarist Georgie Seville and drummer Eric "Belvy K" Klein, but the group gelled with guitarist Richard "Atomic Elf" Bacchus and Sage's drummer brother Michael Wildwood. The "No Way Out" and "Wasted Years" singles of 1993 set in motion an EMI deal. To promote 1994's David Bianco–produced *D Generation*, Malin appeared on a *Paper* cover story (styled by Stephen Sprouse and penned by this writer). After an EMI corporate shake-up, D Gen left to Columbia. Ric Ocasek produced 1996's *No Lunch* with bigger-budget recordings of the EMI album's songs. They toured with friends such as Green Day and the Offspring and opened for Kiss at the Garden, July 25, 1996. Todd Youth (Agnostic Front/Murphy's Law) replaced Bacchus on 1998's *Through the Darkness*, their Tony Visconti–produced, Richard Kern–photo'd coda. D Gen did a "final" gig on April 24, 1999, at Coney Island High.

JESSE MALIN: We caught the tail end of the '70s, and we got to see bands that really meant a lot. There was a mystery, a passion, anger, rebellion and a chance to save lives. And rock and roll doesn't really do that anymore. (1993)

DANNY SAGE: We loved the Dolls and the Ramones, and we loved the neighborhood, which we saw as changing quickly. Some people gave us shit because we were perceived as pop, but we came out of hardcore and had a feel of real New York. They couldn't take anything away from us because we were genuine. (2004)

RICHARD BACCHUS: We made this five-year pact between us, and after 1996 things started to change. Jesse had this club to be involved with almost day-to-day and this was pre-cell-phone days, so he always needed to get back to New York. I remember feeling like a second-class citizen. I always felt that distraction hurt us, Jesse mentally wasn't really there, his business got in the way of our business. We were trying so hard to get where we wanted, and it became a hostile environment. It wasn't working. (2011)

DANNY SAGE: We tried to hang on as long as we could, but I was miserable after 1996. After *No Lunch* it was all downhill. We did some great shows but it lost its magic. From '91 to '95 was magic and the rest was a fucking drain, and that was at least three years. It technically didn't die until 2000, but it became a totally different thing. I wasn't getting along with Jesse and wanted to quit every day. I called our guy at Columbia on a pay phone and told him to send me the paperwork to drop me. I didn't care anymore. Then the label said what if we delivered *Through the Darkness* by June 1, they'd offer a good release date. So we finished it with Tony Visconti; we knew we delivered a good record, and we emerged without imploding. Then I went on vacation, and found out Columbia delayed the release anyway. We did everything they asked, and got fucked totally. (2011)

> *When I get up, feel like shit*
> *Bummin' my trip*
> —ACTION SWINGERS, "BUM MY TRIP"

Action Swingers baffled alt-rockers with regressive punk, starting with 1989's "Kicked in the Head" / "Bum My Trip" and 1990's "Fear of a Fucked Up Planet" / "Blow Job." Ex-members of Ned Hayden's gnarly group include Bob Bert (Sonic Youth), Julia Cafritz (Pussy Galore), Pete Shore (Unsane), Don Fleming (Gumball), and Howie Pyro.

The Waldos, named for Johnny Thunders's nickname for guitarist Walter Lure ("One Track Mind," "All by Myself," "Too Much Junkie Business") carried on after JT's death. Lure (guitarist on Ramones' *Subterranean Jungle* and *Too Tough to Die*) with Joey Pinter, Tony Coiro, and Jeff West did 1991's "Crazy Little Baby" 45 ("Dedicated to the memory of our friend Johnny Thunders") and 1994's Andy Shernoff–produced *Rent Party.*

Devil Dogs rocked a raw garage-punk later popularized by Dwarves, Supersuckers, and Turbonegro. NYHC guitarist Andy Gortler played in the Rat Bastards. Then Gortler, Steve Baise, and Paul Corio with Raunch Hands' Mike Mariconda, recut an aborted Bastards album as 1989's *Devil Dogs* (Crypt). They debuted in March '89 at the Pyramid as "The World Famous Raunch Bastards." Their "Real Slop O' New Yawk City" included tunes like "Hosebag" and "North Shore Bitch."

Vacant Lot got compared to Devil Dogs since Pete Ciccone sang in Rat Bastards. But unlike DD's dirty doggerel, Lot's foundation was Ramones love songs. Ninety-two's Andy Shernoff–produced . . . *Because They Can* ended with a loyal rip on Dictators' "Loyola." Ninety-three's *Wrong* contained "Dee Dee Said," about that Ramone.

Gutterboy, an Astoria quartet from the ashes of Kraut and Major Conflict, suffered a major-label meltdown that showed many locals what not to do. Dito Montiel rose from barback at Mars and 420 Lafayette to a Bruce Weber underwear model on billboards and busses. He, guitarist Danny Hulsizer, bassist Eric Hulsizer, and drummer Johnny Koncz flopped on 1990's *Gutterboy* (DGC) with its Springsteen sound, NY themes ("Rainy Day on Mulberry St."), and homoerotic Weber photos in crew cuts and wifebeaters.

Viva La Wattage, first called Sprokkett, starred Richard Bacchus and Brijitte West and over time included Dee Dee Ramone, Harry Bogdan (Helmet), Steven Cerio (Railroad Jerk), and Reed St. Mark (Celtic Frost). Greg Santoro wrote in the *Post* of August 4, 1987's Ritz show with the Pixies and Happy Mondays: "Dee Dee & Co. pack the charismatic variety of a fast-food outlet." Sprokkett's wrenching four-song demo yielded an Anthrax tour offer before they imploded over the love triangle involving Brijitte, Rick, and Dee Dee.

She was such a pretty suicide
Snap a photo so you don't forget it
—THE NEW YORK LOOSE, "PRETTY SUICIDE"

The New York Loose rocked a melodic but angry NYC punk. Brijitte West lived with Dee Dee and jammed with him and Rick in Sprokkett. Ninety-four's Bacchus-produced "Bitch" and 1995's *Loosen Up* portended a move to L.A. Madonna courted West for her Maverick label but did not sign her. Ninety-six's *Year of the Rat* (Hollywood) won them a song in *The Crow: City of Angels* and a Marilyn Manson tour, before disbanding. **Fur** was big on this scene: Holly Ramos had dated Jesse Malin, while Danusia Roberts (Danuta Gozdziewicz) dated Dee Dee. David Tritt, Dee Pop, Rob Sefcik, and Peter Klinger all drummed. Ninety-seven's "Don't Need No Xmas Tree" single starred a young Antony Hegarty. Their demise was Blackout! Records' folding with their *True American Underground* LP in the can. Tim Stegall spewed in *Alternative Press*: "That Fur aren't huger than God herself is a rock tragedy."

Spanky, with guitarist Daniel Rey and singer Jenny Decker, played a spunky Blondie-esque pop/punk. The buzz over 1995's "Out of It" 45 (Honey Roasted) initiated a bidding war. On the verge of an Epic deal, Decker couldn't deal. Rey, John Connor (Golden Horde), and Roger Murdock (King Missile) later reunited on her 1998 demo for Warner-Chappell. **Clowns for Progress** were like the Misfits in clown makeup. Drummer Johnny T. Yerington lived with singer Deano Jones at "The Big Clown House" on Avenue B. They excelled with guitarist Coco Cohen and bassist Nutley LaRoux on 1994's "Killing Time" and 1995's *Clowns for Progress*. Ninety-six's split-7" with Joe Sib's band 22 Jacks featured Danton Mayorga artwork of CFP as *Rock N Roll Over*–era Kiss.

Trick Babys starred Da Willys' Lynn Von Schlichting singing to Vacant Lot's Demitrios "Uncle Mitro" Valsamas, Brett Wilder, and Paul Corio, and they retained the best of both bands. Ira Robbins wrote in *Trouser Press*: "Von's throaty Shangri-La-from-hell growling is the deciding factor in Trick Babys' lovability." Ninety-five's Nitebob-coproduced *Player* offered barroom blues with LES rage, covering Brenda Lee's "Sweet Nothins" and Isley Brothers' "Warpath." Their end was 1996's *A Fool and His Money Will Be Partying*. **The Kowalskis** were called Killer Kowalskis until a cease-and-desist letter from the wrestler. Kitty Kowalski (Lindsey Anderson), a Coney Island High owner, star of the Troma film *Terror Firmer,* in the CT punk band Disorder with a young Moby, and of the Avenue A band Starkist, fueled their "powerpoppunk."

For Blackout! they did 1997's "First Date" and 1998's *All Hopped up on Goof-balls* accompanied by Adrenalin O.D.'s Paul Richard and Jack Steeples.

The Radicts, Clash-style street punks, influenced bands like Rancid and Green Day. Guitarist/vocalist Todd Radict (Berrios), guitarist Curt Radict (Gove), and bassist Karl Radict (Carl Leblanc) left Portsmouth, NH, punx 5 Balls of Power, and teamed with drummer Johnny Radict (Fanning). First came "Six of Them" on 1990's seminal *Squat or Rot* comp. *Rebel Sound* kicked up a racket in 1991. **The Goops** (Eleanor Whitledge, Brad Worrell, Steve Mazur, and Jeff Bennison) won fans at CBGB and Squeezebox, and on tours with Rancid and Offspring. Ninety-two's *The Goops* (Blackout!) outsold 1995's *Lucky* (Reprise). Ninety-four's "One Kiss Left" 45 came with a twelve-page comic, and its B-side of "Build Me up Buttercup" was heard in Kevin Smith's *Mallrats*.

The Stiffs starred frontman Whitey Sterling, stylish in bowler hat, specs, and pancake makeup. His Damned/Pistols-ish act with guitarist Paul Boering and bassist R. X. Mauser came to the LES from Philly in 1992 as the Stiffs and in 1994 did their "Destroy All Art" and "Blown Away Baby" 7″s. Then they signed with Rick Rubin's Def American as Stiffs, Inc. for 1995's Antony Hegarty–produced *Nix Nought Nothing*. **Blanks 77** began in NJ as the Blanks. Their "total fucking pogo punk" made the "77" tag work. In true punk fashion, Mike Blank, Chad 77, and Renee Wasted slept in a van and caught scabies. Ninety-five's Don Fury–produced *Killer Blanks* portended the Daniel Rey–produced 1997 *Tanked and Pogoed* and 1998's *C.B.H.* Jack Rabid said in *Seconds* (#39, 1996): "They even do songs 'Search and Destroy' and 'Final Solution' without covering The Stooges or Pere Ubu!"

(L.E.S.) Stitches, a gutter-punk band fronted by Mick Stitch (Brown) with Radicts guitarists Todd Berrios and Curt Stitch, drummer James Baggs, and bassist Damien Branica, began with 1995's "Rustic City," 1996's "Could Just Die," 1997's *Snapped*, and 1998's "Down the Drain." Their cameo in Spike Lee's *Summer of Sam* coincided with 1999's *Staja '98 LES* and 2000's *Lower East Side*. **Yuppicide** was a crusty quartet big at the Pyramid and ABC No Rio. Eighty-nine's *Yuppicide* EP and split-single with Born Against resulted in lost gems for Pavlos Ioanidis's Wreck-Age label: 1990's *Fear Love*, 1993's *Shinebox*, and 1995's *Dead Man Walking*; the latter covering both R.E.M and Negative Approach. In May '94's *Interview*, singer Jesse KFW Jones modeled Jean Paul Gaultier!

Furious George began as Curious George, until publisher Houghton Mifflin demanded a name change. Dee Dee Ramone often joined 'em live on "Betty Krocker Punk Rocker," and leader George Tabb (Roach Motel, False Prophets, Iron Prostate) almost replaced C. J. Ramone. George starred as

"Spider" in *Summer of Sam* (in Adrian Brody's "band" that played Tabb's "Hello from the Gutters"). **Stop**, grunge-y trio of Joey Ramone's brother Mickey Leigh, was popular at the Continental, CBGB, and Coney Island High. Ninety-five's *Never*—with Dick Manitoba on "Cake and Eat It"—blared punk guitars with pop tones. The band allegedly broke up after Joey offered to manage—for a 50 percent take!

Bebe Buell (Beverle Lorence Buell), fired by the Ford Modeling Agency for her 1974 *Playboy* spread, counts among her conquests Mick Jagger, Jimmy Page, Todd Rundgren, and Steven Tyler. Buell managed daughter Liv Tyler's career yet still made music, like 1981's Ric Ocasek/Rick Derringer–produced *Covers Girl*, 1984's Rundgren-overseen *A Side of the B Sides*, and '02's *Free to Rock* with Don Fleming. **Coyote Shivers** (Francis Coyote Shivers) left Toronto to join Dave Rave Conspiracy with Billy Ficca (Television), Lauren Agnelli (Washington Squares), and Dave Desroches (Teenage Head). His bad marriage to Bebe Buell coincided with roles in *Johnny Mnemonic* and *Empire Records*, and 1996's *Coyote Shivers* CD, promoted by dates on Kiss's comeback tour. *Mojo* mused: "If Johnny Thunders shot up bubblegum instead of dope, you'd have Coyote Shivers."

The Prissteens blended bratty punk with '60s malt-shop harmonies. Manager/WFMU DJ Jim Marshall was the muse for 1996's debut "The Hound." Richard Gottehrer (Blondie, Go-Gos) produced Lori Yorkman, Tina Canellas, and Leslie Day with drummer Joe Vincent on 1998's *Scandal, Controversy & Romance* (Almo). Highlights included New Year's Eve 1999's Coney Island High show with the Dictators and Fleshtones, and "Beat You Up" in the film *Jawbreaker*. **Nancy Boy**, a glitter-ish quintet named for Brit slang for queer, starred Calvin Klein model Donovan Leitch (son of '60s star Donovan), Jason Nesmith (son of Monkee Michael Nesmith), and Nigel Mogg (London Quireboys). *Alternative Press* raved of 1995's *Promosexual*: "guitars with more guts than gumption send every song rocketing to glam heaven!" But '96's *Nancy Boy* (Sire) sold 4,000 units.

Suicide King starred intimidating Jeff "4-Way" Miller of SF HC stars Bad Posture and Stimulators bassist Nick Marden, blaring at the junction of Haight-Ashbury and St. Marks Place. "The Punk Rock Thin Lizzy" shone on 1996's yellow-vinyl "She's Dead" (with 3-D cover and glasses) and 1998's pink-vinyl *New York* LP. After that, 4-Way quit to coach inner-city high school girl's soccer. **World/Inferno Friendship Society**, the Brooklyn punk cabaret of sharp-dressed Peter "Jack Terricloth" Ventantonio, meld punk, ska, klezmer, and swing. His ten-piece with strings and horns made 1997's *The True Story of the Bridgewater Astral League* and 2002's *Just the Best Party* before 2006's *Red-Eyed*

Soul—of which Punknews.org wrote, "It doesn't defy categorization, it spits in its face."

Working on the avenue: Jesse Malin, D Generation, *Paper* magazine cover story by the author, 1994. Styled by the late great Stephen Sprouse. Thanks to David Hershkovits and Kim Hastreiter.

Turpentine, with a twist of lime
It's high time I blew my mind
—THE TURBO A.C.'S, "GONNA GET IT"

The Turbo A.C.'s (for the Turnbull A.C.'s gang in *The Warriors*) called themselves "Dick Dale meets the Misfits." The Social Distortion–ish trio of Kevin Cole, Michael Dolan, and Kevin Prunty wrenched high-octane vinyl on 1996's *Damnation Overdrive* (Blackout!), 2001's Roger Miret–produced *Fuel for Life* (Nitro), and 2005's Brooklyn-themed *Avenue X* (Gearhead). **Dripping Goss** came out of the Warmjets, who made a 1989 7" for Bob Mould's Singles Only Label. Their punk/psych began on 1991's *Flake* and 1993's *The Shifter*, self-released by the band's Brian and Tommy Goss. *Blowtorch Consequence* (Another Planet) could not overcome bassist Chuck Valle's senseless murder at a taco stand in LA. Tommy, a Ramones roadie and Ritz employee, quit before 1996's *The Gift of Demise* (Popsmart), promoted by gigs with Fugazi. *Blue Collar Black Future* with Mick Rock shots had no shot on the CBGB label in 1998.

Sweet Diesel began when Ben Smith, Nat Murray, Zack Kurland, and Nick Heller met at a Mudhoney gig at the Marquee in 1991. Their punk/rock debuted at W-burg's first rock club, Keep Refrigerated, long before 1995's *The Kids Are Dead*, 1996's *Search & Annoy*, or 1997's *Wrongville*. As per Jack Rabid in *Seconds #39*: "The speeds aren't breakneck thrash but are as fast as Deion Sanders." **The Kill Van Kull** (the waterway separating Staten Island and Bayonne) flowed when Ben Smith and Cooper Copernicus, after the final Sweet Diesel tour, teamed with Janis Cakers (Citizens Arrest, Hell No), James Paradise (Hell No), and Robert Russell. They excelled on 1998's *Human Bomb* (with "You Keep Yourself from Loving Me Because You Think I Am a Bastard").

Speed McQueen, a Cheap Trick–ish punk/pop trio, got lost in the Green Day era. Mark Troth Lewis's trio made an album with Ramones emgineer Ed Stasium that Mercury shelved, so they coproduced 1997's underrated *Speed McQueen* (Mutiny/Zoo). **Electric Monster**, a Motörhead-style trio with Kiss theatrics, began in Manchester, NH, as Flying 69, who backed GG Allin on 1987's *Live Fast Die Fast*. Their shows blew minds, from Beowolf and Atlantis to Limelight and Coney Island High. The Holy Plastic label bailed on 1993's Rick Bacchus–produced "Star Child" single for it being too cock-rock.

Special Head, the pussy-powered quartet of Andrea Kusten (ex-Freaks), Laurie Es (ex-Krave), bassist Tracie Hex Hag, and drummer Edward "Odude" Odowd (pre–Toilet Boys), rocked a kitschy stoner punk with Lunachicks at CBGB and D Gen at Coney Island High. Ninety-four's fuzz-ed Joe Hogan–produced "Hag" / "Mental Dam" single did not rock the world. **Sisters Grimm** starred big-haired Sheepshead-babe twins Victoria and Marissa Stern, whose father nixed an offer to join Paul McCartney's Wings. They achieved near-fame as Coney Island High coat-check girls in glitter, fishnets, and fuck-me pumps. After 1994's *I Hate My Boyfriend* EP and 1996's *Sisters by Birth Grimm by the Grace of God*, they moved to L.A.

Motorbaby starred Sharon Middendorf, the Cleveland-bred Ford model in the Beastie Boys' "She's on It" video, and on a *High Times* cover as the singer of Blacklight Chameleons. She, the Cult drummer Lez Warner, and Beggars & Thieves bassist Ron Mancuso, made 1996's *Motorbaby*, an alt-era Joan Jett–ish effort for rap label Rawkus. Lisa Robinson purred in the *Post* (9/4/96): "You'll be hearing more about Motorbaby." **Wives**—guitarist Susan "Zu" Horwitz, bassist Mary Dunham, and drummer Tracy Almazon (pre–Nashville Pussy)—played trashy punk/metal in ripped rock tees and jeans. Neither 1994's "Girly Girl," 1995's Dean Rispler–produced *Ask Me How*, 1997's Don Fury–overseen *Wives* EP, nor 1999's *Ripped* cut by Genya Ravan for CBGB Records, with photos of the girls "peeing" at the CBGB urinals, panned out.

This is New York, man
And I'm a New York man
—THE BULLYS, "NEW YORK CITY MAN"

The Bullys blared a blue-collar punk. Rockaway Beach–bred drummer Johnny Heff (Heffernan) and frontman Joey Lanz created a gritty CBGB-style band. Ninety-eight's Marky Ramone–produced *Stomposition*, hailed by *Punk* editor John Holmstrom, resulted in 2001's *Tonight We Fight Again*, 2004's *Rumble Fist*, and 2006's *BQE Overdrive*. Hero fireman Heff died on 9/11; the other Bullys at times perform in his memory. **The Krays**, Brooklynites named for the British gangsters, made 1998's *Inside Warfare*, 1999's *Battle for the Truth*, and 2002's *A Time for Action* plus Oi!-inspired split-singles with the Infiltrators, the Truents, and N.Y. Rel-X. An ill-fated tour with Blanks 77 was the beginning of the end, though they kicked ass at "The Polish Woodstock" in Przystanek.

Deviant Behavior, quais-pornographic, antiestablishment LES punks, starred street-rats Kaya Chaos and Pat Pervert. Rudy Giuliani inspired their ire. *Giuliani Years* assailed neo-Republicans in 2000-era squatter psalms such as "Government Screwing Punks" and "Fuck the System." *New York Press* picked them as the 2001 "Punk Band of the Year." **Dirty Mary**, a sexily crass East Village lady trio, toured with Joe Strummer and the Donnas after 1999's *Livin' La Vida Loca* and 2001's *Gorge Us*. Their tribute page read: "Our bond was our undying love for punk and our need to show up everyone around us. It was this love that drove us to be rock stars (in our own minds)."

Hesher, the project of Queens graffiti artist and Bad Brains "spliff coordinator" Chip Love (Wolfson), began after his alt-rap group Roguish Armament disbanded. Dante Ross and John Gamble produced 2000's *Hesher* (Warner Bros.)—with input by Everlast, Doc and Darryl (Bad Brains), Warren Haynes (Allmans), Chino Moreno (Deftones), Biz Markie, and Cibo Matto—which fused NYHC street smarts and spicy riddim. **Dufus** was the folk/punk act of Seth Faergolzia, a sculptor, C Squat denizen, and rock opera writer of *Fun Wearing Underwear*. Live, with bands like Animal Collective and the Yeah Yeah Yeahs, he'd have fifteen or more people onstage; like Regina Spektor, Imani Coppola, or Kimya Dawson. Others worthy of mention include **Gyda Gash**'s "I Kill with My Cunt" that spawned Lunachicks drummer Chip English and Betty Blowtorch guitarist Blair Bitch, and **Psycho 69**, who did a 1995 album with Brazilian singer Supla (Eduardo Smith de Vasconcellos Suplicy), son of the mayor of São Paulo.

Kids of the nation: Coney Island High all-access pass, 1998. Collection of Mike Schnapp.

THE FALL

Some call it art and make it clean
You're not so smart, you're no machine
—D Generation, "Too Loose"

The '90s punk revival did not pan out in New York, and succumbed to rising indie rock. D Generation's 1999 breakup, Coney Island High's closure, and Squeezebox's demise all pointed to the end of an era. That all coincided with the 2000 film *Coyote Ugly*, based on life at the Avenue A yuppie bar, which foretold the East Village's makeover from artist slum to party zone.

MISS GUY (Toilet Boys): There was still a real sense of scene in the late '90s. There were more bands friendly with each other and playing together: Toilet Boys, Lunachicks, Karen Black and D Generation. That ended and the press started writing of a scene with the Strokes and Yeah Yeah Yeahs, which was a very different thing. Our thing was so underground, it never caught mass appeal, but it paved the way for new bands to gain mass appeal. When something gets a lot of press, it's usually already over. (2004)

JESSE MALIN (D Generation): We gave our best for New York, and we totally did it for rock and roll. D Generation, Green Door, Coney Island High, and all the bands and friends, we really made things happen. And that's something to be proud of. (2012)

Another day in the life: Toilet Boys, Cat Club, 1999. Photo by Frank White.

NEW YORK ROCK REVIVAL

1999–2006: TOILET BOYS, CANDY ASS, SEX SLAVES, *NEW YORK CITY ROCK N ROLL*, RÖCK CÄNDY, DOSAGE, THE CLOSING OF CBGB, THE CONTINENTAL AND DON HILL'S

THE RISE

Rock city's got teeth that bite
Shoot it up, we're going strong, up all night
—Toilet Boys, "Ride"

New York Rock subculture smoldered into the twenty-first century, through the last burning embers of CBGB, the Continental, and Don Hill's. The most palpable rock action occurred for seven years at Röck Cändy parties at Don Hill's that involved the all-girl "Bitch" events, and 2003's *New York City Rock*

N Roll compilation CD, all of which this writer was behind. Then after CBGB closed in 2006, everything fell apart. It was truly the end of an era.

ZANE FIX (Starr): We're the last of our tribe and the first of a new tribe. We represent the invincible power of rock. Hopefully, we'll be messiahs for the new generation. (2000)

QUEEN V (musician): CBGB and Don Hill's held magic because of the vibe. At Don's people knew there was something happening, and Röck Cändy and the "Bitch" night solidified that for people making our kind of music. It was right after 9/11 so the scene was changing. Rock was not in vogue, and the greatest thing of these nights was hundreds of people there who also felt that rock and roll never died. That's what makes a scene. That sense of community is rare. If it still exists, I'd love to see it. (2013)

THE SCENE

Tonight, tonight
I got a party wreckin' appetite
—BANANA FISH ZERO, "PARTY WRECKER"

Dosage, Laurie Es's weekly end of the century stoner-rock parties at the Continental, catered to the heaviest metal. Cool quasi-psychedelic posters promoted packed shows, many with a half-dozen bands. Upon entering the club, one got overcome by the marijuana haze and post-Sabbath sounds. It wasn't a stylish scene but Dosage circa 1999 catered to a hairy male subculture ruled by bands such as Chrome Locust, Bottom, or any side project of Monster Magnet or Kyuss.

LAURIE ES (New York scene): Dosage parties went down when stoner rock became an official term and was really being embraced. The Continental was doing well and Trigger gave me Tuesday nights.

The *High Times* folks came to every show, so bands wanted to play. I did the bookings and it got very popular; the door was $3 and of course everyone wanted to be on the guest list! It was an incredible party and a surreal scene: Spirit Caravan, Atomic Bitchwax, Chrome Locust, Bottom—all doing their first shows. All those *High Times* guys, wow, it was like aromatherapy! (2011)

Don Hill's (511 Greenwich Street) opened in 1994 on the northern fringes of Tribeca. Don Hill (Mulvihill) had managed Kenny's Castaways and Cat Club. With insurance money from a car accident, Don opened a club. Unlike most fly-by-night venues, Don built his brand with weekly parties. The club's apex was 1999–2002 Wednesday night Röck Cändy shows, Thursday night Beaver dance parties, Friday night Squeezebox events, and Saturday Britpop with Tiswas. Don was a true New York Rock patron, helping struggling musicians with money, drinks, and a club to perform in. Don died on March 31, 2011, and the place shut days later. More than a thousand assorted friends, from rock stars to bankers to gangsters to bikers to trannies, attended his funeral.

MISS GUY (Toilet Boys): Don made a lot of things possible. He was cool to me and made me feel welcome. With Squeezebox, he literally let us do what we wanted. Toilet Boys never would've existed without him. I pretty much owe everything to him. He's the only person in New York to offer openness. (2004)

MOBY (DJ): Don was willing to let people express themselves however they chose. He encouraged everyone, and was supportive and gracious in circumstances where lots of people would've been petty and mean. (2011)

DAVID JOHANSEN (New York Dolls): Don Hill was a total gentleman. Of all the club owners out there, he was one of the good guys. My life was better from knowing him. That's a big compliment—I can't say that about many folks in this business. (2011)

NITEBOB (soundman/producer): Don Hill was ahead of his times. There'd be none of these bands without Don; he offered a place for people to work it out. Squeezebox was a groundbreaking scene, Tiswas helped launch the Strokes, and there were those bands on *New York*

City Rock N Roll. He gave people a chance and let it to grow. He had a vision. He let marginal people create. So many bands came out of that. (2011)

DON HILL (club owner): When most people think of clubs, they think of the worst. Clubland today is predicated on credit cards and $400 bottles of vodka. My longevity is people come for the music and it's art-driven, all about the bands and DJs, and their own celebrities. And I think consistent theme nights make a club, to make people feel welcome to create your own scene. I think a lot of people forget that it's supposed to be fun. (2004)

Röck Cändy, a New York Rock party at Don Hill's (1999–2006) featured metal bands and others ill-suited for the Williamsburg explosion. The DJ-promoter ("Best Rock DJ" in *New York Press* for 2002 and 2004) spun late night to inebriated rockers in denim and leather. Female singers partook in "Bitch," a monthly Röck Cändy event with punky females belting out metal classics (backed by a band led by Bruce "Brucifer" Edwards). Röck Cändy headliners included Ace Frehley, Buckcherry, Murder Junkies, Britny Fox, and Thor.

TONY MANN (New York scene): Röck Cändy at Don Hill's had a great mix of famous, not-so-famous, and young hopefuls. It was a party with someone interesting always hanging out. The promoter and others helped to make us rockers feel welcome and at home. One night John Waters, another Ace Frehley; a real rock atmosphere. (2013)

TRIGGER (The Continental): After D Generation broke up and Toilet Boys started to take off, came great new bands—Slunt, Banana Fish Zero, Sex Slaves, Queen V, Joker Five Speed—that played great shows and drew very well. It was a classic New York Rock scene, a lot of community and energy, but competitive and jealous! They all played Don Hill's and the Continental. It was all connected and nourished a scene. (2006)

Destination: Meltdown: Röck Cändy party, original flyer, 1999. Artwork by George Petros and Steven Blush.

New York City is a drug
I need a fix in a bad way
—THE DIRTY PEARLS, "NYC IS A DRUG"

Three of Cups (85 First Avenue), a restaurant's cellar bar, became the degenerate rock drinking spot after a night at Röck Cändy or the Continental. **The Delancey** (168 Delancey Street), a 6,000-square-foot, three-level club by the Williamsburg Bridge, opened by original D Gen guitarist Georgie Seville in 2004, also offered such DJs and bands. **Trash Bar** (256 Grand Street, Brooklyn), Aaron Pierce's den of iniquity, opened in 2003 at the site of Electroclash club Luxx, was a rock bar in a decidedly "anti-rock" W-burg. **Duff's** (28 North Third Street, now 168 Marcy Street, Brooklyn), dates back to 1999, when Jimmy Duff ran Bellevue Bar in Hell's Kitchen. He'd find success in 2004, moving to W-burg—attracting tattooed rock drunks and the women who love 'em.

METAL MIKE (New York scene): Yo, we'd get so fucked up at Cups. Late night it was a zoo, total fuckin' metal. The drinking was off-the-hook, and the coke and sex in the bathroom was crazy. Same went down at Trash Bar and Duff's. I love that shit. (2006)

New York City Rock N Roll came out in late 2002 on Radical Records. The release party at Don Hill's drew more than seven hundred people. To push the CD of Röck Cändy bands, some of them played a Virgin Megastore in-store, and at the opening party for 2003's Slamdance Film Festival in Park City, Utah. *Village Voice* writer Robert Christgau rated *New York City Rock N Roll* "Dud of the Month." Most of the groups broke up soon after. In 2005 and 2006, the Continental stopped booking bands, and CBGB and Don Hill's closed.

JOHN LAW (Bananafish Zero): There's a lot of unity between the bands. We stand up for each other because we know that it's a real uphill battle. A lot of people in New York totally look down on this rock scene, so all we have is each other and our music. (2005)

NITEBOB: Most of these bands fell short of the mark. They couldn't get to the next step; they really didn't want it enough. It's tough to sur-vive as a national act; you gotta go for it. That's why most bands have limited life spans. None of those bands survived because in the end they didn't do the hard work. They all sat back and waited for it to happen, and then got disappointed and pointed fingers. (2011)

THE MUSIC

Rocket turn up the red Marshall half stack
Mission control we're not coming back
—Toilet Boys, "Another Day in the Life"

Toilet Boys was a glam/metal band fronted by a drag queen with pyrotechnics and fire-breathing. Like the Dolls, they ruled Downtown with a requisite queer fabulosity. It all began at Squeezebox started by the party's DJ Miss Guy, de-buting as Miss Guy & the Toilet Boys. The 1996 *Toilet Boys* EP set in motion 1997's *Male Itch*, 1998's *Livin' Like a Millionaire*, and 1999's split-single with the Donnas. Deborah Harry had them open Blondie's 2000 *No Exit* tour, and joined 'em onstage. The band argued so much with Roadrunner Records, they were allowed to self-release 2002's *Toilet Boys* with its MTV2 hit "Another Day in the Life." While on tour with the Red Hot Chili Peppers came that tragic 2003 Great White concert fire that killed one hundred people, ending all pyrotechnics in clubs.

MISS GUY (Toilet Boys): I was working at Squeezebox and wanted to start a band, but I'd never been in an environment to meet people who thought the same way as me. Most of the rock scenes I'd seen were very straight. I wanted a band that was fun and visual, based on things I liked—glam and punk. (2004)

RIK ROCKET (Toilet Boys): I want my rock stars to be rock stars. I don't want them to be the dude from down the block that works in the coffee shop. It's all part of building your show. It goes back to theater. You're onstage. (2000)

SEAN PIERCE (Toilet Boys): People don't wanna see dudes standing around looking like gas station attendants. They wanna see a real rock-and-roll show. (2000)

MISS GUY: The Great White thing stopped us 'cause half the band wanted to continue without the fire, the other half didn't—which I thought was lame because I thought we were fine enough without all that, that there was enough going on without the fire, which started off as an addition to what we were doing. I thought it was fucked up. (2004)

Can you spare some sympathy?
Don't you feel sorry for me
—Manscouts of America, "Nightmare"

Manscouts of America, gnarly tattooed punkers led by Rik Slave, sported Boy Scout uniforms and flamethrower guitars. Ray Martin–coproduced 1999's *Crash Course,* equal parts Misfits and Metallica. Its cover caused a local scene stir for its Huja Brothers sketch of MOA as Kiss-style heroes atop a trash heap, with "Toilet Boys" in the debris. **Candy Ass** was like a female Toilet Boys. Their 2000 *Orgy* took its name for Orgy's CD *Candy Ass. Lip Lockin' Live* in 2002 included tunes that Galadriel Masterson's quartet played at Squeezebox. Their

2003 tour with Pink came after Candy Ass girls got nude on *Howard Stern* and a Metallica video spot ("Whiskey in the Jar").

Honky Toast rocked an ironic, funky punk. Eric J. Toast (Eric M. Jakobsson, Jr.) came to the LES in 1995 from Champaign-Urbana, IL, where as a teenager, Black Flag played at his house. First came 1997's *Meat the Honky*. *Spin* wrote of 1999's *Whatcha Gonna Do Honky?* (Epic): "When it comes to trailer park boogie, Honky Toast delivers a full loaf." **The Unband** from Northampton, MA, moved to the LES. The trio's intoxicated AC/DC party-rock on 2000's *Retarder* was the worst-selling record in TVT label history. Their drug train derailed after singer Matt Pierce blew off shows with Motörhead and Def Leppard. Bassist Mike Ruffino's Unband-era autobiography, *Confessions of a Debauched Rock 'N' Roller*, is a must-read. **Frankenorange** were big in local stoner-rock circles. Their only real release was "PTA" on *Live at the Continental: Vol. 2*. Drummer Matt Flynn joined Maroon 5.

Chrome Locust—NYHC vet Todd Youth, D Gen's Michael Wildwood, and bassist Jim Heneghan—blasted a leather-pants blend of stoner rock and street punk. "The Pioneers of Smoke Coke Rock" blew away Queens of the Stone Age at Coney Island High on January 22, 1999. Then Todd quit and left town after 1999's *Chrome Locust* (Tee Pee) to join Danzig. **Atomic Bitchwax** was Ed Mundell's psychedelic-laced project during his time off from Monster Magnet. He, Chris Kosnik, and Keith Ackerman awed fin-de-siècle stoners. Ed finally put down the bong after 1999's *Atomic Bitchwax I* and 2000's *Atomic Bitchwax II*. **Bottom**, a heavy-ass lady trio (Sina, Nila, and Clementine) ruled the Dosage scene with trippy VU/Sab blasts. Greg Gordon (Helmet/Slayer) produced 1999's *Made in Voyage*. They plowed "The Garden" on 2005's *Live at the Continental* before moving to SF.

Bad Wizard (a drunken riff on "Budweiser") moved from Georgia to W-burg in 1999. Curtis Brown and Scott Nutt created out-of-control '70s-style rock on 2001's *Free and Easy* and 2002's *Sophisticated Mouth*. Tommy Hill's Howler label released 2004's *#1 Tonight* produced by Dean Rispler (of Karen Black) and 2006's *Sky High* by Jennifer Herrema (Royal Trux). **The Brought Low**, a biblical reference (Isaiah 2:17), came from NYC pedigree (Sweet Diesel, Murphy's Law, Karen Black, Kill Van Kull) to blare ironic Grand Funk boogie. The B'klyn crew begun by Ben "B.H." Smith and Nick Heller excelled on 2001's *The Brought Low* (Tee Pee) and 2006's *Right on Time* (Small Stone). **Brain Surgeons**, with Blue Öyster Cult drummer Albert Bouchard and rock critic wife Deborah Frost, excelled with Cult obscurae (for encores, Albert wore the Godzilla mask). Al endured hard times: fired by BÖC in 1981 before they reworked his tabled solo album as 1988's *Imaginos*. His Cellsum Records put out BS like 1994's *Eponymous*, 1995's *Trepanation*, and 1997's *Malpractise*.

L-U-V N-Y-C
We're makin' rock and roll history
—STARR, "LUV, NYC"

Starr teased indie-rockers with big hair and red patent leather. Zane Fixx, Luke Luv, Kenny Max, and Nicky Shea won fifteen minutes of fame on a 2001 *New York Press* cover and a Don Hill's residency. Starr cut demos with Johnny Indovina (Human Drama), one of which included "LUV NYC" on 2002's *New York City Rock N Roll*. **Pisser** flowed from Honky Toast, with a similar Dolls-style sleaze. Eric J. Toast, guitarist Richard Fortus, and drummer Frank Ferrer, with bassists from Mike Ruffino (Unband) to Anthony Esposito (Lynch Mob), drew crowds, often with Hilfiger-link designer Michael H. (Houghton), but burned out soon after "Wifey" on *New York City Rock N Roll*. **Bantam** was Lunachicks guitarist Gina Volpe's punk/metal trio. After 2002's Ray Martin–produced *Bantam* (with "The Car" on *New York City Rock N Roll*) and 2005's *Suicide Tourist*, Gina composed music for *Butterflies and Hurricanes*, a doc film on female Thai-boxer Alisanne "Ali" Casey.

Queen V (Veronica Stigeler) arose as a star of the early '00s scene. From sold-out Don Hill's gigs came a showcase for Gene Simmons, and gigs with Twisted Sister, Billy Idol, and Bon Jovi. Lemmy, Tom Morello, and Vernon Reid all played on 2006's *Death or Glory*. **Sex Slaves** began around the recreational activities of Queen V guitarist Eric "13" Sanchez and Chain Angel's Ancel Bowlin, and finally came to form as a trio with Sanchez, Manscouts bassist Del Cheetah, and QV drummer Jason "J. Bomb" Harrison. The band led off *New York City Rock N Roll* ("2AM") and soared on 2004's lost slice of Downtown, *Bite Your Tongue* (Radical). **The Compulsions** blared Stones/Dolls stomp. Rob Carlyle's sidemen included Sami Yaffa (Hanoi Rocks), Jay Dee Daugherty (Patti Smith), and Richard Fortus (GN'R). *Classic Rock* (7/09): "A genre-blending bag of whoop-ass that offers everything from disco hump to full-throttle, meth-in-the-eyeballs sleaze-punk."

Joker Five Speed were cocked and loaded like L.A. Guns, but more punk rock. Sweet Pain bassist Scarlet Rowe, singer Victor "Tor" Caracappa, drummer Roger Benton, and original guitarist Dave Blackshire (bonded by J5S tattoos) blared a denim-and-leather rock big at CBGB and Röck Cändy.

"Destination: Meltdown" was a highlight of *New York City Rock N Roll*. **Banana Fish Zero** cut more than fifty songs, sold on CDs at gigs ("Party Wrecker" on *New York City Rock N Roll* their only official release). The unruly trio led by male model John Law (Adams) in a guitar, Speedo, and faux-hawk wowed from CBGB and Don Hill's to Utica and Elmira. **Slunt**—Abby Gennet, Jenny Gunns, Pat Harrington, and Charles Ruggiero—did "The Best Thing" on *New York City Rock N Roll*, 2005's *Get a Load of This*, and 2006's *One Night Stand*, and toured with Motörhead and Marilyn Manson, before Abby retired with Fuel and latter-era Doors singer Brett Scallions.

Satanicide, an alt-rock *Spinal Tap*, claim to have "collectively kicked more rock-and-roll ass than Kiss and Zep and AC/DC and Skid Row and Crüe put together." Two thousand three's *Heather* ("'69 Chevy," "Jer-Z Nites") embodied the cock-rock mock of Devlin Mayhem (Dale May), Aleister Cradley (Phil Costello), Baron Klaus Van Goaten (Pemberton Roach), and Sloth Vader (Andrew Griffiths). **Uncle Fucker**, Izzy Zaidman's "Grasscore" ensemble, blended punk/metal and bluegrass that they called "Flatts & Scruggs on meth at a Napalm Death show." Live, Izzy painted himself red with a black pentagram across his back, as "Satan" with his cowgirl go-go dancers. The Fuckerettes. Their first show at Meow Mix yielded a Mindless Self Indulgence tour, and 2003's *Usurpers of the Tradition* ("Ole Slew Foot," "Shapiro Creek"). **Alabama Blacksnake** (slang for a large African-American organ) was a '70s-style three-guitar sextet with punk attitude. Their 2004 CD *Weapons of Ass Destruction* was the beginning of their end. Guitarist Mick Man said: "We're not out to save the rock world, we're here to destroy it."

Pink Steel, the faux German metal act of Udo Von DüYü and Hanson Jobb in leather, spikes, and chains, claim to have "made good on their sacred oath to conquer the world, one bathhouse at a time." A 2003 *Voice* spread came with the award of "Best Gay Heavy Metal Band" for high-register romps like "We Fight for Cock" and "Sausage Party." **Erocktica** starred the late Andover, Mass. piece-o'-ass, cabaret singer-cum-eroticist Pink Snow (Selena Crabbe). Her act, with naked ladies in soft-core orgies or whipped-cream fights, gelled with guitarist Justin Masters on 2004's *Porn Again* and 2006's *Second Cuming*. They got deemed high art in Europe, where contracts required guitar picks and sex toys.

Young & Fabulous, Jimmy Maresca's (Sic F*cks) cross-dressing glam spoof, rocked Squeezebox, and shocked Woodstock '99. *The Greatest Album in the History of Music* tape of 1996 paved the way for 2000's *Young & Fabulous* with rips on "I Get More Pussy than Frank Sinatra," Manitoba's Wild Kingdom's "The Party Starts Now," and the Beasties' "Fight for Your Right to Party."

Sküm formed when Young & Fabulous/Sic F*cks bassist Jimmy Maresca and singer Stacy "Fern Burns" Chbosky took a stab at writing pop-punk with foul lyrics. With guitarist Chris "Cupcake" Goercke and drummer Tyler Land, they belted out 2004's *Sküm* with "Big Black Cock" and "Your Mother Sucks Cocks in Hell."

Detox Darlings carried on Johnny Thunders's junkie punk. Spyder Darling (Young & Fabulous) worked best with girlfriend Jet Set Jenna and drummer John Gabriel. Their "7 Songs in the Jukebox" appeared on *New York City Rock N Roll*. "No Sleep Til Detox" got graffitied on EV walls and toilet stalls. **The Slags** starred Danny Biondo, a D.C. punk/metal scene vet. The LES hairstylist did a gnarly 2003 CD that included "She Said" on *New York City Rock N Roll*. **Daddy**, part Patti Smith, part Jane's Addiction, made great CDs that never got noticed. Poet Laurel Barclay and guitarist Matt Katz-Bohen modeled in Levi's ads and Anna Sui shows, and scored a play by the Fugs' Ed Sanders.

> *I'm just around for the ride*
> *And I've got nothin' to hide*
> —SHE WOLVES, "OUT OF ORDER"

She Wolves began as Syl Sylvain's backup band. That's how Syl played with Donna Lupie (Cycle Sluts), Gyda Gash (Angel Rot), Laura Sativa (Mongrel Bitch), and Tony Mann (Electric Monster) on 2006's *Mach One*. George Smith wrote in the *Voice* (4/07): "She Wolves are in a good place if you desire equal portions of catchy tunes and heavy rock." **Mad Juana** blended punk/gypsy spirit with laid-back sensuality. Caterwauling Karmen Guy's bohemian acoustic act with guitarist Sami Yaffa (Hanoi Rocks) and saxist Danny Ray began with 2006's *Acoustic Voodoo* with a soft rip on the VU's "Venus in Furs."

Theo and the Skyscrapers starred Lunachicks tattooed supermodel Theo Kogan. Her towering Skyscrapers, fire-breathing Toilet Boys guitarist Sean Pierce, and programmer Chris Kling, erected NYC electro-punk. *Ink 19* hailed 2006's CD, "an explosive combo that leaves you no option but to bow to the tectonic rumble." **Lady Unluck**, "NYC's Finest All-Girl Punk & Roll Review," featured guitarist Suzi Hotrod and vocalist Vicky Voltage ("the bastard love child of Bon Scott"). A 2005 Van's Warped Tour seemed like their big break, but it killed the band. (Suzi became a star of Gotham Girls Roller Derby.)

Supervillain defined street-tough NYHC-fueled metal. Onetime Bad Brains roadie Morgan Liebman fronted a revolving five-piece that soared with

Louie Gasparro (Murphy's Law/Blitzspeer) and Fernando Rosario, Jr. (Michael Monroe, Cycle Sluts). Their Soundgarden-ish "War Torn" stood out on *New York City Rock N Roll*. **Grounded**, Sapphic LES stoner rockers, featured the fuzz guitar of Allegra Rose and Dio-style vocals of Pam "The Metal Queen" Grande. They cut demos at Anthony Esposito's Schoolhouse Studios; one included "Torpedo" on *NYCRNR*. **Metal John**, a twenty-first-century answer to Yngwie Malmsteen without the hair or ego, traversed a rugged terrain between guitar wizardry and '80s irony, replete with hipsters headbangin' or Bic-flickin' to his noodling.

Dirty Rig, driven by Steve "Buckshot" Seabury, moved to NYC to make it, and didn't. An EP, 2003's *Blood, Sweat and Beer Make America Strong* for Eric Lemasters' The Music Cartel, came out before Warrior Soul singer Kory Clarke joined. *Rock Did It* imploded in 2005 fast after firing Clarke. Steve wrote a popular metal cookbook, *Mosh Potatoes*. **Crusade**, a goth/metal act emoting a love-lorn punk-metal akin to Pete Steele's Type O Negative, also came from the deep 718. Lawrence Susi, of the NYHC acts Breakdown and Subzero, excelled on 2003's *The Beauty within the Decay* and 2005's *Last Days of Romance*. **Phoenix Reign**, from working-class Astoria, blazed like Iron Maiden or Manowar. Theresa Gaffney led her Herculean warriors Billy Chrissochos, Kostas Psarros, and Chris Pollatos. *Destination Unknown* included "The Gates of Bosphorus" and "Constantinople 1453 (On the Eve of the Fall)." **Borgo Pass** (for the mountain pass near Dracula's Castle) blared a rootsy Skynyrd/Sabbath sludge. The LI longhairs dug by Hatebreed's Jamey Jasta delivered 1996's *Borgo Pass* and 1999's *Powered by Sludge*. Jibed Mike Bazini (*Voice*, 8/24/99): "If you've never heard Borgo Pass, you've hung out in sports bars too much."

> *I have a bone to pick*
> *Maybe it's yours*
> —Khanate, "Release"

Khanate—O.L.D. guitarist James Plotkin and singer Adam Dubin with Burning Witch bassist Stephen O'Malley and Blind Idiot God drummer Tim Wyskida—turned doom-metal artsy. *Khanate* (2001) featured extended songs; *Capture & Release* (2005) included "Capture" (18:13) and "Release" (25:03). Plotkin then quit "due to lack of commitment of certain members." **Early Man** evolved from Ohio alt-rockers Mike Conte and Adam Bennati. In New York with guitarist Pete Macy, they signed to anti-metal label Matador. Their 2004

Early Man EP with the Ozzy-ish "Death Is the Answer to My Prayers" preceded 2005's Matt Sweeney–produced *Closing In*. It took them five years to get out of that deal.

Cheeseburger grilled indie-rockers with metal irony. Joe Bradley's wry-soaked RISDI crew cooked up 2005's *Gang's All Here* EP as a sampler for 2006's *Cheeseburger*—with "Let the Good Times Roll" (not The Cars) and "Co-caine" (not J. J. Cale). Flavorpill wrote: "Crass, foul and politically incorrect? That's the point!" **The Giraffes** made noise in W-burg, incited by singer Aaron Lazar. Both 2002's *Helping You Help Yourself* and 2003's *A Gentleman Never Dies* (rehearsed under a Hasidic dry cleaner) portended 2005's *The Giraffes* (Razor & Tie), which yielded great reviews before the quartet and the label parted ways. Lazar suffered two heart attacks, so at press time, they tour with a defibrillator.

The Black Hollies blasted LSD-enhanced jams like "Crimson Reflections through the Looking Glass" (off 2005's *Crimson Reflections*) and "Paisley Pattern Ground" (2007's *Casting Shadows*). *Rolling Stone* said of stylish Rye Coalition vets Justin Angelo Morey, Jon Gonnelli, Herb Joseph Wiley V, Scott Thomas Bolasci, and their vintage gear: "Their mash-up of British Invasion and psychedelia would bring a smile to Brian Jones." **The Stalkers** began in 2003 after they backed UK punk star TV Smith. Andy "Animal" Doocey and Josh Styles's hipster quartet of cool record collectors cut 2006's *Yesterday Is No Tomorrow*—as per *Music OHM*, "it reminds you why it's necessary to spend half your life in sweaty venues and the other half recovering."

Some Action—Ian McGee, Ethan Campbell, Jon Gatland, and Zac Shaw—evoked the Stooges or the Saints. The Action ended after '06's *The Band That Sucked the Life out of Rock N Roll and Killed Itself in the Process*. Jennifer Kelly extolled in *Pop Matters*: "the snarl, the strut, the come-on, the spit, that's all here." **Goodfinger**—"the future of New York music" according to Tom Verlaine—began with Nancy Boy drummer Mike Williams and singer Stephanie "Scrappy" Calloway, a former high-end pole-dancer who, according to Don Hill, was once fired for grinding her stiletto heel through a patron's cheek. Williams produced 2005's *Goodfinger* EP; Tim O'Heir (stellastarr*) oversaw 2006's *Killing with Kindness*.

The Visitors (not the '70s punk act) got started through Evan Cohen (author of *The Last Days of GG Allin*) at Trash Bar and Don Hill's. Two thousand six's *The Visitors* (Eschatone) spewed post-garage, like wrecking Roky Ericson's "I Walked with a Zombie" (live at CBGB). **Drag Citizen**, a glammy band led by Nick Vivid (ex-Bisapiens), with Marcan "Blitch" Arneau (Mark Vizioli) and Richie White (Rich Bienstock), soared on 2004's self-released *You Can Thank Us Later* before drummer Steve Asbury departed for River City Rebels.

The Dirty Pearls carried on the New York Rock spirit. Singer Tommy London (Fornario) formed a band that sold out Bowery Ballroom or Gramercy Theatre with no record deal. *Classic Rock* (9/08) wrote: "Dirty Pearls are balls-out torch-the-joint fucking great!" Other bands of note included: **Vasquez**, Rick Bacchus's VU-ish follow-up to D Gen, with Hanoi Rocks' Sami Yaffa; **Sammytown Jones** with Hogs & Heifers bouncer Anthony Allen Van Hoek (Anthony Allen Begnal), made a 2002 EP produced by Jerry Teel; and **Monolith,** who made news after their singer Paul Cortez killed his ex-girlfriend, going to practice right after, as if nothing happened.

HERE TODAY, GONE TOMORROW

FALL OF CBGB

End of the Century: Hilly Krystal, 2005.
Photo by Tony Mann.

FALL OF CBGB

When every memory is gone
And every thing you know is wrong
—The Dictators, "Avenue A"

The global media coverage and 24/7 vigils outside CBGB following Joey Ramone's April 15, 2001, death from lymphatic cancer at age forty-nine became a moment of the city's pop culture pride, and brought renewed interest in New York Rock. Joey was a ubiquitous, positive force; he helped bands (by booking them at his annual b-day parties at Limelight and the Continental), played solo (as Joey Ramone and the Resistance), and used his fame to promote the scene.

Joey hid his illness for years and continued to play for his fans. He was so deep while all around him seemed so petty. Ramones factions still feud over the scraps. On March 18, 2002, Joey was granted a posthumous Rock and Roll Hall of Fame induction. Also that year came his Daniel Rey–produced *Don't Worry about Me* solo CD. Those honors preceded the city's November 30, 2003, naming of Bowery & 2nd Street, maybe a hundred feet from the club's entry, Joey Ramone Place.

CBGB's final night, October 15, 2006, was the end of the era. The mainstream appeal of punk had made the club a terminus for touring bands and tourists. And for musicians onstage, that aura remained until the end. But a half-filled room typified the club's final years. Sightseers would instead go next door to CBGB Gallery to buy CBGB T-shirts. A certain type of band found refuge at CBs, but there wasn't enough commerce to sustain it all. When it first opened, the fact that you arrived safely meant you could do whatever you wanted because no sane person went to the Bowery at night. By the final days, pot smokers got evicted. Punk no longer reflected the 'hood.

HILLY KRISTAL (CBGB): When I started, I paid $700 a month rent, now I pay $23,000. Unfortunately, I never really tried to make money—I just tried to do what I wanted to do. Aside from the revenue, the T-shirts act as a marketing tool. Everything we sell says "home of underground rock"—and that trademark does have meaning. It stands for people doing their own thing with rock and roll. People still make pilgrimages to play here—when they come in, they're in awe. It's hallowed ground. (2005)

PALEFACE (musician): I had mixed emotions about CBs' closing because it stopped being the place it was. I played there many times, it was a cool place, and it had great sound, which was the best thing about it. It was still happening in the early '90s. Then all of a sudden they started to book lots of Jersey and Long Island metal bands. Maybe that's all they had left to stay alive, but these shows with eight or nine bands of which you wouldn't know any, I don't think that helped. New York was changing, and you have to get out of that mindset of letting it bum you out, because otherwise you'll be bummed out all the time. (2011)

JOE COLEMAN (artist): In a way it should've closed earlier. The Bowery was a place of dive bars, and there were no more Bowery bars left on the Bowery! CBs didn't fit with anything around it, so it didn't belong there anymore. It was from a certain era that's gone. And maybe in some ways that's pathetic. They could've turned it into a museum but that wouldn't be the same. It all already happened. (2011)

RICHARD BACCHUS (D Generation): I spent almost every day at CBGB from 1983 to 1987. Seeing how it was run, I was surprised it didn't close years earlier! The name became so emblematic, touring bands saw it as a notch in their belt, and everybody in rock wanted to be associated with the history. But no one that got big ever came back and supported it, until the very end when they were closing. I mean, who really hung out there? Nobody! I was dumbfounded by the reaction of people. (2011)

GLENN MORROW (The Individuals): CBs had run its course. I didn't go there much in its last five-ten years. Its closing was not as sentimental as I thought it'd be. But it's sad to look down Bowery and not see it there. As far as the music, the club had become more about T-shirt sales than bands. I went to his memorial, and Hilly's death was much sadder. I felt worse when a beer distributor bought Maxwell's, and the action went to Williamsburg. (2011)

CBGB's demise made headlines, but the room went out with a whimper. Few of the big names that Hilly "made" came back to save him; most of the benefit gigs starred out-of-town acts. In the end, a greedy landlord—Bowery Residents' Committee, a nonprofit homeless advocacy group—evicted CBGB!

NICK MARDEN (The Stimulators): CBs could be happening perfectly well. It had the best PA in the city. It's pathetic and it still makes me angry how it went down. That scumbag landlord, he always had a bone to pick with Hilly. But he was the one who moved in on top of a club and then complained about the club. He had it in for Hilly, like busting holes in the floors and blaming CBs. Premeditated underhanded shit went down. Then Hilly got sick from the irritation of working in the club. He always had it hard, and deserved better. He was a blessing, and the person upstairs is not. That guy makes millions under the pretense of "I run a housing shelter." He went out of his way to kill Hilly, and he succeeded. (2011)

Hilly saw CBGB's closure as a mercy killing. On that final night before showtime, Patti Smith exhibited diva behavior, so Hilly threatened to shut it down then and there. That's how CBs went out. The club faded as Hilly faded; a piece of him went when CBs shut. He died the next year, August 28, 2007, of lung cancer. Then came October 30's ugly racially motivated murder of Hilly's dear friend Linda Stein, Seymour Stein's ex-wife turned Realtor-to-the-stars. At press time, Hilly's heirs still bicker over his $3.7 million estate.

SONNY VINCENT (Testors): The last time I was there, Hilly was still humping cases of beer. He was one of the great supporters of American music and doesn't get the credit he deserves. He wasn't only after money like others who came later with gentrification fever. The guy was soulful. He supported American music that went the distance from Patti Smith's poetry to the hardcore matinees. Hilly is missed and the house he built is missed. (2011)

PARKER DULANY (Certain General): When CBs closed, I didn't go. It felt like a funeral to me. Hilly asked me to come but I didn't want to deal with it. I completely loved Hilly, and it was part of my youth being erased. And after that there was that stupid clothing store, I felt like it was desecrated. That whole thing bothered me; it didn't seem right in some sense. I still won't go near the Limelight. I guess I'm superstitious. (2011)

RUSSELL WOLINSKY (Sic F*cks): My emotions about the closing were very personal because for at least five or six years of my life, every night of the year, the place was my home. I could walk in there broke, and walk out drunk with $20 in my pocket. It was very communal and loving, though very dirty and ugly from the outside. To me the closing represented the end of the mindset. The closing was the last page of a chapter in my life, although it ended years before. The very important truth of the matter was five years before it closed I barely went—yet there was a sad finality to it all. (2011)

CHEETAH CHROME (Dead Boys): I was sad to see it go. But it had to go; the city was changing all around it. The problem with CBGB was it was just a matter of time, but it went on and on and on. It became more of a cultural icon, a museum, as opposed to a club. Hilly talked of moving to Las Vegas, and I wished he lived long enough to see that happen. It was a great idea. It was time for a change. (2011)

WALTER LURE (The Heartbreakers): The closing of CBGB was a sad event but not entirely unexpected. CBs had really lost its cachet in recent years as the home of new, indie rock but it did have a lot of historical value. New York rarely designates cultural sites for preservation, which is sad. They recognized that the place was an institution but wouldn't do anything to save it. The determining factor in the end was money. That is the god that New York worships, and the people who owned the building could get more money by selling it to a retail chain store than by keeping it as an artistic destination. The city will eventually regret it, but it's too late to change anything now. (2010)

The anarchists as they get old
Start searchin' for that pot of gold
—FOETUS, "THE NEED"

Manhattan now caters to a different populace, which is great for real estate but not for art. Women once came to the city like Deborah Harry, not like Sarah Jessica Parker's "Carrie Bradshaw" character. Their Doc Martens gave way to open-toed shoes. SoHo condos sell for more than entire blocks did in the no wave days. The Meatpacking District's cobblestone streets, once the domain of meat processors and transvestite hookers, now cater to limousine loudmouths. St. Marks Place's counterculture ceded to cantinas and frat pubs. Little is left of militant bohemia. The dirty Apple went "green" (who'da thunk!). Red Sox caps abound (fuggedaboutit!). That plus the music business's demise means NYC's no longer the epicenter of rock. A sanitized city can be fun, but it's not very rock and roll.

Fifty million tourists annually since 9/11 and new technologies have changed the city. New York Rock's grungy frontlines have been tidied beyond recognition. With dizzying speed, the intense artists and rockers lost out. Decades ago, activists angrily picketed the Gap on St. Marks. Now 7-Elevens and gelato shops outnumber head shops. Hotel brunches replaced after-hours clubs. Rich armchair progressives replaced down-and-dirty radicals.

The next tenant of 315 Bowery, high-end clothier John Varvatos's "rock" store, hosted gigs sort of in keeping with the CBs spirit. Things began poorly with protests at April 2008's "VH1 Save the Music" gala. Signs read "$800 jeans don't make music in New York City" and "CBGB was not a museum and we're not dead yet." But the designer's New York Rock devotion remains true, in spite of some dubious fashion. And he was correct: his threads echo the times, and his vision of rock reflects Bowery's new demographic. A block away from Varvatos opened DBGB, chef Daniel Boulud's alleged homage serving $37 main courses.

JOHN VARVATOS (designer): I want the kids to come here. They don't have to buy anything; that's not the intention. I want them to come in here and feel like, "Wow, I can still feel it, I can still smell it, and I can still get that aura." (2008)

REBECCA MOORE (Varvatos protester): Who can afford these clothes? Mr. Varvatos caters to a wealthy, male-dominated major label mainstream rock world that has no claim on the CBs legacy whatsoever. (2008)

New York has changed, but it's still New York. The Big Apple attracts great minds, so it'll never lose that energy. It may still be the world's best place to find artistic activity.

Suzanne Wasserman, director of Gotham Center for New York City History at CUNY, told the *New York Post* (1/24/11) that there are two constants in New York: change, and people worrying about change. The best and smartest folks roll with the changes. Others cling to memories, wishing for a return to their own cool youth of art, music, and other moments. So, there is no end to the evolution/devolution that is New York Rock.

PHIL HARTMAN (Howl Festival): There's still a great amount of creative energy in the East Village. It's a magnet for people who have the East Village inside of them. No matter what, people still look to the East Village as a counterculture mecca. (2004)

TRIGGER (The Continental): The East Village has surely changed. But things are always changing: things changed a lot before I ever got here. It was exciting in the '50s, '60s, '70s before my time, and it was exciting for much of my time. So I'm cool with what's going on. I don't get cynical, I stay positive. (2003)

MORGAN LIEBMAN (New York scene): The East Village is a different place, but still the same. It's still a hotbed of drugs, alcohol, self-abuse and despair. Great creativity and incredible characters still come out of it. The scene's always thrived, it's just the older guys get replaced and move on. I love it; it's my home. It's where I belong. (2004)

Spikes in real estate and declines in crime led to a '90s population boom: 1.5 million more inhabitants in the eight years after Mayor Giuliani's 1994 election, and 500,000 more in the post-9/11 decade. Creative types looked across the East River to Brooklyn's ruins. These days Brooklyn feels like an East Coast

Austin or Berkeley, a college town without the college, hipper than Manhattan. The oasis spread deep into the borough, and into Queens, part of a new vibe. Now the once unimaginable happens—reverse bridge-and-tunnel traffic!

MISS GUY (Toilet Boys): The Brooklyn scene is based on a Downtown feel. For a while, it was the only affordable place to live in New York, though never inexpensive. But I don't think anyone forced Brooklyn to become a scene. It happened naturally. (2004)

AARON WARREN (Black Dice): Living in Brooklyn and the people around us inspire our music. Every night there's shows I can see cheap or free, and there we meet other musicians and exchange ideas. I guess that's how the East Village used to be. (2004)

ASK THE ANGELS

EPILOGUE

Wasted years: Neon Leon, Chelsea Hotel lobby, 1977. Photo by Eileen Polk.

EPILOGUE

Manhattan are you up or down? I feel like dancing
Manhattan are you still around? I'm only asking
—ELEFANT, "THE LUNATIC"

IGGY POP (The Stooges): I don't miss New York, not since they whitened up Manhattan. I mean, I see a lot of chiefs here, but where are all the Indians? Puerto Ricans are getting driven into the sea, or into the East River. I don't hear anybody saying "Yo, Vinnie" anymore. There's less and less of that. There are more chain stores, and every guy on the street looks like Conan O'Brien or Letterman. It's gotten a bit too straight for my tastes. (1998)

ALAN VEGA (Suicide): It's ridiculous there is no atmosphere for the New York artist now, like the late '70s. The only atmosphere is CO_2. You might as well be living on Mars. (1992)

CHEETAH CHROME (Dead Boys): I love New York but it's become just another stop on the tour. The places I played are gone, all the people died or moved to Brooklyn. We used to be dying to go there but now it's not the same. The city's changed; the last time I was there I didn't even leave my hotel room. The New York I knew is gone. (2010)

NICK MARDEN (The Stimulators): New York is the same but different. We could use cheaper rents, so some reasonable people can live here, not just kids trust-funding their way through college to party. But the city's always been corrupt, nothing's changed in that regard since Tammany Hall. There are still mayors trying to stomp out freaks and keep the bad expensive art galleries. As long as you're a millionaire it's fine if you live here. There's still plenty of kids hungry to go out and create that came here for a place to work, and there's lots of similar-minded people to interact with. People who could work at a record store to pay the rent are now priced out. And the city's still not that safe. People come here and are disappointed that they can't find it. (2011)

SEAN YSEULT (White Zombie): A lot of friends my age hate what's happened to the city, with all the cool stuff gone. I have a little more objective view. I still love New York but I also agree it's been turned into a big shopping mall with most of the flavor gone. But I still find the East Village and Lower East Side exciting and cool, it still has one-of-a-kind shops and restaurants and bars. But it is much cleaner and safer and expensive. It's a shame the creative types got priced out and there's no scene anymore. I know I'd be annoyed as fuck with all the people and the babies and the strollers. It's a whole other world. (2011)

JILL CUNNIFF (Luscious Jackson): As I've grown and changed, the city has grown and changed. We've both changed, some for the better, some for the worse. I see New York, and every other city, as a living entity, though at one time New York was more vibrant than most. There's still good aspects, but I can't ignore that some of what made the city great has been prettified to make it more accessible to tourists, and that's hurt the city in my view. (2007)

HUEY MORGAN (Fun Lovin' Criminals): New York is still a clique-y small town. You got the hip-hoppers hangin' with the models Uptown, and you have the rock-and-rollers down on the East Side, where I'm from. I feel I'm disappointed the cultural scene ain't producing anything mind-blowin' like it used to. Crazy shit now happens elsewhere. The city's getting like Jersey, a nice little town where everyone has a Range Rover and shit. (2001)

DREW STONE (Antidote): Where are the whores? Where are the drugs? I know they're out there but you used to go down Tenth, Eleventh Avenue, and it was part of the flavor of New York. It's what made New York edgy. Nowadays, if you want to shoot a film and you need a New York location, you go to Toronto. (2008)

MIKE DOUGHTY (Soul Coughing): New York isn't New York anymore. It's the city that just recently got up to speed with the rest of the nation. New York is the Banana Republic town. A Häagen-Dazs town. Starbucks fucking runs this joint! There are three within four blocks of each other on Second Ave. But dude, I'm not knocking Starbucks, I was just there. (2000)

JULIA CAFRITZ (Pussy Galore): If you had asked me this in the '90s, I would've predicted New York was going towards Tokyo or *Blade Runner*. New York was going to get taller; there'd be sex clubs in buildings that catered to hospital fetishes. And there'd be freeze-dried drinks at bars. In reality because of 9/11 it's a run for comfort. It's the proliferation of cupcake shops. New York has tried to recast itself to look like the rest of America. Instead of rising like a phoenix, it retreated into itself. There are Crate and Barrels here. And you can get your Ikea crib in Brooklyn. (2008)

PETER MISSING (Missing Foundation): The Lower East Side in the 1980s, we had like a hundred art galleries. Now we have like a hundred bars and restaurants, which I think is extremely boring. When you had the galleries, there was wine and cheese flowing in the neighborhood. There was a lot more communication and there was community. (2005)

CHRIS STEIN (Blondie): I walk around the Lower East Side for a bit of refreshing, but it's gotten bad down there too. The atmosphere's been sucked right out. Total mall shit. Not very conducive to art. If it were up to me, New York would be like *Escape from New York*, but in reverse, where you'd have to show your papers to get in. (1999)

HANDSOME DICK MANITOBA (The Dictators): The people who complain about the changes don't get New York. The essence of this city is change. The New York of my dad isn't the New York of mine, and the New York of mine isn't the New York of my son. It's more conservative and yuppified, which aren't great. But I accept it. (2003)

PALEFACE (musician): New York is about constant change, and some people can't get used to that. Change isn't always joyous; often it hurts. It always changes, and if you're not happening then you're out. It seems to me I've heard generations of New York artists all say it was cooler before: '60s people about the '70s, '70s people about the '80s, '80s about the '90s; it was always cooler when they were happening. Then they got too comfy and without them knowing, things changed and they're not cool anymore. Stuff you like or got used to isn't there anymore. That's still going on, there's constant new blood. (2011)

PETER LANDAU (White Zombie/Da Willys): New York changes; that's what it does. It just hasn't changed the way I wanted. It was such an incubator of incredible ideas, so it's a shame to lose that creative capital. But the city is not respectful of its own history and keeps moving on to the next thing. It's now more like a Monopoly board in which you get priced out, with the expenses ramping up each year. People have these Damon Runyan visions of a punk rock '70s that'll never happen again. For some, the city's like a narcotic, but the only thing that held me were memories. Unless something devastating happens that people can afford it again, it'll remain a playground for the rich. (2011)

CARLO McCORMICK (author/journalist): To complain about the state of the city for people like me is to lament no longer being young oneself. As far as I can tell, the kids are all right. At times I wish they'd challenge the status quo more, and give up their sense of entitlement, but by my measure they're still having fun, which is what this town is about. There are so many more kids here that it's easy to look at the frat boys, bankers, brokers—and perhaps more insidiously the hordes who've banked their spot-on taste in youth culture in the myriad day jobs of our creative industries—and forget that within the cluster of small scenes amid the flurry of wanton consumption there are just as many freethinking people trying to do their own thing as ever. Only fools predict the future. (2011)

JIM CARROLL (poet): I wish all the addictions in my life, now and in the past, were as easy to drop as how I feel for New York. I could leave it without thinking too much. I think people who weren't born and raised in New York feel more of that sense of addiction. (1993)

JIM THIRLWELL (Foetus): The fact is New York is still the place people congregate because it's where everything happens and everything passes through. It's the best city in the world to see art, as there is so much of it. It's such a confluence of styles, and you can be aware of what's happening. If people want to, there are ways to do it. (2004)

JAKE SHEARS (Scissor Sisters): It's still exciting here. I don't think it's ruined. People who say it's not good anymore are just talking about themselves. Maybe it's them who's over-with, maybe it's time for them to go out to pasture. I can't believe how many amazing creative people I know here. It's what feeds you. (2005)

Diggin' in the crates: Kid at Oldies But Goodies, Bleecker Street, 1967. Photo by Ron Da Silva/Frank White Photo Agency.

SOURCES

All interviews by **STEVEN BLUSH** unless otherwise indicated.

HOWIE ABRAMS (New York scene): *American Hardcore* book transcript, 1997

LEONARD ABRAMS (*East Village Eye*): *Gothamist*, by David Insley, July 2005

BILL ADLER (Def Jam publicist): *New York Rock*, May 2014

VINCE ALETTI (journalist): DJHistory.com, by Bill Brewster and Frank Broughton, 1998

ARTHUR ALEXANDER (Sorrows/Poppees): *The Beat Army*, by Paul Collins, 2010

WILLIE "LOCO" ALEXANDER (The Velvet Underground): *Goldmine*, by Dave Thompson, 2004

ERIC ANDERSEN: *Performing Songwriter*, uncited, Jan./Feb. 2005

LINDSEY ANDERSON (New York scene): *New York Rock*, 2005

GABE ANDRUZZI (The Rapture): *Paper*, 2004

STUART ARGABRIGHT (Ike Yard): *Ithaca Times* blog, uncited, 2010

JOEY ARIAS (Strange Party): *L.A. Record*, by Charles Mallison, Dec. 6, 2009; *New York Rock*, by Tony Mann, 2012

TOD ASHLEY (Cop Shoot Cop): *Seconds #21*, by Carlo McCormick, 1993

LIZZIE AVONDET (Piss Factory): *Seconds #23*, 1993

RICHARD BACCHUS (D Generation): *New York Rock*, March 2011

AFRIKA BAMBAATAA (DJ): *Seconds #31*, by Adam Keane Stern, 1995

LESTER BANGS (journalist): DePaul.edu, credited online to "C.S.," May 1980

MARK BARKAN (songwriter): *New York Rock*, 2011

RICHARD BARONE (The Bongos): *New York Rock*, March 2011

CHRIS BARRON (Spin Doctors): *Downtown* Express, by Cree McCree, Oct. 1, 1990; *Spin Doctors*, by Carol Brennan, 1994

PAUL BEARER (Sheer Terror): Blackout!/MCA band bio, original version, 1995

SNOOKY BELLOMO (Manic Panic): *Sic F*cks* EP reissue liner notes, 2006

BOB BERT (Sonic Youth/Pussy Galore): *Flesh & Bones* #7, by Jeff-O, spring 1988

ADELE BERTEI (The Contortions/The Bloods): *East Village Eye*, by L. Abrams, Feb. 1980; *Out*, by Evelyn McDonnell, April 2000

GINGER BIANCO (Goldie and the Gingerbreads): *New York Rock*, 2011

RICHIE BIRKENHEAD (Underdog/Into Another): *Barebones Hardcore*, by Ronny Little, Sept. 11, 2005

HAROLD C. BLACK (Teenage Lust): *New York Rock*, 2011

BOB BLANK (producer): DJHistory.com, by Bill Brewster, 2006

LARRY BLOCH (Wetlands Preserve): *Jam Bands*, by Dean Budnick, 1998

ERIC BLOOM (Blue Öyster Cult): *Seconds* #41, 1996

LIZZIE BOUGATSOS (Gang Gang Dance): *BlackBook*, by Ben Barna, Oct. 8, 2008

BUDDY BOWZER (saxophonist): *New York Rock*, by Tony Mann, March 2011

GLENN BRANCA (composer): ZG, uncited, 1981; *Seconds* #9, by Steve Fritz, 1989

JERRY BRANDT (club owner): *New York*, by Steven Gaines, June 25, 1979

JUSTIN BRANNAN (Indecision/Most Precious Blood): *Ear Candy*, by Mike SOS, April 2006

PAT BRIGGS (Psychotica/Squeezebox): *Genre*, by Morris Weissinger, August 1999

BILL BRONSON (The Spitters): *Seconds* #25, 1994

DJINJI E. BROWN (Absolution): *Double Cross*, by Tim McMahon, April 2008

BEBE BUELL (musician): *Paper*, 2004; *The Aquarian*

SANDY BULL (songwriter): *Friends* (UK), by John Coleman, Oct. 16, 1970

MIKE BULLSHIT (SFA/Go!): *Jersey Beat* #39, by Jim Testa, December 1990

CLEM BURKE (Blondie): *Paper*, 1999

BLAIR BUSCARENO (editor, *Teen Scene*): CheepskatesMovie.com, s/w, 2004

LYNN BYRD (Comateens): *New York Post*, by Elisabeth Vincentelli, Oct. 24, 2010

DAVID BYRNE (Talking Heads): Sire bio, uncited, 1980; RAI-TV "Rock Café," 1990

IRVING CAESAR (songwriter): *Milwaukee Journal*, by Fred Ferretti, July 22, 1971

JULIA CAFRITZ (Pussy Galore): *Paper*, 1988; *Village Voice*, Michael D. Ayers, Sept. 2, 2008

JOHN CAGE (composer): KPFA-FM interview, by Richard Friedman, Dec. 6, 1969

JOHN CALE (Velvet Underground): *Paper*, 2004; *New York Times*, by Ben Sisario, May 5, 2011

NINA CANAL (UT/Dark Day): *Warped Reality*, by Andrea Feldman, June 2006

JIM CARROLL (poet): *Seconds* #23, 1993

JIMMY CASTOR (Jimmy Castor Bunch): *Baltimore Afro-American*, by Frederick I. Douglass, June 26, 1973

PEPPY CASTRO (The Blues Magoos): *New York Rock*, 2011

STEVEN CERIO (Railroad Jerk/Drunk Tank): *New York Rock*, 2003

JAMES CHANCE (The Contortions): *The Blow Up*, by Alexis Georgopoulos, 2005

MICHAEL CHANDLER (Raunch Hands): CheepskatesMovie.com, s/w, 2004

RHYS CHATHAM (composer): *Composer's Notebook 1990*, by Rhys Chatham

BRIAN CHILDERS (Crawlpappy): *Seconds* #15, 1991

LEEE BLACK CHILDERS (photographer): *New York Rock*, 2011

DAN CHRISTENSEN (painter): *New York Times*, May 11, 2003

SHAWN CHRISTENSEN (stellastarr*): *New York Rock*, 2004

CHEETAH CHROME (Dead Boys): *New York Rock*, February 2011

POPA CHUBBY (musician): *New York Rock*, September 2011

JOE COLEMAN (artist): *Seconds* #50, by Steven Cerio, 1999; *New York Rock*, March 2011

SESU COLEMAN (The Magic Tramps): *New York Rock*, 2010

JOHN COLLINS (John Collins Band/The Terrorists): *New York Rock*, March 2011

GENE CORNISH (The Rascals): *New York Rock*, 2012

DANNY CORNYETZ (videographer): *New York Rock*, 2004

JAYNE COUNTY (musician): *Seconds* #24, by George Petros, 1993

FREDDY CRICIEN (Madball): *Sound Views*, by Vincent N. Cecolini, Sept./Oct. 1994

LYDIA CRISS (Kiss wife): *New York Rock*, 2011

ROBIN CRUTCHFIELD (DNA/Dark Day): Totally Wired blog, by Simon Reynolds, July 26, 2009

JILL CUNNIFF (Luscious Jackson): *Spin*, by Maureen Callahan, June 1999; Blog-critics Music, by Larry Sakin, March 2007

MARK CUNNINGHAM (Mars): *Fake Jazz*, by Adam Strohm, April 2, 2004

DONNA DAMAGE (No Thanks): *Mad at the World*, by Dan Scheme, Mar. 26, 2007

GLENN DANZIG (The Misfits): *Seconds* #44, 1997

JIMMY DESTRI (Blondie): *Paper*, 1999

WILLY DeVILLE (Mink DeVille): *Sounds*, by Sylvie Simmons, August 1977

MIKE DIAMOND (Beastie Boys): *RIP*, 1994

VIC DiCARA (108): *Allschools Network*, by Rene, 2007

DION DiMUCCI (musician): *Elmore*, by Arnie Goodman, November 2008

DIANE DI PRIMA (artist): *Village Voice*, Letter to Editor, April 16, 1964, from *Café Cino*, by Wendell C. Stone, 2005

MIKE DOUGHTY (Soul Coughing): *The Onion*, by Joshua Klein, April 19, 2000; *Village Voice*, by Scott Indrisek, Oct. 29, 2009; *New York Post*, by Larry Getlen, Jan. 29, 2012

PARKER DULANY (Certain General): *FR3* TV, February 1986; *New York Rock*, March 2011

NORMAN DUNN (soundman): *This Ain't No Disco: Story of CBGB*, by Roman Kozak, 1988

WALTER DURKACZ (promoter): *Downtown Express*, by Cree McCree, Oct. 1, 1990

ROY EDROSO (Reverb Motherfuckers): *The Ballad of the RMF*, s/w, Sept. 2002

BRIAN ENO (musician): *Musician*, by Lester Bangs, 1979

LAURIE ES (New York scene): *New York Rock*, March 2011

JOHN FAY (The Tryfles/The Outta Place): CheepskatesMovie.com, s/w, 2004

ZANE FIX (Starr): *New York Press*, by Allyson Schrager, Feb. 8, 2000

HARLEY FLANAGAN (Cro-Mags): *American Hardcore* book interview, 1996; *New York Rock*, 2009, 2013

RICHIE FONTANA (Piper): *New York Rock*, March 2011

JIM FOURATT (Danceteria): *New York*, by Henry Post, May 3, 1982

CHRIS FRANTZ (Talking Heads): *Pittsburgh Post-Gazette*, by Scott Mervis, Oct. 5, 2001

ACE FREHLEY (Kiss): *Seconds #6*, 1988

JANE FRIEDMAN (publicist/manager): *New York Rock*, March 2011

DON FURY (producer): *Seconds #46*, 1998

GERARD GARONE (Radio 4): *The Portable Infinite*, Alexander Lawrence, Oct. 2, 2004

GYDA GASH (New York scene): *Pop Smear #20*, by Ula Pain-Proof, 2004

PETER GATIEN (The Limelight): *People*, by Laura Sanderson, Nov. 28, 1983

GEORGE GERSHWIN (composer): George Gershwin bio, source unknown, 1935

JIMMY GESTAPO (Murphy's Law): *Murphy's Law/Back with a Bong!* liner notes, 1994

GREG GINN (Black Flag): *American Hardcore* film interview, 2004

MICHAEL GIRA (Swans): *Seconds #44*, by Michael Moynihan, 1995

GABBY GLASER (Luscious Jackson): *Seconds #22*, by Eric Wielander, 1993; *Spin*, by Maureen Callahan, June 1999

ANNIE GOLDEN (The Shirts): Broadway.com, by Robert Sandia, 2006

GIORGIO GOMELSKY (producer): *New York Press*, by George Tabb and John Strausbaugh, April 26, 2000

PETER GORDON (composer): *Bomb*, by Nick Hallett, October 2010

ANDY GORTLER (The Devil Dogs): *Sound Views*, Sept./Oct. 1994 by David Grad

CURT GOVE (The Radicts): *New York Waste*, by Lucky Lawler, 1999

PAM GRANDE (New York scene): *New York Rock*, 2006

BOB GRUEN (photographer): *Paper*, 2004; *New York Trash* by Carlo McCormick, 2006

CORKY GUNN (Sweet Pain): *Frank 151 #20* by Melanie Scherenzel, 2005

ARLO GUTHRIE (musician): PBS *American Roots Music*, by the Ginger Group, 2001

ANTHONY HADEN-GUEST (writer): *The Observer* (UK), s/w, July 18, 2004

PAGE HAMILTON (Helmet): *New York Rock*, 2006

OSCAR HAMMERSTEIN II (composer): *The Mike Wallace Interview*, March 15, 1958

CHRIS HARLOT (Harlots of 42nd Street): *New York Rock*, 2011

JODY HARRIS (The Contortions): *Dusted*, by Sam Frank, 2005

PHIL HARRIS (The Jades): by Olivier Landemaine, 2003

SHAYNE HARRIS (Luger): *New York Rock*, 2011

DEBORAH HARRY (Blondie): *Paper*, 1999

PHIL HARTMAN (Howl! Festival): *New York Post*, by Billy Heller, Aug. 17, 2004

TODD HAYNES (filmmaker): *Paper*, 1998

RICHARD HELL: *Pittsburgh Post-Gazette*, by Scott Mervis, May 25, 2006

JOHN HERALD (Greenbriar Boys): *Daily Freeman*, by Mary Fairchild, July 21, 2005

DAVID HERSHKOVITS (*Paper*): *New York Rock*, 2005

DON HILL (club owner): *New York Rock*, 2004; *Frank 151*, 2005

KRISTIAN HOFFMAN (Mumps/Swinging Madisons): *Daily News*, by Janiel Bladow, Nov. 11, 1977

JOHN HOLMSTROM (*Punk Magazine*): *New York Rock*, 2004

PETER HOLSAPPLE (The dB's): *North Carolina Punk 1977–1984* for *ArtsyNC #1*, 2008

ADAM HOROVITZ (Beastie Boys): *Seconds #1*, 1985; *Paper*, 1989

HOYA (Madball): *Sound Views*, by Vincent N. Cecolini, Sept./Oct. 1994

H.R. (Bad Brains): *Sold Out*, #9 by Otto Buj, 1989; *American Hardcore* film, 2004

GEORGIA HUBLEY (Yo La Tengo): RAI-TV *Rock Café* (Italy), 1989

DAVE INSURGENT (Reagan Youth): *Paper*, 1988

TIMOTHY A. JACKSON (Dorian Zero): *70s Invasion Presents*, uncited, 2005

HILARY JAEGER (Tier 3): *Perfect Sound Forever*, by Andy Schwartz, December 2008

MICK JAGGER (The Rolling Stones): Timeisonourside.com, uncredited quote, 2011

JIM JARMUSCH (filmmaker): *Notes from the Pop Underground*, by Paul Belsito, 1985; *Seconds #37*, 1996

DAVID JOHANSEN: *Paper*, 1997; *New York Post*, by Larry Getlen, July 23, 2006

JOHN JOSEPH (Cro-Mags): *American Hardcore*, 1996

MARK JOSEPHSON (*Rockpool*): *Billboard*, by Roman Kozak, April 17, 1982

IVAN JULIAN (Voidoids): *Paper*, 2004; *Our Stage*, by Jim Allen, March 2011

SAMMY JAMES JUNIOR (The Mooney Suzuki): Furious.com, by Will Shade, Feb. 2001

DARYL KAHAN (Citizens Arrest): *You Breed Like Rats*, by Rob T, 2006

MARK KAMINS (producer/DJ): *Black Book*, by Steve Lewis, Dec. 15, 2008

IRA KAPLAN (Yo La Tengo): *Harp*, by Andria Lisle, May 2005

JAMES KAVOUSSI (Uncle Wiggly): *Waste Paper #34*, uncredited, 1993

LENNY KAYE (Patti Smith Group): *Paper*, 2004

SCOTT KEMPNER (The Dictators/Del-Lords): *The Clifford Method*, by Clifford Meth, July 19, 2010

RICHARD KERN (filmmaker): *Paper*, 2004

THEO KOGAN (Lunachicks): *New York Rock*, 2004

LOU KOLLER (Sick of It All): *Paper*, 1994

PETE KOLLER (Sick of It All): *Paper*, 1994

HILLY KRISTAL (CBGB): *Daily News*, by Janiel Bladow, Nov. 11, 1977; *New York Rock*, 2005

LACH (musician): *Chorus & Verse*, by Josh Davidson, 2002

PETER LANDAU (White Zombie/Da Willys): *New York Rock*, March 2011

FRANKIE LaROCKA (drummer/A&R): *New York Rocker*, by Andy Schwartz [1991 quote to Jonathan Grevatt], May 12, 2010

CHARLES LARKEY (The Fugs/The Myddle Class): *Lost Rockers*, February 2015

JOHN LAW (Banana Fish Zero): *New York Waste*, by Lucky, 2003; *New York Rock*, 2005

JASON LEDYARD (DJ/promoter): *New York Rock*, July 2013

JOHN LENNON: *Melody Maker*, by Chris Charlesworth, Nov. 3, 1973

CRAIG LEON (producer): *New York Rock*, 2006

RIK LETENDRE (Circle X): *Dusted*, by Jordan N. Mamone, 2009

MORGAN LIEBMAN (New York scene): *New York Rock*, 2004

ARTO LINDSAY (guitarist): *Perfect Sound Forever*, by Jason Gross, November 1997

BUZZY LINHART (vibraphonist): *Rolling Stone*, by Timothy Ferris, Nov. 25, 1971

DAVID LINTON (Interference): *Bad Vibes*, uncited, 2012

RICHARD LLOYD (Television): *Perfect Sounds*, by Eric Veillettel, 1999

JEFFREY LOHN (Theoretical Girls): *JunkMedia*, by Robert Young, December 2002

LYDIA LUNCH (Teenage Jesus and the Jerks): *Seconds #24*, 1993; *Perfect Sound Forever*, by Jason Gross, October 1997

DONNA LUPIE (Cycle Sluts from Hell): *Popular 1*, by Robert Barry Francos, 2010

WALTER LURE (The Heartbreakers): *White Trash Soul*, by Mihaleez, January 2010

FRANKIE LYMON (The Teenagers): *Ebony*, by Art Peters, January 1967

ANN MAGNUSON (Bongwater): *Interview*, by Beverly D'Angelo, September 1995

SAL MAIDA (Milk 'N' Cookies/Velveteen): *New York Rock*, March 2011

CHAKA MALIK (Burn/Orange 9mm): *Seconds #46*, 1998

JESSE MALIN (D Generation): *Paper*, 1997; *Paper*, 1999; *Paper*, 2004; *Frank 151*, 2005, *New York Rock*, 2012

DAVID MANCUSO (DJ): *The Record Players: DJ Revolutionaries*, by Bill Brewster and Frank Broughton, 2010

HANDSOME DICK MANITOBA (The Dictators): *New York Rock,* 2003

TONY MANN (New York scene): *New York Rock,* 2013

PHILIPPE MARCADE (The Senders): *White Trash Soul,* by Mihaleez, February 2010

CHRISTIAN MARCLAY (composer): *Kulture Flash,* by Catherine Yass, 2003

NICK MARDEN (The Stimulators): *New York Rock,* March 2011

MIKE MARICONDA (Raunch Hands): *Life in a Bungalo Digest,* by Rev. Sal Lucci, 2001

FRANK MARINO (Step2Far): 100Interviews.com, uncited, 2011

JOE MARTIN (Citizens Arrest): *Jersey Beat #56,* by Jim Testa, spring 1996

PAUL MARTIN (The Vipers): CheepskatesMovie.com, s/w, 2004

BOBBY McADAMS (New York scene): *New York Rock,* 2011

CARLO McCORMICK (author/journalist): *New York Rock,* 2011

RICHARD McGUIRE (Liquid Liquid): Scaruffi.com, by Carlo Maramotti, 2000

SAM McPHEETERS (Born Against): *Vol. 1 Brooklyn,* by Aaron Lake Smith, October 2009

GLENN MERCER (The Feelies): *New York Rocker,* by Kevin Underwood, May–June 1977

MIKE METAL (New York scene): *New York Rock,* 2013

MIKE MILLIUS (Five Dollar Shoes): *New York Rock,* 2011

ROGER MIRET (Agnostic Front): *Seconds #9,* 1989; *American Hardcore,* 1996

PETER MISSING (Missing Foundation): *Augenmusik,* by Vincent Dominion, March 29, 2009

ALEX MITCHELL (Circus of Power): *SugarBuzz,* by Geordie Pleathur, 2007

MOBY (DJ): *New York Rock,* 2004; *Interview,* by Brendan Sullivan, 2011

JON MONTGOMERY (Street Punk): *New York Rock,* 2008

REBECCA MOORE (John Varvatos protester): *Post,* by Richard Johnson, April 19, 2008

THURSTON MOORE (Sonic Youth): *RIP,* by Mark Dery, August 1987; *Flipside #58,* by Krk and Al Flipside, winter 1989; *CMJ,* by Kurt B. Reighley, April 2000

BEN MOREA (Up Against the Wall Motherfuckers): libcom.org, by Iain McIntyre, 2006

HUEY MORGAN (Fun Lovin' Criminals): *Seconds #43,* 1996; *Paper,* 2001

IKUE MORI (DNA): *Perfect Sound,* by Jason Gross, November 1997

STERLING MORRISON (The Velvet Underground): *Fusion,* by Robert Greenfield, March 6, 1970; *NME,* by Mary Harron, April 25, 1981

PAUL MORRISSEY (filmmaker): *Seconds #49,* by John Aes-Nihil, 1999

GLENN MORROW (The Individuals): *New York Rock,* May 2011

JAMES MURPHY (LCD Soundsystem/DFA Records): *New York Rock,* 2005

MICHAEL MUSTO (writer): *Guardian* (UK), by Anthony Haden-Guest, July 18, 2004

JACK NATZ (Cop Shoot Cop): *Seconds* #23, by Carlo McCormick, 1993

PAUL NELSON (journalist): RockCritics.com, by Steven Ward, 2005

BOB NICKAS (curator): *Sympathy for the Devil,* by Dominic Molon and Diedrich Diederichsen, 2007

FRANZ NICOLAY (The Hold Steady): *No Ripcord,* by Matt Erler, March 25, 2007

NITEBOB (soundman/producer): *New York Rock,* 2011

JERRY NOLAN (New York Dolls): *Zigzag,* by Kris Needs, March 1977; *Daily News,* by David Hinckley, 1990 quote from March 2, 2005

ROB NORRIS (The Bongos): *New York Rock,* April 2011

JESSE OBSTBAUM (The Thing): *Seconds* #13, by George Petros, 1990

DEB O'NAIR (The Fuzztones): *Sounds,* by Lindsay Hutton, Oct. 6, 1984; *New York Rock,* by Tony Mann, January 2012

JERRY ONLY (The Misfits): *Seconds* #44, 1997

YOKO ONO (artist): *Seconds* #36, by George Petros, 1996

JASON O'TOOLE (Life's Blood): *True Punk & Metal,* by Nate Gloom, February 2009

PALEFACE (musician): *New York Rock,* March 2011

CLAYTON PATTERSON (artist): *BlackBook,* by Steven Lewis, March 20, 2009

ADAM PEACOCK (Hugo Largo): *Contrast* #3, by Philip Drucker, fall 1987

DAVID PEEL (David Peel & The Lower East Side): *Lost Rockers,* 2009

KEMBRA PFAHLER (Karen Black): *New York Rock,* 2006

BOB PFEIFER (Human Switchboard): *FFanzine* #14, by Jim Downs & Barry Francos, 1986

BILLY PHILIPS (Urban Waste/Major Conflict): *Mad at the World,* by Dan Scheme, 2006

BINKY PHILIPS (The Planets): *New York Rock,* 2011

STEVE PICCOLO (Lounge Lizards): *Melody Maker,* by Mary Harron, Feb. 16, 1980

RUDOLF PIEPER (Danceteria): *New York,* by David L. Lewis, June 8, 1987; *New York,* by Hal Rubenstein, April 17, 1989

SEAN PIERCE (Toilet Boys): NYRock.com, by Alice Hammond, January 2000

AMOS POE (filmmaker): *Films in Review,* by Glenn Andreiev, April 7, 2011

VICTOR POISON-TETE (Rat At Rat R): *Seconds* #8, by Carlo McCormick, 1989

IGGY POP (The Stooges): *Paper,* 1998

JOHN POPPER (Blues Traveler): *Paper,* 1994; *Relix,* by Mike Greenhaus, April 2011

RUDI PROTRUDI (The Fuzztones): *Lowcut* #43, by Jens, May/June 2007; *SugarBuzz,* by Geordie Pleathur, 2010

HOWIE PYRO (D Generation): *New York Rock,* 2004

QUEEN V (musician): *New York Rock,* July 2013

JACK RABID (*The Big Takeover*): *American Hardcore* book interview, 1996

MARY RAFFAELE (Cycle Sluts from Hell): *New York Rock,* 2006

C. J. RAMONE (The Ramones): *Livewire*, by Maggie St. Thomas, December 2001

DEE DEE RAMONE (The Ramones): *Metal Madness* (UK), by Mickey Madness, 1986, *SoundSpike*, by Alexa Williamson, October 2000

JOEY RAMONE (The Ramones): *Seconds* #3, 1986

MARKY RAMONE (The Ramones): *Paper*, 1996; NYRock.com, by Glyn Emmerson, February 2003

TOMMY RAMONE (The Ramones): *SoHo Weekly News*, by Alan Betrock, 1975

HOLLY RAMOS (Fur): *American Hardcore*, 1996

GENYA RAVAN (Goldie and the Gingerbreads): *New York Rock*, 2005

RAYBEEZ (Warzone): *Schism* #7, by Porcell, 1987; *American Hardcore*, 1996

LOU REED (The Velvet Underground): *Rolling Stone*, by Mick Rock, Oct. 26, 1972; *Let It Rock*, by Lester Bangs, November 1973; *Record Collector*, by Peter Doggett, June 1992; *Mojo*, by Barney Hoskyns, March 1996; *Hits*, 2000

VERNON REID (Living Colour): *NME*, by Mark Sinker, April 1988

JOE RENZETTI (arranger): *New York Rock*, March 2011

MARTIN REV (Suicide): *Nightwaves*, by Gary Flanagan, 2005

ULLI RIMKUS (Max Fish): Grub Street blog, by Daniel Maurer, Dec. 8, 2010

BILL RISBROOK (B.T. Express): *Jet*, by M. Cordell Thompson, April 1, 1976

IRA ROBBINS (*Trouser Press*): RockCritics.com, by Steven Ward, 2006

BILLY ROBERTSON (Polyrock): *No Love Lost* liner notes, s/w, 1986

SYLVIA ROBINSON (singer): *The Big Payback*, by Dan Charnas, 2010

RICK ROCKET (Toilet Boys): NYRock.com, by Alice Hammond, January 2000

RED RODNEY (trumpeter): *Smack and the American City*, by Eric C. Schneider, 2013

ANTHONY ROMAN (Radio 4): *Gigwise*, by Mike Davidson, Sept. 23, 2003

POISON IVY RORSCHACH (The Cramps): *Seconds* #29, 1994

ALLEGRA ROSE (New York scene): *New York Rock*, 2006

T ROTH (Another Pretty Face): *New York Rock*, 2011

TODD RUNDGREN (musician): *Seconds* #24, 1993

CHUCK RUSINAK (DJ/promoter): Nerve.com, by Steven Kurutz, 2005

MICKEY RUSKIN (Max's Kansas City): *Interview*, by Danny Fields, April 1973

JOY RYDER (Joy Ryder & Avis Davis): *New York Rock*, 2011

DANNY SAGE (D Generation): *American Hardcore*, 1996; *New York Rock*, 2004, 2011

CHRIS SANCHEZ (The Fever): *New York Rock*, 2005

ED SANDERS (The Fugs): *Seconds* #27, by George Petros, 1994

JOE VALENTINE SAUSA (The Rags): *New York Rock*, 2011

KATE SCHELLENBACH (Luscious Jackson): *CMJ*, by Heidi MacDonald, December 1996; *SF Chronicle*, by Marlene Goldman, July 14, 1999

MIKE SCHNAPP (New York scene): *New York Rock*, 2003

MITCH SCHNEIDER (publicist): *New York Rock*, 2005

WALTER SCHREIFELS (Gorilla Biscuits/Quicksand): *Longshot #4*, by Ronny, 1989; *It's for Life*, uncited, 2008

JIM SCLAVUNOS (Teenage Jesus): *Penny Black Music*, by John Clarkson, 2008

JAKE SHEARS (Scissor Sisters): *New York Rock*, 2004

BOBBY SHEEHAN (Blues Traveler): *Celebrity Café*, by Dominick Miserandino, November 2000

SAM SHEPARD (playwright): *Interview*, by Michael Alymereyda, October 2011

ANDY SHERNOFF (The Dictators): *Perfect Sound Forever*, by Jason Gross, May 1996; *Punk Globe*, by Ginger Coyote, 2011

IRWIN SILBER (*Sing Out!*): *Perfect Sound Forever*, by Richie Unterberger, 2002

TOM SILVERMAN (New Music Seminar): *New York Times*, by Neil Strauss, July 20, 1994

GENE SIMMONS (Kiss): *Seconds #18*, 1992; *Goldmine*, by Ken Sharp, April 11, 2008

CYNTHIA SLEY (Bush Tetras): *Paper*, 2004

STU SPASM (Lubricated Goat): *New York Rock*, July 2013

CHRIS SPENCER (Unsane): *Seconds #17*, 1991

JON SPENCER (Pussy Galore): *Paper*, 1988; *Rock's Backpages*, by Al Friston, March 2002; *Pop Catastrophe #2*, uncited, August 1996

STEPHEN SPROUSE (designer): *5000 Artists Return to Artists Space*, by Claudia Gould and Valerie Smith, 1998

NANCY SPUNGEN (New York scene): *Record Mirror*, by Rosalind Russell, August 4, 1978

PETER STAMPFEL (Holy Modal Rounders): *New York Rock*, March 2011

PAUL STANLEY (Kiss): *High Times*, 1993; *Goldmine*, by Ken Sharp, April 11, 2008

MICHAEL STARK (New York scene): CheepskatesMovie.com, s/w, 2004

WALTER STEDING (artist/musician): *New York Rock*, 2011

BOBBY STEELE (The Undead): *American Hardcore*, 1996

PETE STEELE (Type O Negative): *American Hardcore* book interview, 1997

CHRIS STEIN (Blondie): *Paper*, 1999

SEYMOUR STEIN (Sire Records): NPR, *Fresh Air with Terry Gross*, Oct. 15, 2009

SEBASTIAN STEINBERG (Soul Coughing): *City Paper*, by Margit Detweiler, July 4, 1996

ELYSE STEINMAN (Raging Slab): *Seconds #3*, 1986

DREW STONE (Antidote): *American Hardcore*, 1997; *New York Rock*, 2008

STRAFE (musician): *Spin*, by John Leland, May 1986

JOE STRUMMER (The Clash): *Paper*, by Carlo McCormick, 1999

GREG STRZEMPKA (Raging Slab): *Seconds #22*, 1993

PAUL SUB (owner, The Coventry): *Goldmine,* by Ken Sharp, April 11, 2008

PRINCESS SUPERSTAR: *Paper,* 2004

TARO SUZUKI (Youth in Asia): *New York Observer,* by Michael H. Miller, Nov. 10, 2000

MATT SWEENEY (Chavez): *New York Rock,* July 2013

SYLVAIN SYLVAIN (New York Dolls): NYRock.com, by Roger Scott, April 1998; *Brooklyn Vegan,* by "J," September 2006

GEORGE TABB (journalist/musician): *New York Rock,* 2004

SEAN TAGGART (artist): *American Hardcore* book interview, 1997

GREG TATE (Black Rock Coalition): *BRC Newsletter,* s/w, January 2001

MARTY THAU (Red Star Records): *New York Rock,* March 2011

JIM THIRLWELL (Foetus): *Seconds #35,* 1995; *New York Rock,* 2005

JOHNNY THUNDERS (The Heartbreakers): *Zigzag,* by Kris Needs, March 1977; by Nikki Sudden, November 1980

JON TIVEN (Prix): *New York Rock,* February 2011

TRIGGER (The Continental): *Frank 151,* 2005

EDDIE TRUNK (DJ): *New York Rock,* July 2013

MAUREEN TUCKER (The Velvet Underground): *Perfect Sound Forever,* by Jason Gross, May 1998

GRAHAM TYLER (The Mooney Suzuki): *Soho Strut,* by Graham Coxon, 2004

JAMES BLOOD ULMER (guitarist): *Seconds #25,* by George Petros, 1994

AURELIO VALLE (Calla): *The Dumbing of America,* by Todd C, May 15, 2009

CHERRY VANILLA (musician): *Lost Rockers,* 2011

DAVE VAN RONK (musician): *World Socialist,* by David Walsh, May 7, 1998

JOHN VARVATOS (designer): *New York Post,* by Serena French, April 7, 2008

JUNIOR VASQUEZ (DJ): *Billboard,* by Larry Flick

ALAN VEGA (Suicide): *Seconds #19,* by Richard Fantina, 1992

TOM VERLAINE (Television): *Boston Phoenix,* by Frank Rose, October 1977; *Hit Parader,* by Richard Robinson, September 1978; *Pittsburgh Post-Gazette,* by Scott Mervis, June 8, 2006

TOMMY VICTOR (Prong): *Seconds #11,* 1990

SONNY VINCENT (Testors): *New York Rock,* May 2011

LYNNE VON SCHLICHTING (Da Willys/Trick Babys): *New York Rock,* March 2011

ANDY WARHOL: *Interview,* by Glenn O'Brien, June 1977; *Melody Maker,* by Mary Harron, Feb. 16, 1980; *Popism: The Warhol Sixties,* by Andy Warhol and Pat Hackett, 1980

AARON WARREN (Black Dice): *Paper,* 2004

JOHNNY WASTE (Urban Waste): *Barebones Hardcore,* by Sarge, Feb. 2, 2006

KEN WEAVER (The Fugs): *Perfect Sound,* by Ashley Meeks, August 2005

ARTHUR WEINSTEIN (owner, Hurrah/The World): *New York Times,* by Howard Blum, Feb. 22, 1983; *New York Rock,* 2005

SCOTT WEIS (Ed Gein's Car/Iron Prostate): *New York Rock,* by Tony Mann, March 2011

JON WEISS (The Vipers): *Fuzzbrains #9,* by Rev. Joe Longone, 1985

JIM WELCH (New York scene): *American Hardcore* book interview, 1996

NEVILLE WELLS (promoter): *USA Today,* by Tim Friend, Nov. 10, 1994

JEFF WENGROFSKY (New York scene): *New York Rock,* 2012

KEITH WEST (The Brats): *New York Rock,* March 2011

LESLIE WEST (Mountain): *New York Rock,* August 2011

TINA WEYMOUTH (Talking Heads): *Rolling Stone,* by Ed McCormick, Oct. 23, 1975

JERRY WILLIAMS (producer): *New York Rock,* 2008

JIMMY WILLIAMS (Maximum Penalty): Tripod.com, by Dope Sick Girl, Sept. 18, 1998

TOM WYNBRANDT (The Miamis/Queen Elizabeth): *New York Rock,* 2011

ADAM YAUCH (Beastie Boys): *American Hardcore* book transcript, 1998

LA MONTE YOUNG (composer): *Seconds #50,* by David Paul, 1998

TODD YOUTH (Agnostic Front/Murphy's Law): *American Hardcore* film transcript, 2004

SEAN YSEULT (White Zombie): *Seconds #18,* 1992; *New York Rock,* April 2011

JIMMY YU (Judge): *Double Cross,* by Tim McMahon, July 2008

BILLY YULE (The Velvet Underground): *Modern Drummer,* by Adam Budofsky, 2005

DOUG YULE (The Velvet Underground): *The Violin Maker,* dir. by Greg Brotherton, 2010; *New York Rock,* 2011

IZZY ZAIDMAN (Uncle Fucker): *Thrasher,* uncredited, 2004

PETER ZAREMBA (The Fleshtones): *Sounds,* by Sylvie Simmons, 1983; *Interview,* by Dimitri Erlich, 2007

NICK ZEDD (filmmaker): *Oakazine,* by Marlo Kronberg and Peter Humphrey, March 2011

JOHNNY ZEEK (The Shirts): *Daily News,* by Janiel Bladow, Nov. 11, 1977

NICK ZINNER (Yeah Yeah Yeahs): *Supersweet,* by Choltida Pekanan, 2005

ROB ZOMBIE (White Zombie): *Seconds #3,* 1986

MIKI ZONE (The Fast): video interview by Dave Street, 1978

PAUL ZONE (The Fast): video interview by Dave Street, 1978

ABOUT THE AUTHOR

STEVEN BLUSH has written four books on rock music: 2001's *American Hardcore*, 2005's *.45 Dangerous Minds*, 2006's *American Hair Metal*, and the recent *Lost Rockers*. His writing has appeared in more than fifty publications, including *Spin*, *Details*, *Interview*, *Village Voice*, and *The Times* of London. He long served as a contributing music editor to *Paper*.

Blush got his start promoting punk rock shows in Washington, D.C., in the early '80s. He moved to New York in 1986, where he published fifty-two issues of *Seconds* magazine, interviewing amazing musicians through 2000. He spun vinyl at clubs like Mars, Limelight, Carmelita's, and the Pyramid with the likes of Moby, Spooky, Grandmaster Flash, and Jellybean Benitez. As a Downtown club promoter, he booked the earliest shows by bands like Dinosaur, Jr. and White Zombie. He programmed the music for designer Stephen Sprouse's runway shows, and threw the long-running "Röck Cändy" parties at Don Hill's. He wrote and coproduced the documentary film *American Hardcore*, which premiered at 2006's Sundance Film Festival and was theatrically distributed by Sony Pictures Classics. He lives in New York.

INDEX